Credits

Author
Dusty Phillips

Reviewers
AMahdy AbdElAziz
Grigoriy Beziuk
Krishna Bharadwaj
Justin Cano
Anthony Petitbois
Claudio Rodriguez

Commissioning Editor
Edward Gordon

Acquisition Editors
Indrajit Das
Rebecca Pedley
Greg Wild

Content Development Editors
Divij Kotian
Arvind Koul
Anila Vincent

Technical Editor
Siddhi Rane

Copy Editor
Janbal Dharmaraj

Project Coordinator
Neha Bhatnagar

Proofreader
Safis Editing

Indexer
Hemangini Bari

Graphics
Sheetal Aute
Jason Monteiro

Production Coordinator
Komal Ramchandani

Cover Work
Komal Ramchandani

About the Author

Dusty Phillips is a Canadian software developer and author currently living in Seattle, Washington. He has been active in the open source community for a decade and a half and programming in Python for nearly all of it. He cofounded the popular Puget Sound Programming Python meetup group; drop by and say hi if you're in the area.

Python 3 Object Oriented Programming, Packt Publishing, was the first of his books. He has also written *Creating Apps In Kivy, O'Reilly,* the mobile Python library, and self-published *Hacking Happy,* a journey to mental wellness for the technically inclined. He was hospitalized for suicidal tendencies shortly after the first edition of this book was published and has been an outspoken proponent for positive mental health ever since.

About the Reviewers

AMahdy AbdElAziz has more than 8 years of experience in software engineering using several languages and frameworks. Over the last 5 years, he has focused on Android and mobile development, including cross-platform tools, and Android internals, such as building custom ROMs and customizing AOSP for embedded devices.

He is currently teaching Python at Information Technology Institution. You can visit his website, `http://www.amahdy.net/`, to find out more about him.

Grigoriy Beziuk is a former CIO of Crowdage Foundation, acting as an independent software developer as this book was being written. He has worked with a wide variety of programming languages and technologies, including different versions of Python in different environments, ranging from purely scientific ones to modern production-scale web development issues.

> I would like to thank my mom, Larisa Beziuk, for giving me the gift of life; all of my teachers and friends for making my life more interesting; and all of my beloved ones, former and present for… well, everything.

Krishna Bharadwaj is the cofounder of SMERGERS (`https://www.smergers.com/`), a Fintech start-up helping small and medium businesses raise capital from investors and different financial institutions. In the past, he has worked with early stage start-ups such as BlockBeacon (Santa Monica) and PricePoint (CA) and large organizations such as National Instruments, Bangalore, and Google, New York. Krishna got introduced to Python and FOSS during his college days and has continued to use it extensively in his personal projects and also professionally at work. Because of his liking for teaching and mentoring, he visits different universities, conducting workshops whenever he gets an opportunity.

He holds a master's degree in computer science from the University of Southern California, Los Angeles, and a bachelor's degree in information science and engineering from the BMS College of Engineering, Bangalore. He can be reached through his e-mail, `krishna@krishnabharadwaj.info`, or his website, `http://www.krishnabharadwaj.info/`.

Justin Cano is a recent graduate from the University of California, Riverside, with a BS in computer engineering and is currently working as a software engineer in the Silicon Valley area with hopes of moving to a big tech company such as Google or Apple.

He first started programming in the sixth grade, creating small, primitive websites in HTML and CSS. He started to learn computer science theory and C++ in his first year at UC Riverside and then started learning Python in his third year.

Justin admits that at first, he wasn't immediately attracted to Python, since abstractions between C++ and Python are very different. It wasn't until he began to express more of an interest in coding contests and challenges that he began to show interest in Python, mainly because he feels that the readability and elegance of the Python syntax allows him to quickly and more naturally turn ideas and thought processes into Python code. He now writes Python code regularly, often to create mock-ups or prototypes of software applications before moving on to a more domain-specific language.

> I would like to thank the author for taking the time to write this book as I have received a lot of valuable insights and information on the Python language and design patterns. This book has strengthened my understanding of Python, and I believe that I am now a more knowledgeable Python programmer.

Anthony Petitbois is an online architect in the video game industry with 13 years of professional experience in operations and development and more than 20 years of software development experience. He is passionate about new technologies and loves to take creative approaches to solve complex problems.

In his spare time, he learns new languages and new platforms, plays video games, and spends time with his family in the beautiful region of British Columbia, Canada, where he now lives after emigrating from France in 2009.

Claudio Rodriguez started working on PLCs for GE, but his main goal has always been research and development and turning dreams into reality. This made him move from automation engineering to software engineering and the structured way of software, OOD; the remote team working from the comfort of his computer was just too powerful not to take advantage of. During his master's, he got to learn the proper place to look for resources and found a friend in books and research papers and conferences. Eventually, he started working on a system to control an electric arc furnace, but the needs of his clients moved him into taking further control of technology. He has a deep love for complex AI and can be seen surrounded by papers, books, and a computer to test things, but he keeps things real by delivering beautiful and dynamic applications for his customers.

www.PacktPub.com

Support files, eBooks, discount offers, and more

For support files and downloads related to your book, please visit www.PacktPub.com.

Did you know that Packt offers eBook versions of every book published, with PDF and ePub files available? You can upgrade to the eBook version at www.PacktPub.com and as a print book customer, you are entitled to a discount on the eBook copy. Get in touch with us at service@packtpub.com for more details.

At www.PacktPub.com, you can also read a collection of free technical articles, sign up for a range of free newsletters and receive exclusive discounts and offers on Packt books and eBooks.

https://www2.packtpub.com/books/subscription/packtlib

Do you need instant solutions to your IT questions? PacktLib is Packt's online digital book library. Here, you can search, access, and read Packt's entire library of books.

Why subscribe?
- Fully searchable across every book published by Packt
- Copy and paste, print, and bookmark content
- On demand and accessible via a web browser

Free access for Packt account holders

If you have an account with Packt at www.PacktPub.com, you can use this to access PacktLib today and view 9 entirely free books. Simply use your login credentials for immediate access.

Introduction to the second edition

I have a confession to make. When I wrote the first edition of this book, I didn't have a clue what I was doing. I thought I knew Python and I thought I knew how to write. I quickly learned that this was false. Luckily, I became adept at both by finishing the book!

I was so afraid that people wouldn't like *Python 3 Object Oriented Programming* that I skipped Pycon for two years straight. After a couple dozen positive reviews, my confidence was boosted and I finally attended Pycon 2012 in Santa Clara. I soon discovered that nobody had ever heard of me or my book. So much for arrogance!

I was also afraid to reread the book after completing it. So while it has received many accolades, the copy on my shelf has remained firmly shut, save for when I open it for reference to answer a reader's query. In preparing this second edition, I was finally forced to face my demons. To my surprise and joy, I discovered that the book I wrote five years ago was both accurate and enjoyable, just as many reviewers had suggested.

Shortly after that initial rereading, I got my first ever negative review on Amazon. It would have been devastating had I read it directly after completing the project. Fortunately, four years of good reviews and my own confidence in the writing allowed me to ignore the vitriol and take the remainder as constructive feedback. The truth is many of the flaws the reviewer had pointed out were features at the time the book was originally published. *Python 3 Object Oriented Programming* was showing its age, and it was clearly time for an update. You're holding the result in your hands (or flipping through it on your e-reader).

I've often wondered why authors describe in detail what has changed between the editions of a technical book. I mean, seriously, how many people reading this second edition have read the first one? As with software versions, you safely assume the latest edition is the best, and you don't really care about the project's history. And yet, this project has consumed so much of my life over the past year that I can't leave without a few words about how much better the book has become.

The original book was a little disorganized. Many chapters flowed directly into the next one, but there were a few key places where the topic change was jarring, or worse, irrelevant. The two chapters preceding the discussions about design patterns have been reorganized, reversed, and split into three chapters that flow cleanly into the next topic.

I've also removed an entire chapter on third-party libraries for Python 3. This chapter made more sense when both the book and Python 3 were new. There were only a few libraries that had been ported to Python 3 and it was reasonable to have a best of breed discussion about each of them. However, I was unable to cover any of those topics in detail, and frankly, I could write an entire book on any one of them.

Finally, I've added an entire new chapter on concurrency. I struggled with this chapter and I can freely admit that it's not directly related to object-oriented programming. However, much like the chapter on unit testing, I think that understanding concurrency is an integral part of all programming and especially of object-oriented programming in the Python ecosystem. You are, of course, free to skip those chapters if you disagree (or until you discover a reason to change your mind).

Enjoy the book and your journey into the world of object-oriented programming.

Dusty Phillips

Table of Contents

Preface   vii

Chapter 1: Object-oriented Design   1

Introducing object-oriented   1

Objects and classes   3

Specifying attributes and behaviors   5

   Data describes objects   6

   Behaviors are actions   7

Hiding details and creating the public interface   9

Composition   11

Inheritance   14

   Inheritance provides abstraction   16

   Multiple inheritance   17

Case study   18

Exercises   25

Summary   26

Chapter 2: Objects in Python   27

Creating Python classes   27

   Adding attributes   29

   Making it do something   30

     Talking to yourself   30

     More arguments   31

   Initializing the object   33

   Explaining yourself   35

Modules and packages   37

   Organizing the modules   40

     Absolute imports   40

     Relative imports   41

Organizing module contents   43

Who can access my data?	**46**
Third-party libraries	**48**
Case study	**49**
Exercises	**58**
Summary	**58**
Chapter 3: When Objects Are Alike	**59**
Basic inheritance	**59**
Extending built-ins	62
Overriding and super	63
Multiple inheritance	**65**
The diamond problem	67
Different sets of arguments	72
Polymorphism	**75**
Abstract base classes	**78**
Using an abstract base class	78
Creating an abstract base class	79
Demystifying the magic	81
Case study	**82**
Exercises	**95**
Summary	**96**
Chapter 4: Expecting the Unexpected	**97**
Raising exceptions	**98**
Raising an exception	99
The effects of an exception	101
Handling exceptions	102
The exception hierarchy	108
Defining our own exceptions	109
Case study	**114**
Exercises	**123**
Summary	**124**
Chapter 5: When to Use Object-oriented Programming	**125**
Treat objects as objects	**125**
Adding behavior to class data with properties	**129**
Properties in detail	132
Decorators – another way to create properties	134
Deciding when to use properties	136
Manager objects	**138**
Removing duplicate code	140
In practice	142

Case study **145**
Exercises **153**
Summary **154**

Chapter 6: Python Data Structures **155**
Empty objects **155**
Tuples and named tuples **157**
Named tuples 159
Dictionaries **160**
Dictionary use cases 164
Using defaultdict 164
Counter 166
Lists **167**
Sorting lists 169
Sets **173**
Extending built-ins **177**
Queues **182**
FIFO queues 183
LIFO queues 185
Priority queues 186
Case study **188**
Exercises **194**
Summary **195**

Chapter 7: Python Object-oriented Shortcuts **197**
Python built-in functions **197**
The len() function 198
Reversed 198
Enumerate 200
File I/O 201
Placing it in context 203
An alternative to method overloading **205**
Default arguments 206
Variable argument lists 208
Unpacking arguments 212
Functions are objects too **213**
Using functions as attributes 217
Callable objects 218
Case study **219**
Exercises **226**
Summary **227**

Chapter 8: Strings and Serialization   229

Strings   229
String manipulation   230
String formatting   232
Escaping braces   233
Keyword arguments   234
Container lookups   235
Object lookups   236
Making it look right   237
Strings are Unicode   239
Converting bytes to text   240
Converting text to bytes   241
Mutable byte strings   243
Regular expressions   244
Matching patterns   245
Matching a selection of characters   246
Escaping characters   247
Matching multiple characters   248
Grouping patterns together   249
Getting information from regular expressions   250
Making repeated regular expressions efficient   252
Serializing objects   252
Customizing pickles   254
Serializing web objects   257
Case study   260
Exercises   265
Summary   267

Chapter 9: The Iterator Pattern   269

Design patterns in brief   269
Iterators   270
The iterator protocol   271
Comprehensions   273
List comprehensions   273
Set and dictionary comprehensions   276
Generator expressions   277
Generators   279
Yield items from another iterable   281
Coroutines   284
Back to log parsing   287
Closing coroutines and throwing exceptions   289
The relationship between coroutines, generators, and functions   290

Case study	**291**
Exercises	**298**
Summary	**299**
Chapter 10: Python Design Patterns I	**301**
The decorator pattern	**301**
A decorator example	302
Decorators in Python	305
The observer pattern	**307**
An observer example	308
The strategy pattern	**310**
A strategy example	311
Strategy in Python	313
The state pattern	**313**
A state example	314
State versus strategy	320
State transition as coroutines	320
The singleton pattern	**320**
Singleton implementation	321
The template pattern	**325**
A template example	325
Exercises	**329**
Summary	**329**
Chapter 11: Python Design Patterns II	**331**
The adapter pattern	**331**
The facade pattern	**335**
The flyweight pattern	**337**
The command pattern	**341**
The abstract factory pattern	**346**
The composite pattern	**351**
Exercises	**355**
Summary	**356**
Chapter 12: Testing Object-oriented Programs	**357**
Why test?	**357**
Test-driven development	359
Unit testing	**360**
Assertion methods	362
Reducing boilerplate and cleaning up	364
Organizing and running tests	365
Ignoring broken tests	366

Testing with py.test	**368**
One way to do setup and cleanup	370
A completely different way to set up variables	373
Skipping tests with py.test	377
Imitating expensive objects	**378**
How much testing is enough?	**382**
Case study	**385**
Implementing it	386
Exercises	**391**
Summary	**392**
Chapter 13: Concurrency	**393**
Threads	**394**
The many problems with threads	397
Shared memory	397
The global interpreter lock	398
Thread overhead	399
Multiprocessing	**399**
Multiprocessing pools	401
Queues	404
The problems with multiprocessing	406
Futures	**406**
AsyncIO	**409**
AsyncIO in action	410
Reading an AsyncIO future	411
AsyncIO for networking	412
Using executors to wrap blocking code	415
Streams	417
Executors	417
Case study	**418**
Exercises	**425**
Summary	**426**
Index	**427**

Preface

This book introduces the terminology of the object-oriented paradigm. It focuses on object-oriented design with step-by-step examples. It guides us from simple inheritance, one of the most useful tools in the object-oriented programmer's toolbox through exception handling to design patterns, an object-oriented way of looking at object-oriented concepts.

Along the way, we'll learn to integrate the object-oriented and not-so-object-oriented aspects of the Python programming language. We will learn the complexities of string and file manipulation, emphasizing (as Python 3 does) the difference between binary and textual data.

We'll then cover the joys of unit testing, using not one, but two unit testing frameworks. Finally, we'll explore, through Python's various concurrency paradigms, how to make objects work well together at the same time.

What this book covers

This book is loosely divided into four major parts. In the first four chapters, we will dive into the formal principles of object-oriented programming and how Python leverages them. In chapters 5 through 8, we will cover some of Python's idiosyncratic applications of these principles by learning how they are applied to a variety of Python's built-in functions. Chapters 9 through 11 cover design patterns, and the final two chapters discuss two bonus topics related to Python programming that may be of interest.

Chapter 1, Object-oriented Design, covers important object-oriented concepts. It deals mainly with terminology such as abstraction, classes, encapsulation, and inheritance. We also briefly look at UML to model our classes and objects.

Chapter 2, Objects in Python, discusses classes and objects and how they are used in Python. We will learn about attributes and behaviors on Python objects, and also the organization of classes into packages and modules. Lastly, we will see how to protect our data.

Chapter 3, When Objects Are Alike, gives us a more in-depth look into inheritance. It covers multiple inheritance and shows us how to extend built-ins. This chapter also covers how polymorphism and duck typing work in Python.

Chapter 4, Expecting the Unexpected, looks into exceptions and exception handling. We will learn how to create our own exceptions and how to use exceptions for program flow control.

Chapter 5, When to Use Object-oriented Programming, deals with creating and using objects. We will see how to wrap data using properties and restrict data access. This chapter also discusses the DRY principle and how not to repeat code.

Chapter 6, Python Data Structures, covers the object-oriented features of Python's built-in classes. We'll cover tuples, dictionaries, lists, and sets, as well as a few more advanced collections. We'll also see how to extend these standard objects.

Chapter 7, Python Object-oriented Shortcuts, as the name suggests, deals with time-savers in Python. We will look at many useful built-in functions such as method overloading using default arguments. We'll also see that functions themselves are objects and how this is useful.

Chapter 8, Strings and Serialization, looks at strings, files, and formatting. We'll discuss the difference between strings, bytes, and bytearrays, as well as various ways to serialize textual, object, and binary data to several canonical representations.

Chapter 9, The Iterator Pattern, introduces us to the concept of design patterns and covers Python's iconic implementation of the iterator pattern. We'll learn about list, set, and dictionary comprehensions. We'll also demystify generators and coroutines.

Chapter 10, Python Design Patterns I, covers several design patterns, including the decorator, observer, strategy, state, singleton, and template patterns. Each pattern is discussed with suitable examples and programs implemented in Python.

Chapter 11, Python Design Patterns II, wraps up our discussion of design patterns with coverage of the adapter, facade, flyweight, command, abstract, and composite patterns. More examples of how idiomatic Python code differs from canonical implementations are provided.

Chapter 12, Testing Object-oriented Programs, opens with why testing is so important in Python applications. It emphasizes test-driven development and introduces two different testing suites: unittest and py.test. Finally, it discusses mocking test objects and code coverage.

Chapter 13, Concurrency, is a whirlwind tour of Python's support (and lack thereof) of concurrency patterns. It discusses threads, multiprocessing, futures, and the new AsyncIO library.

Each chapter includes relevant examples and a case study that collects the chapter's contents into a working (if not complete) program.

What you need for this book

All the examples in this book rely on the Python 3 interpreter. Make sure you are not using Python 2.7 or earlier. At the time of writing, Python 3.4 was the latest release of Python. Most examples will work on earlier revisions of Python 3, but you are encouraged to use the latest version to minimize frustration.

All of the examples should run on any operating system supported by Python. If this is not the case, please report it as a bug.

Some of the examples need a working Internet connection. You'll probably want to have one of these for extracurricular research and debugging anyway!

In addition, some of the examples in this book rely on third-party libraries that do not ship with Python. These are introduced within the book at the time they are used, so you do not need to install them in advance. However, for completeness, here is a list:

- pip
- requests
- pillow
- bitarray

Who this book is for

This book specifically targets people who are new to object-oriented programming. It assumes you have basic Python skills. You'll learn object-oriented principles in depth. It is particularly useful for system administrator types who have used Python as a "glue" language and would like to improve their programming skills.

If you are familiar with object-oriented programming in other languages, then this book will help you understand the idiomatic ways to apply your knowledge in the Python ecosystem.

Conventions

This book uses a variety of text styles to distinguish between different kinds of information. Here are some examples of these styles, and an explanation of their meaning.

Code words in text, database table names, folder names, filenames, file extensions, pathnames, dummy URLs, user input, and Twitter handles are shown as follows: "We look up the class in the dictionary and store it in a variable named `PropertyClass`."

A block of code is set as follows:

```python
def add_property(self):
    property_type = get_valid_input(
            "What type of property? ",
            ("house", "apartment")).lower()
    payment_type = get_valid_input(
            "What payment type? ",
            ("purchase", "rental")).lower()
```

When we wish to draw your attention to a particular part of a code block, the relevant lines or items are set in bold:

```python
def add_property(self):
    property_type = get_valid_input(
            "What type of property? ",
            ("house", "apartment")).lower()
    payment_type = get_valid_input(
            "What payment type? ",
            ("purchase", "rental")).lower()
```

Any command-line input or output is written as follows:

```
>>> c1 = Contact("John A", "johna@example.net")
>>> c2 = Contact("John B", "johnb@example.net")
>>> c3 = Contact("Jenna C", "jennac@example.net")
>>> [c.name for c in Contact.all_contacts.search('John')]
['John A', 'John B']
```

New terms and **important words** are shown in bold. Words that you see on the screen, in menus or dialog boxes for example, appear in the text like this: "It will fail with a **not enough arguments** error similar to the one we received earlier when we forgot the self argument."

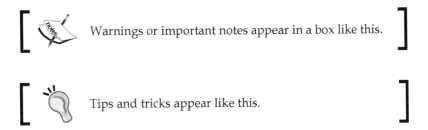

Warnings or important notes appear in a box like this.

Tips and tricks appear like this.

Reader feedback

Feedback from our readers is always welcome. Let us know what you think about this book—what you liked or disliked. Reader feedback is important for us as it helps us develop titles that you will really get the most out of.

To send us general feedback, simply e-mail feedback@packtpub.com, and mention the book's title in the subject of your message.

If there is a topic that you have expertise in and you are interested in either writing or contributing to a book, see our author guide at www.packtpub.com/authors.

Customer support

Now that you are the proud owner of a Packt book, we have a number of things to help you to get the most from your purchase.

Downloading the example code

You can download the example code files from your account at `http://www.packtpub.com` for all the Packt Publishing books you have purchased. If you purchased this book elsewhere, you can visit `http://www.packtpub.com/support` and register to have the files e-mailed directly to you.

Errata

Although we have taken every care to ensure the accuracy of our content, mistakes do happen. If you find a mistake in one of our books—maybe a mistake in the text or the code—we would be grateful if you could report this to us. By doing so, you can save other readers from frustration and help us improve subsequent versions of this book. If you find any errata, please report them by visiting `http://www.packtpub.com/submit-errata`, selecting your book, clicking on the **Errata Submission Form** link, and entering the details of your errata. Once your errata are verified, your submission will be accepted and the errata will be uploaded to our website or added to any list of existing errata under the Errata section of that title.

To view the previously submitted errata, go to `https://www.packtpub.com/books/content/support` and enter the name of the book in the search field. The required information will appear under the **Errata** section.

Piracy

Piracy of copyrighted material on the Internet is an ongoing problem across all media. At Packt, we take the protection of our copyright and licenses very seriously. If you come across any illegal copies of our works in any form on the Internet, please provide us with the location address or website name immediately so that we can pursue a remedy.

Please contact us at `copyright@packtpub.com` with a link to the suspected pirated material.

We appreciate your help in protecting our authors and our ability to bring you valuable content.

Questions

If you have a problem with any aspect of this book, you can contact us at `questions@packtpub.com`, and we will do our best to address the problem.

1
Object-oriented Design

In software development, design is often considered as the step done *before* programming. This isn't true; in reality, analysis, programming, and design tend to overlap, combine, and interweave. In this chapter, we will cover the following topics:

- What object-oriented means
- The difference between object-oriented design and object-oriented programming
- The basic principles of an object-oriented design
- Basic **Unified Modeling Language** (**UML**) and when it isn't evil

Introducing object-oriented

Everyone knows what an object is—a tangible thing that we can sense, feel, and manipulate. The earliest objects we interact with are typically baby toys. Wooden blocks, plastic shapes, and over-sized puzzle pieces are common first objects. Babies learn quickly that certain objects do certain things: bells ring, buttons press, and levers pull.

The definition of an object in software development is not terribly different. Software objects are not typically tangible things that you can pick up, sense, or feel, but they are models of something that can do certain things and have certain things done to them. Formally, an object is a collection of **data** and associated **behaviors**.

So, knowing what an object is, what does it mean to be object-oriented? Oriented simply means *directed toward*. So object-oriented means functionally directed towards modeling objects. This is one of the many techniques used for modeling complex systems by describing a collection of interacting objects via their data and behavior.

If you've read any hype, you've probably come across the terms object-oriented analysis, object-oriented design, object-oriented analysis and design, and object-oriented programming. These are all highly related concepts under the general object-oriented umbrella.

In fact, analysis, design, and programming are all stages of software development. Calling them object-oriented simply specifies what style of software development is being pursued.

Object-oriented analysis (OOA) is the process of looking at a problem, system, or task (that somebody wants to turn into an application) and identifying the objects and interactions between those objects. The analysis stage is all about *what* needs to be done.

The output of the analysis stage is a set of requirements. If we were to complete the analysis stage in one step, we would have turned a task, such as, I need a website, into a set of requirements. For example:

Website visitors need to be able to (*italic* represents actions, **bold** represents objects):

- *review* our **history**
- *apply* for **jobs**
- *browse*, *compare*, and *order* **products**

In some ways, analysis is a misnomer. The baby we discussed earlier doesn't analyze the blocks and puzzle pieces. Rather, it will explore its environment, manipulate shapes, and see where they might fit. A better turn of phrase might be object-oriented exploration. In software development, the initial stages of analysis include interviewing customers, studying their processes, and eliminating possibilities.

Object-oriented design (OOD) is the process of converting such requirements into an implementation specification. The designer must name the objects, define the behaviors, and formally specify which objects can activate specific behaviors on other objects. The design stage is all about *how* things should be done.

The output of the design stage is an implementation specification. If we were to complete the design stage in a single step, we would have turned the requirements defined during object-oriented analysis into a set of classes and interfaces that could be implemented in (ideally) any object-oriented programming language.

Object-oriented programming (OOP) is the process of converting this perfectly defined design into a working program that does exactly what the CEO originally requested.

Yeah, right! It would be lovely if the world met this ideal and we could follow these stages one by one, in perfect order, like all the old textbooks told us to. As usual, the real world is much murkier. No matter how hard we try to separate these stages, we'll always find things that need further analysis while we're designing. When we're programming, we find features that need clarification in the design.

Most twenty-first century development happens in an iterative development model. In iterative development, a small part of the task is modeled, designed, and programmed, then the program is reviewed and expanded to improve each feature and include new features in a series of short development cycles.

The rest of this book is about object-oriented programming, but in this chapter, we will cover the basic object-oriented principles in the context of design. This allows us to understand these (rather simple) concepts without having to argue with software syntax or Python interpreters.

Objects and classes

So, an object is a collection of data with associated behaviors. How do we differentiate between types of objects? Apples and oranges are both objects, but it is a common adage that they cannot be compared. Apples and oranges aren't modeled very often in computer programming, but let's pretend we're doing an inventory application for a fruit farm. To facilitate the example, we can assume that apples go in barrels and oranges go in baskets.

Now, we have four kinds of objects: apples, oranges, baskets, and barrels. In object-oriented modeling, the term used for *kind of object* is **class**. So, in technical terms, we now have four classes of objects.

What's the difference between an object and a class? Classes describe objects. They are like blueprints for creating an object. You might have three oranges sitting on the table in front of you. Each orange is a distinct object, but all three have the attributes and behaviors associated with one class: the general class of oranges.

The relationship between the four classes of objects in our inventory system can be described using a **Unified Modeling Language** (invariably referred to as **UML**, because three letter acronyms never go out of style) class diagram. Here is our first class diagram:

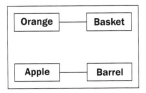

This diagram shows that an **Orange** is somehow associated with a **Basket** and that an **Apple** is also somehow associated with a **Barrel**. Association is the most basic way for two classes to be related.

UML is very popular among managers, and occasionally disparaged by programmers. The syntax of a UML diagram is generally pretty obvious; you don't have to read a tutorial to (mostly) understand what is going on when you see one. UML is also fairly easy to draw, and quite intuitive. After all, many people, when describing classes and their relationships, will naturally draw boxes with lines between them. Having a standard based on these intuitive diagrams makes it easy for programmers to communicate with designers, managers, and each other.

However, some programmers think UML is a waste of time. Citing iterative development, they will argue that formal specifications done up in fancy UML diagrams are going to be redundant before they're implemented, and that maintaining these formal diagrams will only waste time and not benefit anyone.

Depending on the corporate structure involved, this may or may not be true. However, every programming team consisting of more than one person will occasionally has to sit down and hash out the details of the subsystem it is currently working on. UML is extremely useful in these brainstorming sessions for quick and easy communication. Even those organizations that scoff at formal class diagrams tend to use some informal version of UML in their design meetings or team discussions.

Further, the most important person you will ever have to communicate with is yourself. We all think we can remember the design decisions we've made, but there will always be the *Why did I do that?* moments hiding in our future. If we keep the scraps of papers we did our initial diagramming on when we started a design, we'll eventually find them a useful reference.

This chapter, however, is not meant to be a tutorial in UML. There are many of these available on the Internet, as well as numerous books available on the topic. UML covers far more than class and object diagrams; it also has a syntax for use cases, deployment, state changes, and activities. We'll be dealing with some common class diagram syntax in this discussion of object-oriented design. You'll find that you can pick up the structure by example, and you'll subconsciously choose the UML-inspired syntax in your own team or personal design sessions.

Our initial diagram, while correct, does not remind us that apples go in barrels or how many barrels a single apple can go in. It only tells us that apples are somehow associated with barrels. The association between classes is often obvious and needs no further explanation, but we have the option to add further clarification as needed.

The beauty of UML is that most things are optional. We only need to specify as much information in a diagram as makes sense for the current situation. In a quick whiteboard session, we might just quickly draw lines between boxes. In a formal document, we might go into more detail. In the case of apples and barrels, we can be fairly confident that the association is, **many apples go in one barrel**, but just to make sure nobody confuses it with, **one apple spoils one barrel**, we can enhance the diagram as shown:

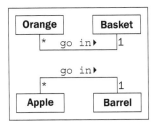

This diagram tells us that oranges **go in** baskets with a little arrow showing what goes in what. It also tells us the number of that object that can be used in the association on both sides of the relationship. One **Basket** can hold many (represented by a *) **Orange** objects. Any one **Orange** can go in exactly one **Basket**. This number is referred to as the multiplicity of the object. You may also hear it described as the cardinality. These are actually slightly distinct terms. Cardinality refers to the actual number of items in the set, whereas multiplicity specifies how small or how large this number could be.

I frequently forget which side of a relationship the multiplicity goes on. The multiplicity nearest to a class is the number of objects of that class that can be associated with any one object at the other end of the association. For the apple goes in barrel association, reading from left to right, many instances of the **Apple** class (that is many **Apple** objects) can go in any one **Barrel**. Reading from right to left, exactly one **Barrel** can be associated with any one **Apple**.

Specifying attributes and behaviors

We now have a grasp of some basic object-oriented terminology. Objects are instances of classes that can be associated with each other. An object instance is a specific object with its own set of data and behaviors; a specific orange on the table in front of us is said to be an instance of the general class of oranges. That's simple enough, but what are these data and behaviors that are associated with each object?

Data describes objects

Let's start with data. Data typically represents the individual characteristics of a certain object. A class can define specific sets of characteristics that are shared by all objects of that class. Any specific object can have different data values for the given characteristics. For example, our three oranges on the table (if we haven't eaten any) could each weigh a different amount. The orange class could then have a weight **attribute**. All instances of the orange class have a weight attribute, but each orange has a different value for this attribute. Attributes don't have to be unique, though; any two oranges may weigh the same amount. As a more realistic example, two objects representing different customers might have the same value for a first name attribute.

Attributes are frequently referred to as **members** or **properties**. Some authors suggest that the terms have different meanings, usually that attributes are settable, while properties are read-only. In Python, the concept of "read-only" is rather pointless, so throughout this book, we'll see the two terms used interchangeably. In addition, as we'll discuss in *Chapter 5, When to Use Object-oriented Programming*, the property keyword has a special meaning in Python for a particular kind of attribute.

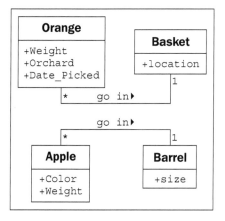

In our fruit inventory application, the fruit farmer may want to know what orchard the orange came from, when it was picked, and how much it weighs. They might also want to keep track of where each basket is stored. Apples might have a color attribute, and barrels might come in different sizes. Some of these properties may also belong to multiple classes (we may want to know when apples are picked, too), but for this first example, let's just add a few different attributes to our class diagram:

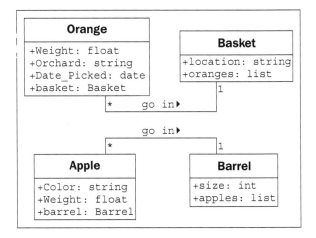

Depending on how detailed our design needs to be, we can also specify the type for each attribute. Attribute types are often primitives that are standard to most programming languages, such as integer, floating-point number, string, byte, or Boolean. However, they can also represent data structures such as lists, trees, or graphs, or most notably, other classes. This is one area where the design stage can overlap with the programming stage. The various primitives or objects available in one programming language may be somewhat different from what is available in other languages.

Usually, we don't need to be overly concerned with data types at the design stage, as implementation-specific details are chosen during the programming stage. Generic names are normally sufficient for design. If our design calls for a list container type, the Java programmers can choose to use a `LinkedList` or an `ArrayList` when implementing it, while the Python programmers (that's us!) can choose between the `list` built-in and a `tuple`.

In our fruit-farming example so far, our attributes are all basic primitives. However, there are some implicit attributes that we can make explicit—the associations. For a given orange, we might have an attribute containing the basket that holds that orange.

Behaviors are actions

Now, we know what data is, but what are behaviors? Behaviors are actions that can occur on an object. The behaviors that can be performed on a specific class of objects are called **methods**. At the programming level, methods are like functions in structured programming, but they magically have access to all the data associated with this object. Like functions, methods can also accept **parameters** and return **values**.

Parameters to a method are a list of objects that need to be **passed** into the method that is being called (the objects that are passed in from the calling object are usually referred to as **arguments**). These objects are used by the method to perform whatever behavior or task it is meant to do. Returned values are the results of that task.

We've stretched our "comparing apples and oranges" example into a basic (if far-fetched) inventory application. Let's stretch it a little further and see if it breaks. One action that can be associated with oranges is the **pick** action. If you think about implementation, **pick** would place the orange in a basket by updating the **basket** attribute of the orange, and by adding the orange to the **oranges** list on the **Basket**. So, **pick** needs to know what basket it is dealing with. We do this by giving the **pick** method a **basket** parameter. Since our fruit farmer also sells juice, we can add a **squeeze** method to **Orange**. When squeezed, **squeeze** might return the amount of juice retrieved, while also removing the **Orange** from the **basket** it was in.

Basket can have a **sell** action. When a basket is sold, our inventory system might update some data on as-yet unspecified objects for accounting and profit calculations. Alternatively, our basket of oranges might go bad before we can sell them, so we add a **discard** method. Let's add these methods to our diagram:

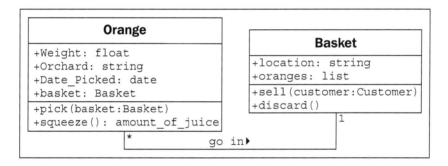

Adding models and methods to individual objects allows us to create a **system** of interacting objects. Each object in the system is a member of a certain class. These classes specify what types of data the object can hold and what methods can be invoked on it. The data in each object can be in a different state from other objects of the same class, and each object may react to method calls differently because of the differences in state.

Object-oriented analysis and design is all about figuring out what those objects are and how they should interact. The next section describes principles that can be used to make those interactions as simple and intuitive as possible.

Hiding details and creating the public interface

The key purpose of modeling an object in object-oriented design is to determine what the public **interface** of that object will be. The interface is the collection of attributes and methods that other objects can use to interact with that object. They do not need, and are often not allowed, to access the internal workings of the object. A common real-world example is the television. Our interface to the television is the remote control. Each button on the remote control represents a method that can be called on the television object. When we, as the calling object, access these methods, we do not know or care if the television is getting its signal from an antenna, a cable connection, or a satellite dish. We don't care what electronic signals are being sent to adjust the volume, or whether the sound is destined to speakers or headphones. If we open the television to access the internal workings, for example, to split the output signal to both external speakers and a set of headphones, we will void the warranty.

This process of hiding the implementation, or functional details, of an object is suitably called **information hiding**. It is also sometimes referred to as **encapsulation**, but encapsulation is actually a more all-encompassing term. Encapsulated data is not necessarily hidden. Encapsulation is, literally, creating a capsule and so think of creating a time capsule. If you put a bunch of information into a time capsule, lock and bury it, it is both encapsulated and the information is hidden. On the other hand, if the time capsule has not been buried and is unlocked or made of clear plastic, the items inside it are still encapsulated, but there is no information hiding.

The distinction between encapsulation and information hiding is largely irrelevant, especially at the design level. Many practical references use these terms interchangeably. As Python programmers, we don't actually have or need true information hiding, (we'll discuss the reasons for this in *Chapter 2*, *Objects in Python*) so the more encompassing definition for encapsulation is suitable.

The public interface, however, is very important. It needs to be carefully designed as it is difficult to change it in the future. Changing the interface will break any client objects that are calling it. We can change the internals all we like, for example, to make it more efficient, or to access data over the network as well as locally, and the client objects will still be able to talk to it, unmodified, using the public interface. On the other hand, if we change the interface by changing attribute names that are publicly accessed, or by altering the order or types of arguments that a method can accept, all client objects will also have to be modified. While on the topic of public interfaces, keep it simple. Always design the interface of an object based on how easy it is to use, not how hard it is to code (this advice applies to user interfaces as well).

Remember, program objects may represent real objects, but that does not make them real objects. They are models. One of the greatest gifts of modeling is the ability to ignore irrelevant details. The model car I built as a child may look like a real 1956 Thunderbird on the outside, but it doesn't run and the driveshaft doesn't turn. These details were overly complex and irrelevant before I started driving. The model is an **abstraction** of a real concept.

Abstraction is another object-oriented concept related to encapsulation and information hiding. Simply put, abstraction means dealing with the level of detail that is most appropriate to a given task. It is the process of extracting a public interface from the inner details. A driver of a car needs to interact with steering, gas pedal, and brakes. The workings of the motor, drive train, and brake subsystem don't matter to the driver. A mechanic, on the other hand, works at a different level of abstraction, tuning the engine and bleeding the breaks. Here's an example of two abstraction levels for a car:

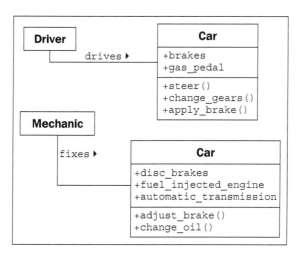

Now, we have several new terms that refer to similar concepts. Condensing all this jargon into a couple of sentences: abstraction is the process of encapsulating information with separate public and private interfaces. The private interfaces can be subject to information hiding.

The important lesson to take from all these definitions is to make our models understandable to other objects that have to interact with them. This means paying careful attention to small details. Ensure methods and properties have sensible names. When analyzing a system, objects typically represent nouns in the original problem, while methods are normally verbs. Attributes can often be picked up as adjectives, although if the attribute refers to another object that is part of the current object, it will still likely be a noun. Name classes, attributes, and methods accordingly.

Don't try to model objects or actions that *might* be useful in the future. Model exactly those tasks that the system needs to perform, and the design will naturally gravitate towards the one that has an appropriate level of abstraction. This is not to say we should not think about possible future design modifications. Our designs should be open ended so that future requirements can be satisfied. However, when abstracting interfaces, try to model exactly what needs to be modeled and nothing more.

When designing the interface, try placing yourself in the object's shoes and imagine that the object has a strong preference for privacy. Don't let other objects have access to data about you unless you feel it is in your best interest for them to have it. Don't give them an interface to force you to perform a specific task unless you are certain you want them to be able to do that to you.

Composition

So far, we learned to design systems as a group of interacting objects, where each interaction involves viewing objects at an appropriate level of abstraction. But we don't know yet how to create these levels of abstraction. There are a variety of ways to do this; we'll discuss some advanced design patterns in *Chapter 8, Strings and Serialization* and *Chapter 9, The Iterator Pattern*. But even most design patterns rely on two basic object-oriented principles known as **composition** and **inheritance**. Composition is simpler, so let's start with it.

Composition is the act of collecting several objects together to create a new one. Composition is usually a good choice when one object is part of another object. We've already seen a first hint of composition in the mechanic example. A car is composed of an engine, transmission, starter, headlights, and windshield, among numerous other parts. The engine, in turn, is composed of pistons, a crank shaft, and valves. In this example, composition is a good way to provide levels of abstraction. The car object can provide the interface required by a driver, while also providing access to its component parts, which offers the deeper level of abstraction suitable for a mechanic. Those component parts can, of course, be further broken down if the mechanic needs more information to diagnose a problem or tune the engine.

This is a common introductory example of composition, but it's not overly useful when it comes to designing computer systems. Physical objects are easy to break into component objects. People have been doing this at least since the ancient Greeks originally postulated that atoms were the smallest units of matter (they, of course, didn't have access to particle accelerators). Computer systems are generally less complicated than physical objects, yet identifying the component objects in such systems does not happen as naturally.

The objects in an object-oriented system occasionally represent physical objects such as people, books, or telephones. More often, however, they represent abstract ideas. People have names, books have titles, and telephones are used to make calls. Calls, titles, accounts, names, appointments, and payments are not usually considered objects in the physical world, but they are all frequently-modeled components in computer systems.

Let's try modeling a more computer-oriented example to see composition in action. We'll be looking at the design of a computerized chess game. This was a very popular pastime among academics in the 80s and 90s. People were predicting that computers would one day be able to defeat a human chess master. When this happened in 1997 (IBM's Deep Blue defeated world chess champion, Gary Kasparov), interest in the problem waned, although there are still contests between computer and human chess players. (The computers usually win.)

As a basic, high-level analysis, a game of chess is played between two *players*, using a *chess set* featuring a *board* containing sixty-four *positions* in an 8 X 8 grid. The board can have two sets of sixteen *pieces* that can be **moved**, in alternating *turns* by the two players in different ways. Each piece can **take** other pieces. The board will be required to **draw** itself on the computer screen after each turn.

I've identified some of the possible objects in the description using *italics*, and a few key methods using **bold**. This is a common first step in turning an object-oriented analysis into a design. At this point, to emphasize composition, we'll focus on the board, without worrying too much about the players or the different types of pieces.

Let's start at the highest level of abstraction possible. We have two players interacting with a chess set by taking turns making moves:

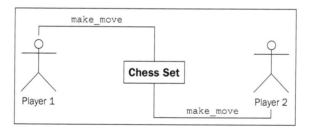

What is this? It doesn't quite look like our earlier class diagrams. That's because it isn't a class diagram! This is an **object diagram**, also called an instance diagram. It describes the system at a specific state in time, and is describing specific instances of objects, not the interaction between classes. Remember, both players are members of the same class, so the class diagram looks a little different:

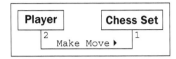

The diagram shows that exactly two players can interact with one chess set. It also indicates that any one player can be playing with only one chess set at a time.

However, we're discussing composition, not UML, so let's think about what the **Chess Set** is composed of. We don't care what the player is composed of at this time. We can assume that the player has a heart and brain, among other organs, but these are irrelevant to our model. Indeed, there is nothing stopping said player from being Deep Blue itself, which has neither a heart nor a brain.

The chess set, then, is composed of a board and 32 pieces. The board further comprises 64 positions. You could argue that pieces are not part of the chess set because you could replace the pieces in a chess set with a different set of pieces. While this is unlikely or impossible in a computerized version of chess, it introduces us to **aggregation**.

Aggregation is almost exactly like composition. The difference is that aggregate objects can exist independently. It would be impossible for a position to be associated with a different chess board, so we say the board is composed of positions. But the pieces, which might exist independently of the chess set, are said to be in an aggregate relationship with that set.

Another way to differentiate between aggregation and composition is to think about the lifespan of the object. If the composite (outside) object controls when the related (inside) objects are created and destroyed, composition is most suitable. If the related object is created independently of the composite object, or can outlast that object, an aggregate relationship makes more sense. Also, keep in mind that composition is aggregation; aggregation is simply a more general form of composition. Any composite relationship is also an aggregate relationship, but not vice versa.

Let's describe our current chess set composition and add some attributes to the objects to hold the composite relationships:

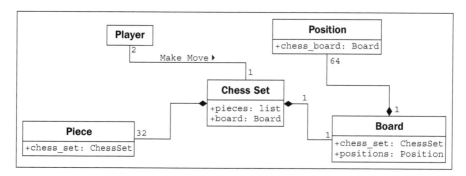

The composition relationship is represented in UML as a solid diamond. The hollow diamond represents the aggregate relationship. You'll notice that the board and pieces are stored as part of the chess set in exactly the same way a reference to them is stored as an attribute on the chess set. This shows that, once again, in practice, the distinction between aggregation and composition is often irrelevant once you get past the design stage. When implemented, they behave in much the same way. However, it can help to differentiate between the two when your team is discussing how the different objects interact. Often, you can treat them as the same thing, but when you need to distinguish between them, it's great to know the difference (this is abstraction at work).

Inheritance

We discussed three types of relationships between objects: association, composition, and aggregation. However, we have not fully specified our chess set, and these tools don't seem to give us all the power we need. We discussed the possibility that a player might be a human or it might be a piece of software featuring artificial intelligence. It doesn't seem right to say that a player is *associated* with a human, or that the artificial intelligence implementation is *part of* the player object. What we really need is the ability to say that "Deep Blue *is a* player" or that "Gary Kasparov *is a* player".

The *is a* relationship is formed by **inheritance**. Inheritance is the most famous, well-known, and over-used relationship in object-oriented programming. Inheritance is sort of like a family tree. My grandfather's last name was Phillips and my father inherited that name. I inherited it from him (along with blue eyes and a penchant for writing). In object-oriented programming, instead of inheriting features and behaviors from a person, one class can inherit attributes and methods from another class.

For example, there are 32 chess pieces in our chess set, but there are only six different types of pieces (pawns, rooks, bishops, knights, king, and queen), each of which behaves differently when it is moved. All of these classes of piece have properties, such as color and the chess set they are part of, but they also have unique shapes when drawn on the chess board, and make different moves. Let's see how the six types of pieces can inherit from a **Piece** class:

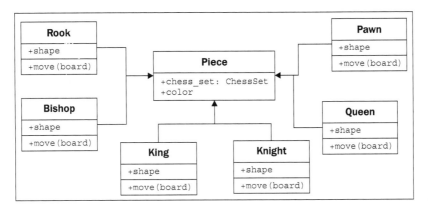

The hollow arrows indicate that the individual classes of pieces inherit from the **Piece** class. All the subtypes automatically have a **chess_set** and **color** attribute inherited from the base class. Each piece provides a different shape property (to be drawn on the screen when rendering the board), and a different **move** method to move the piece to a new position on the board at each turn.

We actually know that all subclasses of the **Piece** class need to have a **move** method; otherwise, when the board tries to move the piece, it will get confused. It is possible that we would want to create a new version of the game of chess that has one additional piece (the wizard). Our current design allows us to design this piece without giving it a **move** method. The board would then choke when it asked the piece to move itself.

We can implement this by creating a dummy move method on the **Piece** class. The subclasses can then **override** this method with a more specific implementation. The default implementation might, for example, pop up an error message that says: **That piece cannot be moved**.

Overriding methods in subtypes allows very powerful object-oriented systems to be developed. For example, if we wanted to implement a player class with artificial intelligence, we might provide a `calculate_move` method that takes a **Board** object and decides which piece to move where. A very basic class might randomly choose a piece and direction and move it accordingly. We could then override this method in a subclass with the Deep Blue implementation. The first class would be suitable for play against a raw beginner, the latter would challenge a grand master. The important thing is that other methods in the class, such as the ones that inform the board as to which move was chose need not be changed; this implementation can be shared between the two classes.

In the case of chess pieces, it doesn't really make sense to provide a default implementation of the move method. All we need to do is specify that the move method is required in any subclasses. This can be done by making **Piece** an **abstract class** with the move method declared **abstract**. Abstract methods basically say, "We demand this method exist in any non-abstract subclass, but we are declining to specify an implementation in this class."

Indeed, it is possible to make a class that does not implement any methods at all. Such a class would simply tell us what the class should do, but provides absolutely no advice on how to do it. In object-oriented parlance, such classes are called **interfaces**.

Inheritance provides abstraction

Let's explore the longest word in object-oriented argot. **Polymorphism** is the ability to treat a class differently depending on which subclass is implemented. We've already seen it in action with the pieces system we've described. If we took the design a bit further, we'd probably see that the **Board** object can accept a move from the player and call the **move** function on the piece. The board need not ever know what type of piece it is dealing with. All it has to do is call the **move** method, and the proper subclass will take care of moving it as a **Knight** or a **Pawn**.

Polymorphism is pretty cool, but it is a word that is rarely used in Python programming. Python goes an extra step past allowing a subclass of an object to be treated like a parent class. A board implemented in Python could take any object that has a **move** method, whether it is a bishop piece, a car, or a duck. When **move** is called, the **Bishop** will move diagonally on the board, the car will drive someplace, and the duck will swim or fly, depending on its mood.

This sort of polymorphism in Python is typically referred to as **duck typing**: "If it walks like a duck or swims like a duck, it's a duck". We don't care if it really *is a* duck (inheritance), only that it swims or walks. Geese and swans might easily be able to provide the duck-like behavior we are looking for. This allows future designers to create new types of birds without actually specifying an inheritance hierarchy for aquatic birds. It also allows them to create completely different drop-in behaviors that the original designers never planned for. For example, future designers might be able to make a walking, swimming penguin that works with the same interface without ever suggesting that penguins are ducks.

Multiple inheritance

When we think of inheritance in our own family tree, we can see that we inherit features from more than just one parent. When strangers tell a proud mother that her son has, "his fathers eyes", she will typically respond along the lines of, "yes, but he got my nose."

Object-oriented design can also feature such **multiple inheritance**, which allows a subclass to inherit functionality from multiple parent classes. In practice, multiple inheritance can be a tricky business, and some programming languages (most notably, Java) strictly prohibit it. However, multiple inheritance can have its uses. Most often, it can be used to create objects that have two distinct sets of behaviors. For example, an object designed to connect to a scanner and send a fax of the scanned document might be created by inheriting from two separate `scanner` and `faxer` objects.

As long as two classes have distinct interfaces, it is not normally harmful for a subclass to inherit from both of them. However, it gets messy if we inherit from two classes that provide overlapping interfaces. For example, if we have a motorcycle class that has a `move` method, and a boat class also featuring a `move` method, and we want to merge them into the ultimate amphibious vehicle, how does the resulting class know what to do when we call `move`? At the design level, this needs to be explained, and at the implementation level, each programming language has different ways of deciding which parent class's method is called, or in what order.

Often, the best way to deal with it is to avoid it. If you have a design showing up like this, you're *probably* doing it wrong. Take a step back, analyze the system again, and see if you can remove the multiple inheritance relationship in favor of some other association or composite design.

Inheritance is a very powerful tool for extending behavior. It is also one of the most marketable advancements of object-oriented design over earlier paradigms. Therefore, it is often the first tool that object-oriented programmers reach for. However, it is important to recognize that owning a hammer does not turn screws into nails. Inheritance is the perfect solution for obvious *is a* relationships, but it can be abused. Programmers often use inheritance to share code between two kinds of objects that are only distantly related, with no *is a* relationship in sight. While this is not necessarily a bad design, it is a terrific opportunity to ask just why they decided to design it that way, and whether a different relationship or design pattern would have been more suitable.

Case study

Let's tie all our new object-oriented knowledge together by going through a few iterations of object-oriented design on a somewhat real-world example. The system we'll be modeling is a library catalog. Libraries have been tracking their inventory for centuries, originally using card catalogs, and more recently, electronic inventories. Modern libraries have web-based catalogs that we can query from our homes.

Let's start with an analysis. The local librarian has asked us to write a new card catalog program because their ancient DOS-based program is ugly and out of date. That doesn't give us much detail, but before we start asking for more information, let's consider what we already know about library catalogs.

Catalogs contain lists of books. People search them to find books on certain subjects, with specific titles, or by a particular author. Books can be uniquely identified by an **International Standard Book Number (ISBN)**. Each book has a **Dewey Decimal System (DDS)** number assigned to help find it on a particular shelf.

This simple analysis tells us some of the obvious objects in the system. We quickly identify **Book** as the most important object, with several attributes already mentioned, such as author, title, subject, ISBN, and DDS number, and catalog as a sort of manager for books.

We also notice a few other objects that may or may not need to be modeled in the system. For cataloging purposes, all we need to search a book by author is an `author_name` attribute on the book. However, authors are also objects, and we might want to store some other data about the author. As we ponder this, we might remember that some books have multiple authors. Suddenly, the idea of having a single `author_name` attribute on objects seems a bit silly. A list of authors associated with each book is clearly a better idea.

The relationship between author and book is clearly association, since you would never say, "a book is an author" (it's not inheritance), and saying "a book has an author", though grammatically correct, does not imply that authors are part of books (it's not aggregation). Indeed, any one author may be associated with multiple books.

We should also pay attention to the noun (nouns are always good candidates for objects) *shelf*. Is a shelf an object that needs to be modeled in a cataloging system? How do we identify an individual shelf? What happens if a book is stored at the end of one shelf, and later moved to the beginning of the next shelf because another book was inserted in the previous shelf?

DDS was designed to help locate physical books in a library. As such, storing a DDS attribute with the book should be enough to locate it, regardless of which shelf it is stored on. So we can, at least for the moment, remove shelf from our list of contending objects.

Another questionable object in the system is the user. Do we need to know anything about a specific user, such as their name, address, or list of overdue books? So far, the librarian has told us only that they want a catalog; they said nothing about tracking subscriptions or overdue notices. In the back of our minds, we also note that authors and users are both specific kinds of people; there might be a useful inheritance relationship here in the future.

For cataloging purposes, we decide we don't need to identify the user for now. We can assume that a user will be searching the catalog, but we don't have to actively model them in the system, beyond providing an interface that allows them to search.

We have identified a few attributes on the book, but what properties does a catalog have? Does any one library have more than one catalog? Do we need to uniquely identify them? Obviously, the catalog has to have a collection of the books it contains, somehow, but this list is probably not part of the public interface.

What about behaviors? The catalog clearly needs a search method, possibly separate ones for authors, titles, and subjects. Are there any behaviors on books? Would it need a preview method? Or could preview be identified by a first pages attribute instead of a method?

The questions in the preceding discussion are all part of the object-oriented analysis phase. But intermixed with the questions, we have already identified a few key objects that are part of the design. Indeed, what you have just seen are several microiterations between analysis and design.

Likely, these iterations would all occur in an initial meeting with the librarian. Before this meeting, however, we can already sketch out a most basic design for the objects we have concretely identified:

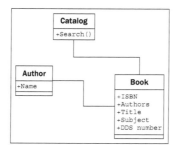

Armed with this basic diagram and a pencil to interactively improve it, we meet up with the librarian. They tell us that this is a good start, but libraries don't serve only books, they also have DVDs, magazines, and CDs, none of which have an ISBN or DDS number. All of these types of items can be uniquely identified by a UPC number though. We remind the librarian that they have to find the items on the shelf, and these items probably aren't organized by UPC. The librarian explains that each type is organized in a different way. The CDs are mostly audio books, and they only have a couple of dozen in stock, so they are organized by the author's last name. DVDs are divided into genre and further organized by title. Magazines are organized by title and then refined by the volume and issue number. Books are, as we had guessed, organized by the DDS number.

With no previous object-oriented design experience, we might consider adding separate lists of DVDs, CDs, magazines, and books to our catalog, and search each one in turn. The trouble is, except for certain extended attributes, and identifying the physical location of the item, these items all behave as much the same. This is a job for inheritance! We quickly update our UML diagram:

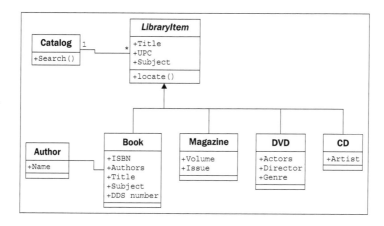

The librarian understands the gist of our sketched diagram, but is a bit confused by the **locate** functionality. We explain using a specific use case where the user is searching for the word "bunnies". The user first sends a search request to the catalog. The catalog queries its internal list of items and finds a book and a DVD with "bunnies" in the title. At this point, the catalog doesn't care if it is holding a DVD, book, CD, or magazine; all items are the same, as far as the catalog is concerned. However, the user wants to know how to find the physical items, so the catalog would be remiss if it simply returned a list of titles. So, it calls the **locate** method on the two items it has uncovered. The book's **locate** method returns a DDS number that can be used to find the shelf holding the book. The DVD is located by returning the genre and title of the DVD. The user can then visit the DVD section, find the section containing that genre, and find the specific DVD as sorted by the titles.

As we explain, we sketch a UML **sequence diagram** explaining how the various objects are communicating:

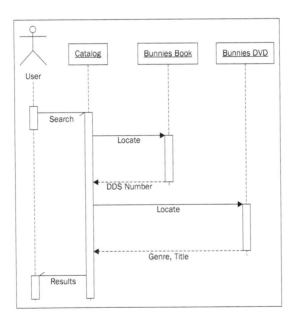

Where, class diagrams describe the relationships between classes, and sequence diagrams describe specific sequences of messages passed between objects. The dashed line hanging from each object is a **lifeline** describing the lifetime of the object. The wider boxes on each lifeline represent active processing in that object (where there's no box, the object is basically sitting idle, waiting for something to happen). The horizontal arrows between the lifelines indicate specific messages. The solid arrows represent methods being called, while the dashed arrows with solid heads represent the method return values.

The half arrowheads indicate asynchronous messages sent to or from an object. An asynchronous message typically means the first object calls a method on the second object, which returns immediately. After some processing, the second object calls a method on the first object to give it a value. This is in contrast to normal method calls, which do the processing in the method, and return a value immediately.

Sequence diagrams, like all UML diagrams, are best used only when they are needed. There is no point in drawing a UML diagram for the sake of drawing a diagram. However, when you need to communicate a series of interactions between two objects, the sequence diagram is a very useful tool.

Unfortunately, our class diagram so far is still a messy design. We notice that actors on DVDs and artists on CDs are all types of people, but are being treated differently from the book authors. The librarian also reminds us that most of their CDs are audio books, which have authors instead of artists.

How can we deal with different kinds of people that contribute to a title? An obvious implementation is to create a `Person` class with the person's name and other relevant details, and then create subclasses of this for the artists, authors, and actors. However, is inheritance really necessary here? For searching and cataloging purposes, we don't really care that acting and writing are two very different activities. If we were doing an economic simulation, it would make sense to give separate actor and author classes, and different `calculate_income` and `perform_job` methods, but for cataloging purposes, it is probably enough to know how the person contributed to the item. We recognize that all items have one or more `Contributor` objects, so we move the author relationship from the book to its parent class:

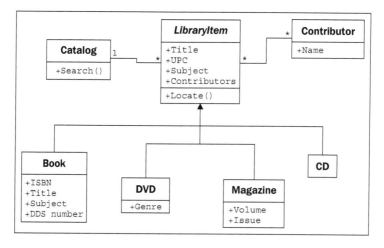

The multiplicity of the **Contributor/LibraryItem** relationship is **many-to-many**, as indicated by the * character at both ends of one relationship. Any one library item might have more than one contributor (for example, several actors and a director on a DVD). And many authors write many books, so they would be attached to multiple library items.

This little change, while it looks a bit cleaner and simpler, has lost some vital information. We can still tell who contributed to a specific library item, but we don't know how they contributed. Were they the director or an actor? Did they write the audio book, or were they the voice that narrated the book?

It would be nice if we could just add a `contributor_type` attribute on the **Contributor** class, but this will fall apart when dealing with multitalented people who have both authored books and directed movies.

One option is to add attributes to each of our **LibraryItem** subclasses that hold the information we need, such as **Author** on **Book**, or **Artist** on **CD**, and then make the relationship to those properties all point to the **Contributor** class. The problem with this is that we lose a lot of polymorphic elegance. If we want to list the contributors to an item, we have to look for specific attributes on that item, such as **Authors** or **Actors**. We can alleviate this by adding a **GetContributors** method on the **LibraryItem** class that subclasses can override. Then the catalog never has to know what attributes the objects are querying; we've abstracted the public interface:

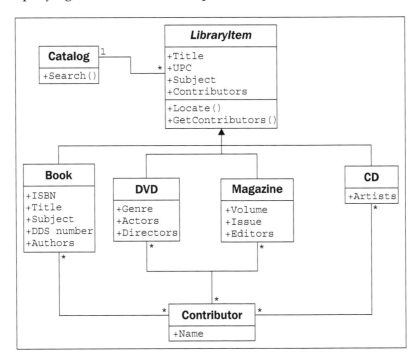

Just looking at this class diagram, it feels like we are doing something wrong. It is bulky and fragile. It may do everything we need, but it feels like it will be hard to maintain or extend. There are too many relationships, and too many classes would be affected by modifications to any one class. It looks like spaghetti and meatballs.

Now that we've explored inheritance as an option, and found it wanting, we might look back at our previous composition-based diagram, where **Contributor** was attached directly to **LibraryItem**. With some thought, we can see that we actually only need to add one more relationship to a brand-new class to identify the type of contributor. This is an important step in object-oriented design. We are now adding a class to the design that is intended to *support* the other objects, rather than modeling any part of the initial requirements. We are **refactoring** the design to facilitate the objects in the system, rather than objects in real life. Refactoring is an essential process in the maintenance of a program or design. The goal of refactoring is to improve the design by moving code around, removing duplicate code or complex relationships in favor of simpler, more elegant designs.

This new class is composed of a **Contributor** and an extra attribute identifying the type of contribution the person has made to the given **LibraryItem**. There can be many such contributions to a particular **LibraryItem**, and one contributor can contribute in the same way to different items. The diagram communicates this design very well:

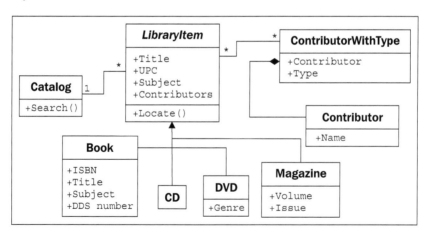

At first, this composition relationship looks less natural than the inheritance-based relationships. However, it has the advantage of allowing us to add new types of contributions without adding a new class to the design. Inheritance is most useful when the subclasses have some kind of specialization. Specialization is creating or changing attributes or behaviors on the subclass to make it somehow different from the parent class. It seems silly to create a bunch of empty classes solely for identifying different types of objects (this attitude is less prevalent among Java and other "everything is an object" programmers, but it is common among more practical Python designers). If we look at the inheritance version of the diagram, we can see a bunch of subclasses that don't actually do anything:

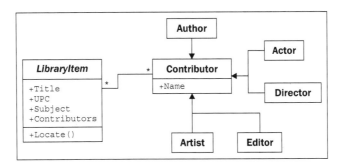

Sometimes it is important to recognize when not to use object-oriented principles. This example of when not to use inheritance is a good reminder that objects are just tools, and not rules.

Exercises

This is a practical book, not a textbook. As such, I'm not about to assign you a bunch of fake object-oriented analysis problems to create designs for bunch of fake object-oriented problems to analyze and design. Instead, I want to give you some thoughts that you can apply to your own projects. If you have previous object-oriented experience, you won't need to put much effort into these. However, they are useful mental exercises if you've been using Python for a while, but never really cared about all that class stuff.

First, think about a recent programming project you've completed. Identify the most prominent object in the design. Try to think of as many attributes for this object as possible. Did it have: Color? Weight? Size? Profit? Cost? Name? ID number? Price? Style? Think about the attribute types. Were they primitives or classes? Were some of those attributes actually behaviors in disguise? Sometimes what looks like data is actually calculated from other data on the object, and you can use a method to do those calculations. What other methods or behaviors did the object have? Which objects called those methods? What kinds of relationships did they have with this object?

Now, think about an upcoming project. It doesn't matter what the project is; it might be a fun free-time project or a multimillion dollar contract. It doesn't have to be a complete application; it could just be one subsystem. Perform a basic object-oriented analysis. Identify the requirements and the interacting objects. Sketch out a class diagram featuring the highest level of abstraction on that system. Identify the major interacting objects. Identify minor supporting objects. Go into detail for the attributes and methods of some of the most interesting ones. Take different objects to different levels of abstraction. Look for places you can use inheritance or composition. Look for places you should avoid inheritance.

The goal is not to design a system (although you're certainly welcome to do so if inclination meets both ambition and available time). The goal is to think about object-oriented designs. Focusing on projects that you have worked on, or are expecting to work on in the future, simply makes it real.

Now, visit your favorite search engine and look up some tutorials on UML. There are dozens, so find the one that suits your preferred method of study. Sketch some class diagrams or a sequence diagram for the objects you identified earlier. Don't get too hung up on memorizing the syntax (after all, if it is important, you can always look it up again), just get a feel for the language. Something will stay lodged in your brain, and it can make communicating a bit easier if you can quickly sketch a diagram for your next OOP discussion.

Summary

In this chapter, we took a whirlwind tour through the terminology of the object-oriented paradigm, focusing on object-oriented design. We can separate different objects into a taxonomy of different classes and describe the attributes and behaviors of those objects via the class interface. Classes describe objects, abstraction, encapsulation, and information hiding are highly related concepts. There are many different kinds of relationships between objects, including association, composition, and inheritance. UML syntax can be useful for fun and communication.

In the next chapter, we'll explore how to implement classes and methods in Python.

2
Objects in Python

So, we now have a design in hand and are ready to turn that design into a working program! Of course, it doesn't usually happen this way. We'll be seeing examples and hints for good software design throughout the book, but our focus is object-oriented programming. So, let's have a look at the Python syntax that allows us to create object-oriented software.

After completing this chapter, we will understand:

- How to create classes and instantiate objects in Python
- How to add attributes and behaviors to Python objects
- How to organize classes into packages and modules
- How to suggest people don't clobber our data

Creating Python classes

We don't have to write much Python code to realize that Python is a very "clean" language. When we want to do something, we just do it, without having to go through a lot of setup. The ubiquitous "hello world" in Python, as you've likely seen, is only one line.

Similarly, the simplest class in Python 3 looks like this:

```
class MyFirstClass:
    pass
```

There's our first object-oriented program! The class definition starts with the `class` keyword. This is followed by a name (of our choice) identifying the class, and is terminated with a colon.

The class name must follow standard Python variable naming rules (it must start with a letter or underscore, and can only be comprised of letters, underscores, or numbers). In addition, the Python style guide (search the web for "PEP 8") recommends that classes should be named using **CamelCase** notation (start with a capital letter; any subsequent words should also start with a capital).

The class definition line is followed by the class contents indented. As with other Python constructs, indentation is used to delimit the classes, rather than braces or brackets as many other languages use. Use four spaces for indentation unless you have a compelling reason not to (such as fitting in with somebody else's code that uses tabs for indents). Any decent programming editor can be configured to insert four spaces whenever the *Tab* key is pressed.

Since our first class doesn't actually do anything, we simply use the `pass` keyword on the second line to indicate that no further action needs to be taken.

We might think there isn't much we can do with this most basic class, but it does allow us to instantiate objects of that class. We can load the class into the Python 3 interpreter, so we can interactively play with it. To do this, save the class definition mentioned earlier into a file named `first_class.py` and then run the command `python -i first_class.py`. The `-i` argument tells Python to "run the code and then drop to the interactive interpreter". The following interpreter session demonstrates basic interaction with this class:

```
>>> a = MyFirstClass()
>>> b = MyFirstClass()
>>> print(a)
<__main__.MyFirstClass object at 0xb7b7faec>
>>> print(b)
<__main__.MyFirstClass object at 0xb7b7fbac>
>>>
```

This code instantiates two objects from the new class, named a and b. Creating an instance of a class is a simple matter of typing the class name followed by a pair of parentheses. It looks much like a normal function call, but Python knows we're "calling" a class and not a function, so it understands that its job is to create a new object. When printed, the two objects tell us which class they are and what memory address they live at. Memory addresses aren't used much in Python code, but here, they demonstrate that there are two distinct objects involved.

Downloading the example code

You can download the example code files for all Packt books you have purchased from your account at http://www.packtpub.com. If you purchased this book elsewhere, you can visit http://www.packtpub.com/support and register to have the files e-mailed directly to you.

Adding attributes

Now, we have a basic class, but it's fairly useless. It doesn't contain any data, and it doesn't do anything. What do we have to do to assign an attribute to a given object?

It turns out that we don't have to do anything special in the class definition. We can set arbitrary attributes on an instantiated object using the dot notation:

```
class Point:
    pass

p1 = Point()
p2 = Point()

p1.x = 5
p1.y = 4

p2.x = 3
p2.y = 6

print(p1.x, p1.y)
print(p2.x, p2.y)
```

If we run this code, the two `print` statements at the end tell us the new attribute values on the two objects:

```
5 4
```

```
3 6
```

This code creates an empty `Point` class with no data or behaviors. Then it creates two instances of that class and assigns each of those instances x and y coordinates to identify a point in two dimensions. All we need to do to assign a value to an attribute on an object is use the *<object>.<attribute>* = *<value>* syntax. This is sometimes referred to as **dot notation**. The value can be anything: a Python primitive, a built-in data type, or another object. It can even be a function or another class!

Making it do something

Now, having objects with attributes is great, but object-oriented programming is really about the interaction between objects. We're interested in invoking actions that cause things to happen to those attributes. It is time to add behaviors to our classes.

Let's model a couple of actions on our `Point` class. We can start with a called `reset` that moves the point to the origin (the origin is the point where x and y are both zero). This is a good introductory action because it doesn't require any parameters:

```
class Point:
    def reset(self):
        self.x = 0
        self.y = 0

p = Point()
p.reset()
print(p.x, p.y)
```

This `print` statement shows us the two zeros on the attributes:

```
0 0
```

A method in Python is formatted identically to a function. It starts with the keyword `def` followed by a space and the name of the method. This is followed by a set of parentheses containing the parameter list (we'll discuss that `self` parameter in just a moment), and terminated with a colon. The next line is indented to contain the statements inside the method. These statements can be arbitrary Python code operating on the object itself and any parameters passed in as the method sees fit.

Talking to yourself

The one difference between methods and normal functions is that all methods have one required argument. This argument is conventionally named `self`; I've never seen a programmer use any other name for this variable (convention is a very powerful thing). There's nothing stopping you, however, from calling it `this` or even `Martha`.

The `self` argument to a method is simply a reference to the object that the method is being invoked on. We can access attributes and methods of that object as if it were any another object. This is exactly what we do inside the `reset` method when we set the x and y attributes of the `self` object.

Notice that when we call the `p.reset()` method, we do not have to pass the `self` argument into it. Python automatically takes care of this for us. It knows we're calling a method on the `p` object, so it automatically passes that object to the method.

However, the method really is just a function that happens to be on a class. Instead of calling the method on the object, we can invoke the function on the class, explicitly passing our object as the `self` argument:

```
p = Point()
Point.reset(p)
print(p.x, p.y)
```

The output is the same as the previous example because internally, the exact same process has occurred.

What happens if we forget to include the `self` argument in our class definition? Python will bail with an error message:

```
>>> class Point:
...     def reset():
...         pass
...
>>> p = Point()
>>> p.reset()
Traceback (most recent call last):
  File "<stdin>", line 1, in <module>
TypeError: reset() takes no arguments (1 given)
```

The error message is not as clear as it could be ("You silly fool, you forgot the `self` argument" would be more informative). Just remember that when you see an error message that indicates missing arguments, the first thing to check is whether you forgot `self` in the method definition.

More arguments

So, how do we pass multiple arguments to a method? Let's add a new method that allows us to move a point to an arbitrary position, not just to the origin. We can also include one that accepts another `Point` object as input and returns the distance between them:

```
import math

class Point:
```

```python
    def move(self, x, y):
        self.x = x
        self.y = y

    def reset(self):
        self.move(0, 0)

    def calculate_distance(self, other_point):
        return math.sqrt(
                (self.x - other_point.x)**2 +
                (self.y - other_point.y)**2)

# how to use it:
point1 = Point()
point2 = Point()

point1.reset()
point2.move(5,0)
print(point2.calculate_distance(point1))
assert (point2.calculate_distance(point1) ==
        point1.calculate_distance(point2))
point1.move(3,4)
print(point1.calculate_distance(point2))
print(point1.calculate_distance(point1))
```

The `print` statements at the end give us the following output:

```
5.0
4.472135955
0.0
```

A lot has happened here. The class now has three methods. The `move` method accepts two arguments, x and y, and sets the values on the `self` object, much like the old `reset` method from the previous example. The old `reset` method now calls `move`, since a reset is just a move to a specific known location.

The `calculate_distance` method uses the not-too-complex Pythagorean theorem to calculate the distance between two points. I hope you understand the math (`**` means squared, and `math.sqrt` calculates a square root), but it's not a requirement for our current focus, learning how to write methods.

The sample code at the end of the preceding example shows how to call a method with arguments: simply include the arguments inside the parentheses, and use the same dot notation to access the method. I just picked some random positions to test the methods. The test code calls each method and prints the results on the console. The `assert` function is a simple test tool; the program will bail if the statement after `assert` is `False` (or zero, empty, or `None`). In this case, we use it to ensure that the distance is the same regardless of which point called the other point's `calculate_distance` method.

Initializing the object

If we don't explicitly set the x and y positions on our `Point` object, either using `move` or by accessing them directly, we have a broken point with no real position. What will happen when we try to access it?

Well, let's just try it and see. "Try it and see" is an extremely useful tool for Python study. Open up your interactive interpreter and type away. The following interactive session shows what happens if we try to access a missing attribute. If you saved the previous example as a file or are using the examples distributed with the book, you can load it into the Python interpreter with the command `python -i filename.py`:

```
>>> point = Point()
>>> point.x = 5
>>> print(point.x)
5
>>> print(point.y)
Traceback (most recent call last):
  File "<stdin>", line 1, in <module>
AttributeError: 'Point' object has no attribute 'y'
```

Well, at least it threw a useful exception. We'll cover exceptions in detail in *Chapter 4, Expecting the Unexpected*. You've probably seen them before (especially the ubiquitous **SyntaxError**, which means you typed something incorrectly!). At this point, simply be aware that it means something went wrong.

The output is useful for debugging. In the interactive interpreter, it tells us the error occurred at **line 1**, which is only partially true (in an interactive session, only one line is executed at a time). If we were running a script in a file, it would tell us the exact line number, making it easy to find the offending code. In addition, it tells us the error is an `AttributeError`, and gives a helpful message telling us what that error means.

We can catch and recover from this error, but in this case, it feels like we should have specified some sort of default value. Perhaps every new object should be reset() by default, or maybe it would be nice if we could force the user to tell us what those positions should be when they create the object.

Most object-oriented programming languages have the concept of a **constructor**, a special method that creates and initializes the object when it is created. Python is a little different; it has a constructor *and* an initializer. The constructor function is rarely used unless you're doing something exotic. So, we'll start our discussion with the initialization method.

The Python initialization method is the same as any other method, except it has a special name, __init__. The leading and trailing double underscores mean this is a special method that the Python interpreter will treat as a special case.

 Never name a function of your own with leading and trailing double underscores. It may mean nothing to Python, but there's always the possibility that the designers of Python will add a function that has a special purpose with that name in the future, and when they do, your code will break.

Let's start with an initialization function on our Point class that requires the user to supply x and y coordinates when the Point object is instantiated:

```python
class Point:
    def __init__(self, x, y):
        self.move(x, y)

    def move(self, x, y):
        self.x = x
        self.y = y

    def reset(self):
        self.move(0, 0)

# Constructing a Point
point = Point(3, 5)
print(point.x, point.y)
```

Now, our point can never go without a y coordinate! If we try to construct a point without including the proper initialization parameters, it will fail with a **not enough arguments** error similar to the one we received earlier when we forgot the self argument.

What if we don't want to make those two arguments required? Well, then we can use the same syntax Python functions use to provide default arguments. The keyword argument syntax appends an equals sign after each variable name. If the calling object does not provide this argument, then the default argument is used instead. The variables will still be available to the function, but they will have the values specified in the argument list. Here's an example:

```
class Point:
    def __init__(self, x=0, y=0):
        self.move(x, y)
```

Most of the time, we put our initialization statements in an __init__ function. But as mentioned earlier, Python has a constructor in addition to its initialization function. You may never need to use the other Python constructor, but it helps to know it exists, so we'll cover it briefly.

The constructor function is called __new__ as opposed to __init__, and accepts exactly one argument; the class that is being constructed (it is called *before* the object is constructed, so there is no self argument). It also has to return the newly created object. This has interesting possibilities when it comes to the complicated art of metaprogramming, but is not very useful in day-to-day programming. In practice, you will rarely, if ever, need to use __new__ and __init__ will be sufficient.

Explaining yourself

Python is an extremely easy-to-read programming language; some might say it is self-documenting. However, when doing object-oriented programming, it is important to write API documentation that clearly summarizes what each object and method does. Keeping documentation up-to-date is difficult; the best way to do it is to write it right into our code.

Python supports this through the use of **docstrings**. Each class, function, or method header can have a standard Python string as the first line following the definition (the line that ends in a colon). This line should be indented the same as the following code.

Docstrings are simply Python strings enclosed with apostrophe (') or quote (") characters. Often, docstrings are quite long and span multiple lines (the style guide suggests that the line length should not exceed 80 characters), which can be formatted as multi-line strings, enclosed in matching triple apostrophe (''') or triple quote (""") characters.

A docstring should clearly and concisely summarize the purpose of the class or method it is describing. It should explain any parameters whose usage is not immediately obvious, and is also a good place to include short examples of how to use the API. Any caveats or problems an unsuspecting user of the API should be aware of should also be noted.

To illustrate the use of docstrings, we will end this section with our completely documented Point class:

```python
import math

class Point:
    'Represents a point in two-dimensional geometric coordinates'

    def __init__(self, x=0, y=0):
        '''Initialize the position of a new point. The x and y
        coordinates can be specified. If they are not, the
            point defaults to the origin.'''
        self.move(x, y)

    def move(self, x, y):
        "Move the point to a new location in 2D space."
        self.x = x
        self.y = y

    def reset(self):
        'Reset the point back to the geometric origin: 0, 0'
        self.move(0, 0)

    def calculate_distance(self, other_point):
        """Calculate the distance from this point to a second
        point passed as a parameter.

        This function uses the Pythagorean Theorem to calculate
        the distance between the two points. The distance is
        returned as a float."""

        return math.sqrt(
                (self.x - other_point.x)**2 +
                (self.y - other_point.y)**2)
```

Try typing or loading (remember, it's `python -i filename.py`) this file into the interactive interpreter. Then, enter `help(Point)<enter>` at the Python prompt. You should see nicely formatted documentation for the class, as shown in the following screenshot:

```
Terminal - dusty@cactus:~/writing/packt/Chapter2/code
File  Edit  View  Terminal  Go  Help
Help on class Point in module __main__:

class Point(builtins.object)
 |  Represents a point in two-dimensional geometric coordinates
 |
 |  Methods defined here:
 |
 |  __init__(self, x=0, y=0)
 |      Initialize the position of a new point. The x and y coordinates can
 |      be specified. If they are not, the point defaults to the origin.
 |
 |  calculate_distance(self, other_point)
 |      Calculate the distance from this point to a second point passed
 |      as a parameter.
 |
 |      This function uses the Pythagorean Theorem to calculate the distance
 |      between the two points.  The distance is returned as a float.
 |
 |  move(self, x, y)
 |      Move the point to a new location in two-dimensional space.
 |
 |  reset(self)
 |      Reset the point back to the geometric origin: 0, 0
```

Modules and packages

Now, we know how to create classes and instantiate objects, but how do we organize them? For small programs, we can just put all our classes into one file and add a little script at the end of the file to start them interacting. However, as our projects grow, it can become difficult to find the one class that needs to be edited among the many classes we've defined. This is where **modules** come in. Modules are simply Python files, nothing more. The single file in our small program is a module. Two Python files are two modules. If we have two files in the same folder, we can load a class from one module for use in the other module.

For example, if we are building an e-commerce system, we will likely be storing a lot of data in a database. We can put all the classes and functions related to database access into a separate file (we'll call it something sensible: `database.py`). Then, our other modules (for example, customer models, product information, and inventory) can import classes from that module in order to access the database.

The `import` statement is used for importing modules or specific classes or functions from modules. We've already seen an example of this in our `Point` class in the previous section. We used the `import` statement to get Python's built-in `math` module and use its `sqrt` function in our `distance` calculation.

Here's a concrete example. Assume we have a module called `database.py` that contains a class called `Database`, and a second module called `products.py` that is responsible for product-related queries. At this point, we don't need to think too much about the contents of these files. What we know is that `products.py` needs to instantiate the `Database` class from `database.py` so that it can execute queries on the product table in the database.

There are several variations on the `import` statement syntax that can be used to access the class:

```
import database
db = database.Database()
# Do queries on db
```

This version imports the `database` module into the `products` namespace (the list of names currently accessible in a module or function), so any class or function in the `database` module can be accessed using the `database.<something>` notation. Alternatively, we can import just the one class we need using the `from...import` syntax:

```
from database import Database
db = Database()
# Do queries on db
```

If, for some reason, `products` already has a class called `Database`, and we don't want the two names to be confused, we can rename the class when used inside the `products` module:

```
from database import Database as DB
db = DB()
# Do queries on db
```

We can also import multiple items in one statement. If our `database` module also contains a `Query` class, we can import both classes using:

```
from database import Database, Query
```

Some sources say that we can import all classes and functions from the `database` module using this syntax:

```
from database import *
```

Don't do this. Every experienced Python programmer will tell you that you should never use this syntax. They'll use obscure justifications such as "it clutters up the namespace", which doesn't make much sense to beginners. One way to learn why to avoid this syntax is to use it and try to understand your code two years later. But we can save some time and two years of poorly written code with a quick explanation now!

When we explicitly import the `database` class at the top of our file using `from database import Database`, we can easily see where the `Database` class comes from. We might use `db = Database()` 400 lines later in the file, and we can quickly look at the imports to see where that `Database` class came from. Then, if we need clarification as to how to use the `Database` class, we can visit the original file (or import the module in the interactive interpreter and use the `help(database.Database)` command). However, if we use the `from database import *` syntax, it takes a lot longer to find where that class is located. Code maintenance becomes a nightmare.

In addition, most editors are able to provide extra functionality, such as reliable code completion, the ability to jump to the definition of a class, or inline documentation, if normal imports are used. The `import *` syntax usually completely destroys their ability to do this reliably.

Finally, using the `import *` syntax can bring unexpected objects into our local namespace. Sure, it will import all the classes and functions defined in the module being imported from, but it will also import any classes or modules that were themselves imported into that file!

Every name used in a module should come from a well-specified place, whether it is defined in that module, or explicitly imported from another module. There should be no magic variables that seem to come out of thin air. We should *always* be able to immediately identify where the names in our current namespace originated. I promise that if you use this evil syntax, you will one day have extremely frustrating moments of "where on earth can this class be coming from?".

Organizing the modules

As a project grows into a collection of more and more modules, we may find that we want to add another level of abstraction, some kind of nested hierarchy on our modules' levels. However, we can't put modules inside modules; one file can hold only one file after all, and modules are nothing more than Python files.

Files, however, can go in folders and so can modules. A **package** is a collection of modules in a folder. The name of the package is the name of the folder. All we need to do to tell Python that a folder is a package is place a (normally empty) file in the folder named __init__.py. If we forget this file, we won't be able to import modules from that folder.

Let's put our modules inside an ecommerce package in our working folder, which will also contain a main.py file to start the program. Let's additionally add another package in the ecommerce package for various payment options. The folder hierarchy will look like this:

```
parent_directory/
    main.py
    ecommerce/
        __init__.py
        database.py
        products.py
        payments/
            __init__.py
            square.py
            stripe.py
```

When importing modules or classes between packages, we have to be cautious about the syntax. In Python 3, there are two ways of importing modules: absolute imports and relative imports.

Absolute imports

Absolute imports specify the complete path to the module, function, or path we want to import. If we need access to the Product class inside the products module, we could use any of these syntaxes to do an absolute import:

```
import ecommerce.products
product = ecommerce.products.Product()
```

or

```
from ecommerce.products import Product
product = Product()
```

or

```
from ecommerce import products
product = products.Product()
```

The `import` statements use the period operator to separate packages or modules.

These statements will work from any module. We could instantiate a `Product` class using this syntax in `main.py`, in the `database` module, or in either of the two payment modules. Indeed, assuming the packages are available to Python, it will be able to import them. For example, the packages can also be installed to the Python site packages folder, or the `PYTHONPATH` environment variable could be customized to dynamically tell Python what folders to search for packages and modules it is going to import.

So, with these choices, which syntax do we choose? It depends on your personal taste and the application at hand. If there are dozens of classes and functions inside the `products` module that I want to use, I generally import the module name using the `from ecommerce import products` syntax, and then access the individual classes using `products.Product`. If I only need one or two classes from the `products` module, I can import them directly using the `from ecommerce.proucts import Product` syntax. I don't personally use the first syntax very often unless I have some kind of name conflict (for example, I need to access two completely different modules called `products` and I need to separate them). Do whatever you think makes your code look more elegant.

Relative imports

When working with related modules in a package, it seems kind of silly to specify the full path; we know what our parent module is named. This is where **relative imports** come in. Relative imports are basically a way of saying find a class, function, or module as it is positioned relative to the current module. For example, if we are working in the `products` module and we want to import the `Database` class from the `database` module next to it, we could use a relative import:

```
from .database import Database
```

The period in front of `database` says "u*se the database module inside the current package*". In this case, the current package is the package containing the `products.py` file we are currently editing, that is, the `ecommerce` package.

If we were editing the `paypal` module inside the `ecommerce.payments` package, we would want to say "u*se the database package inside the parent package*" instead. This is easily done with two periods, as shown here:

```
from ..database import Database
```

We can use more periods to go further up the hierarchy. Of course, we can also go down one side and back up the other. We don't have a deep enough example hierarchy to illustrate this properly, but the following would be a valid import if we had an `ecommerce.contact` package containing an `email` module and wanted to import the `send_mail` function into our `paypal` module:

```
from ..contact.email import send_mail
```

This import uses two periods to say, *the parent of the payments package*, and then uses the normal `package.module` syntax to go back *up* into the contact package.

Finally, we can import code directly from packages, as opposed to just modules inside packages. In this example, we have an `ecommerce` package containing two modules named `database.py` and `products.py`. The database module contains a `db` variable that is accessed from a lot of places. Wouldn't it be convenient if this could be imported as `import ecommerce.db` instead of `import ecommerce.database.db`?

Remember the `__init__.py` file that defines a directory as a package? This file can contain any variable or class declarations we like, and they will be available as part of the package. In our example, if the `ecommerce/__init__.py` file contained this line:

```
from .database import db
```

We can then access the `db` attribute from `main.py` or any other file using this import:

```
from ecommerce import db
```

It might help to think of the `__init__.py` file as if it was an `ecommerce.py` file if that file were a module instead of a package. This can also be useful if you put all your code in a single module and later decide to break it up into a package of modules. The `__init__.py` file for the new package can still be the main point of contact for other modules talking to it, but the code can be internally organized into several different modules or subpackages.

I recommend not putting all your code in an `__init__.py` file, though. Programmers do not expect actual logic to happen in this file, and much like with `from x import *`, it can trip them up if they are looking for the declaration of a particular piece of code and can't find it until they check `__init__.py`.

Organizing module contents

Inside any one module, we can specify variables, classes, or functions. They can be a handy way to store the global state without namespace conflicts. For example, we have been importing the `Database` class into various modules and then instantiating it, but it might make more sense to have only one `database` object globally available from the `database` module. The `database` module might look like this:

```
class Database:
    # the database implementation
    pass


database = Database()
```

Then we can use any of the import methods we've discussed to access the `database` object, for example:

```
from ecommerce.database import database
```

A problem with the preceding class is that the `database` object is created immediately when the module is first imported, which is usually when the program starts up. This isn't always ideal since connecting to a database can take a while, slowing down startup, or the database connection information may not yet be available. We could delay creating the database until it is actually needed by calling an `initialize_database` function to create the module-level variable:

```
class Database:
    # the database implementation
    pass


database = None


def initialize_database():
    global database
    database = Database()
```

The `global` keyword tells Python that the database variable inside `initialize_database` is the module level one we just defined. If we had not specified the variable as global, Python would have created a new local variable that would be discarded when the method exits, leaving the module-level value unchanged.

As these two examples illustrate, all module-level code is executed immediately at the time it is imported. However, if it is inside a method or function, the function will be created, but its internal code will not be executed until the function is called. This can be a tricky thing for scripts (such as the main script in our e-commerce example) that perform execution. Often, we will write a program that does something useful, and then later find that we want to import a function or class from that module in a different program. However, as soon as we import it, any code at the module level is immediately executed. If we are not careful, we can end up running the first program when we really only meant to access a couple functions inside that module.

To solve this, we should always put our startup code in a function (conventionally, called main) and only execute that function when we know we are running the module as a script, but not when our code is being imported from a different script. But how do we know this?

```
class UsefulClass:
    '''This class might be useful to other modules.'''
    pass

def main():
    '''creates a useful class and does something with it for our
module.'''
    useful = UsefulClass()
    print(useful)

if __name__ == "__main__":
    main()
```

Every module has a __name__ special variable (remember, Python uses double underscores for special variables, such as a class's __init__ method) that specifies the name of the module when it was imported. When the module is executed directly with python module.py, it is never imported, so the __name__ is arbitrarily set to the string "__main__". Make it a policy to wrap all your scripts in an if __name__ == "__main__": test, just in case you write a function you will find useful to be imported by other code someday.

So, methods go in classes, which go in modules, which go in packages. Is that all there is to it?

Actually, no. This is the typical order of things in a Python program, but it's not the only possible layout. Classes can be defined anywhere. They are typically defined at the module level, but they can also be defined inside a function or method, like this:

```python
def format_string(string, formatter=None):
    '''Format a string using the formatter object, which
    is expected to have a format() method that accepts
    a string.'''
    class DefaultFormatter:
        '''Format a string in title case.'''
        def format(self, string):
            return str(string).title()

    if not formatter:
        formatter = DefaultFormatter()

    return formatter.format(string)

hello_string = "hello world, how are you today?"
print(" input: " + hello_string)
print("output: " + format_string(hello_string))
```

The output will be as follows:

```
input: hello world, how are you today?
output: Hello World, How Are You Today?
```

The `format_string` function accepts a string and optional formatter object, and then applies the formatter to that string. If no formatter is supplied, it creates a formatter of its own as a local class and instantiates it. Since it is created inside the scope of the function, this class cannot be accessed from anywhere outside of that function. Similarly, functions can be defined inside other functions as well; in general, any Python statement can be executed at any time.

These inner classes and functions are occasionally useful for one-off items that don't require or deserve their own scope at the module level, or only make sense inside a single method. However, it is not common to see Python code that frequently uses this technique.

Who can access my data?

Most object-oriented programming languages have a concept of access control. This is related to abstraction. Some attributes and methods on an object are marked private, meaning only that object can access them. Others are marked protected, meaning only that class and any subclasses have access. The rest are public, meaning any other object is allowed to access them.

Python doesn't do this. Python doesn't really believe in enforcing laws that might someday get in your way. Instead, it provides unenforced guidelines and best practices. Technically, all methods and attributes on a class are publicly available. If we want to suggest that a method should not be used publicly, we can put a note in docstrings indicating that the method is meant for internal use only (preferably, with an explanation of how the public-facing API works!).

By convention, we should also prefix an attribute or method with an underscore character, _. Python programmers will interpret this as *"this is an internal variable, think three times before accessing it directly"*. But there is nothing inside the interpreter to stop them from accessing it if they think it is in their best interest to do so. Because if they think so, why should we stop them? We may not have any idea what future uses our classes may be put to.

There's another thing you can do to strongly suggest that outside objects don't access a property or method: prefix it with a double underscore, __. This will perform **name mangling** on the attribute in question. This basically means that the method can still be called by outside objects if they really want to do it, but it requires extra work and is a strong indicator that you demand that your attribute remains private. For example:

```python
class SecretString:
    '''A not-at-all secure way to store a secret string.'''

    def __init__(self, plain_string, pass_phrase):
        self.__plain_string = plain_string
        self.__pass_phrase = pass_phrase

    def decrypt(self, pass_phrase):
        '''Only show the string if the pass_phrase is correct.'''
        if pass_phrase == self.__pass_phrase:
            return self.__plain_string
        else:
            return ''
```

If we load this class and test it in the interactive interpreter, we can see that it hides the plain text string from the outside world:

```
>>> secret_string = SecretString("ACME: Top Secret", "antwerp")
>>> print(secret_string.decrypt("antwerp"))
ACME: Top Secret
>>> print(secret_string.__plain_text)
Traceback (most recent call last):
  File "<stdin>", line 1, in <module>
AttributeError: 'SecretString' object has no attribute
'__plain_text'
```

It looks like it works; nobody can access our `plain_text` attribute without the passphrase, so it must be safe. Before we get too excited, though, let's see how easy it can be to hack our security:

```
>>> print(secret_string._SecretString__plain_string)
ACME: Top Secret
```

Oh no! Somebody has hacked our secret string. Good thing we checked! This is Python name mangling at work. When we use a double underscore, the property is prefixed with `_<classname>`. When methods in the class internally access the variable, they are automatically unmangled. When external classes wish to access it, they have to do the name mangling themselves. So, name mangling does not guarantee privacy, it only strongly recommends it. Most Python programmers will not touch a double underscore variable on another object unless they have an extremely compelling reason to do so.

However, most Python programmers will not touch a single underscore variable without a compelling reason either. Therefore, there are very few good reasons to use a name-mangled variable in Python, and doing so can cause grief. For example, a name-mangled variable may be useful to a subclass, and it would have to do the mangling itself. Let other objects access your hidden information if they want to, just let them know, using a single-underscore prefix or some clear docstrings, that you think this is not a good idea.

Third-party libraries

Python ships with a lovely standard library, which is a collection of packages and modules that are available on every machine that runs Python. However, you'll soon find that it doesn't contain everything you need. When this happens, you have two options:

- Write a supporting package yourself
- Use somebody else's code

We won't be covering the details about turning your packages into libraries, but if you have a problem you need to solve and you don't feel like coding it (the best programmers are extremely lazy and prefer to reuse existing, proven code, rather than write their own), you can probably find the library you want on the **Python Package Index (PyPI)** at `http://pypi.python.org/`. Once you've identified a package that you want to install, you can use a tool called `pip` to install it. However, `pip` does not come with Python, but Python 3.4 contains a useful tool called `ensurepip`, which will install it:

```
python -m ensurepip
```

This may fail for you on Linux, Mac OS, or other Unix systems, in which case, you'll need to become root to make it work. On most modern Unix systems, this can be done with `sudo python -m ensurepip`.

> If you are using an older version of Python than Python 3.4, you'll need to download and install `pip` yourself, since `ensurepip` doesn't exist. You can do this by following the instructions at `http://pip.readthedocs.org/`.

Once `pip` is installed and you know the name of the package you want to install, you can install it using syntax such as:

```
pip install requests
```

However, if you do this, you'll either be installing the third-party library directly into your system Python directory, or more likely, get an error that you don't have permission to do so. You could force the installation as an administrator, but common consensus in the Python community is that you should only use system installers to install the third-party library to your system Python directory.

Instead, Python 3.4 supplies the `venv` tool. This utility basically gives you a mini Python installation called a *virtual environment* in your working directory. When you activate the mini Python, commands related to Python will work on that directory instead of the system directory. So when you run `pip` or `python`, it won't touch the system Python at all. Here's how to use it:

```
cd project_directory
python -m venv env
source env/bin/activate   # on Linux or MacOS
env/bin/activate.bat      # on Windows
```

Typically, you'll create a different virtual environment for each Python project you work on. You can store your virtual environments anywhere, but I keep mine in the same directory as the rest of my project files (but ignored in version control), so first we `cd` into that directory. Then we run the `venv` utility to create a virtual environment named `env`. Finally, we use one of the last two lines (depending on the operating system, as indicated in the comments) to activate the environment. We'll need to execute this line each time we want to use that particular virtualenv, and then use the command `deactivate` when we are done working on this project.

Virtual environments are a terrific way to keep your third-party dependencies separate. It is common to have different projects that depend on different versions of a particular library (for example, an older website might run on Django 1.5, while newer versions run on Django 1.8). Keeping each project in separate virtualenvs makes it easy to work in either version of Django. Further, it prevents conflicts between system-installed packages and `pip` installed packages if you try to install the same package using different tools.

Case study

To tie it all together, let's build a simple command-line notebook application. This is a fairly simple task, so we won't be experimenting with multiple packages. We will, however, see common usage of classes, functions, methods, and docstrings.

Let's start with a quick analysis: notes are short memos stored in a notebook. Each note should record the day it was written and can have tags added for easy querying. It should be possible to modify notes. We also need to be able to search for notes. All of these things should be done from the command line.

The obvious object is the Note object; less obvious one is a Notebook container object. Tags and dates also seem to be objects, but we can use dates from Python's standard library and a comma-separated string for tags. To avoid complexity, in the prototype, let's not define separate classes for these objects.

Note objects have attributes for memo itself, tags, and creation_date. Each note will also need a unique integer id so that users can select them in a menu interface. Notes could have a method to modify note content and another for tags, or we could just let the notebook access those attributes directly. To make searching easier, we should put a match method on the Note object. This method will accept a string and can tell us if a note matches the string without accessing the attributes directly. This way, if we want to modify the search parameters (to search tags instead of note contents, for example, or to make the search case-insensitive), we only have to do it in one place.

The Notebook object obviously has the list of notes as an attribute. It will also need a search method that returns a list of filtered notes.

But how do we interact with these objects? We've specified a command-line app, which can mean either that we run the program with different options to add or edit commands, or we have some kind of a menu that allows us to pick different things to do to the notebook. We should try to design it such that either interface is supported and future interfaces, such as a GUI toolkit or web-based interface, could be added in the future.

As a design decision, we'll implement the menu interface now, but will keep the command-line options version in mind to ensure we design our Notebook class with extensibility in mind.

If we have two command-line interfaces, each interacting with the Notebook object, then Notebook will need some methods for those interfaces to interact with. We need to be able to add a new note, and modify an existing note by id, in addition to the search method we've already discussed. The interfaces will also need to be able to list all notes, but they can do that by accessing the notes list attribute directly.

We may be missing a few details, but that gives us a really good overview of the code we need to write. We can summarize all this in a simple class diagram:

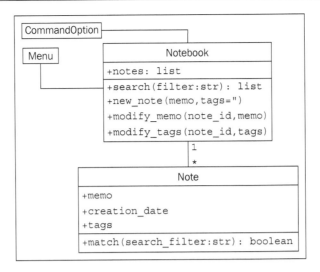

Before writing any code, let's define the folder structure for this project. The menu interface should clearly be in its own module, since it will be an executable script, and we may have other executable scripts accessing the notebook in the future. The `Notebook` and `Note` objects can live together in one module. These modules can both exist in the same top-level directory without having to put them in a package. An empty `command_option.py` module can help remind us in the future that we were planning to add new user interfaces.

```
parent_directory/
    notebook.py
    menu.py
    command_option.py
```

Now let's see some code. We start by defining the `Note` class as it seems simplest. The following example presents `Note` in its entirety. Docstrings within the example explain how it all fits together.

```
import datetime

# Store the next available id for all new notes
last_id = 0

class Note:
    '''Represent a note in the notebook. Match against a
```

```
        string in searches and store tags for each note.'''

    def __init__(self, memo, tags=''):
        '''initialize a note with memo and optional
        space-separated tags. Automatically set the note's
        creation date and a unique id.'''
        self.memo = memo
        self.tags = tags
        self.creation_date = datetime.date.today()
        global last_id
        last_id += 1
        self.id = last_id

    def match(self, filter):
        '''Determine if this note matches the filter
        text. Return True if it matches, False otherwise.

        Search is case sensitive and matches both text and
        tags.'''
        return filter in self.memo or filter in self.tags
```

Before continuing, we should quickly fire up the interactive interpreter and test our code so far. Test frequently and often because things never work the way you expect them to. Indeed, when I tested my first version of this example, I found out I had forgotten the self argument in the match function! We'll discuss automated testing in *Chapter 10, Python Design Patterns I*. For now, it suffices to check a few things using the interpreter:

```
>>> from notebook import Note
>>> n1 = Note("hello first")
>>> n2 = Note("hello again")
>>> n1.id
1
>>> n2.id
2
>>> n1.match('hello')
True
>>> n2.match('second')
False
```

It looks like everything is behaving as expected. Let's create our notebook next:

```python
class Notebook:
    '''Represent a collection of notes that can be tagged,
    modified, and searched.'''

    def __init__(self):
        '''Initialize a notebook with an empty list.'''
        self.notes = []

    def new_note(self, memo, tags=''):
        '''Create a new note and add it to the list.'''
        self.notes.append(Note(memo, tags))

    def modify_memo(self, note_id, memo):
        '''Find the note with the given id and change its
        memo to the given value.'''
        for note in self.notes:
            if note.id == note_id:
                note.memo = memo
                break

    def modify_tags(self, note_id, tags):
        '''Find the note with the given id and change its
        tags to the given value.'''
        for note in self.notes:
            if note.id == note_id:
                note.tags = tags
                break

    def search(self, filter):
        '''Find all notes that match the given filter
        string.'''
        return [note for note in self.notes if
                note.match(filter)]
```

We'll clean this up in a minute. First, let's test it to make sure it works:

```
>>> from notebook import Note, Notebook
>>> n = Notebook()
>>> n.new_note("hello world")
>>> n.new_note("hello again")
>>> n.notes
[<notebook.Note object at 0xb730a78c>, <notebook.Note object at
  0xb73103ac>]
```

```
>>> n.notes[0].id
1
>>> n.notes[1].id
2
>>> n.notes[0].memo
'hello world'
>>> n.search("hello")
[<notebook.Note object at 0xb730a78c>, <notebook.Note object at
  0xb73103ac>]
>>> n.search("world")
[<notebook.Note object at 0xb730a78c>]
>>> n.modify_memo(1, "hi world")
>>> n.notes[0].memo
'hi world'
```

It does work. The code is a little messy though; our modify_tags and modify_memo
methods are almost identical. That's not good coding practice. Let's see how we can
improve it.

Both methods are trying to identify the note with a given ID before doing something
to that note. So, let's add a method to locate the note with a specific ID. We'll prefix
the method name with an underscore to suggest that the method is for internal use
only, but of course, our menu interface can access the method if it wants to:

```
def _find_note(self, note_id):
    '''Locate the note with the given id.'''
    for note in self.notes:
        if note.id == note_id:
            return note
    return None


def modify_memo(self, note_id, memo):
    '''Find the note with the given id and change its
    memo to the given value.'''
    self._find_note(note_id).memo = memo
```

This should work for now. Let's have a look at the menu interface. The interface
simply needs to present a menu and allow the user to input choices. Here's our
first try:

```
import sys
```

```python
from notebook import Notebook, Note

class Menu:
    '''Display a menu and respond to choices when run.'''
    def __init__(self):
        self.notebook = Notebook()
        self.choices = {
                "1": self.show_notes,
                "2": self.search_notes,
                "3": self.add_note,
                "4": self.modify_note,
                "5": self.quit
                }

    def display_menu(self):
        print("""
Notebook Menu

1. Show all Notes
2. Search Notes
3. Add Note
4. Modify Note
5. Quit
""")

    def run(self):
        '''Display the menu and respond to choices.'''
        while True:
            self.display_menu()
            choice = input("Enter an option: ")
            action = self.choices.get(choice)
            if action:
                action()
            else:
                print("{0} is not a valid choice".format(choice))

    def show_notes(self, notes=None):
        if not notes:
            notes = self.notebook.notes
        for note in notes:
            print("{0}: {1}\n{2}".format(
                note.id, note.tags, note.memo))

    def search_notes(self):
```

```
            filter = input("Search for: ")
            notes = self.notebook.search(filter)
            self.show_notes(notes)

    def add_note(self):
        memo = input("Enter a memo: ")
        self.notebook.new_note(memo)
        print("Your note has been added.")

    def modify_note(self):
        id = input("Enter a note id: ")
        memo = input("Enter a memo: ")
        tags = input("Enter tags: ")
        if memo:
            self.notebook.modify_memo(id, memo)
        if tags:
            self.notebook.modify_tags(id, tags)

    def quit(self):
        print("Thank you for using your notebook today.")
        sys.exit(0)

if __name__ == "__main__":
    Menu().run()
```

This code first imports the notebook objects using an absolute import. Relative imports wouldn't work because we haven't placed our code inside a package. The Menu class's run method repeatedly displays a menu and responds to choices by calling functions on the notebook. This is done using an idiom that is rather peculiar to Python; it is a lightweight version of the command pattern that we will discuss in *Chapter 10, Python Design Patterns I*. The choices entered by the user are strings. In the menu's __init__ method, we create a dictionary that maps strings to functions on the menu object itself. Then, when the user makes a choice, we retrieve the object from the dictionary. The action variable actually refers to a specific method, and is called by appending empty brackets (since none of the methods require parameters) to the variable. Of course, the user might have entered an inappropriate choice, so we check if the action really exists before calling it.

Each of the various methods request user input and call appropriate methods on the Notebook object associated with it. For the search implementation, we notice that after we've filtered the notes, we need to show them to the user, so we make the show_notes function serve double duty; it accepts an optional notes parameter. If it's supplied, it displays only the filtered notes, but if it's not, it displays all notes. Since the notes parameter is optional, show_notes can still be called with no parameters as an empty menu item.

If we test this code, we'll find that modifying notes doesn't work. There are two bugs, namely:

- The notebook crashes when we enter a note ID that does not exist. We should never trust our users to enter correct data!

- Even if we enter a correct ID, it will crash because the note IDs are integers, but our menu is passing a string.

The latter bug can be solved by modifying the `Notebook` class's `_find_note` method to compare the values using strings instead of the integers stored in the note, as follows:

```
def _find_note(self, note_id):
    '''Locate the note with the given id.'''
    for note in self.notes:
        if str(note.id) == str(note_id):
            return note
    return None
```

We simply convert both the input (`note_id`) and the note's ID to strings before comparing them. We could also convert the input to an integer, but then we'd have trouble if the user had entered the letter "a" instead of the number "1".

The problem with users entering note IDs that don't exist can be fixed by changing the two `modify` methods on the notebook to check whether `_find_note` returned a note or not, like this:

```
def modify_memo(self, note_id, memo):
    '''Find the note with the given id and change its
    memo to the given value.'''
    note = self._find_note(note_id)
    if note:
        note.memo = memo
        return True
    return False
```

This method has been updated to return `True` or `False`, depending on whether a note has been found. The menu could use this return value to display an error if the user entered an invalid note. This code is a bit unwieldy though; it would look a bit better if it raised an exception instead. We'll cover those in *Chapter 4, Expecting the Unexpected*.

Exercises

Write some object-oriented code. The goal is to use the principles and syntax you learned in this chapter to ensure you can use it, instead of just reading about it. If you've been working on a Python project, go back over it and see if there are some objects you can create and add properties or methods to. If it's large, try dividing it into a few modules or even packages and play with the syntax.

If you don't have such a project, try starting a new one. It doesn't have to be something you intend to finish, just stub out some basic design parts. You don't need to fully implement everything, often just a `print("this method will do something")` is all you need to get the overall design in place. This is called **top-down design**, in which you work out the different interactions and describe how they should work before actually implementing what they do. The converse, **bottom-up design**, implements details first and then ties them all together. Both patterns are useful at different times, but for understanding object-oriented principles, a top-down workflow is more suitable.

If you're having trouble coming up with ideas, try writing a to-do application. (Hint: It would be similar to the design of the notebook application, but with extra date management methods.) It can keep track of things you want to do each day, and allow you to mark them as completed.

Now, try designing a bigger project. It doesn't have to actually do anything, but make sure you experiment with the package and module importing syntax. Add some functions in various modules and try importing them from other modules and packages. Use relative and absolute imports. See the difference, and try to imagine scenarios where you would want to use each one.

Summary

In this chapter, we learned how simple it is to create classes and assign properties and methods in Python. Unlike many languages, Python differentiates between a constructor and an initializer. It has a relaxed attitude toward access control. There are many different levels of scope, including packages, modules, classes, and functions. We understood the difference between relative and absolute imports, and how to manage third-party packages that don't come with Python.

In the next chapter, we'll learn how to share implementation using inheritance.

3
When Objects Are Alike

In the programming world, duplicate code is considered evil. We should not have multiple copies of the same, or similar, code in different places.

There are many ways to merge pieces of code or objects that have a similar functionality. In this chapter, we'll be covering the most famous object-oriented principle: inheritance. As discussed in *Chapter 1, Object-oriented Design*, inheritance allows us to create *is a* relationships between two or more classes, abstracting common logic into superclasses and managing specific details in the subclass. In particular, we'll be covering the Python syntax and principles for:

- Basic inheritance
- Inheriting from built-ins
- Multiple inheritance
- Polymorphism and duck typing

Basic inheritance

Technically, every class we create uses inheritance. All Python classes are subclasses of the special class named `object`. This class provides very little in terms of data and behaviors (the behaviors it does provide are all double-underscore methods intended for internal use only), but it does allow Python to treat all objects in the same way.

If we don't explicitly inherit from a different class, our classes will automatically inherit from `object`. However, we can openly state that our class derives from `object` using the following syntax:

```
class MySubClass(object):
    pass
```

This is inheritance! This example is, technically, no different from our very first example in *Chapter 2, Objects in Python*, since Python 3 automatically inherits from `object` if we don't explicitly provide a different superclass. A superclass, or parent class, is a class that is being inherited from. A subclass is a class that is inheriting from a superclass. In this case, the superclass is `object`, and `MySubClass` is the subclass. A subclass is also said to be derived from its parent class or that the subclass extends the parent.

As you've probably figured out from the example, inheritance requires a minimal amount of extra syntax over a basic class definition. Simply include the name of the parent class inside parentheses after the class name but before the colon terminating the class definition. This is all we have to do to tell Python that the new class should be derived from the given superclass.

How do we apply inheritance in practice? The simplest and most obvious use of inheritance is to add functionality to an existing class. Let's start with a simple contact manager that tracks the name and e-mail address of several people. The contact class is responsible for maintaining a list of all contacts in a class variable, and for initializing the name and address for an individual contact:

```python
class Contact:
    all_contacts = []

    def __init__(self, name, email):
        self.name = name
        self.email = email
        Contact.all_contacts.append(self)
```

This example introduces us to class variables. The `all_contacts` list, because it is part of the class definition, is shared by all instances of this class. This means that there is only one `Contact.all_contacts` list, which we can access as `Contact.all_contacts`. Less obviously, we can also access it as `self.all_contacts` on any object instantiated from `Contact`. If the field can't be found on the object, then it will be found on the class and thus refer to the same single list.

Be careful with this syntax, for if you ever *set* the variable using `self.all_contacts`, you will actually be creating a **new** instance variable associated only with that object. The class variable will still be unchanged and accessible as `Contact.all_contacts`.

This is a simple class that allows us to track a couple pieces of data about each contact. But what if some of our contacts are also suppliers that we need to order supplies from? We could add an order method to the Contact class, but that would allow people to accidentally order things from contacts who are customers or family friends. Instead, let's create a new Supplier class that acts like our Contact class, but has an additional order method:

```
class Supplier(Contact):
    def order(self, order):
        print("If this were a real system we would send "
                "'{}' order to '{}'".format(order, self.name))
```

Now, if we test this class in our trusty interpreter, we see that all contacts, including suppliers, accept a name and e-mail address in their __init__, but only suppliers have a functional order method:

```
>>> c = Contact("Some Body", "somebody@example.net")
>>> s = Supplier("Sup Plier", "supplier@example.net")
>>> print(c.name, c.email, s.name, s.email)
Some Body somebody@example.net Sup Plier supplier@example.net
>>> c.all_contacts
[<__main__.Contact object at 0xb7375ecc>,
 <__main__.Supplier object at 0xb7375f8c>]
>>> c.order("I need pliers")
Traceback (most recent call last):
  File "<stdin>", line 1, in <module>
AttributeError: 'Contact' object has no attribute 'order'
>>> s.order("I need pliers")
If this were a real system we would send 'I need pliers' order to
'Sup Plier '
```

So, now our Supplier class can do everything a contact can do (including adding itself to the list of all_contacts) and all the special things it needs to handle as a supplier. This is the beauty of inheritance.

Extending built-ins

One interesting use of this kind of inheritance is adding functionality to built-in classes. In the Contact class seen earlier, we are adding contacts to a list of all contacts. What if we also wanted to search that list by name? Well, we could add a method on the Contact class to search it, but it feels like this method actually belongs to the list itself. We can do this using inheritance:

```python
class ContactList(list):
    def search(self, name):
        '''Return all contacts that contain the search value
        in their name.'''
        matching_contacts = []
        for contact in self:
            if name in contact.name:
                matching_contacts.append(contact)
        return matching_contacts

class Contact:
    all_contacts = ContactList()

    def __init__(self, name, email):
        self.name = name
        self.email = email
        self.all_contacts.append(self)
```

Instead of instantiating a normal list as our class variable, we create a new ContactList class that extends the built-in list. Then, we instantiate this subclass as our all_contacts list. We can test the new search functionality as follows:

```python
>>> c1 = Contact("John A", "johna@example.net")
>>> c2 = Contact("John B", "johnb@example.net")
>>> c3 = Contact("Jenna C", "jennac@example.net")
>>> [c.name for c in Contact.all_contacts.search('John')]
['John A', 'John B']
```

Are you wondering how we changed the built-in syntax [] into something we can inherit from? Creating an empty list with [] is actually a shorthand for creating an empty list using list(); the two syntaxes behave identically:

```python
>>> [] == list()
True
```

In reality, the `[]` syntax is actually so-called **syntax sugar** that calls the `list()` constructor under the hood. The `list` data type is a class that we can extend. In fact, the list itself extends the `object` class:

```
>>> isinstance([], object)
True
```

As a second example, we can extend the `dict` class, which is, similar to the list, the class that is constructed when using the `{}` syntax shorthand:

```
class LongNameDict(dict):
    def longest_key(self):
        longest = None
        for key in self:
            if not longest or len(key) > len(longest):
                longest = key
        return longest
```

This is easy to test in the interactive interpreter:

```
>>> longkeys = LongNameDict()
>>> longkeys['hello'] = 1
>>> longkeys['longest yet'] = 5
>>> longkeys['hello2'] = 'world'
>>> longkeys.longest_key()
'longest yet'
```

Most built-in types can be similarly extended. Commonly extended built-ins are `object`, `list`, `set`, `dict`, `file`, and `str`. Numerical types such as `int` and `float` are also occasionally inherited from.

Overriding and super

So, inheritance is great for *adding* new behavior to existing classes, but what about *changing* behavior? Our `contact` class allows only a name and an e-mail address. This may be sufficient for most contacts, but what if we want to add a phone number for our close friends?

As we saw in *Chapter 2, Objects in Python,* we can do this easily by just setting a `phone` attribute on the contact after it is constructed. But if we want to make this third variable available on initialization, we have to override `__init__`. Overriding means altering or replacing a method of the superclass with a new method (with the same name) in the subclass. No special syntax is needed to do this; the subclass's newly created method is automatically called instead of the superclass's method. For example:

```
class Friend(Contact):
    def __init__(self, name, email, phone):
        self.name = name
        self.email = email
        self.phone = phone
```

Any method can be overridden, not just `__init__`. Before we go on, however, we need to address some problems in this example. Our `Contact` and `Friend` classes have duplicate code to set up the `name` and `email` properties; this can make code maintenance complicated as we have to update the code in two or more places. More alarmingly, our `Friend` class is neglecting to add itself to the `all_contacts` list we have created on the `Contact` class.

What we really need is a way to execute the original `__init__` method on the `Contact` class. This is what the `super` function does; it returns the object as an instance of the parent class, allowing us to call the parent method directly:

```
class Friend(Contact):
    def __init__(self, name, email, phone):
        super().__init__(name, email)
        self.phone = phone
```

This example first gets the instance of the parent object using `super`, and calls `__init__` on that object, passing in the expected arguments. It then does its own initialization, namely, setting the `phone` attribute.

Note that the `super()` syntax does not work in older versions of Python. Like the [] and {} syntaxes for lists and dictionaries, it is a shorthand for a more complicated construct. We'll learn more about this shortly when we discuss multiple inheritance, but know for now that in Python 2, you would have to call `super(EmailContact, self).__init__()`. Specifically notice that the first argument is the name of the child class, not the name as the parent class you want to call, as some might expect. Also, remember the class comes before the object. I always forget the order, so the new syntax in Python 3 has saved me hours of having to look it up.

A `super()` call can be made inside any method, not just `__init__`. This means all methods can be modified via overriding and calls to `super`. The call to `super` can also be made at any point in the method; we don't have to make the call as the first line in the method. For example, we may need to manipulate or validate incoming parameters before forwarding them to the superclass.

Multiple inheritance

Multiple inheritance is a touchy subject. In principle, it's very simple: a subclass that inherits from more than one parent class is able to access functionality from both of them. In practice, this is less useful than it sounds and many expert programmers recommend against using it.

 As a rule of thumb, if you think you need multiple inheritance, you're probably wrong, but if you know you need it, you're probably right.

The simplest and most useful form of multiple inheritance is called a **mixin**. A mixin is generally a superclass that is not meant to exist on its own, but is meant to be inherited by some other class to provide extra functionality. For example, let's say we wanted to add functionality to our `Contact` class that allows sending an e-mail to `self.email`. Sending e-mail is a common task that we might want to use on many other classes. So, we can write a simple mixin class to do the e-mailing for us:

```
class MailSender:
    def send_mail(self, message):
        print("Sending mail to " + self.email)
        # Add e-mail logic here
```

For brevity, we won't include the actual e-mail logic here; if you're interested in studying how it's done, see the `smtplib` module in the Python standard library.

This class doesn't do anything special (in fact, it can barely function as a standalone class), but it does allow us to define a new class that describes both a `Contact` and a `MailSender`, using multiple inheritance:

```
class EmailableContact(Contact, MailSender):
    pass
```

The syntax for multiple inheritance looks like a parameter list in the class definition. Instead of including one base class inside the parentheses, we include two (or more), separated by a comma. We can test this new hybrid to see the mixin at work:

```
>>> e = EmailableContact("John Smith", "jsmith@example.net")
```

```
>>> Contact.all_contacts
[<__main__.EmailableContact object at 0xb7205fac>]
>>> e.send_mail("Hello, test e-mail here")
Sending mail to jsmith@example.net
```

The Contact initializer is still adding the new contact to the all_contacts list, and the mixin is able to send mail to self.email so we know everything is working.

This wasn't so hard, and you're probably wondering what the dire warnings about multiple inheritance are. We'll get into the complexities in a minute, but let's consider some other options we had, rather than using a mixin here:

- We could have used single inheritance and added the send_mail function to the subclass. The disadvantage here is that the e-mail functionality then has to be duplicated for any other classes that need e-mail.

- We can create a standalone Python function for sending an e-mail, and just call that function with the correct e-mail address supplied as a parameter when the e-mail needs to be sent.

- We could have explored a few ways of using composition instead of inheritance. For example, EmailableContact could have a MailSender object instead of inheriting from it.

- We could monkey-patch (we'll briefly cover monkey-patching in *Chapter 7, Python Object-oriented Shortcuts*) the Contact class to have a send_mail method after the class has been created. This is done by defining a function that accepts the self argument, and setting it as an attribute on an existing class.

Multiple inheritance works all right when mixing methods from different classes, but it gets very messy when we have to call methods on the superclass. There are multiple superclasses. How do we know which one to call? How do we know what order to call them in?

Let's explore these questions by adding a home address to our Friend class. There are a few approaches we might take. An address is a collection of strings representing the street, city, country, and other related details of the contact. We could pass each of these strings as a parameter into the Friend class's __init__ method. We could also store these strings in a tuple or dictionary and pass them into __init__ as a single argument. This is probably the best course of action if there are no methods that need to be added to the address.

Another option would be to create a new `Address` class to hold those strings together, and then pass an instance of this class into the `__init__` method of our `Friend` class. The advantage of this solution is that we can add behavior (say, a method to give directions or to print a map) to the data instead of just storing it statically. This is an example of composition, as we discussed in *Chapter 1, Object-oriented Design*. The "has a" relationship of composition is a perfectly viable solution to this problem and allows us to reuse `Address` classes in other entities such as buildings, businesses, or organizations.

However, inheritance is also a viable solution, and that's what we want to explore. Let's add a new class that holds an address. We'll call this new class "AddressHolder" instead of "Address" because inheritance defines an *is a* relationship. It is not correct to say a "Friend" is an "Address" , but since a friend can have an "Address" , we can argue that a "Friend" is an "AddressHolder". Later, we could create other entities (companies, buildings) that also hold addresses. Here's our `AddressHolder` class:

```
class AddressHolder:
    def __init__(self, street, city, state, code):
        self.street = street
        self.city = city
        self.state = state
        self.code = code
```

Very simple; we just take all the data and toss it into instance variables upon initialization.

The diamond problem

We can use multiple inheritance to add this new class as a parent of our existing `Friend` class. The tricky part is that we now have two parent `__init__` methods both of which need to be initialized. And they need to be initialized with different arguments. How do we do this? Well, we could start with a naive approach:

```
class Friend(Contact, AddressHolder):
    def __init__(
        self, name, email, phone,street, city, state, code):
        Contact.__init__(self, name, email)
        AddressHolder.__init__(self, street, city, state, code)
        self.phone = phone
```

In this example, we directly call the __init__ function on each of the superclasses and explicitly pass the self argument. This example technically works; we can access the different variables directly on the class. But there are a few problems.

First, it is possible for a superclass to go uninitialized if we neglect to explicitly call the initializer. That wouldn't break this example, but it could cause hard-to-debug program crashes in common scenarios. Imagine trying to insert data into a database that has not been connected to, for example.

Second, and more sinister, is the possibility of a superclass being called multiple times because of the organization of the class hierarchy. Look at this inheritance diagram:

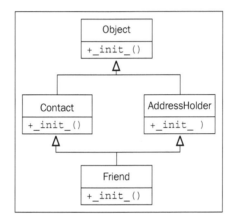

The __init__ method from the Friend class first calls __init__ on Contact, which implicitly initializes the object superclass (remember, all classes derive from object). Friend then calls __init__ on AddressHolder, which implicitly initializes the object superclass *again*. This means the parent class has been set up twice. With the object class, that's relatively harmless, but in some situations, it could spell disaster. Imagine trying to connect to a database twice for every request!

The base class should only be called once. Once, yes, but when? Do we call Friend, then Contact, then Object, then AddressHolder? Or Friend, then Contact, then AddressHolder, then Object?

The order in which methods can be called can be adapted on the fly by modifying the __mro__ (**Method Resolution Order**) attribute on the class. This is beyond the scope of this book. If you think you need to understand it, I recommend *Expert Python Programming, Tarek Ziadé, Packt Publishing*, or read the original documentation on the topic at http://www.python.org/download/releases/2.3/mro/.

Let's look at a second contrived example that illustrates this problem more clearly. Here we have a base class that has a method named `call_me`. Two subclasses override that method, and then another subclass extends both of these using multiple inheritance. This is called diamond inheritance because of the diamond shape of the class diagram:

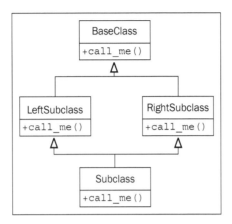

Let's convert this diagram to code; this example shows when the methods are called:

```
class BaseClass:
    num_base_calls = 0
    def call_me(self):
        print("Calling method on Base Class")
        self.num_base_calls += 1


class LeftSubclass(BaseClass):
    num_left_calls = 0
    def call_me(self):
        BaseClass.call_me(self)
        print("Calling method on Left Subclass")
        self.num_left_calls += 1


class RightSubclass(BaseClass):
    num_right_calls = 0
    def call_me(self):
        BaseClass.call_me(self)
        print("Calling method on Right Subclass")
        self.num_right_calls += 1


class Subclass(LeftSubclass, RightSubclass):
```

```
        num_sub_calls = 0
        def call_me(self):
            LeftSubclass.call_me(self)
            RightSubclass.call_me(self)
            print("Calling method on Subclass")
            self.num_sub_calls += 1
```

This example simply ensures that each overridden `call_me` method directly calls the parent method with the same name. It lets us know each time a method is called by printing the information to the screen. It also updates a static variable on the class to show how many times it has been called. If we instantiate one `Subclass` object and call the method on it once, we get this output:

```
>>> s = Subclass()
>>> s.call_me()
Calling method on Base Class
Calling method on Left Subclass
Calling method on Base Class
Calling method on Right Subclass
Calling method on Subclass
>>> print(
... s.num_sub_calls,
... s.num_left_calls,
... s.num_right_calls,
... s.num_base_calls)
1 1 1 2
```

Thus we can clearly see the base class's `call_me` method being called twice. This could lead to some insidious bugs if that method is doing actual work—like depositing into a bank account—twice.

The thing to keep in mind with multiple inheritance is that we only want to call the "next" method in the class hierarchy, not the "parent" method. In fact, that next method may not be on a parent or ancestor of the current class. The `super` keyword comes to our rescue once again. Indeed, `super` was originally developed to make complicated forms of multiple inheritance possible. Here is the same code written using `super`:

```
    class BaseClass:
        num_base_calls = 0
        def call_me(self):
```

```
        print("Calling method on Base Class")
        self.num_base_calls += 1

class LeftSubclass(BaseClass):
    num_left_calls = 0
    def call_me(self):
        super().call_me()
        print("Calling method on Left Subclass")
        self.num_left_calls += 1

class RightSubclass(BaseClass):
    num_right_calls = 0
    def call_me(self):
        super().call_me()
        print("Calling method on Right Subclass")
        self.num_right_calls += 1

class Subclass(LeftSubclass, RightSubclass):
    num_sub_calls = 0
    def call_me(self):
        super().call_me()
        print("Calling method on Subclass")
        self.num_sub_calls += 1
```

The change is pretty minor; we simply replaced the naive direct calls with calls to super(), although the bottom subclass only calls super once rather than having to make the calls for both the left and right. The change is simple enough, but look at the difference when we execute it:

```
>>> s = Subclass()
>>> s.call_me()
Calling method on Base Class
Calling method on Right Subclass
Calling method on Left Subclass
Calling method on Subclass
>>> print(s.num_sub_calls, s.num_left_calls, s.num_right_calls,
s.num_base_calls)
1 1 1 1
```

Looks good, our base method is only being called once. But what is super() actually doing here? Since the print statements are executed after the super calls, the printed output is in the order each method is actually executed. Let's look at the output from back to front to see who is calling what.

First, call_me of Subclass calls super().call_me(), which happens to refer to LeftSubclass.call_me(). The LeftSubclass.call_me() method then calls super().call_me(), but in this case, super() is referring to RightSubclass.call_me().

Pay particular attention to this: the super call is *not* calling the method on the superclass of LeftSubclass (which is BaseClass). Rather, it is calling RightSubclass, even though it is not a direct parent of LeftSubclass! This is the *next* method, not the parent method. RightSubclass then calls BaseClass and the super calls have ensured each method in the class hierarchy is executed once.

Different sets of arguments

This is going to make things complicated as we return to our Friend multiple inheritance example. In the __init__ method for Friend, we were originally calling __init__ for both parent classes, *with different sets of arguments*:

```
Contact.__init__(self, name, email)
AddressHolder.__init__(self, street, city, state, code)
```

How can we manage different sets of arguments when using super? We don't necessarily know which class super is going to try to initialize first. Even if we did, we need a way to pass the "extra" arguments so that subsequent calls to super, on other subclasses, receive the right arguments.

Specifically, if the first call to super passes the name and email arguments to Contact.__init__, and Contact.__init__ then calls super, it needs to be able to pass the address-related arguments to the "next" method, which is AddressHolder.__init__.

This is a problem whenever we want to call superclass methods with the same name, but with different sets of arguments. Most often, the only time you would want to call a superclass with a completely different set of arguments is in __init__, as we're doing here. Even with regular methods, though, we may want to add optional parameters that only make sense to one subclass or set of subclasses.

Sadly, the only way to solve this problem is to plan for it from the beginning. We have to design our base class parameter lists to accept keyword arguments for any parameters that are not required by every subclass implementation. Finally, we must ensure the method freely accepts unexpected arguments and passes them on to its super call, in case they are necessary to later methods in the inheritance order.

Python's function parameter syntax provides all the tools we need to do this, but it makes the overall code look cumbersome. Have a look at the proper version of the `Friend` multiple inheritance code:

```python
class Contact:
    all_contacts = []

    def __init__(self, name='', email='', **kwargs):
        super().__init__(**kwargs)
        self.name = name
        self.email = email
        self.all_contacts.append(self)

class AddressHolder:
    def __init__(self, street='', city='', state='', code='',
            **kwargs):
        super().__init__(**kwargs)
        self.street = street
        self.city = city
        self.state = state
        self.code = code

class Friend(Contact, AddressHolder):
    def __init__(self, phone='', **kwargs):
        super().__init__(**kwargs)
        self.phone = phone
```

We've changed all arguments to keyword arguments by giving them an empty string as a default value. We've also ensured that a `**kwargs` parameter is included to capture any additional parameters that our particular method doesn't know what to do with. It passes these parameters up to the next class with the `super` call.

If you aren't familiar with the `**kwargs` syntax, it basically collects any keyword arguments passed into the method that were not explicitly listed in the parameter list. These arguments are stored in a dictionary named `kwargs` (we can call the variable whatever we like, but convention suggests kw, or kwargs). When we call a different method (for example, `super().__init__`) with a `**kwargs` syntax, it unpacks the dictionary and passes the results to the method as normal keyword arguments. We'll cover this in detail in *Chapter 7, Python Object-oriented Shortcuts*.

The previous example does what it is supposed to do. But it's starting to look messy, and it has become difficult to answer the question, *What arguments do we need to pass into* Friend.__init__? This is the foremost question for anyone planning to use the class, so a docstring should be added to the method to explain what is happening.

Further, even this implementation is insufficient if we want to *reuse* variables in parent classes. When we pass the **kwargs variable to super, the dictionary does not include any of the variables that were included as explicit keyword arguments. For example, in Friend.__init__, the call to super does not have phone in the kwargs dictionary. If any of the other classes need the phone parameter, we need to ensure it is in the dictionary that is passed. Worse, if we forget to do this, it will be tough to debug because the superclass will not complain, but will simply assign the default value (in this case, an empty string) to the variable.

There are a few ways to ensure that the variable is passed upwards. Assume the Contact class does, for some reason, need to be initialized with a phone parameter, and the Friend class will also need access to it. We can do any of the following:

- Don't include phone as an explicit keyword argument. Instead, leave it in the kwargs dictionary. Friend can look it up using the syntax kwargs['phone']. When it passes **kwargs to the super call, phone will still be in the dictionary.

- Make phone an explicit keyword argument but update the kwargs dictionary before passing it to super, using the standard dictionary syntax kwargs['phone'] = phone.

- Make phone an explicit keyword argument, but update the kwargs dictionary using the kwargs.update method. This is useful if you have several arguments to update. You can create the dictionary passed into update using either the dict(phone=phone) constructor, or the dictionary syntax {'phone': phone}.

- Make phone an explicit keyword argument, but pass it to the super call explicitly with the syntax super().__init__(phone=phone, **kwargs).

We have covered many of the caveats involved with multiple inheritance in Python. When we need to account for all the possible situations, we have to plan for them and our code will get messy. Basic multiple inheritance can be handy but, in many cases, we may want to choose a more transparent way of combining two disparate classes, usually using composition or one of the design patterns we'll be covering in *Chapter 10, Python Design Patterns I* and *Chapter 11, Python Design Patterns II*.

Polymorphism

We were introduced to polymorphism in *Chapter 1, Object-oriented Design*. It is a fancy name describing a simple concept: different behaviors happen depending on which subclass is being used, without having to explicitly know what the subclass actually is. As an example, imagine a program that plays audio files. A media player might need to load an `AudioFile` object and then `play` it. We'd put a `play()` method on the object, which is responsible for decompressing or extracting the audio and routing it to the sound card and speakers. The act of playing an `AudioFile` could feasibly be as simple as:

```
audio_file.play()
```

However, the process of decompressing and extracting an audio file is very different for different types of files. The `.wav` files are stored uncompressed, while `.mp3`, `.wma`, and `.ogg` files all have totally different compression algorithms.

We can use inheritance with polymorphism to simplify the design. Each type of file can be represented by a different subclass of `AudioFile`, for example, `WavFile`, `MP3File`. Each of these would have a `play()` method, but that method would be implemented differently for each file to ensure the correct extraction procedure is followed. The media player object would never need to know which subclass of `AudioFile` it is referring to; it just calls `play()` and polymorphically lets the object take care of the actual details of playing. Let's look at a quick skeleton showing how this might look:

```python
class AudioFile:
    def __init__(self, filename):
        if not filename.endswith(self.ext):
            raise Exception("Invalid file format")

        self.filename = filename

class MP3File(AudioFile):
    ext = "mp3"
    def play(self):
        print("playing {} as mp3".format(self.filename))

class WavFile(AudioFile):
    ext = "wav"
    def play(self):
```

```
            print("playing {} as wav".format(self.filename))

    class OggFile(AudioFile):
        ext = "ogg"
        def play(self):
            print("playing {} as ogg".format(self.filename))
```

All audio files check to ensure that a valid extension was given upon initialization. But did you notice how the __init__ method in the parent class is able to access the ext class variable from different subclasses? That's polymorphism at work. If the filename doesn't end with the correct name, it raises an exception (exceptions will be covered in detail in the next chapter). The fact that AudioFile doesn't actually store a reference to the ext variable doesn't stop it from being able to access it on the subclass.

In addition, each subclass of AudioFile implements play() in a different way (this example doesn't actually play the music; audio compression algorithms really deserve a separate book!). This is also polymorphism in action. The media player can use the exact same code to play a file, no matter what type it is; it doesn't care what subclass of AudioFile it is looking at. The details of decompressing the audio file are *encapsulated*. If we test this example, it works as we would hope:

```
>>> ogg = OggFile("myfile.ogg")
>>> ogg.play()
playing myfile.ogg as ogg
>>> mp3 = MP3File("myfile.mp3")
>>> mp3.play()
playing myfile.mp3 as mp3
>>> not_an_mp3 = MP3File("myfile.ogg")
Traceback (most recent call last):
  File "<stdin>", line 1, in <module>
  File "polymorphic_audio.py", line 4, in __init__
    raise Exception("Invalid file format")
Exception: Invalid file format
```

See how AudioFile.__init__ is able to check the file type without actually knowing what subclass it is referring to?

Polymorphism is actually one of the coolest things about object-oriented programming, and it makes some programming designs obvious that weren't possible in earlier paradigms. However, Python makes polymorphism less cool because of duck typing. Duck typing in Python allows us to use *any* object that provides the required behavior without forcing it to be a subclass. The dynamic nature of Python makes this trivial. The following example does not extend `AudioFile`, but it can be interacted with in Python using the exact same interface:

```python
class FlacFile:
    def __init__(self, filename):
        if not filename.endswith(".flac"):
            raise Exception("Invalid file format")

        self.filename = filename

    def play(self):
        print("playing {} as flac".format(self.filename))
```

Our media player can play this object just as easily as one that extends `AudioFile`.

Polymorphism is one of the most important reasons to use inheritance in many object-oriented contexts. Because any objects that supply the correct interface can be used interchangeably in Python, it reduces the need for polymorphic common superclasses. Inheritance can still be useful for sharing code but, if all that is being shared is the public interface, duck typing is all that is required. This reduced need for inheritance also reduces the need for multiple inheritance; often, when multiple inheritance appears to be a valid solution, we can just use duck typing to mimic one of the multiple superclasses.

Of course, just because an object satisfies a particular interface (by providing required methods or attributes) does not mean it will simply work in all situations. It has to fulfill that interface in a way that makes sense in the overall system. Just because an object provides a `play()` method does not mean it will automatically work with a media player. For example, our chess AI object from *Chapter 1, Object-oriented Design*, may have a `play()` method that moves a chess piece. Even though it satisfies the interface, this class would likely break in spectacular ways if we tried to plug it into a media player!

Another useful feature of duck typing is that the duck-typed object only needs to provide those methods and attributes that are actually being accessed. For example, if we needed to create a fake file object to read data from, we can create a new object that has a `read()` method; we don't have to override the `write` method if the code that is going to interact with the object will only be reading from the file. More succinctly, duck typing doesn't need to provide the entire interface of an object that is available, it only needs to fulfill the interface that is actually accessed.

Abstract base classes

While duck typing is useful, it is not always easy to tell in advance if a class is going to fulfill the protocol you require. Therefore, Python introduced the idea of abstract base classes. **Abstract base classes**, or **ABCs**, define a set of methods and properties that a class must implement in order to be considered a duck-type instance of that class. The class can extend the abstract base class itself in order to be used as an instance of that class, but it must supply all the appropriate methods.

In practice, it's rarely necessary to create new abstract base classes, but we may find occasions to implement instances of existing ABCs. We'll cover implementing ABCs first, and then briefly see how to create your own if you should ever need to.

Using an abstract base class

Most of the abstract base classes that exist in the Python Standard Library live in the `collections` module. One of the simplest ones is the `Container` class. Let's inspect it in the Python interpreter to see what methods this class requires:

```
>>> from collections import Container
>>> Container.__abstractmethods__
frozenset(['__contains__'])
```

So, the `Container` class has exactly one abstract method that needs to be implemented, `__contains__`. You can issue `help(Container.__contains__)` to see what the function signature should look like:

```
Help on method __contains__ in module _abcoll:
__contains__(self, x) unbound _abcoll.Container method
```

So, we see that `__contains__` needs to take a single argument. Unfortunately, the help file doesn't tell us much about what that argument should be, but it's pretty obvious from the name of the ABC and the single method it implements that this argument is the value the user is checking to see if the container holds.

This method is implemented by `list`, `str`, and `dict` to indicate whether or not a given value is in that data structure. However, we can also define a silly container that tells us whether a given value is in the set of odd integers:

```
class OddContainer:
    def __contains__(self, x):
        if not isinstance(x, int) or not x % 2:
            return False
        return True
```

Now, we can instantiate an `OddContainer` object and determine that, even though we did not extend `Container`, the class *is a* `Container` object:

```
>>> from collections import Container
>>> odd_container = OddContainer()
>>> isinstance(odd_container, Container)
True
>>> issubclass(OddContainer, Container)
True
```

And that is why duck typing is way more awesome than classical polymorphism. We can create *is a* relationships without the overhead of using inheritance (or worse, multiple inheritance).

The interesting thing about the `Container` ABC is that any class that implements it gets to use the `in` keyword for free. In fact, `in` is just syntax sugar that delegates to the `__contains__` method. Any class that has a `__contains__` method is a `Container` and can therefore be queried by the `in` keyword, for example:

```
>>> 1 in odd_container
True
>>> 2 in odd_container
False
>>> 3 in odd_container
True
>>> "a string" in odd_container
False
```

Creating an abstract base class

As we saw earlier, it's not necessary to have an abstract base class to enable duck typing. However, imagine we were creating a media player with third-party plugins. It is advisable to create an abstract base class in this case to document what API the third-party plugins should provide. The `abc` module provides the tools you need to do this, but I'll warn you in advance, this requires some of Python's most arcane concepts:

```
import abc

class MediaLoader(metaclass=abc.ABCMeta):
    @abc.abstractmethod
    def play(self):
        pass

    @abc.abstractproperty
    def ext(self):
```

```
            pass

        @classmethod
        def __subclasshook__(cls, C):
            if cls is MediaLoader:
                attrs = set(dir(C))
                if set(cls.__abstractmethods__) <= attrs:
                    return True

        return NotImplemented
```

This is a complicated example that includes several Python features that won't be explained until later in this book. It is included here for completeness, but you don't need to understand all of it to get the gist of how to create your own ABC.

The first weird thing is the `metaclass` keyword argument that is passed into the class where you would normally see the list of parent classes. This is a rarely used construct from the mystic art of metaclass programming. We won't be covering metaclasses in this book, so all you need to know is that by assigning the `ABCMeta` metaclass, you are giving your class superpower (or at least superclass) abilities.

Next, we see the `@abc.abstractmethod` and `@abc.abstractproperty` constructs. These are Python decorators. We'll discuss those in *Chapter 5, When to Use Object-oriented Programming*. For now, just know that by marking a method or property as being abstract, you are stating that any subclass of this class must implement that method or supply that property in order to be considered a proper member of the class.

See what happens if you implement subclasses that do or don't supply those properties:

```
>>> class Wav(MediaLoader):
...     pass
...
>>> x = Wav()
Traceback (most recent call last):
  File "<stdin>", line 1, in <module>
TypeError: Can't instantiate abstract class Wav with abstract methods
ext, play
>>> class Ogg(MediaLoader):
...     ext = '.ogg'
...     def play(self):
...         pass
...
>>> o = Ogg()
```

Since the `Wav` class fails to implement the abstract attributes, it is not possible to instantiate that class. The class is still a legal abstract class, but you'd have to subclass it to actually do anything. The `Ogg` class supplies both attributes, so it instantiates cleanly.

Going back to the `MediaLoader` ABC, let's dissect that `__subclasshook__` method. It is basically saying that any class that supplies concrete implementations of all the abstract attributes of this ABC should be considered a subclass of `MediaLoader`, even if it doesn't actually inherit from the `MediaLoader` class.

More common object-oriented languages have a clear separation between the interface and the implementation of a class. For example, some languages provide an explicit `interface` keyword that allows us to define the methods that a class must have without any implementation. In such an environment, an abstract class is one that provides both an interface and a concrete implementation of some but not all methods. Any class can explicitly state that it implements a given interface.

Python's ABCs help to supply the functionality of interfaces without compromising on the benefits of duck typing.

Demystifying the magic

You can copy and paste the subclass code without understanding it if you want to make abstract classes that fulfill this particular contract. We'll cover most of the unusual syntaxes throughout the book, but let's go over it line by line to get an overview.

```
@classmethod
```

This decorator marks the method as a class method. It essentially says that the method can be called on a class instead of an instantiated object:

```
def __subclasshook__(cls, C):
```

This defines the `__subclasshook__` class method. This special method is called by the Python interpreter to answer the question, *Is the class C a subclass of this class?*

```
if cls is MediaLoader:
```

We check to see if the method was called specifically on this class, rather than, say a subclass of this class. This prevents, for example, the `Wav` class from being thought of as a parent class of the `Ogg` class:

```
attrs = set(dir(C))
```

All this line does is get the set of methods and properties that the class has, including any parent classes in its class hierarchy:

```
if set(cls.__abstractmethods__) <= attrs:
```

This line uses set notation to see whether the set of abstract methods in this class have been supplied in the candidate class. Note that it doesn't check to see whether the methods have been implemented, just if they are there. Thus, it's possible for a class to be a subclass and yet still be an abstract class itself.

```
return True
```

If all the abstract methods have been supplied, then the candidate class is a subclass of this class and we return `True`. The method can legally return one of the three values: `True`, `False`, or `NotImplemented`. `True` and `False` indicate that the class is or is not definitively a subclass of this class:

```
return NotImplemented
```

If any of the conditionals have not been met (that is, the class is not `MediaLoader` or not all abstract methods have been supplied), then return `NotImplemented`. This tells the Python machinery to use the default mechanism (does the candidate class explicitly extend this class?) for subclass detection.

In short, we can now define the `Ogg` class as a subclass of the `MediaLoader` class without actually extending the `MediaLoader` class:

```
>>> class Ogg():
...      ext = '.ogg'
...      def play(self):
...          print("this will play an ogg file")
...
>>> issubclass(Ogg, MediaLoader)
True
>>> isinstance(Ogg(), MediaLoader)
True
```

Case study

Let's try to tie everything we've learned together with a larger example. We'll be designing a simple real estate application that allows an agent to manage properties available for purchase or rent. There will be two types of properties: apartments and houses. The agent needs to be able to enter a few relevant details about new properties, list all currently available properties, and mark a property as sold or rented. For brevity, we won't worry about editing property details or reactivating a property after it is sold.

The project will allow the agent to interact with the objects using the Python interpreter prompt. In this world of graphical user interfaces and web applications, you might be wondering why we're creating such old-fashioned looking programs. Simply put, both windowed programs and web applications require a lot of overhead knowledge and boilerplate code to make them do what is required. If we were developing software using either of these paradigms, we'd get so lost in GUI programming or web programming that we'd lose sight of the object-oriented principles we're trying to master.

Luckily, most GUI and web frameworks utilize an object-oriented approach, and the principles we're studying now will help in understanding those systems in the future. We'll discuss them both briefly in *Chapter 13, Concurrency*, but complete details are far beyond the scope of a single book.

Looking at our requirements, it seems like there are quite a few nouns that might represent classes of objects in our system. Clearly, we'll need to represent a property. Houses and apartments may need separate classes. Rentals and purchases also seem to require separate representation. Since we're focusing on inheritance right now, we'll be looking at ways to share behavior using inheritance or multiple inheritance.

`House` and `Apartment` are both types of properties, so `Property` can be a superclass of those two classes. `Rental` and `Purchase` will need some extra thought; if we use inheritance, we'll need to have separate classes, for example, for `HouseRental` and `HousePurchase`, and use multiple inheritance to combine them. This feels a little clunky compared to a composition or association-based design, but let's run with it and see what we come up with.

Now then, what attributes might be associated with a `Property` class? Regardless of whether it is an apartment or a house, most people will want to know the square footage, number of bedrooms, and number of bathrooms. (There are numerous other attributes that might be modeled, but we'll keep it simple for our prototype.)

If the property is a house, it will want to advertise the number of stories, whether it has a garage (attached, detached, or none), and whether the yard is fenced. An apartment will want to indicate if it has a balcony, and if the laundry is ensuite, coin, or off-site.

Both property types will require a method to display the characteristics of that property. At the moment, no other behaviors are apparent.

Rental properties will need to store the rent per month, whether the property is furnished, and whether utilities are included, and if not, what they are estimated to be. Properties for purchase will need to store the purchase price and estimated annual property taxes. For our application, we'll only need to display this data, so we can get away with just adding a `display()` method similar to that used in the other classes.

Finally, we'll need an `Agent` object that holds a list of all properties, displays those properties, and allows us to create new ones. Creating properties will entail prompting the user for the relevant details for each property type. This could be done in the `Agent` object, but then `Agent` would need to know a lot of information about the types of properties. This is not taking advantage of polymorphism. Another alternative would be to put the prompts in the initializer or even a constructor for each class, but this would not allow the classes to be applied in a GUI or web application in the future. A better idea is to create a static method that does the prompting and returns a dictionary of the prompted parameters. Then, all the `Agent` has to do is prompt the user for the type of property and payment method, and ask the correct class to instantiate itself.

That's a lot of designing! The following class diagram may communicate our design decisions a little more clearly:

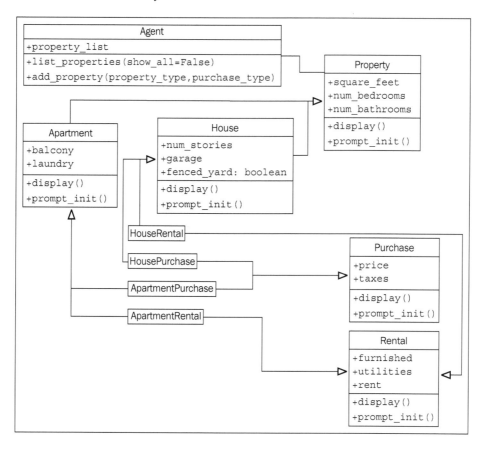

Wow, that's a lot of inheritance arrows! I don't think it would be possible to add another level of inheritance without crossing arrows. Multiple inheritance is a messy business, even at the design stage.

The trickiest aspects of these classes is going to be ensuring superclass methods get called in the inheritance hierarchy. Let's start with the `Property` implementation:

```python
class Property:
    def __init__(self, square_feet='', beds='',
            baths='', **kwargs):
        super().__init__(**kwargs)
        self.square_feet = square_feet
        self.num_bedrooms = beds
        self.num_baths = baths

    def display(self):
        print("PROPERTY DETAILS")
        print("================")
        print("square footage: {}".format(self.square_feet))
        print("bedrooms: {}".format(self.num_bedrooms))
        print("bathrooms: {}".format(self.num_baths))
        print()

    def prompt_init():
        return dict(square_feet=input("Enter the square feet: "),
                beds=input("Enter number of bedrooms: "),
                baths=input("Enter number of baths: "))
    prompt_init = staticmethod(prompt_init)
```

This class is pretty straightforward. We've already added the extra `**kwargs` parameter to `__init__` because we know it's going to be used in a multiple inheritance situation. We've also included a call to `super().__init__` in case we are not the last call in the multiple inheritance chain. In this case, we're *consuming* the keyword arguments because we know they won't be needed at other levels of the inheritance hierarchy.

We see something new in the `prompt_init` method. This method is made into a static method immediately after it is initially created. Static methods are associated only with a class (something like class variables), rather than a specific object instance. Hence, they have no `self` argument. Because of this, the `super` keyword won't work (there is no parent object, only a parent class), so we simply call the static method on the parent class directly. This method uses the Python `dict` constructor to create a dictionary of values that can be passed into `__init__`. The value for each key is prompted with a call to `input`.

The `Apartment` class extends `Property`, and is similar in structure:

```
class Apartment(Property):
    valid_laundries = ("coin", "ensuite", "none")
    valid_balconies = ("yes", "no", "solarium")

    def __init__(self, balcony='', laundry='', **kwargs):
        super().__init__(**kwargs)
        self.balcony = balcony
        self.laundry = laundry

    def display(self):
        super().display()
        print("APARTMENT DETAILS")
        print("laundry: %s" % self.laundry)
        print("has balcony: %s" % self.balcony)

    def prompt_init():
        parent_init = Property.prompt_init()
        laundry = ''
        while laundry.lower() not in \
                Apartment.valid_laundries:
            laundry = input("What laundry facilities does "
                    "the property have? ({})".format(
                    ", ".join(Apartment.valid_laundries)))
        balcony = ''
        while balcony.lower() not in \
                Apartment.valid_balconies:
            balcony = input(
                "Does the property have a balcony? "
                "({})".format(
                ", ".join(Apartment.valid_balconies)))
        parent_init.update({
            "laundry": laundry,
            "balcony": balcony
        })
        return parent_init
    prompt_init = staticmethod(prompt_init)
```

The `display()` and `__init__()` methods call their respective parent class methods using `super()` to ensure the `Property` class is properly initialized.

The `prompt_init` static method is now getting dictionary values from the parent class, and then adding some additional values of its own. It calls the `dict.update` method to merge the new dictionary values into the first one. However, that `prompt_init` method is looking pretty ugly; it loops twice until the user enters a valid input using structurally similar code but different variables. It would be nice to extract this validation logic so we can maintain it in only one location; it will likely also be useful to later classes.

With all the talk on inheritance, we might think this is a good place to use a mixin. Instead, we have a chance to study a situation where inheritance is not the best solution. The method we want to create will be used in a static method. If we were to inherit from a class that provided validation functionality, the functionality would also have to be provided as a static method that did not access any instance variables on the class. If it doesn't access any instance variables, what's the point of making it a class at all? Why don't we just make this validation functionality a module-level function that accepts an input string and a list of valid answers, and leave it at that?

Let's explore what this validation function would look like:

```
def get_valid_input(input_string, valid_options):
    input_string += " ({}) ".format(", ".join(valid_options))
    response = input(input_string)
    while response.lower() not in valid_options:
        response = input(input_string)
    return response
```

We can test this function in the interpreter, independent of all the other classes we've been working on. This is a good sign, it means different pieces of our design are not tightly coupled to each other and can later be improved independently, without affecting other pieces of code.

```
>>> get_valid_input("what laundry?", ("coin", "ensuite", "none"))
what laundry? (coin, ensuite, none) hi
what laundry? (coin, ensuite, none) COIN
'COIN'
```

Now, let's quickly update our `Apartment.prompt_init` method to use this new function for validation:

```
def prompt_init():
    parent_init = Property.prompt_init()
    laundry = get_valid_input(
```

```
                "What laundry facilities does "
                "the property have? ",
                Apartment.valid_laundries)
        balcony = get_valid_input(
            "Does the property have a balcony? ",
            Apartment.valid_balconies)
        parent_init.update({
            "laundry": laundry,
            "balcony": balcony
        })
        return parent_init
    prompt_init = staticmethod(prompt_init)
```

That's much easier to read (and maintain!) than our original version. Now we're ready to build the `House` class. This class has a parallel structure to `Apartment`, but refers to different prompts and variables:

```
class House(Property):
    valid_garage = ("attached", "detached", "none")
    valid_fenced = ("yes", "no")

    def __init__(self, num_stories='',
            garage='', fenced='', **kwargs):
        super().__init__(**kwargs)
        self.garage = garage
        self.fenced = fenced
        self.num_stories = num_stories

    def display(self):
        super().display()
        print("HOUSE DETAILS")
        print("# of stories: {}".format(self.num_stories))
        print("garage: {}".format(self.garage))
        print("fenced yard: {}".format(self.fenced))


    def prompt_init():
        parent_init = Property.prompt_init()
        fenced = get_valid_input("Is the yard fenced? ",
                House.valid_fenced)
        garage = get_valid_input("Is there a garage? ",
                House.valid_garage)
```

```
            num_stories = input("How many stories? ")

            parent_init.update({
                "fenced": fenced,
                "garage": garage,
                "num_stories": num_stories
            })
            return parent_init
        prompt_init = staticmethod(prompt_init)
```

There's nothing new to explore here, so let's move on to the `Purchase` and `Rental` classes. In spite of having apparently different purposes, they are also similar in design to the ones we just discussed:

```
    class Purchase:
        def __init__(self, price='', taxes='', **kwargs):
            super().__init__(**kwargs)
            self.price = price
            self.taxes = taxes

        def display(self):
            super().display()
            print("PURCHASE DETAILS")
            print("selling price: {}".format(self.price))
            print("estimated taxes: {}".format(self.taxes))

        def prompt_init():
            return dict(
                price=input("What is the selling price? "),
                taxes=input("What are the estimated taxes? "))
        prompt_init = staticmethod(prompt_init)

    class Rental:
        def __init__(self, furnished='', utilities='',
                rent='', **kwargs):
            super().__init__(**kwargs)
            self.furnished = furnished
            self.rent = rent
            self.utilities = utilities

        def display(self):
            super().display()
            print("RENTAL DETAILS")
```

```
            print("rent: {}".format(self.rent))
            print("estimated utilities: {}".format(
                self.utilities))
            print("furnished: {}".format(self.furnished))
        def prompt_init():
            return dict(
                rent=input("What is the monthly rent? "),
                utilities=input(
                    "What are the estimated utilities? "),
                furnished = get_valid_input(
                    "Is the property furnished? ",
                        ("yes", "no")))
        prompt_init = staticmethod(prompt_init)
```

These two classes don't have a superclass (other than `object`), but we still call `super().__init__` because they are going to be combined with the other classes, and we don't know what order the `super` calls will be made in. The interface is similar to that used for `House` and `Apartment`, which is very useful when we combine the functionality of these four classes in separate subclasses. For example:

```
    class HouseRental(Rental, House):
        def prompt_init():
            init = House.prompt_init()
            init.update(Rental.prompt_init())
            return init
        prompt_init = staticmethod(prompt_init)
```

This is slightly surprising, as the class on its own has neither an `__init__` nor `display` method! Because both parent classes appropriately call `super` in these methods, we only have to extend those classes and the classes will behave in the correct order. This is not the case with `prompt_init`, of course, since it is a static method that does not call `super`, so we implement this one explicitly. We should test this class to make sure it is behaving properly before we write the other three combinations:

```
>>> init = HouseRental.prompt_init()
Enter the square feet: 1
Enter number of bedrooms: 2
Enter number of baths: 3
Is the yard fenced?   (yes, no) no
Is there a garage?   (attached, detached, none) none
How many stories? 4
What is the monthly rent? 5
What are the estimated utilities? 6
```

```
Is the property furnished?   (yes, no) no
>>> house = HouseRental(**init)
>>> house.display()
PROPERTY DETAILS
================
square footage: 1
bedrooms: 2
bathrooms: 3

HOUSE DETAILS
# of stories: 4
garage: none
fenced yard: no

RENTAL DETAILS
rent: 5
estimated utilities: 6
furnished: no
```

It looks like it is working fine. The prompt_init method is prompting for initializers to all the super classes, and display() is also cooperatively calling all three superclasses.

The order of the inherited classes in the preceding example is important. If we had written class HouseRental(House, Rental) instead of class HouseRental(Rental, House), display() would not have called Rental.display()! When display is called on our version of HouseRental, it refers to the Rental version of the method, which calls super.display() to get the House version, which again calls super. display() to get the property version. If we reversed it, display would refer to the House class's display(). When super is called, it calls the method on the Property parent class. But Property does not have a call to super in its display method. This means Rental class's display method would not be called! By placing the inheritance list in the order we did, we ensure that Rental calls super, which then takes care of the House side of the hierarchy. You might think we could have added a super call to Property.display(), but that will fail because the next superclass of Property is object, and object does not have a display method. Another way to fix this is to allow Rental and Purchase to extend the Property class instead of deriving directly from object. (Or we could modify the method resolution order dynamically, but that is beyond the scope of this book.)

Now that we have tested it, we are prepared to create the rest of our combined subclasses:

```python
class ApartmentRental(Rental, Apartment):
    def prompt_init():
        init = Apartment.prompt_init()
        init.update(Rental.prompt_init())
        return init
    prompt_init = staticmethod(prompt_init)

class ApartmentPurchase(Purchase, Apartment):
    def prompt_init():
        init = Apartment.prompt_init()
        init.update(Purchase.prompt_init())
        return init
    prompt_init = staticmethod(prompt_init)

class HousePurchase(Purchase, House):
    def prompt_init():
        init = House.prompt_init()
        init.update(Purchase.prompt_init())
        return init
    prompt_init = staticmethod(prompt_init)
```

That should be the most intense designing out of our way! Now all we have to do is create the Agent class, which is responsible for creating new listings and displaying existing ones. Let's start with the simpler storing and listing of properties:

```python
class Agent:
    def __init__(self):
        self.property_list = []

    def display_properties(self):
        for property in self.property_list:
            property.display()
```

Adding a property will require first querying the type of property and whether property is for purchase or rental. We can do this by displaying a simple menu. Once this has been determined, we can extract the correct subclass and prompt for all the details using the prompt_init hierarchy we've already developed. Sounds simple? It is. Let's start by adding a dictionary class variable to the Agent class:

```python
type_map = {
    ("house", "rental"): HouseRental,
    ("house", "purchase"): HousePurchase,
```

```
("apartment", "rental"): ApartmentRental,
("apartment", "purchase"): ApartmentPurchase
}
```

That's some pretty funny looking code. This is a dictionary, where the keys are tuples of two distinct strings, and the values are class objects. Class objects? Yes, classes can be passed around, renamed, and stored in containers just like *normal* objects or primitive data types. With this simple dictionary, we can simply hijack our earlier get_valid_input method to ensure we get the correct dictionary keys and look up the appropriate class, like this:

```
def add_property(self):
    property_type = get_valid_input(
            "What type of property? ",
            ("house", "apartment")).lower()
    payment_type = get_valid_input(
            "What payment type? ",
            ("purchase", "rental")).lower()

    PropertyClass = self.type_map[
        (property_type, payment_type)]
    init_args = PropertyClass.prompt_init()
    self.property_list.append(PropertyClass(**init_args))
```

This may look a bit funny too! We look up the class in the dictionary and store it in a variable named PropertyClass. We don't know exactly which class is available, but the class knows itself, so we can polymorphically call prompt_init to get a dictionary of values appropriate to pass into the constructor. Then we use the keyword argument syntax to convert the dictionary into arguments and construct the new object to load the correct data.

Now our user can use this Agent class to add and view lists of properties. It wouldn't take much work to add features to mark a property as available or unavailable or to edit and remove properties. Our prototype is now in a good enough state to take to a real estate agent and demonstrate its functionality. Here's how a demo session might work:

```
>>> agent = Agent()
>>> agent.add_property()
What type of property?  (house, apartment) house
What payment type?  (purchase, rental) rental
Enter the square feet: 900
Enter number of bedrooms: 2
Enter number of baths: one and a half
```

```
Is the yard fenced?   (yes, no) yes
Is there a garage?   (attached, detached, none) detached
How many stories? 1
What is the monthly rent? 1200
What are the estimated utilities? included
Is the property furnished?   (yes, no) no
>>> agent.add_property()
What type of property?   (house, apartment) apartment
What payment type?   (purchase, rental) purchase
Enter the square feet: 800
Enter number of bedrooms: 3
Enter number of baths: 2
What laundry facilities does the property have?   (coin, ensuite,
one) ensuite
Does the property have a balcony? (yes, no, solarium) yes
What is the selling price? $200,000
What are the estimated taxes? 1500
>>> agent.display_properties()
PROPERTY DETAILS
================
square footage: 900
bedrooms: 2
bathrooms: one and a half

HOUSE DETAILS
# of stories: 1
garage: detached
fenced yard: yes
RENTAL DETAILS
rent: 1200
estimated utilities: included
furnished: no
PROPERTY DETAILS
================
square footage: 800
bedrooms: 3
```

```
bathrooms: 2

APARTMENT DETAILS
laundry: ensuite
has balcony: yes
PURCHASE DETAILS
selling price: $200,000
estimated taxes: 1500
```

Exercises

Look around you at some of the physical objects in your workspace and see if you can describe them in an inheritance hierarchy. Humans have been dividing the world into taxonomies like this for centuries, so it shouldn't be difficult. Are there any non-obvious inheritance relationships between classes of objects? If you were to model these objects in a computer application, what properties and methods would they share? Which ones would have to be polymorphically overridden? What properties would be completely different between them?

Now, write some code. No, not for the physical hierarchy; that's boring. Physical items have more properties than methods. Just think about a pet programming project you've wanted to tackle in the past year, but never got around to. For whatever problem you want to solve, try to think of some basic inheritance relationships. Then implement them. Make sure that you also pay attention to the sorts of relationships that you actually don't need to use inheritance for. Are there any places where you might want to use multiple inheritance? Are you sure? Can you see any place you would want to use a mixin? Try to knock together a quick prototype. It doesn't have to be useful or even partially working. You've seen how you can test code using `python -i` already; just write some code and test it in the interactive interpreter. If it works, write some more. If it doesn't, fix it!

Now, take a look at the real estate example. This turned out to be quite an effective use of multiple inheritance. I have to admit though, I had my doubts when I started the design. Have a look at the original problem and see if you can come up with another design to solve it that uses only single inheritance. How would you do it with abstract base classes? What about a design that doesn't use inheritance at all? Which do you think is the most elegant solution? Elegance is a primary goal in Python development, but each programmer has a different opinion as to what is the most elegant solution. Some people tend to think and understand problems most clearly using composition, while others find multiple inheritance to be the most useful model.

Finally, try adding some new features to the three designs. Whatever features strike your fancy are fine. I'd like to see a way to differentiate between available and unavailable properties, for starters. It's not of much use to me if it's already rented!

Which design is easiest to extend? Which is hardest? If somebody asked you why you thought this, would you be able to explain yourself?

Summary

We've gone from simple inheritance, one of the most useful tools in the object-oriented programmer's toolbox, all the way through to multiple inheritance, one of the most complicated. Inheritance can be used to add functionality to existing classes and built-ins using inheritance. Abstracting similar code into a parent class can help increase maintainability. Methods on parent classes can be called using `super` and argument lists must be formatted safely for these calls to work when using multiple inheritance.

In the next chapter, we'll cover the subtle art of handling exceptional circumstances.

4
Expecting the Unexpected

Programs are very fragile. It would be ideal if code always returned a valid result, but sometimes a valid result can't be calculated. For example, it's not possible to divide by zero, or to access the eighth item in a five-item list.

In the old days, the only way around this was to rigorously check the inputs for every function to make sure they made sense. Typically, functions had special return values to indicate an error condition; for example, they could return a negative number to indicate that a positive value couldn't be calculated. Different numbers might mean different errors occurred. Any code that called this function would have to explicitly check for an error condition and act accordingly. A lot of code didn't bother to do this, and programs simply crashed. However, in the object-oriented world, this is not the case.

In this chapter, we will study **exceptions**, special error objects that only need to be handled when it makes sense to handle them. In particular, we will cover:

- How to cause an exception to occur
- How to recover when an exception has occurred
- How to handle different exception types in different ways
- Cleaning up when an exception has occurred
- Creating new types of exception
- Using the exception syntax for flow control

Raising exceptions

In principle, an exception is just an object. There are many different exception classes available, and we can easily define more of our own. The one thing they all have in common is that they inherit from a built-in class called BaseException. These exception objects become special when they are handled inside the program's flow of control. When an exception occurs, everything that was supposed to happen doesn't happen, unless it was supposed to happen when an exception occurred. Make sense? Don't worry, it will!

The easiest way to cause an exception to occur is to do something silly! Chances are you've done this already and seen the exception output. For example, any time Python encounters a line in your program that it can't understand, it bails with SyntaxError, which is a type of exception. Here's a common one:

```
>>> print "hello world"
  File "<stdin>", line 1
    print "hello world"
                      ^
SyntaxError: invalid syntax
```

This print statement was a valid command in Python 2 and previous versions, but in Python 3, because print is now a function, we have to enclose the arguments in parenthesis. So, if we type the preceding command into a Python 3 interpreter, we get the SyntaxError.

In addition to SyntaxError, some other common exceptions, which we can handle, are shown in the following example:

```
>>> x = 5 / 0
Traceback (most recent call last):
  File "<stdin>", line 1, in <module>
ZeroDivisionError: int division or modulo by zero

>>> lst = [1,2,3]
>>> print(lst[3])
Traceback (most recent call last):
  File "<stdin>", line 1, in <module>
IndexError: list index out of range

>>> lst + 2
Traceback (most recent call last):
```

```
    File "<stdin>", line 1, in <module>
TypeError: can only concatenate list (not "int") to list


>>> lst.add
Traceback (most recent call last):
  File "<stdin>", line 1, in <module>
AttributeError: 'list' object has no attribute 'add'


>>> d = {'a': 'hello'}
>>> d['b']
Traceback (most recent call last):
  File "<stdin>", line 1, in <module>
KeyError: 'b'


>>> print(this_is_not_a_var)
Traceback (most recent call last):
  File "<stdin>", line 1, in <module>
NameError: name 'this_is_not_a_var' is not defined
```

Sometimes these exceptions are indicators of something wrong in our program (in which case we would go to the indicated line number and fix it), but they also occur in legitimate situations. A ZeroDivisionError doesn't always mean we received an invalid input. It could also mean we have received a different input. The user may have entered a zero by mistake, or on purpose, or it may represent a legitimate value, such as an empty bank account or the age of a newborn child.

You may have noticed all the preceding built-in exceptions end with the name Error. In Python, the words error and exception are used almost interchangeably. Errors are sometimes considered more dire than exceptions, but they are dealt with in exactly the same way. Indeed, all the error classes in the preceding example have Exception (which extends BaseException) as their superclass.

Raising an exception

We'll get to handling exceptions in a minute, but first, let's discover what we should do if we're writing a program that needs to inform the user or a calling function that the inputs are somehow invalid. Wouldn't it be great if we could use the same mechanism that Python uses? Well, we can! Here's a simple class that adds items to a list only if they are even numbered integers:

```
class EvenOnly(list):
    def append(self, integer):
        if not isinstance(integer, int):
            raise TypeError("Only integers can be added")
        if integer % 2:
            raise ValueError("Only even numbers can be added")
        super().append(integer)
```

This class extends the `list` built-in, as we discussed in *Chapter 2, Objects in Python*, and overrides the `append` method to check two conditions that ensure the item is an even integer. We first check if the input is an instance of the `int` type, and then use the modulus operator to ensure it is divisible by two. If either of the two conditions is not met, the `raise` keyword causes an exception to occur. The `raise` keyword is simply followed by the object being raised as an exception. In the preceding example, two objects are newly constructed from the built-in classes `TypeError` and `ValueError`. The raised object could just as easily be an instance of a new exception class we create ourselves (we'll see how shortly), an exception that was defined elsewhere, or even an exception object that has been previously raised and handled. If we test this class in the Python interpreter, we can see that it is outputting useful error information when exceptions occur, just as before:

```
>>> e = EvenOnly()
>>> e.append("a string")
Traceback (most recent call last):
  File "<stdin>", line 1, in <module>
  File "even_integers.py", line 7, in add
    raise TypeError("Only integers can be added")
TypeError: Only integers can be added

>>> e.append(3)
Traceback (most recent call last):
  File "<stdin>", line 1, in <module>
  File "even_integers.py", line 9, in add
    raise ValueError("Only even numbers can be added")
ValueError: Only even numbers can be added
>>> e.append(2)
```

While this class is effective for demonstrating exceptions in action, it isn't very good at its job. It is still possible to get other values into the list using index notation or slice notation. This can all be avoided by overriding other appropriate methods, some of which are double-underscore methods.

The effects of an exception

When an exception is raised, it appears to stop program execution immediately. Any lines that were supposed to run after the exception is raised are not executed, and unless the exception is dealt with, the program will exit with an error message. Take a look at this simple function:

```
def no_return():
    print("I am about to raise an exception")
    raise Exception("This is always raised")
    print("This line will never execute")
    return "I won't be returned"
```

If we execute this function, we see that the first `print` call is executed and then the exception is raised. The second `print` statement is never executed, and the `return` statement never executes either:

```
>>> no_return()
I am about to raise an exception
Traceback (most recent call last):
  File "<stdin>", line 1, in <module>
  File "exception_quits.py", line 3, in no_return
    raise Exception("This is always raised")
Exception: This is always raised
```

Furthermore, if we have a function that calls another function that raises an exception, nothing will be executed in the first function after the point where the second function was called. Raising an exception stops all execution right up through the function call stack until it is either handled or forces the interpreter to exit. To demonstrate, let's add a second function that calls the earlier one:

```
def call_exceptor():
    print("call_exceptor starts here...")
    no_return()
    print("an exception was raised...")
    print("...so these lines don't run")
```

When we call this function, we see that the first `print` statement executes, as well as the first line in the `no_return` function. But once the exception is raised, nothing else executes:

```
>>> call_exceptor()
call_exceptor starts here...
I am about to raise an exception
Traceback (most recent call last):
  File "<stdin>", line 1, in <module>
  File "method_calls_excepting.py", line 9, in call_exceptor
    no_return()
  File "method_calls_excepting.py", line 3, in no_return
    raise Exception("This is always raised")
Exception: This is always raised
```

We'll soon see that when the interpreter is not actually taking a shortcut and exiting immediately, we can react to and deal with the exception inside either method. Indeed, exceptions can be handled at any level after they are initially raised.

Look at the exception's output (called a traceback) from bottom to top, and notice how both methods are listed. Inside no_return, the exception is initially raised. Then, just above that, we see that inside `call_exceptor`, that pesky no_return function was called and the exception bubbled up to the calling method. From there, it went up one more level to the main interpreter, which, not knowing what else to do with it, gave up and printed a traceback.

Handling exceptions

Now let's look at the tail side of the exception coin. If we encounter an exception situation, how should our code react to or recover from it? We handle exceptions by wrapping any code that might throw one (whether it is exception code itself, or a call to any function or method that may have an exception raised inside it) inside a try...except clause. The most basic syntax looks like this:

```
try:
    no_return()
except:
    print("I caught an exception")
print("executed after the exception")
```

If we run this simple script using our existing `no_return` function, which as we know very well, always throws an exception, we get this output:

```
I am about to raise an exception
I caught an exception
executed after the exception
```

The `no_return` function happily informs us that it is about to raise an exception, but we fooled it and caught the exception. Once caught, we were able to clean up after ourselves (in this case, by outputting that we were handling the situation), and continue on our way, with no interference from that offensive function. The remainder of the code in the `no_return` function still went unexecuted, but the code that called the function was able to recover and continue.

Note the indentation around `try` and `except`. The `try` clause wraps any code that might throw an exception. The `except` clause is then back on the same indentation level as the `try` line. Any code to handle the exception is indented after the `except` clause. Then normal code resumes at the original indentation level.

The problem with the preceding code is that it will catch any type of exception. What if we were writing some code that could raise both a `TypeError` and a `ZeroDivisionError`? We might want to catch the `ZeroDivisionError`, but let the `TypeError` propagate to the console. Can you guess the syntax?

Here's a rather silly function that does just that:

```python
def funny_division(divider):
    try:
        return 100 / divider
    except ZeroDivisionError:
        return "Zero is not a good idea!"

print(funny_division(0))
print(funny_division(50.0))
print(funny_division("hello"))
```

The function is tested with `print` statements that show it behaving as expected:

```
Zero is not a good idea!
2.0
Traceback (most recent call last):
  File "catch_specific_exception.py", line 9, in <module>
    print(funny_division("hello"))
  File "catch_specific_exception.py", line 3, in funny_division
    return 100 / anumber
TypeError: unsupported operand type(s) for /: 'int' and 'str'.
```

The first line of output shows that if we enter 0, we get properly mocked. If we call with a valid number (note that it's not an integer, but it's still a valid divisor), it operates correctly. Yet if we enter a string (you were wondering how to get a `TypeError`, weren't you?), it fails with an exception. If we had used an empty `except` clause that didn't specify a `ZeroDivisionError`, it would have accused us of dividing by zero when we sent it a string, which is not a proper behavior at all.

We can even catch two or more different exceptions and handle them with the same code. Here's an example that raises three different types of exception. It handles `TypeError` and `ZeroDivisionError` with the same exception handler, but it may also raise a `ValueError` if you supply the number 13:

```python
def funny_division2(anumber):
    try:
        if anumber == 13:
            raise ValueError("13 is an unlucky number")
        return 100 / anumber
    except (ZeroDivisionError, TypeError):
        return "Enter a number other than zero"

for val in (0, "hello", 50.0, 13):

    print("Testing {}:".format(val), end=" ")
    print(funny_division2(val))
```

The `for` loop at the bottom loops over several test inputs and prints the results. If you're wondering about that `end` argument in the `print` statement, it just turns the default trailing newline into a space so that it's joined with the output from the next line. Here's a run of the program:

```
Testing 0: Enter a number other than zero
Testing hello: Enter a number other than zero
Testing 50.0: 2.0
Testing 13: Traceback (most recent call last):
  File "catch_multiple_exceptions.py", line 11, in <module>
    print(funny_division2(val))
  File "catch_multiple_exceptions.py", line 4, in funny_division2
    raise ValueError("13 is an unlucky number")
ValueError: 13 is an unlucky number
```

The number 0 and the string are both caught by the except clause, and a suitable error message is printed. The exception from the number 13 is not caught because it is a ValueError, which was not included in the types of exceptions being handled. This is all well and good, but what if we want to catch different exceptions and do different things with them? Or maybe we want to do something with an exception and then allow it to continue to bubble up to the parent function, as if it had never been caught? We don't need any new syntax to deal with these cases. It's possible to stack except clauses, and only the first match will be executed. For the second question, the raise keyword, with no arguments, will reraise the last exception if we're already inside an exception handler. Observe in the following code:

```
def funny_division3(anumber):
    try:
        if anumber == 13:
            raise ValueError("13 is an unlucky number")
        return 100 / anumber
    except ZeroDivisionError:
        return "Enter a number other than zero"
    except TypeError:
        return "Enter a numerical value"
    except ValueError:
        print("No, No, not 13!")
        raise
```

The last line reraises the ValueError, so after outputting No, No, not 13!, it will raise the exception again; we'll still get the original stack trace on the console.

If we stack exception clauses like we did in the preceding example, only the first matching clause will be run, even if more than one of them fits. How can more than one clause match? Remember that exceptions are objects, and can therefore be subclassed. As we'll see in the next section, most exceptions extend the Exception class (which is itself derived from BaseException). If we catch Exception before we catch TypeError, then only the Exception handler will be executed, because TypeError is an Exception by inheritance.

This can come in handy in cases where we want to handle some exceptions specifically, and then handle all remaining exceptions as a more general case. We can simply catch Exception after catching all the specific exceptions and handle the general case there.

Sometimes, when we catch an exception, we need a reference to the `Exception` object itself. This most often happens when we define our own exceptions with custom arguments, but can also be relevant with standard exceptions. Most exception classes accept a set of arguments in their constructor, and we might want to access those attributes in the exception handler. If we define our own exception class, we can even call custom methods on it when we catch it. The syntax for capturing an exception as a variable uses the `as` keyword:

```
try:
    raise ValueError("This is an argument")
except ValueError as e:
    print("The exception arguments were", e.args)
```

If we run this simple snippet, it prints out the string argument that we passed into `ValueError` upon initialization.

We've seen several variations on the syntax for handling exceptions, but we still don't know how to execute code regardless of whether or not an exception has occurred. We also can't specify code that should be executed only if an exception does not occur. Two more keywords, `finally` and `else`, can provide the missing pieces. Neither one takes any extra arguments. The following example randomly picks an exception to throw and raises it. Then some not-so-complicated exception handling code is run that illustrates the newly introduced syntax:

```
import random
some_exceptions = [ValueError, TypeError, IndexError, None]

try:
    choice = random.choice(some_exceptions)
    print("raising {}".format(choice))
    if choice:
        raise choice("An error")
except ValueError:
    print("Caught a ValueError")
except TypeError:
    print("Caught a TypeError")
except Exception as e:
    print("Caught some other error: %s" %
        ( e.__class__.__name__))
else:
    print("This code called if there is no exception")
finally:
    print("This cleanup code is always called")
```

If we run this example—which illustrates almost every conceivable exception handling scenario—a few times, we'll get different output each time, depending on which exception `random` chooses. Here are some example runs:

```
$ python finally_and_else.py
raising None
This code called if there is no exception
This cleanup code is always called


$ python finally_and_else.py
raising <class 'TypeError'>
Caught a TypeError
This cleanup code is always called


$ python finally_and_else.py
raising <class 'IndexError'>
Caught some other error: IndexError
This cleanup code is always called


$ python finally_and_else.py
raising <class 'ValueError'>
Caught a ValueError
This cleanup code is always called
```

Note how the `print` statement in the `finally` clause is executed no matter what happens. This is extremely useful when we need to perform certain tasks after our code has finished running (even if an exception has occurred). Some common examples include:

- Cleaning up an open database connection
- Closing an open file
- Sending a closing handshake over the network

The `finally` clause is also very important when we execute a `return` statement from inside a `try` clause. The `finally` handle will still be executed before the value is returned.

Also, pay attention to the output when no exception is raised: both the `else` and the `finally` clauses are executed. The `else` clause may seem redundant, as the code that should be executed only when no exception is raised could just be placed after the entire `try...except` block. The difference is that the `else` block will still be executed if an exception is caught and handled. We'll see more on this when we discuss using exceptions as flow control later.

Any of the `except`, `else`, and `finally` clauses can be omitted after a `try` block (although `else` by itself is invalid). If you include more than one, the `except` clauses must come first, then the `else` clause, with the `finally` clause at the end. The order of the `except` clauses normally goes from most specific to most generic.

The exception hierarchy

We've already seen several of the most common built-in exceptions, and you'll probably encounter the rest over the course of your regular Python development. As we noticed earlier, most exceptions are subclasses of the `Exception` class. But this is not true of all exceptions. `Exception` itself actually inherits from a class called `BaseException`. In fact, all exceptions must extend the `BaseException` class or one of its subclasses.

There are two key exceptions, `SystemExit` and `KeyboardInterrupt`, that derive directly from `BaseException` instead of `Exception`. The `SystemExit` exception is raised whenever the program exits naturally, typically because we called the `sys.exit` function somewhere in our code (for example, when the user selected an exit menu item, clicked the "close" button on a window, or entered a command to shut down a server). The exception is designed to allow us to clean up code before the program ultimately exits, so we generally don't need to handle it explicitly (because cleanup code happens inside a `finally` clause).

If we do handle it, we would normally reraise the exception, since catching it would stop the program from exiting. There are, of course, situations where we might want to stop the program exiting, for example, if there are unsaved changes and we want to prompt the user if they really want to exit. Usually, if we handle `SystemExit` at all, it's because we want to do something special with it, or are anticipating it directly. We especially don't want it to be accidentally caught in generic clauses that catch all normal exceptions. This is why it derives directly from `BaseException`.

The `KeyboardInterrupt` exception is common in command-line programs. It is thrown when the user explicitly interrupts program execution with an OS-dependent key combination (normally, *Ctrl* + *C*). This is a standard way for the user to deliberately interrupt a running program, and like `SystemExit`, it should almost always respond by terminating the program. Also, like `SystemExit`, it should handle any cleanup tasks inside `finally` blocks.

Here is a class diagram that fully illustrates the exception hierarchy:

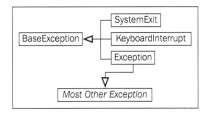

When we use the `except:` clause without specifying any type of exception, it will catch all subclasses of `BaseException`; which is to say, it will catch all exceptions, including the two special ones. Since we almost always want these to get special treatment, it is unwise to use the `except:` statement without arguments. If you want to catch all exceptions other than `SystemExit` and `KeyboardInterrupt`, explicitly catch `Exception`.

Furthermore, if you do want to catch all exceptions, I suggest using the syntax `except BaseException:` instead of a raw `except:`. This helps explicitly tell future readers of your code that you are intentionally handling the special case exceptions.

Defining our own exceptions

Often, when we want to raise an exception, we find that none of the built-in exceptions are suitable. Luckily, it's trivial to define new exceptions of our own. The name of the class is usually designed to communicate what went wrong, and we can provide arbitrary arguments in the initializer to include additional information.

All we have to do is inherit from the `Exception` class. We don't even have to add any content to the class! We can, of course, extend `BaseException` directly, but then it will not be caught by generic `except Exception` clauses.

Here's a simple exception we might use in a banking application:

```
class InvalidWithdrawal(Exception):
    pass

raise InvalidWithdrawal("You don't have $50 in your account")
```

The last line illustrates how to raise the newly defined exception. We are able to pass an arbitrary number of arguments into the exception. Often a string message is used, but any object that might be useful in a later exception handler can be stored. The `Exception.__init__` method is designed to accept any arguments and store them as a tuple in an attribute named `args`. This makes exceptions easier to define without needing to override `__init__`.

Of course, if we do want to customize the initializer, we are free to do so. Here's an exception whose initializer accepts the current balance and the amount the user wanted to withdraw. In addition, it adds a method to calculate how overdrawn the request was:

```
class InvalidWithdrawal(Exception):
    def __init__(self, balance, amount):
        super().__init__("account doesn't have ${}".format(
            amount))
        self.amount = amount
        self.balance = balance

    def overage(self):
        return self.amount - self.balance


raise InvalidWithdrawal(25, 50)
```

The `raise` statement at the end illustrates how to construct this exception. As you can see, we can do anything with an exception that we would do with other objects. We could catch an exception and pass it around as a working object, although it is more common to include a reference to the working object as an attribute on an exception and pass that around instead.

Here's how we would handle an `InvalidWithdrawal` exception if one was raised:

```
try:
    raise InvalidWithdrawal(25, 50)
except InvalidWithdrawal as e:
    print("I'm sorry, but your withdrawal is "
            "more than your balance by "
            "${}".format(e.overage()))
```

Here we see a valid use of the `as` keyword. By convention, most Python coders name the exception variable `e`, although, as usual, you are free to call it `ex`, `exception`, or `aunt_sally` if you prefer.

There are many reasons for defining our own exceptions. It is often useful to add information to the exception or log it in some way. But the utility of custom exceptions truly comes to light when creating a framework, library, or API that is intended for access by other programmers. In that case, be careful to ensure your code is raising exceptions that make sense to the client programmer. They should be easy to handle and clearly describe what went on. The client programmer should easily see how to fix the error (if it reflects a bug in their code) or handle the exception (if it's a situation they need to be made aware of).

Exceptions aren't exceptional. Novice programmers tend to think of exceptions as only useful for exceptional circumstances. However, the definition of exceptional circumstances can be vague and subject to interpretation. Consider the following two functions:

```
def divide_with_exception(number, divisor):
    try:
        print("{} / {} = {}".format(
            number, divisor, number / divisor * 1.0))
    except ZeroDivisionError:
        print("You can't divide by zero")

def divide_with_if(number, divisor):
    if divisor == 0:
        print("You can't divide by zero")
    else:
        print("{} / {} = {}".format(
            number, divisor, number / divisor * 1.0))
```

These two functions behave identically. If `divisor` is zero, an error message is printed; otherwise, a message printing the result of division is displayed. We could avoid a `ZeroDivisionError` ever being thrown by testing for it with an `if` statement. Similarly, we can avoid an `IndexError` by explicitly checking whether or not the parameter is within the confines of the list, and a `KeyError` by checking if the key is in a dictionary.

But we shouldn't do this. For one thing, we might write an `if` statement that checks whether or not the index is lower than the parameters of the list, but forget to check negative values.

 Remember, Python lists support negative indexing; `-1` refers to the last element in the list.

Eventually, we would discover this and have to find all the places where we were checking code. But if we had simply caught the `IndexError` and handled it, our code would just work.

Python programmers tend to follow a model of *Ask forgiveness rather than permission*, which is to say, they execute code and then deal with anything that goes wrong. The alternative, to *look before you leap*, is generally frowned upon. There are a few reasons for this, but the main one is that it shouldn't be necessary to burn CPU cycles looking for an unusual situation that is not going to arise in the normal path through the code. Therefore, it is wise to use exceptions for exceptional circumstances, even if those circumstances are only a little bit exceptional. Taking this argument further, we can actually see that the exception syntax is also effective for flow control. Like an `if` statement, exceptions can be used for decision making, branching, and message passing.

Imagine an inventory application for a company that sells widgets and gadgets. When a customer makes a purchase, the item can either be available, in which case the item is removed from inventory and the number of items left is returned, or it might be out of stock. Now, being out of stock is a perfectly normal thing to happen in an inventory application. It is certainly not an exceptional circumstance. But what do we return if it's out of stock? A string saying out of stock? A negative number? In both cases, the calling method would have to check whether the return value is a positive integer or something else, to determine if it is out of stock. That seems a bit messy. Instead, we can raise `OutOfStockException` and use the `try` statement to direct program flow control. Make sense? In addition, we want to make sure we don't sell the same item to two different customers, or sell an item that isn't in stock yet. One way to facilitate this is to lock each type of item to ensure only one person can update it at a time. The user must lock the item, manipulate the item (purchase, add stock, count items left…), and then unlock the item. Here's an incomplete `Inventory` example with docstrings that describes what some of the methods should do:

```python
class Inventory:
    def lock(self, item_type):
        '''Select the type of item that is going to
        be manipulated. This method will lock the
        item so nobody else can manipulate the
        inventory until it's returned. This prevents
        selling the same item to two different
        customers.'''
        pass

    def unlock(self, item_type):
        '''Release the given type so that other
        customers can access it.'''
        pass

    def purchase(self, item_type):
```

```
'''If the item is not locked, raise an
exception. If the item_type  does not exist,
raise an exception. If the item is currently
out of stock, raise an exception. If the item
is available, subtract one item and return
the number of items left.'''
pass
```

We could hand this object prototype to a developer and have them implement the methods to do exactly as they say while we work on the code that needs to make a purchase. We'll use Python's robust exception handling to consider different branches, depending on how the purchase was made:

```
item_type = 'widget'
inv = Inventory()
inv.lock(item_type)
try:
    num_left = inv.purchase(item_type)
except InvalidItemType:
    print("Sorry, we don't sell {}".format(item_type))
except OutOfStock:
    print("Sorry, that item is out of stock.")
else:
    print("Purchase complete. There are "
            "{} {}s left".format(num_left, item_type))
finally:
    inv.unlock(item_type)
```

Pay attention to how all the possible exception handling clauses are used to ensure the correct actions happen at the correct time. Even though OutOfStock is not a terribly exceptional circumstance, we are able to use an exception to handle it suitably. This same code could be written with an if...elif...else structure, but it wouldn't be as easy to read or maintain.

We can also use exceptions to pass messages between different methods. For example, if we wanted to inform the customer as to what date the item is expected to be in stock again, we could ensure our OutOfStock object requires a back_in_stock parameter when it is constructed. Then, when we handle the exception, we can check that value and provide additional information to the customer. The information attached to the object can be easily passed between two different parts of the program. The exception could even provide a method that instructs the inventory object to reorder or backorder an item.

Using exceptions for flow control can make for some handy program designs. The important thing to take from this discussion is that exceptions are not a bad thing that we should try to avoid. Having an exception occur does not mean that you should have prevented this exceptional circumstance from happening. Rather, it is just a powerful way to communicate information between two sections of code that may not be directly calling each other.

Case study

We've been looking at the use and handling of exceptions at a fairly low level of detail—syntax and definitions. This case study will help tie it all in with our previous chapters so we can see how exceptions are used in the larger context of objects, inheritance, and modules.

Today, we'll be designing a simple central authentication and authorization system. The entire system will be placed in one module, and other code will be able to query that module object for authentication and authorization purposes. We should admit, from the start, that we aren't security experts, and that the system we are designing may be full of security holes. Our purpose is to study exceptions, not to secure a system. It will be sufficient, however, for a basic login and permission system that other code can interact with. Later, if that other code needs to be made more secure, we can have a security or cryptography expert review or rewrite our module, preferably without changing the API.

Authentication is the process of ensuring a user is really the person they say they are. We'll follow the lead of common web systems today, which use a username and private password combination. Other methods of authentication include voice recognition, fingerprint or retinal scanners, and identification cards.

Authorization, on the other hand, is all about determining whether a given (authenticated) user is permitted to perform a specific action. We'll create a basic permission list system that stores a list of the specific people allowed to perform each action.

In addition, we'll add some administrative features to allow new users to be added to the system. For brevity, we'll leave out editing of passwords or changing of permissions once they've been added, but these (highly necessary) features can certainly be added in the future.

There's a simple analysis; now let's proceed with design. We're obviously going to need a User class that stores the username and an encrypted password. This class will also allow a user to log in by checking whether a supplied password is valid. We probably won't need a Permission class, as those can just be strings mapped to a list of users using a dictionary. We should have a central Authenticator class that handles user management and logging in or out. The last piece of the puzzle is an Authorizor class that deals with permissions and checking whether a user can perform an activity. We'll provide a single instance of each of these classes in the auth module so that other modules can use this central mechanism for all their authentication and authorization needs. Of course, if they want to instantiate private instances of these classes, for non-central authorization activities, they are free to do so.

We'll also be defining several exceptions as we go along. We'll start with a special AuthException base class that accepts a username and optional user object as parameters; most of our self-defined exceptions will inherit from this one.

Let's build the User class first; it seems simple enough. A new user can be initialized with a username and password. The password will be stored encrypted to reduce the chances of its being stolen. We'll also need a check_password method to test whether a supplied password is the correct one. Here is the class in full:

```python
import hashlib

class User:
    def __init__(self, username, password):
        '''Create a new user object. The password
        will be encrypted before storing.'''
        self.username = username
        self.password = self._encrypt_pw(password)
        self.is_logged_in = False

    def _encrypt_pw(self, password):
        '''Encrypt the password with the username and return
        the sha digest.'''
        hash_string = (self.username + password)
        hash_string = hash_string.encode("utf8")
        return hashlib.sha256(hash_string).hexdigest()

    def check_password(self, password):
        '''Return True if the password is valid for this
        user, false otherwise.'''
        encrypted = self._encrypt_pw(password)
        return encrypted == self.password
```

Since the code for encrypting a password is required in both __init__ and check_ password, we pull it out to its own method. This way, it only needs to be changed in one place if someone realizes it is insecure and needs improvement. This class could easily be extended to include mandatory or optional personal details, such as names, contact information, and birth dates.

Before we write code to add users (which will happen in the as-yet undefined Authenticator class), we should examine some use cases. If all goes well, we can add a user with a username and password; the User object is created and inserted into a dictionary. But in what ways can all not go well? Well, clearly we don't want to add a user with a username that already exists in the dictionary. If we did so, we'd overwrite an existing user's data and the new user might have access to that user's privileges. So, we'll need a UsernameAlreadyExists exception. Also, for security's sake, we should probably raise an exception if the password is too short. Both of these exceptions will extend AuthException, which we mentioned earlier. So, before writing the Authenticator class, let's define these three exception classes:

```
class AuthException(Exception):
    def __init__(self, username, user=None):
        super().__init__(username, user)
        self.username = username
        self.user = user


class UsernameAlreadyExists(AuthException):
    pass


class PasswordTooShort(AuthException):
    pass
```

The AuthException requires a username and has an optional user parameter. This second parameter should be an instance of the User class associated with that username. The two specific exceptions we're defining simply need to inform the calling class of an exceptional circumstance, so we don't need to add any extra methods to them.

Now let's start on the Authenticator class. It can simply be a mapping of usernames to user objects, so we'll start with a dictionary in the initialization function. The method for adding a user needs to check the two conditions (password length and previously existing users) before creating a new User instance and adding it to the dictionary:

```
class Authenticator:
    def __init__(self):
        '''Construct an authenticator to manage
```

```
            users logging in and out.'''
            self.users = {}

    def add_user(self, username, password):
        if username in self.users:
            raise UsernameAlreadyExists(username)
        if len(password) < 6:
            raise PasswordTooShort(username)
        self.users[username] = User(username, password)
```

We could, of course, extend the password validation to raise exceptions for passwords that are too easy to crack in other ways, if we desired. Now let's prepare the `login` method. If we weren't thinking about exceptions just now, we might just want the method to return `True` or `False`, depending on whether the login was successful or not. But we are thinking about exceptions, and this could be a good place to use them for a not-so-exceptional circumstance. We could raise different exceptions, for example, if the username does not exist or the password does not match. This will allow anyone trying to log a user in to elegantly handle the situation using a `try/except/else` clause. So, first we add these new exceptions:

```
class InvalidUsername(AuthException):
    pass


class InvalidPassword(AuthException):
    pass
```

Then we can define a simple `login` method to our `Authenticator` class that raises these exceptions if necessary. If not, it flags the `user` as logged in and returns:

```
    def login(self, username, password):
        try:
            user = self.users[username]
        except KeyError:
            raise InvalidUsername(username)

        if not user.check_password(password):
            raise InvalidPassword(username, user)

        user.is_logged_in = True
        return True
```

Notice how the `KeyError` is handled. This could have been handled using `if username not in self.users:` instead, but we chose to handle the exception directly. We end up eating up this first exception and raising a brand new one of our own that better suits the user-facing API.

We can also add a method to check whether a particular username is logged in. Deciding whether to use an exception here is trickier. Should we raise an exception if the username does not exist? Should we raise an exception if the user is not logged in?

To answer these questions, we need to think about how the method would be accessed. Most often, this method will be used to answer the yes/no question, "Should I allow them access to *<something>*?" The answer will either be, "Yes, the username is valid and they are logged in", or "No, the username is not valid or they are not logged in". Therefore, a Boolean return value is sufficient. There is no need to use exceptions here, just for the sake of using an exception.

```
def is_logged_in(self, username):
    if username in self.users:
        return self.users[username].is_logged_in
    return False
```

Finally, we can add a default authenticator instance to our module so that the client code can access it easily using `auth.authenticator`:

```
authenticator = Authenticator()
```

This line goes at the module level, outside any class definition, so the authenticator variable can be accessed as `auth.authenticator`. Now we can start on the `Authorizor` class, which maps permissions to users. The `Authorizor` class should not permit user access to a permission if they are not logged in, so they'll need a reference to a specific authenticator. We'll also need to set up the permission dictionary upon initialization:

```
class Authorizor:
    def __init__(self, authenticator):
        self.authenticator = authenticator
        self.permissions = {}
```

Now we can write methods to add new permissions and to set up which users are associated with each permission:

```
def add_permission(self, perm_name):
    '''Create a new permission that users
    can be added to'''
    try:
        perm_set = self.permissions[perm_name]
    except KeyError:
        self.permissions[perm_name] = set()
    else:
```

```
                    raise PermissionError("Permission Exists")

        def permit_user(self, perm_name, username):
            '''Grant the given permission to the user'''
            try:
                perm_set = self.permissions[perm_name]
            except KeyError:
                raise PermissionError("Permission does not exist")
            else:
                if username not in self.authenticator.users:
                    raise InvalidUsername(username)
                perm_set.add(username)
```

The first method allows us to create a new permission, unless it already exists, in which case an exception is raised. The second allows us to add a username to a permission, unless either the permission or the username doesn't yet exist.

We use `set` instead of `list` for usernames, so that even if you grant a user permission more than once, the nature of sets means the user is only in the set once. We'll discuss sets further in a later chapter.

A `PermissionError` is raised in both methods. This new error doesn't require a username, so we'll make it extend `Exception` directly, instead of our custom `AuthException`:

```
    class PermissionError(Exception):
        pass
```

Finally, we can add a method to check whether a user has a specific `permission` or not. In order for them to be granted access, they have to be both logged into the authenticator and in the set of people who have been granted access to that privilege. If either of these conditions is unsatisfied, an exception is raised:

```
        def check_permission(self, perm_name, username):
            if not self.authenticator.is_logged_in(username):
                raise NotLoggedInError(username)
            try:
                perm_set = self.permissions[perm_name]
            except KeyError:
                raise PermissionError("Permission does not exist")
            else:
                if username not in perm_set:
                    raise NotPermittedError(username)
                else:
                    return True
```

There are two new exceptions in here; they both take usernames, so we'll define them as subclasses of `AuthException`:

```
class NotLoggedInError(AuthException):
    pass

class NotPermittedError(AuthException):
    pass
```

Finally, we can add a default `authorizor` to go with our default authenticator:

```
authorizor = Authorizor(authenticator)
```

That completes a basic authentication/authorization system. We can test the system at the Python prompt, checking to see whether a user, `joe`, is permitted to do tasks in the paint department:

```
>>> import auth
>>> auth.authenticator.add_user("joe", "joepassword")
>>> auth.authorizor.add_permission("paint")
>>> auth.authorizor.check_permission("paint", "joe")
Traceback (most recent call last):
  File "<stdin>", line 1, in <module>
  File "auth.py", line 109, in check_permission
    raise NotLoggedInError(username)
auth.NotLoggedInError: joe
>>> auth.authenticator.is_logged_in("joe")
False
>>> auth.authenticator.login("joe", "joepassword")
True
>>> auth.authorizor.check_permission("paint", "joe")
Traceback (most recent call last):
  File "<stdin>", line 1, in <module>
  File "auth.py", line 116, in check_permission
    raise NotPermittedError(username)
auth.NotPermittedError: joe
>>> auth.authorizor.check_permission("mix", "joe")
Traceback (most recent call last):
  File "auth.py", line 111, in check_permission
    perm_set = self.permissions[perm_name]
```

```
KeyError: 'mix'


During handling of the above exception, another exception occurred:
Traceback (most recent call last):
  File "<stdin>", line 1, in <module>
  File "auth.py", line 113, in check_permission
    raise PermissionError("Permission does not exist")
auth.PermissionError: Permission does not exist
>>> auth.authorizor.permit_user("mix", "joe")
Traceback (most recent call last):
  File "auth.py", line 99, in permit_user
    perm_set = self.permissions[perm_name]
KeyError: 'mix'


During handling of the above exception, another exception occurred:


Traceback (most recent call last):
  File "<stdin>", line 1, in <module>
  File "auth.py", line 101, in permit_user
    raise PermissionError("Permission does not exist")
auth.PermissionError: Permission does not exist
>>> auth.authorizor.permit_user("paint", "joe")
>>> auth.authorizor.check_permission("paint", "joe")
True
```

While verbose, the preceding output shows all of our code and most of our exceptions in action, but to really understand the API we've defined, we should write some exception handling code that actually uses it. Here's a basic menu interface that allows certain users to change or test a program:

```
import auth

# Set up a test user and permission
auth.authenticator.add_user("joe", "joepassword")
auth.authorizor.add_permission("test program")
auth.authorizor.add_permission("change program")
auth.authorizor.permit_user("test program", "joe")

class Editor:
```

```
def __init__(self):
    self.username = None
    self.menu_map = {
            "login": self.login,
            "test": self.test,
            "change": self.change,
            "quit": self.quit
        }

def login(self):
    logged_in = False
    while not logged_in:
        username = input("username: ")
        password = input("password: ")
        try:
            logged_in = auth.authenticator.login(
                    username, password)
        except auth.InvalidUsername:
            print("Sorry, that username does not exist")
        except auth.InvalidPassword:
            print("Sorry, incorrect password")
        else:
            self.username = username
def is_permitted(self, permission):
    try:
        auth.authorizor.check_permission(
            permission, self.username)
    except auth.NotLoggedInError as e:
        print("{} is not logged in".format(e.username))
        return False
    except auth.NotPermittedError as e:
        print("{} cannot {}".format(
            e.username, permission))
        return False
    else:
        return True

def test(self):
    if self.is_permitted("test program"):
        print("Testing program now...")

def change(self):
    if self.is_permitted("change program"):
        print("Changing program now...")

def quit(self):
```

```
            raise SystemExit()

    def menu(self):
        try:
            answer = ""
            while True:
                print("""
Please enter a command:
\tlogin\tLogin
\ttest\tTest the program
\tchange\tChange the program
\tquit\tQuit
""")
                answer = input("enter a command: ").lower()
                try:
                    func = self.menu_map[answer]
                except KeyError:
                    print("{} is not a valid option".format(
                        answer))
                else:
                    func()
        finally:
            print("Thank you for testing the auth module")

Editor().menu()
```

This rather long example is conceptually very simple. The is_permitted method is probably the most interesting; this is a mostly internal method that is called by both test and change to ensure the user is permitted access before continuing. Of course, those two methods are stubs, but we aren't writing an editor here; we're illustrating the use of exceptions and exception handlers by testing an authentication and authorization framework!

Exercises

If you've never dealt with exceptions before, the first thing you need to do is look at any old Python code you've written and notice if there are places you should have been handling exceptions. How would you handle them? Do you need to handle them at all? Sometimes, letting the exception propagate to the console is the best way to communicate to the user, especially if the user is also the script's coder. Sometimes, you can recover from the error and allow the program to continue. Sometimes, you can only reformat the error into something the user can understand and display it to them.

Some common places to look are file I/O (is it possible your code will try to read a file that doesn't exist?), mathematical expressions (is it possible that a value you are dividing by is zero?), list indices (is the list empty?), and dictionaries (does the key exist?). Ask yourself if you should ignore the problem, handle it by checking values first, or handle it with an exception. Pay special attention to areas where you might have used `finally` and `else` to ensure the correct code is executed under all conditions.

Now write some new code. Think of a program that requires authentication and authorization, and try writing some code that uses the `auth` module we built in the case study. Feel free to modify the module if it's not flexible enough. Try to handle all the exceptions in a sensible way. If you're having trouble coming up with something that requires authentication, try adding authorization to the notepad example from *Chapter 2, Objects in Python*, or add authorization to the `auth` module itself—it's not a terribly useful module if just anybody can start adding permissions! Maybe require an administrator username and password before allowing privileges to be added or changed.

Finally, try to think of places in your code where you can raise exceptions. It can be in code you've written or are working on; or you can write a new project as an exercise. You'll probably have the best luck for designing a small framework or API that is meant to be used by other people; exceptions are a terrific communication tool between your code and someone else's. Remember to design and document any self-raised exceptions as part of the API, or they won't know whether or how to handle them!

Summary

In this chapter, we went into the gritty details of raising, handling, defining, and manipulating exceptions. Exceptions are a powerful way to communicate unusual circumstances or error conditions without requiring a calling function to explicitly check return values. There are many built-in exceptions and raising them is trivially easy. There are several different syntaxes for handling different exception events.

In the next chapter, everything we've studied so far will come together as we discuss how object-oriented programming principles and structures should best be applied in Python applications.

5

When to Use Object-oriented Programming

In previous chapters, we've covered many of the defining features of object-oriented programming. We now know the principles and paradigms of object-oriented design, and we've covered the syntax of object-oriented programming in Python.

Yet, we don't know exactly how and when to utilize these principles and syntax in practice. In this chapter, we'll discuss some useful applications of the knowledge we've gained, picking up some new topics along the way:

- How to recognize objects
- Data and behaviors, once again
- Wrapping data in behavior using properties
- Restricting data using behavior
- The Don't Repeat Yourself principle
- Recognizing repeated code

Treat objects as objects

This may seem obvious; you should generally give separate objects in your problem domain a special class in your code. We've seen examples of this in the case studies in previous chapters; first, we identify objects in the problem and then model their data and behaviors.

Identifying objects is a very important task in object-oriented analysis and programming. But it isn't always as easy as counting the nouns in a short paragraph, as we've been doing. Remember, objects are things that have both data and behavior. If we are working only with data, we are often better off storing it in a list, set, dictionary, or some other Python data structure (which we'll be covering thoroughly in *Chapter 6, Python Data Structures*). On the other hand, if we are working only with behavior, but no stored data, a simple function is more suitable.

An object, however, has both data and behavior. Proficient Python programmers use built-in data structures unless (or until) there is an obvious need to define a class. There is no reason to add an extra level of abstraction if it doesn't help organize our code. On the other hand, the "obvious" need is not always self-evident.

We can often start our Python programs by storing data in a few variables. As the program expands, we will later find that we are passing the same set of related variables to a set of functions. This is the time to think about grouping both variables and functions into a class. If we are designing a program to model polygons in two-dimensional space, we might start with each polygon being represented as a list of points. The points would be modeled as two-tuples (x, y) describing where that point is located. This is all data, stored in a set of nested data structures (specifically, a list of tuples):

```
square = [(1,1), (1,2), (2,2), (2,1)]
```

Now, if we want to calculate the distance around the perimeter of the polygon, we simply need to sum the distances between the two points. To do this, we also need a function to calculate the distance between two points. Here are two such functions:

```
import math

def distance(p1, p2):
    return math.sqrt((p1[0]-p2[0])**2 + (p1[1]-p2[1])**2)

def perimeter(polygon):
    perimeter = 0
    points = polygon + [polygon[0]]
    for i in range(len(polygon)):
        perimeter += distance(points[i], points[i+1])
    return perimeter
```

Now, as object-oriented programmers, we clearly recognize that a `polygon` class could encapsulate the list of points (data) and the `perimeter` function (behavior). Further, a `point` class, such as we defined in *Chapter 2, Objects in Python*, might encapsulate the x and y coordinates and the `distance` method. The question is: is it valuable to do this?

For the previous code, maybe yes, maybe no. With our recent experience in object-oriented principles, we can write an object-oriented version in record time. Let's compare them

```python
import math

class Point:
    def __init__(self, x, y):
        self.x = x
        self.y = y

    def distance(self, p2):
        return math.sqrt((self.x-p2.x)**2 + (self.y-p2.y)**2)

class Polygon:
    def __init__(self):
        self.vertices = []

    def add_point(self, point):
        self.vertices.append((point))

    def perimeter(self):
        perimeter = 0
        points = self.vertices + [self.vertices[0]]
        for i in range(len(self.vertices)):
            perimeter += points[i].distance(points[i+1])
        return perimeter
```

As we can see from the highlighted sections, there is twice as much code here as there was in our earlier version, although we could argue that the add_point method is not strictly necessary.

Now, to understand the differences a little better, let's compare the two APIs in use. Here's how to calculate the perimeter of a square using the object-oriented code:

```python
>>> square = Polygon()
>>> square.add_point(Point(1,1))
>>> square.add_point(Point(1,2))
>>> square.add_point(Point(2,2))
>>> square.add_point(Point(2,1))
>>> square.perimeter()
4.0
```

That's fairly succinct and easy to read, you might think, but let's compare it to the function-based code:

```
>>> square = [(1,1), (1,2), (2,2), (2,1)]
>>> perimeter(square)
4.0
```

Hmm, maybe the object-oriented API isn't so compact! That said, I'd argue that it was easier to *read* than the functional example: How do we know what the list of tuples is supposed to represent in the second version? How do we remember what kind of object (a list of two-tuples? That's not intuitive!) we're supposed to pass into the `perimeter` function? We would need a lot of documentation to explain how these functions should be used.

In contrast, the object-oriented code is relatively self-documenting, we just have to look at the list of methods and their parameters to know what the object does and how to use it. By the time we wrote all the documentation for the functional version, it would probably be longer than the object-oriented code.

Finally, code length is not a good indicator of code complexity. Some programmers get hung up on complicated "one liners" that do an incredible amount of work in one line of code. This can be a fun exercise, but the result is often unreadable, even to the original author the following day. Minimizing the amount of code can often make a program easier to read, but do not blindly assume this is the case.

Luckily, this trade-off isn't necessary. We can make the object-oriented `Polygon` API as easy to use as the functional implementation. All we have to do is alter our `Polygon` class so that it can be constructed with multiple points. Let's give it an initializer that accepts a list of `Point` objects. In fact, let's allow it to accept tuples too, and we can construct the `Point` objects ourselves, if needed:

```
def __init__(self, points=None):
    points = points if points else []
    self.vertices = []
    for point in points:
        if isinstance(point, tuple):
            point = Point(*point)
        self.vertices.append(point)
```

This initializer goes through the list and ensures that any tuples are converted to points. If the object is not a tuple, we leave it as is, assuming that it is either a `Point` object already, or an unknown duck-typed object that can act like a `Point` object.

Still, there's no clear winner between the object-oriented and more data-oriented versions of this code. They both do the same thing. If we have new functions that accept a polygon argument, such as `area(polygon)` or `point_in_polygon(polygon, x, y)`, the benefits of the object-oriented code become increasingly obvious. Likewise, if we add other attributes to the polygon, such as `color` or `texture`, it makes more and more sense to encapsulate that data into a single class.

The distinction is a design decision, but in general, the more complicated a set of data is, the more likely it is to have multiple functions specific to that data, and the more useful it is to use a class with attributes and methods instead.

When making this decision, it also pays to consider how the class will be used. If we're only trying to calculate the perimeter of one polygon in the context of a much greater problem, using a function will probably be quickest to code and easier to use "one time only". On the other hand, if our program needs to manipulate numerous polygons in a wide variety of ways (calculate perimeter, area, intersection with other polygons, move or scale them, and so on), we have most certainly identified an object; one that needs to be extremely versatile.

Additionally, pay attention to the interaction between objects. Look for inheritance relationships; inheritance is impossible to model elegantly without classes, so make sure to use them. Look for the other types of relationships we discussed in *Chapter 1, Object-oriented Design*, association and composition. Composition can, technically, be modeled using only data structures; for example, we can have a list of dictionaries holding tuple values, but it is often less complicated to create a few classes of objects, especially if there is behavior associated with the data.

 Don't rush to use an object just because you can use an object, but *never* neglect to create a class when you need to use a class.

Adding behavior to class data with properties

Throughout this book, we've been focusing on the separation of behavior and data. This is very important in object-oriented programming, but we're about to see that, in Python, the distinction can be uncannily blurry. Python is very good at blurring distinctions; it doesn't exactly help us to "think outside the box". Rather, it teaches us to stop thinking about the box.

Before we get into the details, let's discuss some bad object-oriented theory. Many object-oriented languages (Java is the most notorious) teach us to never access attributes directly. They insist that we write attribute access like this:

```
class Color:
    def __init__(self, rgb_value, name):
        self._rgb_value = rgb_value
        self._name = name

    def set_name(self, name):
        self._name = name

    def get_name(self):
        return self._name
```

The variables are prefixed with an underscore to suggest that they are private (other languages would actually force them to be private). Then the get and set methods provide access to each variable. This class would be used in practice as follows:

```
>>> c = Color("#ff0000", "bright red")
>>> c.get_name()
'bright red'
>>> c.set_name("red")
>>> c.get_name()
'red'
```

This is not nearly as readable as the direct access version that Python favors:

```
class Color:
    def __init__(self, rgb_value, name):
        self.rgb_value = rgb_value
        self.name = name

c = Color("#ff0000", "bright red")
print(c.name)
c.name = "red"
```

So why would anyone insist upon the method-based syntax? Their reasoning is that someday we may want to add extra code when a value is set or retrieved. For example, we could decide to cache a value and return the cached value, or we might want to validate that the value is a suitable input.

In code, we could decide to change the `set_name()` method as follows:

```
def set_name(self, name):
    if not name:
        raise Exception("Invalid Name")
    self._name = name
```

Now, in Java and similar languages, if we had written our original code to do direct attribute access, and then later changed it to a method like the preceding one, we'd have a problem: anyone who had written code that accessed the attribute directly would now have to access the method. If they don't change the access style from attribute access to a function call, their code will be broken. The mantra in these languages is that we should never make public members private. This doesn't make much sense in Python since there isn't any real concept of private members!

Python gives us the `property` keyword to make methods look like attributes. We can therefore write our code to use direct member access, and if we unexpectedly need to alter the implementation to do some calculation when getting or setting that attribute's value, we can do so without changing the interface. Let's see how it looks:

```
class Color:
    def __init__(self, rgb_value, name):
        self.rgb_value = rgb_value
        self._name = name

    def _set_name(self, name):
        if not name:
            raise Exception("Invalid Name")
        self._name = name

    def _get_name(self):
        return self._name

    name = property(_get_name, _set_name)
```

If we had started with the earlier non-method-based class, which set the `name` attribute directly, we could later change the code to look like the preceding one. We first change the `name` attribute into a (semi-) private `_name` attribute. Then we add two more (semi-) private methods to get and set that variable, doing our validation when we set it.

Finally, we have the `property` declaration at the bottom. This is the magic. It creates a new attribute on the `Color` class called `name`, which now replaces the previous `name` attribute. It sets this attribute to be a property, which calls the two methods we just created whenever the property is accessed or changed. This new version of the `Color` class can be used exactly the same way as the previous version, yet it now does validation when we set the `name` attribute:

```
>>> c = Color("#0000ff", "bright red")
>>> print(c.name)
bright red
>>> c.name = "red"
>>> print(c.name)
red
>>> c.name = ""
Traceback (most recent call last):
  File "<stdin>", line 1, in <module>
  File "setting_name_property.py", line 8, in _set_name
    raise Exception("Invalid Name")
Exception: Invalid Name
```

So, if we'd previously written code to access the `name` attribute, and then changed it to use our `property` object, the previous code would still work, unless it was sending an empty `property` value, which is the behavior we wanted to forbid in the first place. Success!

Bear in mind that even with the `name` property, the previous code is not 100 percent safe. People can still access the `_name` attribute directly and set it to an empty string if they want to. But if they access a variable we've explicitly marked with an underscore to suggest it is private, they're the ones that have to deal with the consequences, not us.

Properties in detail

Think of the `property` function as returning an object that proxies any requests to set or access the attribute value through the methods we have specified. The `property` keyword is like a constructor for such an object, and that object is set as the public facing member for the given attribute.

This `property` constructor can actually accept two additional arguments, a deletion function and a docstring for the property. The `delete` function is rarely supplied in practice, but it can be useful for logging that a value has been deleted, or possibly to veto deleting if we have reason to do so. The docstring is just a string describing what the property does, no different from the docstrings we discussed in *Chapter 2, Objects in Python*. If we do not supply this parameter, the docstring will instead be copied from the docstring for the first argument: the getter method. Here is a silly example that simply states whenever any of the methods are called:

```python
class Silly:
    def _get_silly(self):
        print("You are getting silly")
        return self._silly
    def _set_silly(self, value):
        print("You are making silly {}".format(value))
        self._silly = value
    def _del_silly(self):
        print("Whoah, you killed silly!")
        del self._silly

    silly = property(_get_silly, _set_silly,
            _del_silly, "This is a silly property")
```

If we actually use this class, it does indeed print out the correct strings when we ask it to:

```python
>>> s = Silly()
>>> s.silly = "funny"
You are making silly funny
>>> s.silly
You are getting silly
'funny'
>>> del s.silly
Whoah, you killed silly!
```

Further, if we look at the help file for the `Silly` class (by issuing `help(silly)` at the interpreter prompt), it shows us the custom docstring for our `silly` attribute:

```
Help on class Silly in module __main__:

class Silly(builtins.object)
```

```
 |  Data descriptors defined here:
 |
 |  __dict__
 |      dictionary for instance variables (if defined)
 |
 |  __weakref__
 |      list of weak references to the object (if defined)
 |
 |  silly
 |      This is a silly property
```

Once again, everything is working as we planned. In practice, properties are normally only defined with the first two parameters: the getter and setter functions. If we want to supply a docstring for a property, we can define it on the getter function; the property proxy will copy it into its own docstring. The deletion function is often left empty because object attributes are rarely deleted. If a coder does try to delete a property that doesn't have a deletion function specified, it will raise an exception. Therefore, if there is a legitimate reason to delete our property, we should supply that function.

Decorators – another way to create properties

If you've never used Python decorators before, you might want to skip this section and come back to it after we've discussed the decorator pattern in *Chapter 10*, *Python Design Patterns I*. However, you don't need to understand what's going on to use the decorator syntax to make property methods more readable.

The property function can be used with the decorator syntax to turn a get function into a property:

```
class Foo:
    @property
    def foo(self):
        return "bar"
```

This applies the `property` function as a decorator, and is equivalent to the previous `foo = property(foo)` syntax. The main difference, from a readability perspective, is that we get to mark the `foo` function as a property at the top of the method, instead of after it is defined, where it can be easily overlooked. It also means we don't have to create private methods with underscore prefixes just to define a property.

Going one step further, we can specify a setter function for the new property as follows:

```
class Foo:
    @property
    def foo(self):
        return self._foo

    @foo.setter
    def foo(self, value):
        self._foo = value
```

This syntax looks pretty odd, although the intent is obvious. First, we decorate the foo method as a getter. Then, we decorate a second method with exactly the same name by applying the setter attribute of the originally decorated foo method! The property function returns an object; this object always comes with its own setter attribute, which can then be applied as a decorator to other functions. Using the same name for the get and set methods is not required, but it does help group the multiple methods that access one property together.

We can also specify a deletion function with @foo.deleter. We cannot specify a docstring using property decorators, so we need to rely on the property copying the docstring from the initial getter method.

Here's our previous Silly class rewritten to use property as a decorator:

```
class Silly:
    @property
    def silly(self):
        "This is a silly property"
        print("You are getting silly")
        return self._silly

    @silly.setter
    def silly(self, value):
        print("You are making silly {}".format(value))
        self._silly = value

    @silly.deleter
    def silly(self):
        print("Whoah, you killed silly!")
        del self._silly
```

This class operates *exactly* the same as our earlier version, including the help text. You can use whichever syntax you feel is more readable and elegant.

Deciding when to use properties

With the property built-in clouding the division between behavior and data, it can be confusing to know which one to choose. The example use case we saw earlier is one of the most common uses of properties; we have some data on a class that we later want to add behavior to. There are also other factors to take into account when deciding to use a property.

Technically, in Python, data, properties, and methods are all attributes on a class. The fact that a method is callable does not distinguish it from other types of attributes; indeed, we'll see in *Chapter 7*, *Python Object-oriented Shortcuts*, that it is possible to create normal objects that can be called like functions. We'll also discover that functions and methods are themselves normal objects.

The fact that methods are just callable attributes, and properties are just customizable attributes can help us make this decision. Methods should typically represent actions; things that can be done to, or performed by, the object. When you call a method, even with only one argument, it should *do* something. Method names are generally verbs.

Once confirming that an attribute is not an action, we need to decide between standard data attributes and properties. In general, always use a standard attribute until you need to control access to that property in some way. In either case, your attribute is usually a noun. The only difference between an attribute and a property is that we can invoke custom actions automatically when a property is retrieved, set, or deleted.

Let's look at a more realistic example. A common need for custom behavior is caching a value that is difficult to calculate or expensive to look up (requiring, for example, a network request or database query). The goal is to store the value locally to avoid repeated calls to the expensive calculation.

We can do this with a custom getter on the property. The first time the value is retrieved, we perform the lookup or calculation. Then we could locally cache the value as a private attribute on our object (or in dedicated caching software), and the next time the value is requested, we return the stored data. Here's how we might cache a web page:

```python
from urllib.request import urlopen

class WebPage:
    def __init__(self, url):
        self.url = url
        self._content = None

    @property
```

```
def content(self):
    if not self._content:
        print("Retrieving New Page...")
        self._content = urlopen(self.url).read()
    return self._content
```

We can test this code to see that the page is only retrieved once:

```
>>> import time
>>> webpage = WebPage("http://ccphillips.net/")
>>> now = time.time()
>>> content1 = webpage.content
Retrieving New Page...
>>> time.time() - now
22.433168888809204
>>> now = time.time()
>>> content2 = webpage.content
>>> time.time() - now
1.9266459941864014
>>> content2 == content1
True
```

I was on an awful satellite connection when I originally tested this code and it took 20 seconds the first time I loaded the content. The second time, I got the result in 2 seconds (which is really just the amount of time it took to type the lines into the interpreter).

Custom getters are also useful for attributes that need to be calculated on the fly, based on other object attributes. For example, we might want to calculate the average for a list of integers:

```
class AverageList(list):
    @property
    def average(self):
        return sum(self) / len(self)
```

This very simple class inherits from `list`, so we get list-like behavior for free. We just add a property to the class, and presto, our list can have an average:

```
>>> a = AverageList([1,2,3,4])
>>> a.average
2.5
```

Of course, we could have made this a method instead, but then we should call it `calculate_average()`, since methods represent actions. But a property called `average` is more suitable, both easier to type, and easier to read.

Custom setters are useful for validation, as we've already seen, but they can also be used to proxy a value to another location. For example, we could add a content setter to the `WebPage` class that automatically logs into our web server and uploads a new page whenever the value is set.

Manager objects

We've been focused on objects and their attributes and methods. Now, we'll take a look at designing higher-level objects: the kinds of objects that manage other objects. The objects that tie everything together.

The difference between these objects and most of the examples we've seen so far is that our examples tend to represent concrete ideas. Management objects are more like office managers; they don't do the actual "visible" work out on the floor, but without them, there would be no communication between departments and nobody would know what they are supposed to do (although, this can be true anyway if the organization is badly managed!). Analogously, the attributes on a management class tend to refer to other objects that do the "visible" work; the behaviors on such a class delegate to those other classes at the right time, and pass messages between them.

As an example, we'll write a program that does a find and replace action for text files stored in a compressed ZIP file. We'll need objects to represent the ZIP file and each individual text file (luckily, we don't have to write these classes, they're available in the Python standard library). The manager object will be responsible for ensuring three steps occur in order:

1. Unzipping the compressed file.
2. Performing the find and replace action.
3. Zipping up the new files.

The class is initialized with the `.zip` filename and search and replace strings. We create a temporary directory to store the unzipped files in, so that the folder stays clean. The Python 3.4 `pathlib` library helps out with file and directory manipulation. We'll learn more about that in *Chapter 8, Strings and Serialization*, but the interface should be pretty clear in the following example:

```
import sys
import shutil
import zipfile
```

```
from pathlib import Path

class ZipReplace:
    def __init__(self, filename, search_string, replace_string):
        self.filename = filename
        self.search_string = search_string
        self.replace_string = replace_string
        self.temp_directory = Path("unzipped-{}".format(
                filename))
```

Then, we create an overall "manager" method for each of the three steps. This method delegates responsibility to other methods. Obviously, we could do all three steps in one method, or indeed, in one script without ever creating an object. There are several advantages to separating the three steps:

- **Readability**: The code for each step is in a self-contained unit that is easy to read and understand. The method names describe what the method does, and less additional documentation is required to understand what is going on.

- **Extensibility**: If a subclass wanted to use compressed TAR files instead of ZIP files, it could override the zip and unzip methods without having to duplicate the find_replace method.

- **Partitioning**: An external class could create an instance of this class and call the find_replace method directly on some folder without having to zip the content.

The delegation method is the first in the following code; the rest of the methods are included for completeness:

```
    def zip_find_replace(self):
        self.unzip_files()
        self.find_replace()
        self.zip_files()

    def unzip_files(self):
        self.temp_directory.mkdir()
        with zipfile.ZipFile(self.filename) as zip:
            zip.extractall(str(self.temp_directory))

    def find_replace(self):
        for filename in self.temp_directory.iterdir():
            with filename.open() as file:
                contents = file.read()
            contents = contents.replace(
                    self.search_string, self.replace_string)
```

```
                    with filename.open("w") as file:
                        file.write(contents)

            def zip_files(self):
                with zipfile.ZipFile(self.filename, 'w') as file:
                    for filename in self.temp_directory.iterdir():
                        file.write(str(filename), filename.name)
                    shutil.rmtree(str(self.temp_directory))

        if __name__ == "__main__":
            ZipReplace(*sys.argv[1:4]).zip_find_replace()
```

For brevity, the code for zipping and unzipping files is sparsely documented. Our current focus is on object-oriented design; if you are interested in the inner details of the `zipfile` module, refer to the documentation in the standard library, either online or by typing `import zipfile ; help(zipfile)` into your interactive interpreter. Note that this example only searches the top-level files in a ZIP file; if there are any folders in the unzipped content, they will not be scanned, nor will any files inside those folders.

The last two lines in the example allow us to run the program from the command line by passing the `zip` filename, search string, and replace string as arguments:

python zipsearch.py hello.zip hello hi

Of course, this object does not have to be created from the command line; it could be imported from another module (to perform batch ZIP file processing) or accessed as part of a GUI interface or even a higher-level management object that knows where to get ZIP files (for example, to retrieve them from an FTP server or back them up to an external disk).

As programs become more and more complex, the objects being modeled become less and less like physical objects. Properties are other abstract objects and methods are actions that change the state of those abstract objects. But at the heart of every object, no matter how complex, is a set of concrete properties and well-defined behaviors.

Removing duplicate code

Often the code in management style classes such as `ZipReplace` is quite generic and can be applied in a variety of ways. It is possible to use either composition or inheritance to help keep this code in one place, thus eliminating duplicate code. Before we look at any examples of this, let's discuss a tiny bit of theory. Specifically, why is duplicate code a bad thing?

There are several reasons, but they all boil down to readability and maintainability. When we're writing a new piece of code that is similar to an earlier piece, the easiest thing to do is copy the old code and change whatever needs to be changed (variable names, logic, comments) to make it work in the new location. Alternatively, if we're writing new code that seems similar, but not identical to code elsewhere in the project, it is often easier to write fresh code with similar behavior, rather than figure out how to extract the overlapping functionality.

But as soon as someone has to read and understand the code and they come across duplicate blocks, they are faced with a dilemma. Code that might have made sense suddenly has to be understood. How is one section different from the other? How are they the same? Under what conditions is one section called? When do we call the other? You might argue that you're the only one reading your code, but if you don't touch that code for eight months it will be as incomprehensible to you as it is to a fresh coder. When we're trying to read two similar pieces of code, we have to understand why they're different, as well as how they're different. This wastes the reader's time; code should always be written to be readable first.

> I once had to try to understand someone's code that had three identical copies of the same 300 lines of very poorly written code. I had been working with the code for a month before I finally comprehended that the three "identical" versions were actually performing slightly different tax calculations. Some of the subtle differences were intentional, but there were also obvious areas where someone had updated a calculation in one function without updating the other two. The number of subtle, incomprehensible bugs in the code could not be counted. I eventually replaced all 900 lines with an easy-to-read function of 20 lines or so.

Reading such duplicate code can be tiresome, but code maintenance is even more tormenting. As the preceding story suggests, keeping two similar pieces of code up to date can be a nightmare. We have to remember to update both sections whenever we update one of them, and we have to remember how the multiple sections differ so we can modify our changes when we are editing each of them. If we forget to update both sections, we will end up with extremely annoying bugs that usually manifest themselves as, "but I fixed that already, why is it still happening?"

The result is that people who are reading or maintaining our code have to spend astronomical amounts of time understanding and testing it compared to if we had written the code in a nonrepetitive manner in the first place. It's even more frustrating when we are the ones doing the maintenance; we find ourselves saying, "why didn't I do this right the first time?" The time we save by copy-pasting existing code is lost the very first time we have to maintain it. Code is both read and modified many more times and much more often than it is written. Comprehensible code should always be paramount.

This is why programmers, especially Python programmers (who tend to value elegant code more than average), follow what is known as the **Don't Repeat Yourself** (**DRY**) principle. DRY code is maintainable code. My advice to beginning programmers is to never use the copy and paste feature of their editor. To intermediate programmers, I suggest they think thrice before they hit *Ctrl + C*.

But what should we do instead of code duplication? The simplest solution is often to move the code into a function that accepts parameters to account for whatever parts are different. This isn't a terribly object-oriented solution, but it is frequently optimal.

For example, if we have two pieces of code that unzip a ZIP file into two different directories, we can easily write a function that accepts a parameter for the directory to which it should be unzipped instead. This may make the function itself slightly more difficult to read, but a good function name and docstring can easily make up for that, and any code that invokes the function will be easier to read.

That's certainly enough theory! The moral of the story is: always make the effort to refactor your code to be easier to read instead of writing bad code that is only easier to write.

In practice

Let's explore two ways we can reuse existing code. After writing our code to replace strings in a ZIP file full of text files, we are later contracted to scale all the images in a ZIP file to 640 x 480. Looks like we could use a very similar paradigm to what we used in ZipReplace. The first impulse might be to save a copy of that file and change the find_replace method to scale_image or something similar.

But, that's uncool. What if someday we want to change the unzip and zip methods to also open TAR files? Or maybe we want to use a guaranteed unique directory name for temporary files. In either case, we'd have to change it in two different places!

We'll start by demonstrating an inheritance-based solution to this problem. First we'll modify our original ZipReplace class into a superclass for processing generic ZIP files:

```python
import os
import shutil
import zipfile
from pathlib import Path


class ZipProcessor:
    def __init__(self, zipname):
        self.zipname = zipname
```

```
            self.temp_directory = Path("unzipped-{}".format(
                    zipname[:-4]))

    def process_zip(self):
        self.unzip_files()
        self.process_files()
        self.zip_files()

    def unzip_files(self):
        self.temp_directory.mkdir()
        with zipfile.ZipFile(self.zipname) as zip:
            zip.extractall(str(self.temp_directory))

    def zip_files(self):
        with zipfile.ZipFile(self.zipname, 'w') as file:
            for filename in self.temp_directory.iterdir():
                file.write(str(filename), filename.name)
        shutil.rmtree(str(self.temp_directory))
```

We changed the `filename` property to `zipname` to avoid confusion with the `filename` local variables inside the various methods. This helps make the code more readable even though it isn't actually a change in design.

We also dropped the two parameters to `__init__` (`search_string` and `replace_string`) that were specific to `ZipReplace`. Then we renamed the `zip_find_replace` method to `process_zip` and made it call an (as yet undefined) `process_files` method instead of `find_replace`; these name changes help demonstrate the more generalized nature of our new class. Notice that we have removed the `find_replace` method altogether; that code is specific to `ZipReplace` and has no business here.

This new `ZipProcessor` class doesn't actually define a `process_files` method; so if we ran it directly, it would raise an exception. Because it isn't meant to run directly, we removed the main call at the bottom of the original script.

Now, before we move on to our image processing app, let's fix up our original `zipsearch` class to make use of this parent class:

```
from zip_processor import ZipProcessor
import sys
import os

class ZipReplace(ZipProcessor):
    def __init__(self, filename, search_string,
            replace_string):
        super().__init__(filename)
```

```
            self.search_string = search_string
            self.replace_string = replace_string

    def process_files(self):
        '''perform a search and replace on all files in the
        temporary directory'''
        for filename in self.temp_directory.iterdir():
            with filename.open() as file:
                contents = file.read()
            contents = contents.replace(
                    self.search_string, self.replace_string)
            with filename.open("w") as file:
                file.write(contents)

if __name__ == "__main__":
    ZipReplace(*sys.argv[1:4]).process_zip()
```

This code is a bit shorter than the original version, since it inherits its ZIP processing abilities from the parent class. We first import the base class we just wrote and make ZipReplace extend that class. Then we use super() to initialize the parent class. The find_replace method is still here, but we renamed it to process_files so the parent class can call it from its management interface. Because this name isn't as descriptive as the old one, we added a docstring to describe what it is doing.

Now, that was quite a bit of work, considering that all we have now is a program that is functionally not different from the one we started with! But having done that work, it is now much easier for us to write other classes that operate on files in a ZIP archive, such as the (hypothetically requested) photo scaler. Further, if we ever want to improve or bug fix the zip functionality, we can do it for all classes by changing only the one ZipProcessor base class. Maintenance will be much more effective.

See how simple it is now to create a photo scaling class that takes advantage of the ZipProcessor functionality. (Note: this class requires the third-party pillow library to get the PIL module. You can install it with pip install pillow.)

```
from zip_processor import ZipProcessor
import sys
from PIL import Image

class ScaleZip(ZipProcessor):

    def process_files(self):
        '''Scale each image in the directory to 640x480'''
        for filename in self.temp_directory.iterdir():
            im = Image.open(str(filename))
```

```
        scaled = im.resize((640, 480))
        scaled.save(str(filename))

if __name__ == "__main__":
    ScaleZip(*sys.argv[1:4]).process_zip()
```

Look how simple this class is! All that work we did earlier paid off. All we do is open each file (assuming that it is an image; it will unceremoniously crash if a file cannot be opened), scale it, and save it back. The `ZipProcessor` class takes care of the zipping and unzipping without any extra work on our part.

Case study

For this case study, we'll try to delve further into the question, "when should I choose an object versus a built-in type?" We'll be modeling a `Document` class that might be used in a text editor or word processor. What objects, functions, or properties should it have?

We might start with a `str` for the `Document` contents, but in Python, strings aren't mutable (able to be changed). Once a `str` is defined, it is forever. We can't insert a character into it or remove one without creating a brand new string object. That would be leaving a lot of `str` objects taking up memory until Python's garbage collector sees fit to clean up behind us.

So, instead of a string, we'll use a list of characters, which we can modify at will. In addition, a `Document` class would need to know the current cursor position within the list, and should probably also store a filename for the document.

 Real text editors use a binary-tree based data structure called a `rope` to model their document contents. This book's title isn't "advanced data structures", so if you're interested in learning more about this fascinating topic, you may want to search the web for the rope data structure.

Now, what methods should it have? There are a lot of things we might want to do to a text document, including inserting, deleting, and selecting characters, cut, copy, paste, the selection, and saving or closing the document. It looks like there are copious amounts of both data and behavior, so it makes sense to put all this stuff into its own `Document` class.

A pertinent question is: should this class be composed of a bunch of basic Python objects such as `str` filenames, `int` cursor positions, and a `list` of characters? Or should some or all of those things be specially defined objects in their own right? What about individual lines and characters, do they need to have classes of their own?

We'll answer these questions as we go, but let's start with the simplest possible
Document class first and see what it can do:

```python
class Document:
    def __init__(self):
        self.characters = []
        self.cursor = 0
        self.filename = ''

    def insert(self, character):
        self.characters.insert(self.cursor, character)
        self.cursor += 1

    def delete(self):
        del self.characters[self.cursor]

    def save(self):
        with open(self.filename, 'w') as f:
            f.write(''.join(self.characters))

    def forward(self):
        self.cursor += 1

    def back(self):
        self.cursor -= 1
```

This simple class allows us full control over editing a basic document. Have a look
at it in action:

```python
>>> doc = Document()
>>> doc.filename = "test_document"
>>> doc.insert('h')
>>> doc.insert('e')
>>> doc.insert('l')
>>> doc.insert('l')
>>> doc.insert('o')
>>> "".join(doc.characters)
'hello'
>>> doc.back()
>>> doc.delete()
>>> doc.insert('p')
>>> "".join(doc.characters)
'hellp'
```

Looks like it's working. We could connect a keyboard's letter and arrow keys to these methods and the document would track everything just fine.

But what if we want to connect more than just arrow keys. What if we want to connect the *Home* and *End* keys as well? We could add more methods to the `Document` class that search forward or backwards for newline characters (in Python, a newline character, or \n represents the end of one line and the beginning of a new one) in the string and jump to them, but if we did that for every possible movement action (move by words, move by sentences, *Page Up*, *Page Down*, end of line, beginning of whitespace, and more), the class would be huge. Maybe it would be better to put those methods on a separate object. So, let us turn the cursor attribute into an object that is aware of its position and can manipulate that position. We can move the forward and back methods to that class, and add a couple more for the *Home* and *End* keys:

```
class Cursor:
    def __init__(self, document):
        self.document = document
        self.position = 0

    def forward(self):
        self.position += 1

    def back(self):
        self.position -= 1

    def home(self):
        while self.document.characters[
                self.position-1] != '\n':
            self.position -= 1
            if self.position == 0:
                # Got to beginning of file before newline
                break

    def end(self):
        while self.position < len(self.document.characters
                ) and self.document.characters[
                    self.position] != '\n':
            self.position += 1
```

This class takes the document as an initialization parameter so the methods have access to the content of the document's character list. It then provides simple methods for moving backwards and forwards, as before, and for moving to the `home` and `end` positions.

This code is not very safe. You can very easily move past the ending position, and if you try to go home on an empty file, it will crash. These examples are kept short to make them readable, but that doesn't mean they are defensive! You can improve the error checking of this code as an exercise; it might be a great opportunity to expand your exception handling skills.

The Document class itself is hardly changed, except for removing the two methods that were moved to the Cursor class:

```python
class Document:
    def __init__(self):
        self.characters = []
        self.cursor = Cursor(self)
        self.filename = ''

    def insert(self, character):
        self.characters.insert(self.cursor.position,
                character)
        self.cursor.forward()

    def delete(self):
        del self.characters[self.cursor.position]

    def save(self):
        f = open(self.filename, 'w')
        f.write(''.join(self.characters))
        f.close()
```

We simply updated anything that accessed the old cursor integer to use the new object instead. We can test that the home method is really moving to the newline character:

```python
>>> d = Document()
>>> d.insert('h')
>>> d.insert('e')
>>> d.insert('l')
>>> d.insert('l')
>>> d.insert('o')
>>> d.insert('\n')
>>> d.insert('w')
```

```
>>> d.insert('o')
>>> d.insert('r')
>>> d.insert('l')
>>> d.insert('d')
>>> d.cursor.home()
>>> d.insert("*")
>>> print("".join(d.characters))
hello
*world
```

Now, since we've been using that string `join` function a lot (to concatenate the characters so we can see the actual document contents), we can add a property to the `Document` class to give us the complete string:

```
@property
def string(self):
    return "".join(self.characters)
```

This makes our testing a little simpler:

```
>>> print(d.string)
hello
world
```

This framework is simple (though it might be a bit time consuming!) to extend to create and edit a complete plaintext document. Now, let's extend it to work for rich text; text that can have **bold**, <u>underlined</u>, or *italic* characters.

There are two ways we could process this; the first is to insert "fake" characters into our character list that act like instructions, such as "bold characters until you find a stop bold character". The second is to add information to each character indicating what formatting it should have. While the former method is probably more common, we'll implement the latter solution. To do that, we're obviously going to need a class for characters. This class will have an attribute representing the character, as well as three Boolean attributes representing whether it is bold, italic, or underlined.

Hmm, wait! Is this `Character` class going to have any methods? If not, maybe we should use one of the many Python data structures instead; a tuple or named tuple would probably be sufficient. Are there any actions that we would want to do to, or invoke on a character?

Well, clearly, we might want to do things with characters, such as delete or copy them, but those are things that need to be handled at the Document level, since they are really modifying the list of characters. Are there things that need to be done to individual characters?

Actually, now that we're thinking about what a Character class actually is... what is it? Would it be safe to say that a Character class is a string? Maybe we should use an inheritance relationship here? Then we can take advantage of the numerous methods that str instances come with.

What sorts of methods are we talking about? There's startswith, strip, find, lower, and many more. Most of these methods expect to be working on strings that contain more than one character. In contrast, if Character were to subclass str, we'd probably be wise to override __init__ to raise an exception if a multi-character string were supplied. Since all those methods we'd get for free wouldn't really apply to our Character class, it seems we needn't use inheritance, after all.

This brings us back to our original question; should Character even be a class? There is a very important special method on the object class that we can take advantage of to represent our characters. This method, called __str__ (two underscores, like __init__), is used in string manipulation functions like print and the str constructor to convert any class to a string. The default implementation does some boring stuff like printing the name of the module and class and its address in memory. But if we override it, we can make it print whatever we like. For our implementation, we could make it prefix characters with special characters to represent whether they are bold, italic, or underlined. So, we will create a class to represent a character, and here it is:

```python
class Character:
    def __init__(self, character,
            bold=False, italic=False, underline=False):
        assert len(character) == 1
        self.character = character
        self.bold = bold
        self.italic = italic
        self.underline = underline

    def __str__(self):
        bold = "*" if self.bold else ''
        italic = "/" if self.italic else ''
        underline = "_" if self.underline else ''
        return bold + italic + underline + self.character
```

This class allows us to create characters and prefix them with a special character when the `str()` function is applied to them. Nothing too exciting there. We only have to make a few minor modifications to the `Document` and `Cursor` classes to work with this class. In the `Document` class, we add these two lines at the beginning of the `insert` method:

```
def insert(self, character):
    if not hasattr(character, 'character'):
        character = Character(character)
```

This is a rather strange bit of code. Its basic purpose is to check whether the character being passed in is a `Character` or a `str`. If it is a string, it is wrapped in a `Character` class so all objects in the list are `Character` objects. However, it is entirely possible that someone using our code would want to use a class that is neither `Character` nor string, using duck typing. If the object has a character attribute, we assume it is a "Character-like" object. But if it does not, we assume it is a "str-like" object and wrap it in `Character`. This helps the program take advantage of duck typing as well as polymorphism; as long as an object has a character attribute, it can be used in the `Document` class.

This generic check could be very useful, for example, if we wanted to make a programmer's editor with syntax highlighting: we'd need extra data on the character, such as what type of syntax token the character belongs to. Note that if we are doing a lot of this kind of comparison, it's probably better to implement `Character` as an abstract base class with an appropriate `__subclasshook__`, as discussed in *Chapter 3, When Objects Are Alike*.

In addition, we need to modify the string property on `Document` to accept the new `Character` values. All we need to do is call `str()` on each character before we join it:

```
@property
def string(self):
    return "".join((str(c) for c in self.characters))
```

This code uses a generator expression, which we'll discuss in *Chapter 9, The Iterator Pattern*. It's a shortcut to perform a specific action on all the objects in a sequence.

Finally, we also need to check `Character.character`, instead of just the string character we were storing before, in the `home` and `end` functions when we're looking to see whether it matches a newline character:

```
def home(self):
    while self.document.characters[
            self.position-1].character != '\n':
        self.position -= 1
        if self.position == 0:
```

```
                           # Got to beginning of file before newline
                           break

           def end(self):
               while self.position < len(
                       self.document.characters) and \
                       self.document.characters[
                               self.position
                           ].character != '\n':
                   self.position += 1
```

This completes the formatting of characters. We can test it to see that it works:

```
>>> d = Document()
>>> d.insert('h')
>>> d.insert('e')
>>> d.insert(Character('l', bold=True))
>>> d.insert(Character('l', bold=True))
>>> d.insert('o')
>>> d.insert('\n')
>>> d.insert(Character('w', italic=True))
>>> d.insert(Character('o', italic=True))
>>> d.insert(Character('r', underline=True))
>>> d.insert('l')
>>> d.insert('d')
>>> print(d.string)
he*l*lo
/w/o_rld
>>> d.cursor.home()
>>> d.delete()
>>> d.insert('W')
>>> print(d.string)
he*l*lo
W/o_rld
>>> d.characters[0].underline = True
>>> print(d.string)
_he*l*lo
W/o_rld
```

As expected, whenever we print the string, each bold character is preceded by a
* character, each italic character by a / character, and each underlined character
by a _ character. All our functions seem to work, and we can modify characters in
the list after the fact. We have a working rich text document object that could be
plugged into a proper user interface and hooked up with a keyboard for input and
a screen for output. Naturally, we'd want to display real bold, italic, and underlined
characters on the screen, instead of using our __str__ method, but it was sufficient
for the basic testing we demanded of it.

Exercises

We've looked at various ways that objects, data, and methods can interact with each
other in an object-oriented Python program. As usual, your first thoughts should
be how you can apply these principles to your own work. Do you have any messy
scripts lying around that could be rewritten using an object-oriented manager?
Look through some of your old code and look for methods that are not actions.
If the name isn't a verb, try rewriting it as a property.

Think about code you've written in any language. Does it break the DRY principle?
Is there any duplicate code? Did you copy and paste code? Did you write two
versions of similar pieces of code because you didn't feel like understanding the
original code? Go back over some of your recent code now and see whether you
can refactor the duplicate code using inheritance or composition. Try to pick a
project you're still interested in maintaining; not code so old that you never want
to touch it again. It helps keep your interest up when you do the improvements!

Now, look back over some of the examples we saw in this chapter. Start with the
cached web page example that uses a property to cache the retrieved data. An
obvious problem with this example is that the cache is never refreshed. Add a
timeout to the property's getter, and only return the cached page if the page has
been requested before the timeout has expired. You can use the time module
(time.time() - an_old_time returns the number of seconds that have elapsed
since an_old_time) to determine whether the cache has expired.

Now look at the inheritance-based ZipProcessor. It might be reasonable to use
composition instead of inheritance here. Instead of extending the class in the
ZipReplace and ScaleZip classes, you could pass instances of those classes into the
ZipProcessor constructor and call them to do the processing part. Implement this.

Which version do you find easier to use? Which is more elegant? What is easier to read? These are subjective questions; the answer varies for each of us. Knowing the answer, however, is important; if you find you prefer inheritance over composition, you have to pay attention that you don't overuse inheritance in your daily coding. If you prefer composition, make sure you don't miss opportunities to create an elegant inheritance-based solution.

Finally, add some error handlers to the various classes we created in the case study. They should ensure single characters are entered, that you don't try to move the cursor past the end or beginning of the file, that you don't delete a character that doesn't exist, and that you don't save a file without a filename. Try to think of as many edge cases as you can, and account for them (thinking about edge cases is about 90 percent of a professional programmer's job!) Consider different ways to handle them; should you raise an exception when the user tries to move past the end of the file, or just stay on the last character?

Pay attention, in your daily coding, to the copy and paste commands. Every time you use them in your editor, consider whether it would be a good idea to improve your program's organization so that you only have one version of the code you are about to copy.

Summary

In this chapter, we focused on identifying objects, especially objects that are not immediately apparent; objects that manage and control. Objects should have both data and behavior, but properties can be used to blur the distinction between the two. The DRY principle is an important indicator of code quality and inheritance and composition can be applied to reduce code duplication.

In the next chapter, we'll cover several of the built-in Python data structures and objects, focusing on their object-oriented properties and how they can be extended or adapted.

6
Python Data Structures

In our examples so far, we've already seen many of the built-in Python data structures in action. You've probably also covered many of them in introductory books or tutorials. In this chapter, we'll be discussing the object-oriented features of these data structures, when they should be used instead of a regular class, and when they should not be used. In particular, we'll be covering:

- Tuples and named tuples
- Dictionaries
- Lists and sets
- How and why to extend built-in objects
- Three types of queues

Empty objects

Let's start with the most basic Python built-in, one that we've seen many times already, the one that we've extended in every class we have created: the `object`. Technically, we can instantiate an `object` without writing a subclass:

```
>>> o = object()
>>> o.x = 5
Traceback (most recent call last):
  File "<stdin>", line 1, in <module>
AttributeError: 'object' object has no attribute 'x'
```

Unfortunately, as you can see, it's not possible to set any attributes on an `object` that was instantiated directly. This isn't because the Python developers wanted to force us to write our own classes, or anything so sinister. They did this to save memory; a lot of memory. When Python allows an object to have arbitrary attributes, it takes a certain amount of system memory to keep track of what attributes each object has, for storing both the attribute name and its value. Even if no attributes are stored, memory is allocated for *potential* new attributes. Given the dozens, hundreds, or thousands of objects (every class extends object) in a typical Python program; this small amount of memory would quickly become a large amount of memory. So, Python disables arbitrary properties on `object`, and several other built-ins, by default.

It is possible to restrict arbitrary properties on our own classes using **slots**. Slots are beyond the scope of this book, but you now have a search term if you are looking for more information. In normal use, there isn't much benefit to using slots, but if you're writing an object that will be duplicated thousands of times throughout the system, they can help save memory, just as they do for `object`.

It is, however, trivial to create an empty object class of our own; we saw it in our earliest example:

```
class MyObject:
    pass
```

And, as we've already seen, it's possible to set attributes on such classes:

```
>>> m = MyObject()
>>> m.x = "hello"
>>> m.x
'hello'
```

If we wanted to group properties together, we could store them in an empty object like this. But we are usually better off using other built-ins designed for storing data. It has been stressed throughout this book that classes and objects should only be used when you want to specify *both* data and behaviors. The main reason to write an empty class is to quickly block something out, knowing we'll come back later to add behavior. It is much easier to adapt behaviors to a class than it is to replace a data structure with an object and change all references to it. Therefore, it is important to decide from the outset if the data is just data, or if it is an object in disguise. Once that design decision is made, the rest of the design naturally falls into place.

Tuples and named tuples

Tuples are objects that can store a specific number of other objects in order. They are immutable, so we can't add, remove, or replace objects on the fly. This may seem like a massive restriction, but the truth is, if you need to modify a tuple, you're using the wrong data type (usually a list would be more suitable). The primary benefit of tuples' immutability is that we can use them as keys in dictionaries, and in other locations where an object requires a hash value.

Tuples are used to store data; behavior cannot be stored in a tuple. If we require behavior to manipulate a tuple, we have to pass the tuple into a function (or method on another object) that performs the action.

Tuples should generally store values that are somehow different from each other. For example, we would not put three stock symbols in a tuple, but we might create a tuple of stock symbol, current price, high, and low for the day. The primary purpose of a tuple is to aggregate different pieces of data together into one container. Thus, a tuple can be the easiest tool to replace the "object with no data" idiom.

We can create a tuple by separating the values with a comma. Usually, tuples are wrapped in parentheses to make them easy to read and to separate them from other parts of an expression, but this is not always mandatory. The following two assignments are identical (they record a stock, the current price, the high, and the low for a rather profitable company):

```
>>> stock = "FB", 75.00, 75.03, 74.90
>>> stock2 = ("FB", 75.00, 75.03, 74.90)
```

If we're grouping a tuple inside of some other object, such as a function call, list comprehension, or generator, the parentheses are required. Otherwise, it would be impossible for the interpreter to know whether it is a tuple or the next function parameter. For example, the following function accepts a tuple and a date, and returns a tuple of the date and the middle value between the stock's high and low value:

```
import datetime
def middle(stock, date):
    symbol, current, high, low = stock
    return (((high + low) / 2), date)

mid_value, date = middle(("FB", 75.00, 75.03, 74.90),
        datetime.date(2014, 10, 31))
```

The tuple is created directly inside the function call by separating the values with commas and enclosing the entire tuple in parenthesis. This tuple is then followed by a comma to separate it from the second argument.

This example also illustrates tuple unpacking. The first line inside the function unpacks the `stock` parameter into four different variables. The tuple has to be exactly the same length as the number of variables, or it will raise an exception. We can also see an example of tuple unpacking on the last line, where the tuple returned inside the function is unpacked into two values, `mid_value` and `date`. Granted, this is a strange thing to do, since we supplied the date to the function in the first place, but it gave us a chance to see unpacking at work.

Unpacking is a very useful feature in Python. We can group variables together to make storing and passing them around simpler, but the moment we need to access all of them, we can unpack them into separate variables. Of course, sometimes we only need access to one of the variables in the tuple. We can use the same syntax that we use for other sequence types (lists and strings, for example) to access an individual value:

```
>>> stock = "FB", 75.00, 75.03, 74.90
>>> high = stock[2]
>>> high
75.03
```

We can even use slice notation to extract larger pieces of tuples:

```
>>> stock[1:3]
(75.00, 75.03)
```

These examples, while illustrating how flexible tuples can be, also demonstrate one of their major disadvantages: readability. How does someone reading this code know what is in the second position of a specific tuple? They can guess, from the name of the variable we assigned it to, that it is `high` of some sort, but if we had just accessed the tuple value in a calculation without assigning it, there would be no such indication. They would have to paw through the code to find where the tuple was declared before they could discover what it does.

Accessing tuple members directly is fine in some circumstances, but don't make a habit of it. Such so-called "magic numbers" (numbers that seem to come out of thin air with no apparent meaning within the code) are the source of many coding errors and lead to hours of frustrated debugging. Try to use tuples only when you know that all the values are going to be useful at once and it's normally going to be unpacked when it is accessed. If you have to access a member directly or using a slice and the purpose of that value is not immediately obvious, at least include a comment explaining where it came from.

Named tuples

So, what do we do when we want to group values together, but know we're frequently going to need to access them individually? Well, we could use an empty object, as discussed in the previous section (but that is rarely useful unless we anticipate adding behavior later), or we could use a dictionary (most useful if we don't know exactly how many or which specific data will be stored), as we'll cover in the next section.

If, however, we do not need to add behavior to the object, and we know in advance what attributes we need to store, we can use a named tuple. Named tuples are tuples with attitude. They are a great way to group read-only data together.

Constructing a named tuple takes a bit more work than a normal tuple. First, we have to import `namedtuple`, as it is not in the namespace by default. Then, we describe the named tuple by giving it a name and outlining its attributes. This returns a class-like object that we can instantiate with the required values as many times as we want:

```
from collections import namedtuple
Stock = namedtuple("Stock", "symbol current high low")
stock = Stock("FB", 75.00, high=75.03, low=74.90)
```

The `namedtuple` constructor accepts two arguments. The first is an identifier for the named tuple. The second is a string of space-separated attributes that the named tuple can have. The first attribute should be listed, followed by a space (or comma if you prefer), then the second attribute, then another space, and so on. The result is an object that can be called just like a normal class to instantiate other objects. The constructor must have exactly the right number of arguments that can be passed in as arguments or keyword arguments. As with normal objects, we can create as many instances of this "class" as we like, with different values for each.

The resulting `namedtuple` can then be packed, unpacked, and otherwise treated like a normal tuple, but we can also access individual attributes on it as if it were an object:

```
>>> stock.high
75.03
>>> symbol, current, high, low = stock
>>> current
75.00
```

 Remember that creating named tuples is a two-step process. First, use `collections.namedtuple` to create a class, and then construct instances of that class.

Named tuples are perfect for many "data only" representations, but they are not ideal for all situations. Like tuples and strings, named tuples are immutable, so we cannot modify an attribute once it has been set. For example, the current value of my company's stock has gone down since we started this discussion, but we can't set the new value:

```
>>> stock.current = 74.98
Traceback (most recent call last):
  File "<stdin>", line 1, in <module>
AttributeError: can't set attribute
```

If we need to be able to change stored data, a dictionary may be what we need instead.

Dictionaries

Dictionaries are incredibly useful containers that allow us to map objects directly to other objects. An empty object with attributes to it is a sort of dictionary; the names of the properties map to the property values. This is actually closer to the truth than it sounds; internally, objects normally represent attributes as a dictionary, where the values are properties or methods on the objects (see the __dict__ attribute if you don't believe me). Even the attributes on a module are stored, internally, in a dictionary.

Dictionaries are extremely efficient at looking up a value, given a specific key object that maps to that value. They should always be used when you want to find one object based on some other object. The object that is being stored is called the **value**; the object that is being used as an index is called the **key**. We've already seen dictionary syntax in some of our previous examples.

Dictionaries can be created either using the dict() constructor or using the {} syntax shortcut. In practice, the latter format is almost always used. We can prepopulate a dictionary by separating the keys from the values using a colon, and separating the key value pairs using a comma.

For example, in a stock application, we would most often want to look up prices by the stock symbol. We can create a dictionary that uses stock symbols as keys, and tuples of current, high, and low as values like this:

```
stocks = {"GOOG": (613.30, 625.86, 610.50),
          "MSFT": (30.25, 30.70, 30.19)}
```

As we've seen in previous examples, we can then look up values in the dictionary by requesting a key inside square brackets. If the key is not in the dictionary, it will raise an exception:

```
>>> stocks["GOOG"]
(613.3, 625.86, 610.5)
>>> stocks["RIM"]
Traceback (most recent call last):
  File "<stdin>", line 1, in <module>
KeyError: 'RIM'
```

We can, of course, catch the KeyError and handle it. But we have other options. Remember, dictionaries are objects, even if their primary purpose is to hold other objects. As such, they have several behaviors associated with them. One of the most useful of these methods is the get method; it accepts a key as the first parameter and an optional default value if the key doesn't exist:

```
>>> print(stocks.get("RIM"))
None
>>> stocks.get("RIM", "NOT FOUND")
'NOT FOUND'
```

For even more control, we can use the setdefault method. If the key is in the dictionary, this method behaves just like get; it returns the value for that key. Otherwise, if the key is not in the dictionary, it will not only return the default value we supply in the method call (just like get does), it will also set the key to that same value. Another way to think of it is that setdefault sets a value in the dictionary only if that value has not previously been set. Then it returns the value in the dictionary, either the one that was already there, or the newly provided default value.

```
>>> stocks.setdefault("GOOG", "INVALID")
(613.3, 625.86, 610.5)
>>> stocks.setdefault("BBRY", (10.50, 10.62, 10.39))
(10.50, 10.62, 10.39)
>>> stocks["BBRY"]
(10.50, 10.62, 10.39)
```

The GOOG stock was already in the dictionary, so when we tried to setdefault it to an invalid value, it just returned the value already in the dictionary. BBRY was not in the dictionary, so setdefault returned the default value and set the new value in the dictionary for us. We then check that the new stock is, indeed, in the dictionary.

Three other very useful dictionary methods are keys(), values(), and items(). The first two return an iterator over all the keys and all the values in the dictionary. We can use these like lists or in for loops if we want to process all the keys or values. The items() method is probably the most useful; it returns an iterator over tuples of (key, value) pairs for every item in the dictionary. This works great with tuple unpacking in a for loop to loop over associated keys and values. This example does just that to print each stock in the dictionary with its current value:

```
>>> for stock, values in stocks.items():
...     print("{} last value is {}".format(stock, values[0]))
...
GOOG last value is 613.3
BBRY last value is 10.50
MSFT last value is 30.25
```

Each key/value tuple is unpacked into two variables named stock and values (we could use any variable names we wanted, but these both seem appropriate) and then printed in a formatted string.

Notice that the stocks do not show up in the same order in which they were inserted. Dictionaries, due to the efficient algorithm (known as hashing) that is used to make key lookup so fast, are inherently unsorted.

So, there are numerous ways to retrieve data from a dictionary once it has been instantiated; we can use square brackets as index syntax, the get method, the setdefault method, or iterate over the items method, among others.

Finally, as you likely already know, we can set a value in a dictionary using the same indexing syntax we use to retrieve a value:

```
>>> stocks["GOOG"] = (597.63, 610.00, 596.28)
>>> stocks['GOOG']
(597.63, 610.0, 596.28)
```

Google's price is lower today, so I've updated the tuple value in the dictionary. We can use this index syntax to set a value for any key, regardless of whether the key is in the dictionary. If it is in the dictionary, the old value will be replaced with the new one; otherwise, a new key/value pair will be created.

We've been using strings as dictionary keys, so far, but we aren't limited to string keys. It is common to use strings as keys, especially when we're storing data in a dictionary to gather it together (instead of using an object with named properties). But we can also use tuples, numbers, or even objects we've defined ourselves as dictionary keys. We can even use different types of keys in a single dictionary:

```
random_keys = {}
random_keys["astring"] = "somestring"
random_keys[5] = "aninteger"
random_keys[25.2] = "floats work too"
random_keys[("abc", 123)] = "so do tuples"

class AnObject:
    def __init__(self, avalue):
        self.avalue = avalue

my_object = AnObject(14)
random_keys[my_object] = "We can even store objects"
my_object.avalue = 12
try:
    random_keys[[1,2,3]] = "we can't store lists though"
except:
    print("unable to store list\n")

for key, value in random_keys.items():
    print("{} has value {}".format(key, value))
```

This code shows several different types of keys we can supply to a dictionary. It also shows one type of object that cannot be used. We've already used lists extensively, and we'll be seeing many more details of them in the next section. Because lists can change at any time (by adding or removing items, for example), they cannot hash to a specific value.

Objects that are **hashable** basically have a defined algorithm that converts the object into a unique integer value for rapid lookup. This hash is what is actually used to look up values in a dictionary. For example, strings map to integers based on the characters in the string, while tuples combine hashes of the items inside the tuple. Any two objects that are somehow considered equal (like strings with the same characters or tuples with the same values) should have the same hash value, and the hash value for an object should never ever change. Lists, however, can have their contents changed, which would change their hash value (two lists should only be equal if their contents are the same). Because of this, they can't be used as dictionary keys. For the same reason, dictionaries cannot be used as keys into other dictionaries.

In contrast, there are no limits on the types of objects that can be used as dictionary values. We can use a string key that maps to a list value, for example, or we can have a nested dictionary as a value in another dictionary.

Dictionary use cases

Dictionaries are extremely versatile and have numerous uses. There are two major ways that dictionaries can be used. The first is dictionaries where all the keys represent different instances of similar objects; for example, our stock dictionary. This is an indexing system. We use the stock symbol as an index to the values. The values could even have been complicated self-defined objects that made buy and sell decisions or set a stop-loss, rather than our simple tuples.

The second design is dictionaries where each key represents some aspect of a single structure; in this case, we'd probably use a separate dictionary for each object, and they'd all have similar (though often not identical) sets of keys. This latter situation can often also be solved with named tuples. These should typically be used when we know exactly what attributes the data must store, and we know that all pieces of the data must be supplied at once (when the item is constructed). But if we need to create or change dictionary keys over time or we don't know exactly what the keys might be, a dictionary is more suitable.

Using defaultdict

We've seen how to use `setdefault` to set a default value if a key doesn't exist, but this can get a bit monotonous if we need to set a default value every time we look up a value. For example, if we're writing code that counts the number of times a letter occurs in a given sentence, we could do this:

```python
def letter_frequency(sentence):
    frequencies = {}
    for letter in sentence:
        frequency = frequencies.setdefault(letter, 0)
        frequencies[letter] = frequency + 1
    return frequencies
```

Every time we access the dictionary, we need to check that it has a value already, and if not, set it to zero. When something like this needs to be done every time an empty key is requested, we can use a different version of the dictionary, called `defaultdict`:

```python
from collections import defaultdict
def letter_frequency(sentence):
    frequencies = defaultdict(int)
```

```
    for letter in sentence:
        frequencies[letter] += 1
    return frequencies
```

This code looks like it couldn't possibly work. The `defaultdict` accepts a function in its constructor. Whenever a key is accessed that is not already in the dictionary, it calls that function, with no parameters, to create a default value.

In this case, the function it calls is `int`, which is the constructor for an integer object. Normally, integers are created simply by typing an integer number into our code, and if we do create one using the `int` constructor, we pass it the item we want to create (for example, to convert a string of digits into an integer). But if we call `int` without any arguments, it returns, conveniently, the number zero. In this code, if the letter doesn't exist in the `defaultdict`, the number zero is returned when we access it. Then we add one to this number to indicate we've found an instance of that letter, and the next time we find one, that number will be returned and we can increment the value again.

The `defaultdict` is useful for creating dictionaries of containers. If we want to create a dictionary of stock prices for the past 30 days, we could use a stock symbol as the key and store the prices in `list`; the first time we access the stock price, we would want it to create an empty list. Simply pass `list` into the `defaultdict`, and it will be called every time an empty key is accessed. We can do similar things with sets or even empty dictionaries if we want to associate one with a key.

Of course, we can also write our own functions and pass them into the `defaultdict`. Suppose we want to create a `defaultdict` where each new element contains a tuple of the number of items inserted into the dictionary at that time and an empty list to hold other things. Nobody knows why we would want to create such an object, but let's have a look:

```
from collections import defaultdict
num_items = 0
def tuple_counter():
    global num_items
    num_items += 1
    return (num_items, [])
```

```
d = defaultdict(tuple_counter)
```

When we run this code, we can access empty keys and insert into the list all in one statement:

```
>>> d = defaultdict(tuple_counter)
>>> d['a'][1].append("hello")
>>> d['b'][1].append('world')
```

```
>>> d
defaultdict(<function tuple_counter at 0x82f2c6c>,
{'a': (1, ['hello']), 'b': (2, ['world'])})
```

When we print `dict` at the end, we see that the counter really was working.

This example, while succinctly demonstrating how to create our own function for `defaultdict`, is not actually very good code; using a global variable means that if we created four different `defaultdict` segments that each used `tuple_counter`, it would count the number of entries in all dictionaries, rather than having a different count for each one. It would be better to create a class and pass a method on that class to `defaultdict`.

Counter

You'd think that you couldn't get much simpler than `defaultdict(int)`, but the "I want to count specific instances in an iterable" use case is common enough that the Python developers created a specific class for it. The previous code that counts characters in a string can easily be calculated in a single line:

```
from collections import Counter
def letter_frequency(sentence):
    return Counter(sentence)
```

The `Counter` object behaves like a beefed up dictionary where the keys are the items being counted and the values are the number of such items. One of the most useful functions is the `most_common()` method. It returns a list of (key, count) tuples ordered by the count. You can optionally pass an integer argument into `most_common()` to request only the top most common elements. For example, you could write a simple polling application as follows:

```
from collections import Counter

responses = [
    "vanilla",
    "chocolate",
    "vanilla",
    "vanilla",
    "caramel",
    "strawberry",
    "vanilla"
]

print(
```

```
    "The children voted for {} ice cream".format(
        Counter(responses).most_common(1)[0][0]
    )
)
```

Presumably, you'd get the responses from a database or by using a complicated vision algorithm to count the kids who raised their hands. Here, we hardcode it so that we can test the `most_common` method. It returns a list that has only one element (because we requested one element in the parameter). This element stores the name of the top choice at position zero, hence the double `[0][0]` at the end of the call. I think they look like a surprised face, don't you? Your computer is probably amazed it can count data so easily. It's ancestor, Hollerith's Tabulating Machine for the 1890 US census, must be so jealous!

Lists

Lists are the least object-oriented of Python's data structures. While lists are, themselves, objects, there is a lot of syntax in Python to make using them as painless as possible. Unlike many other object-oriented languages, lists in Python are simply available. We don't need to import them and rarely need to call methods on them. We can loop over a list without explicitly requesting an iterator object, and we can construct a list (as with a dictionary) with custom syntax. Further, list comprehensions and generator expressions turn them into a veritable Swiss-army knife of computing functionality.

We won't go into too much detail of the syntax; you've seen it in introductory tutorials across the Web and in previous examples in this book. You can't code Python very long without learning how to use lists! Instead, we'll be covering when lists should be used, and their nature as objects. If you don't know how to create or append to a list, how to retrieve items from a list, or what "slice notation" is, I direct you to the official Python tutorial, post-haste. It can be found online at `http://docs.python.org/3/tutorial/`.

In Python, lists should normally be used when we want to store several instances of the "same" type of object; lists of strings or lists of numbers; most often, lists of objects we've defined ourselves. Lists should always be used when we want to store items in some kind of order. Often, this is the order in which they were inserted, but they can also be sorted by some criteria.

As we saw in the case study from the previous chapter, lists are also very useful when we need to modify the contents: insert to or delete from an arbitrary location of the list, or update a value within the list.

Like dictionaries, Python lists use an extremely efficient and well-tuned internal data structure so we can worry about what we're storing, rather than how we're storing it. Many object-oriented languages provide different data structures for queues, stacks, linked lists, and array-based lists. Python does provide special instances of some of these classes, if optimizing access to huge sets of data is required. Normally, however, the list data structure can serve all these purposes at once, and the coder has complete control over how they access it.

Don't use lists for collecting different attributes of individual items. We do not want, for example, a list of the properties a particular shape has. Tuples, named tuples, dictionaries, and objects would all be more suitable for this purpose. In some languages, they might create a list in which each alternate item is a different type; for example, they might write `['a', 1, 'b', 3]` for our letter frequency list. They'd have to use a strange loop that accesses two elements in the list at once or a modulus operator to determine which position was being accessed.

Don't do this in Python. We can group related items together using a dictionary, as we did in the previous section (if sort order doesn't matter), or using a list of tuples. Here's a rather convoluted example that demonstrates how we could do the frequency example using a list. It is much more complicated than the dictionary examples, and illustrates the effect choosing the right (or wrong) data structure can have on the readability of our code:

```python
import string
CHARACTERS  = list(string.ascii_letters) + [" "]

def letter_frequency(sentence):
    frequencies = [(c, 0) for c in CHARACTERS]
    for letter in sentence:
        index = CHARACTERS.index(letter)
        frequencies[index] = (letter,frequencies[index][1]+1)
    return frequencies
```

This code starts with a list of possible characters. The `string.ascii_letters` attribute provides a string of all the letters, lowercase and uppercase, in order. We convert this to a list, and then use list concatenation (the plus operator causes two lists to be merged into one) to add one more character, the space. These are the available characters in our frequency list (the code would break if we tried to add a letter that wasn't in the list, but an exception handler could solve this).

The first line inside the function uses a list comprehension to turn the CHARACTERS list into a list of tuples. List comprehensions are an important, non-object-oriented tool in Python; we'll be covering them in detail in the next chapter.

Then we loop over each of the characters in the sentence. We first look up the index of the character in the CHARACTERS list, which we know has the same index in our frequencies list, since we just created the second list from the first. We then update that index in the frequencies list by creating a new tuple, discarding the original one. Aside from the garbage collection and memory waste concerns, this is rather difficult to read!

Like dictionaries, lists are objects too, and they have several methods that can be invoked upon them. Here are some common ones:

- The append(element) method adds an element to the end of the list
- The insert(index, element) method inserts an item at a specific position
- The count(element) method tells us how many times an element appears in the list
- The index() method tells us the index of an item in the list, raising an exception if it can't find it
- The find() method does the same thing, but returns -1 instead of raising an exception for missing items
- The reverse() method does exactly what it says—turns the list around
- The sort() method has some rather intricate object-oriented behaviors, which we'll cover now

Sorting lists

Without any parameters, sort will generally do the expected thing. If it's a list of strings, it will place them in alphabetical order. This operation is case sensitive, so all capital letters will be sorted before lowercase letters, that is z comes before a. If it is a list of numbers, they will be sorted in numerical order. If a list of tuples is provided, the list is sorted by the first element in each tuple. If a mixture containing unsortable items is supplied, the sort will raise a TypeError exception.

If we want to place objects we define ourselves into a list and make those objects sortable, we have to do a bit more work. The special method __lt__, which stands for "less than", should be defined on the class to make instances of that class comparable. The sort method on list will access this method on each object to determine where it goes in the list. This method should return True if our class is somehow less than the passed parameter, and False otherwise. Here's a rather silly class that can be sorted based on either a string or a number:

```
class WeirdSortee:
    def __init__(self, string, number, sort_num):
        self.string = string
        self.number = number
        self.sort_num = sort_num

    def __lt__(self, object):
        if self.sort_num:
            return self.number < object.number
        return self.string < object.string

    def __repr__(self):
        return"{}:{}".format(self.string, self.number)
```

The __repr__ method makes it easy to see the two values when we print a list. The __lt__ method's implementation compares the object to another instance of the same class (or any duck typed object that has string, number, and sort_num attributes; it will fail if those attributes are missing). The following output illustrates this class in action, when it comes to sorting:

```
>>> a = WeirdSortee('a', 4, True)
>>> b = WeirdSortee('b', 3, True)
>>> c = WeirdSortee('c', 2, True)
>>> d = WeirdSortee('d', 1, True)
>>> l = [a,b,c,d]
>>> l
[a:4, b:3, c:2, d:1]
>>> l.sort()
>>> l
[d:1, c:2, b:3, a:4]
```

```
>>> for i in l:
...      i.sort_num = False
...
>>> l.sort()
>>> l
[a:4, b:3, c:2, d:1]
```

The first time we call `sort`, it sorts by numbers because `sort_num` is `True` on all the objects being compared. The second time, it sorts by letters. The `__lt__` method is the only one we need to implement to enable sorting. Technically, however, if it is implemented, the class should normally also implement the similar `__gt__`, `__eq__`, `__ne__`, `__ge__`, and `__le__` methods so that all of the <, >, ==, !=, >=, and <= operators also work properly. You can get this for free by implementing `__lt__` and `__eq__`, and then applying the `@total_ordering` class decorator to supply the rest:

```
from functools import total_ordering

@total_ordering
class WeirdSortee:
    def __init__(self, string, number, sort_num):
        self.string = string
        self.number = number
        self.sort_num = sort_num

    def __lt__(self, object):
        if self.sort_num:
            return self.number < object.number
        return self.string < object.string

    def __repr__(self):
        return"{}:{}".format(self.string, self.number)

    def __eq__(self, object):
        return all((
            self.string == object.string,
            self.number == object.number,
            self.sort_num == object.number
        ))
```

This is useful if we want to be able to use operators on our objects. However, if all we want to do is customize our sort orders, even this is overkill. For such a use case, the `sort` method can take an optional `key` argument. This argument is a function that can translate each object in a list into an object that can somehow be compared. For example, we can use `str.lower` as the key argument to perform a case-insensitive sort on a list of strings:

```
>>> l = ["hello", "HELP", "Helo"]
>>> l.sort()
>>> l
['HELP', 'Helo', 'hello']
>>> l.sort(key=str.lower)
>>> l
['hello', 'Helo', 'HELP']
```

Remember, even though `lower` is a method on string objects, it is also a function that can accept a single argument, `self`. In other words, `str.lower(item)` is equivalent to `item.lower()`. When we pass this function as a key, it performs the comparison on lowercase values instead of doing the default case-sensitive comparison.

There are a few sort key operations that are so common that the Python team has supplied them so you don't have to write them yourself. For example, it is often common to sort a list of tuples by something other than the first item in the list. The `operator.itemgetter` method can be used as a key to do this:

```
>>> from operator import itemgetter
>>> l = [('h', 4), ('n', 6), ('o', 5), ('p', 1), ('t', 3), ('y', 2)]
>>> l.sort(key=itemgetter(1))
>>> l
[('p', 1), ('y', 2), ('t', 3), ('h', 4), ('o', 5), ('n', 6)]
```

The `itemgetter` function is the most commonly used one (it works if the objects are dictionaries, too), but you will sometimes find use for `attrgetter` and `methodcaller`, which return attributes on an object and the results of method calls on objects for the same purpose. See the `operator` module documentation for more information.

Sets

Lists are extremely versatile tools that suit most container object applications. But they are not useful when we want to ensure objects in the list are unique. For example, a song library may contain many songs by the same artist. If we want to sort through the library and create a list of all the artists, we would have to check the list to see if we've added the artist already, before we add them again.

This is where sets come in. Sets come from mathematics, where they represent an unordered group of (usually) unique numbers. We can add a number to a set five times, but it will show up in the set only once.

In Python, sets can hold any hashable object, not just numbers. Hashable objects are the same objects that can be used as keys in dictionaries; so again, lists and dictionaries are out. Like mathematical sets, they can store only one copy of each object. So if we're trying to create a list of song artists, we can create a set of string names and simply add them to the set. This example starts with a list of (song, artist) tuples and creates a set of the artists:

```python
song_library = [("Phantom Of The Opera", "Sarah Brightman"),
        ("Knocking On Heaven's Door", "Guns N' Roses"),
        ("Captain Nemo", "Sarah Brightman"),
        ("Patterns In The Ivy", "Opeth"),
        ("November Rain", "Guns N' Roses"),
        ("Beautiful", "Sarah Brightman"),
        ("Mal's Song", "Vixy and Tony")]

artists = set()
for song, artist in song_library:
    artists.add(artist)

print(artists)
```

There is no built-in syntax for an empty set as there is for lists and dictionaries; we create a set using the `set()` constructor. However, we can use the curly braces (borrowed from dictionary syntax) to create a set, so long as the set contains values. If we use colons to separate pairs of values, it's a dictionary, as in `{'key': 'value', 'key2': 'value2'}`. If we just separate values with commas, it's a set, as in `{'value', 'value2'}`. Items can be added individually to the set using its `add` method. If we run this script, we see that the set works as advertised:

```python
{'Sarah Brightman', "Guns N' Roses", 'Vixy and Tony', 'Opeth'}
```

If you're paying attention to the output, you'll notice that the items are not printed in the order they were added to the sets. Sets, like dictionaries, are unordered. They both use an underlying hash-based data structure for efficiency. Because they are unordered, sets cannot have items looked up by index. The primary purpose of a set is to divide the world into two groups: "things that are in the set", and, "things that are not in the set". It is easy to check whether an item is in the set or to loop over the items in a set, but if we want to sort or order them, we'll have to convert the set to a list. This output shows all three of these activities:

```
>>> "Opeth" in artists
True
>>> for artist in artists:
...     print("{} plays good music".format(artist))
...
Sarah Brightman plays good music
Guns N' Roses plays good music
Vixy and Tony play good music
Opeth plays good music
>>> alphabetical = list(artists)
>>> alphabetical.sort()
>>> alphabetical
["Guns N' Roses", 'Opeth', 'Sarah Brightman', 'Vixy and Tony']
```

While the primary *feature* of a set is uniqueness, that is not its primary *purpose*. Sets are most useful when two or more of them are used in combination. Most of the methods on the set type operate on other sets, allowing us to efficiently combine or compare the items in two or more sets. These methods have strange names, since they use the same terminology used in mathematics. We'll start with three methods that return the same result, regardless of which is the calling set and which is the called set.

The `union` method is the most common and easiest to understand. It takes a second set as a parameter and returns a new set that contains all elements that are in *either* of the two sets; if an element is in both original sets, it will, of course, only show up once in the new set. Union is like a logical `or` operation, indeed, the `|` operator can be used on two sets to perform the union operation, if you don't like calling methods.

Conversely, the intersection method accepts a second set and returns a new set that contains only those elements that are in *both* sets. It is like a logical `and` operation, and can also be referenced using the `&` operator.

Finally, the `symmetric_difference` method tells us what's left; it is the set of objects that are in one set or the other, but not both. The following example illustrates these methods by comparing some artists from my song library to those in my sister's:

```
my_artists = {"Sarah Brightman", "Guns N' Roses",
        "Opeth", "Vixy and Tony"}

auburns_artists = {"Nickelback", "Guns N' Roses",
        "Savage Garden"}

print("All: {}".format(my_artists.union(auburns_artists)))
print("Both: {}".format(auburns_artists.intersection(my_artists)))
print("Either but not both: {}".format(
    my_artists.symmetric_difference(auburns_artists)))
```

If we run this code, we see that these three methods do what the print statements suggest they will do:

```
All: {'Sarah Brightman', "Guns N' Roses", 'Vixy and Tony',
'Savage Garden', 'Opeth', 'Nickelback'}
Both: {"Guns N' Roses"}
Either but not both: {'Savage Garden', 'Opeth', 'Nickelback',
'Sarah Brightman', 'Vixy and Tony'}
```

These methods all return the same result, regardless of which set calls the other. We can say `my_artists.union(auburns_artists)` or `auburns_artists.union(my_artists)` and get the same result. There are also methods that return different results depending on who is the caller and who is the argument.

These methods include `issubset` and `issuperset`, which are the inverse of each other. Both return a `bool`. The `issubset` method returns `True`, if all of the items in the calling set are also in the set passed as an argument. The `issuperset` method returns `True` if all of the items in the argument are also in the calling set. Thus `s.issubset(t)` and `t.issuperset(s)` are identical. They will both return `True` if `t` contains all the elements in `s`.

Finally, the `difference` method returns all the elements that are in the calling set, but not in the set passed as an argument; this is like half a `symmetric_difference`. The `difference` method can also be represented by the - operator. The following code illustrates these methods in action:

```
my_artists = {"Sarah Brightman", "Guns N' Roses",
        "Opeth", "Vixy and Tony"}

bands = {"Guns N' Roses", "Opeth"}

print("my_artists is to bands:")
print("issuperset: {}".format(my_artists.issuperset(bands)))
print("issubset: {}".format(my_artists.issubset(bands)))
print("difference: {}".format(my_artists.difference(bands)))
print("*"*20)
print("bands is to my_artists:")
print("issuperset: {}".format(bands.issuperset(my_artists)))
print("issubset: {}".format(bands.issubset(my_artists)))
print("difference: {}".format(bands.difference(my_artists)))
```

This code simply prints out the response of each method when called from one set on the other. Running it gives us the following output:

```
my_artists is to bands:
issuperset: True
issubset: False
difference: {'Sarah Brightman', 'Vixy and Tony'}
********************
bands is to my_artists:
issuperset: False
issubset: True
difference: set()
```

The `difference` method, in the second case, returns an empty set, since there are no items in `bands` that are not in `my_artists`.

The `union`, `intersection`, and `difference` methods can all take multiple sets as arguments; they will return, as we might expect, the set that is created when the operation is called on all the parameters.

So the methods on sets clearly suggest that sets are meant to operate on other sets, and that they are not just containers. If we have data coming in from two different sources and need to quickly combine them in some way, to determine where the data overlaps or is different, we can use set operations to efficiently compare them. Or if we have data incoming that may contain duplicates of data that has already been processed, we can use sets to compare the two and process only the new data.

Finally, it is valuable to know that sets are much more efficient than lists when checking for membership using the `in` keyword. If you use the syntax `value in container` on a set or a list, it will return `True` if one of the elements in `container` is equal to `value` and `False` otherwise. However, in a list, it will look at every object in the container until it finds the value, whereas in a set, it simply hashes the value and checks for membership. This means that a set will find the value in the same amount of time no matter how big the container is, but a list will take longer and longer to search for a value as the list contains more and more values.

Extending built-ins

We discussed briefly in *Chapter 3, When Objects Are Alike*, how built-in data types can be extended using inheritance. Now, we'll go into more detail as to when we would want to do that.

When we have a built-in container object that we want to add functionality to, we have two options. We can either create a new object, which holds that container as an attribute (composition), or we can subclass the built-in object and add or adapt methods on it to do what we want (inheritance).

Composition is usually the best alternative if all we want to do is use the container to store some objects using that container's features. That way, it's easy to pass that data structure into other methods and they will know how to interact with it. But we need to use inheritance if we want to change the way the container actually works. For example, if we want to ensure every item in a `list` is a string with exactly five characters, we need to extend `list` and override the `append()` method to raise an exception for invalid input. We'd also minimally have to override `__setitem__(self, index, value)`, a special method on lists that is called whenever we use the `x[index] = "value"` syntax, and the `extend()` method.

Yes, lists are objects. All that special non-object-oriented looking syntax we've been looking at for accessing lists or dictionary keys, looping over containers, and similar tasks is actually "syntactic sugar" that maps to an object-oriented paradigm underneath. We might ask the Python designers why they did this. Isn't object-oriented programming *always* better? That question is easy to answer. In the following hypothetical examples, which is easier to read, as a programmer? Which requires less typing?

```
c = a + b
c = a.add(b)

l[0] = 5
l.setitem(0, 5)
d[key] = value
d.setitem(key, value)

for x in alist:
    #do something with x
it = alist.iterator()
while it.has_next():
    x = it.next()
    #do something with x
```

The highlighted sections show what object-oriented code might look like (in practice, these methods actually exist as special double-underscore methods on associated objects). Python programmers agree that the non-object-oriented syntax is easier both to read and to write. Yet all of the preceding Python syntaxes map to object-oriented methods underneath the hood. These methods have special names (with double-underscores before and after) to remind us that there is a better syntax out there. However, it gives us the means to override these behaviors. For example, we can make a special integer that always returns 0 when we add two of them together:

```
class SillyInt(int):
    def __add__(self, num):
        return 0
```

This is an extremely bizarre thing to do, granted, but it perfectly illustrates these object-oriented principles in action:

```
>>> a = SillyInt(1)
>>> b = SillyInt(2)
>>> a + b
0
```

The awesome thing about the `__add__` method is that we can add it to any class we write, and if we use the + operator on instances of that class, it will be called. This is how string, tuple, and list concatenation works, for example.

This is true of all the special methods. If we want to use x in `myobj` syntax for a custom-defined object, we can implement `__contains__`. If we want to use `myobj[i] = value` syntax, we supply a `__setitem__` method and if we want to use `something = myobj[i]`, we implement `__getitem__`.

There are 33 of these special methods on the `list` class. We can use the `dir` function to see all of them:

```
>>> dir(list)
```

```
['__add__', '__class__', '__contains__', '__delattr__','__delitem__',
'__doc__', '__eq__', '__format__', '__ge__', '__getattribute__', '__
getitem__', '__gt__', '__hash__', '__iadd__', '__imul__', '__init__',
'__iter__', '__le__', '__len__', '__lt__', '__mul__', '__ne__', '__
new__', '__reduce__', '__reduce_ex__', '__repr__', '__reversed__',
'__rmul__', '__setattr__', '__setitem__', '__sizeof__', '__str__', '__
subclasshook__', 'append', 'count', 'extend', 'index', 'insert', 'pop',
'remove', 'reverse', 'sort'
```

Further, if we desire additional information on how any of these methods works, we can use the `help` function:

```
>>> help(list.__add__)
Help on wrapper_descriptor:


__add__(self, value, /)
    Return self+value.
```

The plus operator on lists concatenates two lists. We don't have room to discuss all of the available special functions in this book, but you are now able to explore all this functionality with `dir` and `help`. The official online Python reference (https://docs.python.org/3/) has plenty of useful information as well. Focus, especially, on the abstract base classes discussed in the `collections` module.

So, to get back to the earlier point about when we would want to use composition versus inheritance: if we need to somehow change any of the methods on the class—including the special methods—we definitely need to use inheritance. If we used composition, we could write methods that do the validation or alterations and ask the caller to use those methods, but there is nothing stopping them from accessing the property directly. They could insert an item into our list that does not have five characters, and that might confuse other methods in the list.

Often, the need to extend a built-in data type is an indication that we're using the wrong sort of data type. It is not always the case, but if we are looking to extend a built-in, we should carefully consider whether or not a different data structure would be more suitable.

For example, consider what it takes to create a dictionary that remembers the order in which keys were inserted. One way to do this is to keep an ordered list of keys that is stored in a specially derived subclass of dict. Then we can override the methods keys, values, __iter__, and items to return everything in order. Of course, we'll also have to override __setitem__ and setdefault to keep our list up to date. There are likely to be a few other methods in the output of dir(dict) that need overriding to keep the list and dictionary consistent (clear and __delitem__ come to mind, to track when items are removed), but we won't worry about them for this example.

So we'll be extending dict and adding a list of ordered keys. Trivial enough, but where do we create the actual list? We could include it in the __init__ method, which would work just fine, but we have no guarantees that any subclass will call that initializer. Remember the __new__ method we discussed in *Chapter 2, Objects in Python*? I said it was generally only useful in very special cases. This is one of those special cases. We know __new__ will be called exactly once, and we can create a list on the new instance that will always be available to our class. With that in mind, here is our entire sorted dictionary:

```python
from collections import KeysView, ItemsView, ValuesView
class DictSorted(dict):
    def __new__(*args, **kwargs):
        new_dict = dict.__new__(*args, **kwargs)
        new_dict.ordered_keys = []
        return new_dict

    def __setitem__(self, key, value):
        '''self[key] = value syntax'''
        if key not in self.ordered_keys:
            self.ordered_keys.append(key)
        super().__setitem__(key, value)

    def setdefault(self, key, value):
        if key not in self.ordered_keys:
            self.ordered_keys.append(key)
        return super().setdefault(key, value)

    def keys(self):
        return KeysView(self)

    def values(self):
```

```
        return ValuesView(self)

    def items(self):
        return ItemsView(self)

    def __iter__(self):
        '''for x in self syntax'''
        return self.ordered_keys.__iter__()
```

The __new__ method creates a new dictionary and then puts an empty list on that
object. We don't override __init__, as the default implementation works (actually,
this is only true if we initialize an empty DictSorted object, which is standard
behavior. If we want to support other variations of the dict constructor, which accept
dictionaries or lists of tuples, we'd need to fix __init__ to also update our ordered_
keys list). The two methods for setting items are very similar; they both update the list
of keys, but only if the item hasn't been added before. We don't want duplicates in the
list, but we can't use a set here; it's unordered!

The keys, items, and values methods all return views onto the dictionary. The
collections library provides three read-only View objects onto the dictionary; they use
the __iter__ method to loop over the keys, and then use __getitem__ (which we
didn't need to override) to retrieve the values. So, we only need to define our custom
__iter__ method to make these three views work. You would think the superclass
would create these views properly using polymorphism, but if we don't override these
three methods, they don't return properly ordered views.

Finally, the __iter__ method is the really special one; it ensures that if we loop over
the dictionary's keys (using for...in syntax), it will return the values in the correct
order. It does this by returning the __iter__ of the ordered_keys list, which returns
the same iterator object that would be used if we used for...in on the list instead.
Since ordered_keys is a list of all available keys (due to the way we overrode other
methods), this is the correct iterator object for the dictionary as well.

Let's look at a few of these methods in action, compared to a normal dictionary:

```
>>> ds = DictSorted()
>>> d = {}
>>> ds['a'] = 1
>>> ds['b'] = 2
>>> ds.setdefault('c', 3)
3
>>> d['a'] = 1
>>> d['b'] = 2
>>> d.setdefault('c', 3)
3
```

```
>>> for k,v in ds.items():
...     print(k,v)
...
a 1
b 2
c 3
>>> for k,v in d.items():
...     print(k,v)
...
a 1
c 3
b 2
```

Ah, our dictionary is sorted and the normal dictionary is not. Hurray!

> If you wanted to use this class in production, you'd have to override several other special methods to ensure the keys are up to date in all cases. However, you don't need to do this; the functionality this class provides is already available in Python, using the OrderedDict object in the collections module. Try importing the class from collections, and use help(OrderedDict) to find out more about it.

Queues

Queues are peculiar data structures because, like sets, their functionality can be handled entirely using lists. However, while lists are extremely versatile general-purpose tools, they are occasionally not the most efficient data structure for container operations. If your program is using a small dataset (up to hundreds or even thousands of elements on today's processors), then lists will probably cover all your use cases. However, if you need to scale your data into the millions, you may need a more efficient container for your particular use case. Python therefore provides three types of queue data structures, depending on what kind of access you are looking for. All three utilize the same API, but differ in both behavior and data structure.

Before we start our queues, however, consider the trusty list data structure. Python lists are the most advantageous data structure for many use cases:

- They support efficient random access to any element in the list

- They have strict ordering of elements
- They support the append operation efficiently

They tend to be slow, however, if you are inserting elements anywhere but the end of the list (especially so if it's the beginning of the list). As we discussed in the section on sets, they are also slow for checking if an element exists in the list, and by extension, searching. Storing data in a sorted order or reordering the data can also be inefficient.

Let's look at the three types of containers provided by the Python `queue` module.

FIFO queues

FIFO stands for **First In First Out** and represents the most commonly understood definition of the word "queue". Imagine a line of people standing in line at a bank or cash register. The first person to enter the line gets served first, the second person in line gets served second, and if a new person desires service, they join the end of the line and wait their turn.

The Python `Queue` class is just like that. It is typically used as a sort of communication medium when one or more objects is producing data and one or more other objects is consuming the data in some way, probably at a different rate. Think of a messaging application that is receiving messages from the network, but can only display one message at a time to the user. The other messages can be buffered in a queue in the order they are received. FIFO queues are utilized a lot in such concurrent applications. (We'll talk more about concurrency in *Chapter 12, Testing Object-oriented Programs*.)

The `Queue` class is a good choice when you don't need to access any data inside the data structure except the next object to be consumed. Using a list for this would be less efficient because under the hood, inserting data at (or removing from) the beginning of a list can require shifting every other element in the list.

Queues have a very simple API. A `Queue` can have "infinite" (until the computer runs out of memory) capacity, but it is more commonly bounded to some maximum size. The primary methods are `put()` and `get()`, which add an element to the back of the line, as it were, and retrieve them from the front, in order. Both of these methods accept optional arguments to govern what happens if the operation cannot successfully complete because the queue is either empty (can't get) or full (can't put). The default behavior is to block or idly wait until the `Queue` object has data or room available to complete the operation. You can have it raise exceptions instead by passing the `block=False` parameter. Or you can have it wait a defined amount of time before raising an exception by passing a `timeout` parameter.

The class also has methods to check whether the Queue is full() or empty() and there are a few additional methods to deal with concurrent access that we won't discuss here. Here is a interactive session demonstrating these principles:

```
>>> from queue import Queue
>>> lineup = Queue(maxsize=3)
>>> lineup.get(block=False)
Traceback (most recent call last):
  File "<ipython-input-5-a1c8d8492c59>", line 1, in <module>
    lineup.get(block=False)
  File "/usr/lib64/python3.3/queue.py", line 164, in get
    raise Empty
queue.Empty
>>> lineup.put("one")
>>> lineup.put("two")
>>> lineup.put("three")
>>> lineup.put("four", timeout=1)
Traceback (most recent call last):
  File "<ipython-input-9-4b9db399883d>", line 1, in <module>
    lineup.put("four", timeout=1)
  File "/usr/lib64/python3.3/queue.py", line 144, in put
raise Full
queue.Full
>>> lineup.full()
True
>>> lineup.get()
'one'
>>> lineup.get()
'two'
>>> lineup.get()
'three'
>>> lineup.empty()
True
```

Underneath the hood, Python implements queues on top of the `collections.deque` data structure. Deques are advanced data structures that permits efficient access to both ends of the collection. It provides a more flexible interface than is exposed by `Queue`. I refer you to the Python documentation if you'd like to experiment more with it.

LIFO queues

LIFO (**Last In First Out**) queues are more frequently called **stacks**. Think of a stack of papers where you can only access the top-most paper. You can put another paper on top of the stack, making it the new top-most paper, or you can take the top-most paper away to reveal the one beneath it.

Traditionally, the operations on stacks are named push and pop, but the Python `queue` module uses the exact same API as for FIFO queues: `put()` and `get()`. However, in a LIFO queue, these methods operate on the "top" of the stack instead of at the front and back of a line. This is an excellent example of polymorphism. If you look at the `Queue` source code in the Python standard library, you'll actually see that there is a superclass with subclasses for FIFO and LIFO queues that implement the few operations (operating on the top of a stack instead of front and back of a `deque` instance) that are critically different between the two.

Here's an example of the LIFO queue in action:

```
>>> from queue import LifoQueue
>>> stack = LifoQueue(maxsize=3)
>>> stack.put("one")
>>> stack.put("two")
>>> stack.put("three")
>>> stack.put("four", block=False)
Traceback (most recent call last):
  File "<ipython-input-21-5473b359e5a8>", line 1, in <module>
    stack.put("four", block=False)
  File "/usr/lib64/python3.3/queue.py", line 133, in put
    raise Full
queue.Full

>>> stack.get()
'three'
>>> stack.get()
```

```
'two'
>>> stack.get()
'one'
>>> stack.empty()
True
>>> stack.get(timeout=1)
Traceback (most recent call last):
  File "<ipython-input-26-28e084a84a10>", line 1, in <module>
    stack.get(timeout=1)
  File "/usr/lib64/python3.3/queue.py", line 175, in get
    raise Empty
queue.Empty
```

You might wonder why you couldn't just use the `append()` and `pop()` methods on a standard list. Quite frankly, that's probably what I would do. I rarely have occasion to use the `LifoQueue` class in production code. Working with the end of a list is an efficient operation; so efficient, in fact, that the `LifoQueue` uses a standard list under the hood!

There are a couple of reasons that you might want to use `LifoQueue` instead of a list. The most important one is that `LifoQueue` supports clean concurrent access from multiple threads. If you need stack-like behavior in a concurrent setting, you should leave the list at home. Second, `LifoQueue` enforces the stack interface. You can't unwittingly insert a value to the wrong position in a `LifoQueue`, for example (although, as an exercise, you can work out how to do this completely wittingly).

Priority queues

The priority queue enforces a very different style of ordering from the previous queue implementations. Once again, they follow the exact same `get()` and `put()` API, but instead of relying on the order that items arrive to determine when they should be returned, the most "important" item is returned. By convention, the most important, or highest priority item is the one that sorts lowest using the less than operator.

A common convention is to store tuples in the priority queue, where the first element in the tuple is the priority for that element, and the second element is the data. Another common paradigm is to implement the `__lt__` method, as we discussed earlier in this chapter. It is perfectly acceptable to have multiple elements with the same priority in the queue, although there are no guarantees on which one will be returned first.

A priority queue might be used, for example, by a search engine to ensure it refreshes the content of the most popular web pages before crawling sites that are less likely to be searched for. A product recommendation tool might use one to display information about the most highly ranked products while still loading data for the lower ranks.

Note that a priority queue will always return the most important element currently in the queue. The get() method will block (by default) if the queue is empty, but it will not block and wait for a higher priority element to be added if there is already something in the queue. The queue knows nothing about elements that have not been added yet (or even about elements that have been previously extracted), and only makes decisions based on the current contents of the queue.

This interactive session shows a priority queue in action, using tuples as weights to determine what order items are processed in:

```
>>> heap.put((3, "three"))
>>> heap.put((4, "four"))
>>> heap.put((1, "one") )
>>> heap.put((2, "two"))
>>> heap.put((5, "five"), block=False)
Traceback (most recent call last):
  File "<ipython-input-23-d4209db364ed>", line 1, in <module>
    heap.put((5, "five"), block=False)
  File "/usr/lib64/python3.3/queue.py", line 133, in put
    raise Full
Full
>>> while not heap.empty():
    print(heap.get())
(1, 'one')
(2, 'two')
(3, 'three')
(4, 'four')
```

Priority queues are almost universally implemented using the heap data structure. Python's implementation utilizes the heapq module to effectively store a heap inside a normal list. I direct you to an algorithm and data-structure's textbook for more information on heaps, not to mention many other fascinating structures we haven't covered here. No matter what the data structure, you can use object-oriented principles to wrap relevant algorithms (behaviors), such as those supplied in the heapq module, around the data they are structuring in the computer's memory, just as the queue module has done on our behalf in the standard library.

Case study

To tie everything together, we'll be writing a simple link collector, which will visit a website and collect every link on every page it finds in that site. Before we start, though, we'll need some test data to work with. Simply write some HTML files to work with that contain links to each other and to other sites on the Internet, something like this:

```
<html>
    <body>
        <a href="contact.html">Contact us</a>
        <a href="blog.html">Blog</a>
        <a href="esme.html">My Dog</a>
        <a href="/hobbies.html">Some hobbies</a>
        <a href="/contact.html">Contact AGAIN</a>
        <a href="http://www.archlinux.org/">Favorite OS</a>
    </body>
</html>
```

Name one of the files `index.html` so it shows up first when pages are served. Make sure the other files exist, and keep things complicated so there is lots of linking between them. The examples for this chapter include a directory called `case_study_serve` (one of the lamest personal websites in existence!) if you would rather not set them up yourself.

Now, start a simple web server by entering the directory containing all these files and run the following command:

python3 -m http.server

This will start a server running on port 8000; you can see the pages you made by visiting `http://localhost:8000/` in your web browser.

> I doubt anyone can get a website up and running with less work! Never let it be said, "you can't do that easily with Python."

The goal will be to pass our collector the base URL for the site (in this case: `http://localhost:8000/`), and have it create a list containing every unique link on the site. We'll need to take into account three types of URLs (links to external sites, which start with `http://`, absolute internal links, which start with a / character, and relative links, for everything else). We also need to be aware that pages may link to each other in a loop; we need to be sure we don't process the same page multiple times, or it may never end. With all this uniqueness going on, it sounds like we're going to need some sets.

Before we get into that, let's start with the basics. What code do we need to connect to a page and parse all the links from that page?

```
from urllib.request import urlopen
from urllib.parse import urlparse
import re
import sys
LINK_REGEX = re.compile(
        "<a [^>]*href=['\"]([^'\"]+)['\"][^>]*>")

class LinkCollector:
    def __init__(self, url):
        self.url = "" + urlparse(url).netloc

    def collect_links(self, path="/"):
        full_url = self.url + path
        page = str(urlopen(full_url).read())
        links = LINK_REGEX.findall(page)
        print(links)

if __name__ == "__main__":
    LinkCollector(sys.argv[1]).collect_links()
```

This is a short piece of code, considering what it's doing. It connects to the server in the argument passed on the command line, downloads the page, and extracts all the links on that page. The __init__ method uses the urlparse function to extract just the hostname from the URL; so even if we pass in http://localhost:8000/some/page. html, it will still operate on the top level of the host http://localhost:8000/. This makes sense, because we want to collect all the links on the site, although it assumes every page is connected to the index by some sequence of links.

The collect_links method connects to and downloads the specified page from the server, and uses a regular expression to find all the links in the page. Regular expressions are an extremely powerful string processing tool. Unfortunately, they have a steep learning curve; if you haven't used them before, I strongly recommend studying any of the entire books or websites on the topic. If you don't think they're worth knowing, try writing the preceding code without them and you'll change your mind.

The example also stops in the middle of the collect_links method to print the value of links. This is a common way to test a program as we're writing it: stop and output the value to ensure it is the value we expect. Here's what it outputs for our example:

```
['contact.html', 'blog.html', 'esme.html', '/hobbies.html',
'/contact.html', 'http://www.archlinux.org/']
```

So now we have a collection of all the links in the first page. What can we do with it? We can't just pop the links into a set to remove duplicates because links may be relative or absolute. For example, `contact.html` and `/contact.html` point to the same page. So the first thing we should do is normalize all the links to their full URL, including hostname and relative path. We can do this by adding a `normalize_url` method to our object:

```python
def normalize_url(self, path, link):
    if link.startswith("http://"):
        return link
    elif link.startswith("/"):
        return self.url + link
    else:
        return self.url + path.rpartition(
            '/')[0] + '/' + link
```

This method converts each URL to a complete address that includes protocol and hostname. Now the two contact pages have the same value and we can store them in a set. We'll have to modify __init__ to create the set, and `collect_links` to put all the links into it.

Then, we'll have to visit all the non-external links and collect them too. But wait a minute; if we do this, how do we keep from revisiting a link when we encounter the same page twice? It looks like we're actually going to need two sets: a set of collected links, and a set of visited links. This suggests that we were wise to choose a set to represent our data; we know that sets are most useful when we're manipulating more than one of them. Let's set these up:

```python
class LinkCollector:
    def __init__(self, url):
        self.url = "http://+" + urlparse(url).netloc
        self.collected_links = set()
        self.visited_links = set()

    def collect_links(self, path="/"):
        full_url = self.url + path
        self.visited_links.add(full_url)
        page = str(urlopen(full_url).read())
        links = LINK_REGEX.findall(page)
        links = {self.normalize_url(path, link
            ) for link in links}
        self.collected_links = links.union(
                self.collected_links)
        unvisited_links = links.difference(
                self.visited_links)
```

```
print(links, self.visited_links,
        self.collected_links, unvisited_links)
```

The line that creates the normalized list of links uses a `set` comprehension, no different from a list comprehension, except that the result is a set of values. We'll be covering these in detail in the next chapter. Once again, the method stops to print out the current values, so we can verify that we don't have our sets confused, and that `difference` really was the method we wanted to call to collect `unvisited_links`. We can then add a few lines of code that loop over all the unvisited links and add them to the collection as well:

```
for link in unvisited_links:
    if link.startswith(self.url):
        self.collect_links(urlparse(link).path)
```

The `if` statement ensures that we are only collecting links from the one website; we don't want to go off and collect all the links from all the pages on the Internet (unless we're Google or the Internet Archive!). If we modify the main code at the bottom of the program to output the collected links, we can see it seems to have collected them all:

```
if __name__ == "__main__":
    collector = LinkCollector(sys.argv[1])
    collector.collect_links()
    for link in collector.collected_links:
        print(link)
```

It displays all the links we've collected, and only once, even though many of the pages in my example linked to each other multiple times:

```
$ python3 link_collector.py http://localhost:8000
http://localhost:8000/
http://en.wikipedia.org/wiki/Cavalier_King_Charles_Spaniel
http://beluminousyoga.com
http://archlinux.me/dusty/
http://localhost:8000/blog.html
http://ccphillips.net/
http://localhost:8000/contact.html
http://localhost:8000/taichi.html
http://www.archlinux.org/
http://localhost:8000/esme.html
http://localhost:8000/hobbies.html
```

Even though it collected links *to* external pages, it didn't go off collecting links *from* any of the external pages we linked to. This is a great little program if we want to collect all the links in a site. But it doesn't give me all the information I might need to build a site map; it tells me which pages I have, but it doesn't tell me which pages link to other pages. If we want to do that instead, we're going to have to make some modifications.

The first thing we should do is look at our data structures. The set of collected links doesn't work anymore; we want to know which links were linked to from which pages. The first thing we could do, then, is turn that set into a dictionary of sets for each page we visit. The dictionary keys will represent the exact same data that is currently in the set. The values will be sets of all the links on that page. Here are the changes:

```
from urllib.request import urlopen
from urllib.parse import urlparse
import re
import sys
LINK_REGEX = re.compile(
        "<a [^>]*href=['\"]([^'\"]+)['\"][^>]*>")

class LinkCollector:
    def __init__(self, url):
        self.url = "http://%s" % urlparse(url).netloc
        self.collected_links = {}
        self.visited_links = set()

    def collect_links(self, path="/"):
        full_url = self.url + path
        self.visited_links.add(full_url)
        page = str(urlopen(full_url).read())
        links = LINK_REGEX.findall(page)
        links = {self.normalize_url(path, link
            ) for link in links}
        self.collected_links[full_url] = links
        for link in links:
            self.collected_links.setdefault(link, set())
        unvisited_links = links.difference(
                self.visited_links)
        for link in unvisited_links:
            if link.startswith(self.url):
                self.collect_links(urlparse(link).path)

    def normalize_url(self, path, link):
        if link.startswith("http://"):
```

```
                    return link
           elif link.startswith("/"):
                return self.url + link
           else:
                return self.url + path.rpartition('/'
                         )[0] + '/' + link
   if __name__ == "__main__":
       collector = LinkCollector(sys.argv[1])
       collector.collect_links()
       for link, item in collector.collected_links.items():
           print("{}: {}".format(link, item))
```

It is a surprisingly small change; the line that originally created a union of two sets has been replaced with three lines that update the dictionary. The first of these simply tells the dictionary what the collected links for that page are. The second creates an empty set for any items in the dictionary that have not already been added to the dictionary, using `setdefault`. The result is a dictionary that contains all the links as its keys, mapped to sets of links for all the internal links, and empty sets for the external links.

Finally, instead of recursively calling `collect_links`, we can use a queue to store the links that haven't been processed yet. This implementation won't support it, but this would be a good first step to creating a multithreaded version that makes multiple requests in parallel to save time.

```
from urllib.request import urlopen
from urllib.parse import urlparse
import re
import sys
from queue import Queue
LINK_REGEX = re.compile("<a [^>]*href=['\"]([^'\"]+)['\"][^>]*>")


class LinkCollector:
    def __init__(self, url):
        self.url = "http://%s" % urlparse(url).netloc
        self.collected_links = {}
        self.visited_links = set()

    def collect_links(self):
        queue = Queue()
        queue.put(self.url)
        while not queue.empty():
            url = queue.get().rstrip('/')
            self.visited_links.add(url)
            page = str(urlopen(url).read())
```

```
                links = LINK_REGEX.findall(page)
                links = {
                    self.normalize_url(urlparse(url).path, link)
                    for link in links
                }
                self.collected_links[url] = links
                for link in links:
                    self.collected_links.setdefault(link, set())
                unvisited_links = links.difference(self.visited_links)
                for link in unvisited_links:
                    if link.startswith(self.url):
                        queue.put(link)

    def normalize_url(self, path, link):
        if link.startswith("http://"):
            return link.rstrip('/')
        elif link.startswith("/"):
            return self.url + link.rstrip('/')
        else:
            return self.url + path.rpartition('/')[0] + '/' + link.
rstrip('/')


if __name__ == "__main__":
    collector = LinkCollector(sys.argv[1])
    collector.collect_links()
    for link, item in collector.collected_links.items():
        print("%s: %s" % (link, item))
```

I had to manually strip any trailing forward slashes in the `normalize_url` method to remove duplicates in this version of the code.

Because the end result is an unsorted dictionary, there is no restriction on what order the links should be processed in. Therefore, we could just as easily have used a `LifoQueue` instead of a `Queue` here. A priority queue probably wouldn't make a lot of sense since there is no obvious priority to attach to a link in this case.

Exercises

The best way to learn how to choose the correct data structure is to do it wrong a few times. Take some code you've recently written, or write some new code that uses a list. Try rewriting it using some different data structures. Which ones make more sense? Which ones don't? Which have the most elegant code?

Try this with a few different pairs of data structures. You can look at examples you've done for previous chapter exercises. Are there objects with methods where you could have used `namedtuple` or `dict` instead? Attempt both and see. Are there dictionaries that could have been sets because you don't really access the values? Do you have lists that check for duplicates? Would a set suffice? Or maybe several sets? Would one of the queue implementations be more efficient? Is it useful to restrict the API to the top of a stack rather than allowing random access to the list?

If you want some specific examples to work with, try adapting the link collector to also save the title used for each link. Perhaps you can generate a site map in HTML that lists all the pages on the site, and contains a list of links to other pages, named with the same link titles.

Have you written any container objects recently that you could improve by inheriting a built-in and overriding some of the "special" double-underscore methods? You may have to do some research (using `dir` and `help`, or the Python library reference) to find out which methods need overriding. Are you sure inheritance is the correct tool to apply; could a composition-based solution be more effective? Try both (if it's possible) before you decide. Try to find different situations where each method is better than the other.

If you were familiar with the various Python data structures and their uses before you started this chapter, you may have been bored. But if that is the case, there's a good chance you use data structures too much! Look at some of your old code and rewrite it to use more self-made objects. Carefully consider the alternatives and try them all out; which one makes for the most readable and maintainable system?

Always critically evaluate your code and design decisions. Make a habit of reviewing old code and take note if your understanding of "good design" has changed since you've written it. Software design has a large aesthetic component, and like artists with oil on canvas, we all have to find the style that suits us best.

Summary

We've covered several built-in data structures and attempted to understand how to choose one for specific applications. Sometimes, the best thing we can do is create a new class of objects, but often, one of the built-ins provides exactly what we need. When it doesn't, we can always use inheritance or composition to adapt them to our use cases. We can even override special methods to completely change the behavior of built-in syntaxes.

In the next chapter, we'll discuss how to integrate the object-oriented and not-so-object-oriented aspects of Python. Along the way, we'll discover that it's more object-oriented than it looks at first sight!

7
Python Object-oriented Shortcuts

There are many aspects of Python that appear more reminiscent of structural or functional programming than object-oriented programming. Although object-oriented programming has been the most visible paradigm of the past two decades, the old models have seen a recent resurgence. As with Python's data structures, most of these tools are syntactic sugar over an underlying object-oriented implementation; we can think of them as a further abstraction layer built on top of the (already abstracted) object-oriented paradigm. In this chapter, we'll be covering a grab bag of Python features that are not strictly object-oriented:

- Built-in functions that take care of common tasks in one call
- File I/O and context managers
- An alternative to method overloading
- Functions as objects

Python built-in functions

There are numerous functions in Python that perform a task or calculate a result on certain types of objects without being methods on the underlying class. They usually abstract common calculations that apply to multiple types of classes. This is duck typing at its best; these functions accept objects that have certain attributes or methods, and are able to perform generic operations using those methods. Many, but not all, of these are special double underscore methods. We've used many of the built-in functions already, but let's quickly go through the important ones and pick up a few neat tricks along the way.

The len() function

The simplest example is the `len()` function, which counts the number of items in some kind of container object, such as a dictionary or list. You've seen it before:

```
>>> len([1,2,3,4])
4
```

Why don't these objects have a length property instead of having to call a function on them? Technically, they do. Most objects that `len()` will apply to have a method called `__len__()` that returns the same value. So `len(myobj)` seems to call `myobj.__len__()`.

Why should we use the `len()` function instead of the `__len__` method? Obviously `__len__` is a special double-underscore method, suggesting that we shouldn't call it directly. There must be an explanation for this. The Python developers don't make such design decisions lightly.

The main reason is efficiency. When we call `__len__` on an object, the object has to look the method up in its namespace, and, if the special `__getattribute__` method (which is called every time an attribute or method on an object is accessed) is defined on that object, it has to be called as well. Further, `__getattribute__` for that particular method may have been written to do something nasty, like refusing to give us access to special methods such as `__len__`! The `len()` function doesn't encounter any of this. It actually calls the `__len__` function on the underlying class, so `len(myobj)` maps to `MyObj.__len__(myobj)`.

Another reason is maintainability. In the future, the Python developers may want to change `len()` so that it can calculate the length of objects that don't have `__len__`, for example, by counting the number of items returned in an iterator. They'll only have to change one function instead of countless `__len__` methods across the board.

There is one other extremely important and often overlooked reason for `len()` being an external function: backwards compatibility. This is often cited in articles as "for historical reasons", which is a mildly dismissive phrase that an author will use to say something is the way it is because a mistake was made long ago and we're stuck with it. Strictly speaking, `len()` isn't a mistake, it's a design decision, but that decision was made in a less object-oriented time. It has stood the test of time and has some benefits, so do get used to it.

Reversed

The `reversed()` function takes any sequence as input, and returns a copy of that sequence in reverse order. It is normally used in `for` loops when we want to loop over items from back to front.

Similar to `len`, `reversed` calls the `__reversed__()` function on the class for the parameter. If that method does not exist, `reversed` builds the reversed sequence itself using calls to `__len__` and `__getitem__`, which are used to define a sequence. We only need to override `__reversed__` if we want to somehow customize or optimize the process:

```
normal_list=[1,2,3,4,5]

class CustomSequence():
    def __len__(self):
        return 5


    def __getitem__(self, index):
        return "x{0}".format(index)

class FunkyBackwards():

    def __reversed__(self):
        return "BACKWARDS!"

for seq in normal_list, CustomSequence(), FunkyBackwards():
    print("\n{}: ".format(seq.__class__.__name__), end="")
    for item in reversed(seq):
        print(item, end=", ")
```

The `for` loops at the end print the reversed versions of a normal list, and instances of the two custom sequences. The output shows that `reversed` works on all three of them, but has very different results when we define `__reversed__` ourselves:

```
list: 5, 4, 3, 2, 1,
CustomSequence: x4, x3, x2, x1, x0,
FunkyBackwards: B, A, C, K, W, A, R, D, S, !,
```

When we reverse `CustomSequence`, the `__getitem__` method is called for each item, which just inserts an x before the index. For `FunkyBackwards`, the `__reversed__` method returns a string, each character of which is output individually in the `for` loop.

> The preceding two classes aren't very good sequences as they don't define a proper version of `__iter__`, so a forward `for` loop over them will never end.

Enumerate

Sometimes, when we're looping over a container in a `for` loop, we want access to the index (the current position in the list) of the current item being processed. The `for` loop doesn't provide us with indexes, but the `enumerate` function gives us something better: it creates a sequence of tuples, where the first object in each tuple is the index and the second is the original item.

This is useful if we need to use index numbers directly. Consider some simple code that outputs each of the lines in a file with line numbers:

```python
import sys
filename = sys.argv[1]

with open(filename) as file:
    for index, line in enumerate(file):
        print("{0}: {1}".format(index+1, line), end='')
```

Running this code using it's own filename as the input file shows how it works:

```
1: import sys
2: filename = sys.argv[1]
3:
4: with open(filename) as file:
5:     for index, line in enumerate(file):
6:         print("{0}: {1}".format(index+1, line), end='')
```

The `enumerate` function returns a sequence of tuples, our `for` loop splits each tuple into two values, and the `print` statement formats them together. It adds one to the index for each line number, since `enumerate`, like all sequences, is zero-based.

We've only touched on a few of the more important Python built-in functions. As you can see, many of them call into object-oriented concepts, while others subscribe to purely functional or procedural paradigms. There are numerous others in the standard library; some of the more interesting ones include:

- `all` and `any`, which accept an iterable object and return `True` if all, or any, of the items evaluate to true (such as a nonempty string or list, a nonzero number, an object that is not `None`, or the literal `True`).

- `eval`, `exec`, and `compile`, which execute string as code inside the interpreter. Be careful with these ones; they are not safe, so don't execute code an unknown user has supplied to you (in general, assume all unknown users are malicious, foolish, or both).

- `hasattr`, `getattr`, `setattr`, and `delattr`, which allow attributes on an object to be manipulated by their string names.

- `zip`, which takes two or more sequences and returns a new sequence of tuples, where each tuple contains a single value from each sequence.

- And many more! See the interpreter help documentation for each of the functions listed in `dir(__builtins__)`.

File I/O

Our examples so far that touch the filesystem have operated entirely on text files without much thought to what is going on under the hood. Operating systems, however, actually represent files as a sequence of bytes, not text. We'll do a deep dive into the relationship between bytes and text in *Chapter 8, Strings and Serialization*. For now, be aware that reading textual data from a file is a fairly involved process. Python, especially Python 3, takes care of most of this work for us behind the scenes. Aren't we lucky?

The concept of files has been around since long before anyone coined the term object-oriented programming. However, Python has wrapped the interface that operating systems provide in a sweet abstraction that allows us to work with file (or file-like, vis-á-vis duck typing) objects.

The `open()` built-in function is used to open a file and return a file object. For reading text from a file, we only need to pass the name of the file into the function. The file will be opened for reading, and the bytes will be converted to text using the platform default encoding.

Of course, we don't always want to read files; often we want to write data to them! To open a file for writing, we need to pass a `mode` argument as the second positional argument, with a value of `"w"`:

```
contents = "Some file contents"
file = open("filename", "w")
file.write(contents)
file.close()
```

We could also supply the value `"a"` as a mode argument, to append to the end of the file, rather than completely overwriting existing file contents.

These files with built-in wrappers for converting bytes to text are great, but it'd be awfully inconvenient if the file we wanted to open was an image, executable, or other binary file, wouldn't it?

To open a binary file, we modify the mode string to append 'b'. So, 'wb' would open a file for writing bytes, while 'rb' allows us to read them. They will behave like text files, but without the automatic encoding of text to bytes. When we read such a file, it will return bytes objects instead of str, and when we write to it, it will fail if we try to pass a text object.

> These mode strings for controlling how files are opened are rather cryptic and are neither pythonic nor object-oriented. However, they are consistent with virtually every other programming language out there. File I/O is one of the fundamental jobs an operating system has to handle, and all programming languages have to talk to the OS using the same system calls. Just be glad that Python returns a file object with useful methods instead of the integer that most major operating systems use to identify a file handle!

Once a file is opened for reading, we can call the read, readline, or readlines methods to get the contents of the file. The read method returns the entire contents of the file as a str or bytes object, depending on whether there is 'b' in the mode. Be careful not to use this method without arguments on huge files. You don't want to find out what happens if you try to load that much data into memory!

It is also possible to read a fixed number of bytes from a file; we pass an integer argument to the read method describing how many bytes we want to read. The next call to read will load the next sequence of bytes, and so on. We can do this inside a while loop to read the entire file in manageable chunks.

The readline method returns a single line from the file (where each line ends in a newline, a carriage return, or both, depending on the operating system on which the file was created). We can call it repeatedly to get additional lines. The plural readlines method returns a list of all the lines in the file. Like the read method, it's not safe to use on very large files. These two methods even work when the file is open in bytes mode, but it only makes sense if we are parsing text-like data that has newlines at reasonable positions. An image or audio file, for example, will not have newline characters in it (unless the newline byte happened to represent a certain pixel or sound), so applying readline wouldn't make sense.

For readability, and to avoid reading a large file into memory at once, it is often better to use a for loop directly on a file object. For text files, it will read each line, one at a time, and we can process it inside the loop body. For binary files, it's better to read fixed-sized chunks of data using the read() method, passing a parameter for the maximum number of bytes to read.

Writing to a file is just as easy; the `write` method on file objects writes a string (or bytes, for binary data) object to the file. It can be called repeatedly to write multiple strings, one after the other. The `writelines` method accepts a sequence of strings and writes each of the iterated values to the file. The `writelines` method does *not* append a new line after each item in the sequence. It is basically a poorly named convenience function to write the contents of a sequence of strings without having to explicitly iterate over it using a `for` loop.

Lastly, and I do mean lastly, we come to the `close` method. This method should be called when we are finished reading or writing the file, to ensure any buffered writes are written to the disk, that the file has been properly cleaned up, and that all resources associated with the file are released back to the operating system. Technically, this will happen automatically when the script exits, but it's better to be explicit and clean up after ourselves, especially in long-running processes.

Placing it in context

The need to close files when we are finished with them can make our code quite ugly. Because an exception may occur at any time during file I/O, we ought to wrap all calls to a file in a `try...finally` clause. The file should be closed in the `finally` clause, regardless of whether I/O was successful. This isn't very Pythonic. Of course, there is a more elegant way to do it.

If we run `dir` on a file-like object, we see that it has two special methods named `__enter__` and `__exit__`. These methods turn the file object into what is known as a **context manager**. Basically, if we use a special syntax called the `with` statement, these methods will be called before and after nested code is executed. On file objects, the `__exit__` method ensures the file is closed, even if an exception is raised. We no longer have to explicitly manage the closing of the file. Here is what the `with` statement looks like in practice:

```
with open('filename') as file:
    for line in file:
        print(line, end='')
```

The `open` call returns a file object, which has `__enter__` and `__exit__` methods. The returned object is assigned to the variable named `file` by the `as` clause. We know the file will be closed when the code returns to the outer indentation level, and that this will happen even if an exception is raised.

The `with` statement is used in several places in the standard library where startup or cleanup code needs to be executed. For example, the `urlopen` call returns an object that can be used in a `with` statement to clean up the socket when we're done. Locks in the threading module can automatically release the lock when the statement has been executed.

Most interestingly, because the `with` statement can apply to any object that has the appropriate special methods, we can use it in our own frameworks. For example, remember that strings are immutable, but sometimes you need to build a string from multiple parts. For efficiency, this is usually done by storing the component strings in a list and joining them at the end. Let's create a simple context manager that allows us to construct a sequence of characters and automatically convert it to a string upon exit:

```python
class StringJoiner(list):
    def __enter__(self):
        return self

    def __exit__(self, type, value, tb):
        self.result = "".join(self)
```

This code adds the two special methods required of a context manager to the `list` class it inherits from. The `__enter__` method performs any required setup code (in this case, there isn't any) and then returns the object that will be assigned to the variable after `as` in the `with` statement. Often, as we've done here, this is just the context manager object itself. The `__exit__` method accepts three arguments. In a normal situation, these are all given a value of `None`. However, if an exception occurs inside the `with` block, they will be set to values related to the type, value, and traceback for the exception. This allows the `__exit__` method to do any cleanup code that may be required, even if an exception occurred. In our example, we take the irresponsible path and create a result string by joining the characters in the string, regardless of whether an exception was thrown.

While this is one of the simplest context managers we could write, and its usefulness is dubious, it does work with a `with` statement. Have a look at it in action:

```python
import random, string
with StringJoiner() as joiner:
    for i in range(15):
        joiner.append(random.choice(string.ascii_letters))

print(joiner.result)
```

This code constructs a string of 15 random characters. It appends these to a StringJoiner using the append method it inherited from list. When the with statement goes out of scope (back to the outer indentation level), the __exit__ method is called, and the result attribute becomes available on the joiner object. We print this value to see a random string.

An alternative to method overloading

One prominent feature of many object-oriented programming languages is a tool called **method overloading**. Method overloading simply refers to having multiple methods with the same name that accept different sets of arguments. In statically typed languages, this is useful if we want to have a method that accepts either an integer or a string, for example. In non-object-oriented languages, we might need two functions, called add_s and add_i, to accommodate such situations. In statically typed object-oriented languages, we'd need two methods, both called add, one that accepts strings, and one that accepts integers.

In Python, we only need one method, which accepts any type of object. It may have to do some testing on the object type (for example, if it is a string, convert it to an integer), but only one method is required.

However, method overloading is also useful when we want a method with the same name to accept different numbers or sets of arguments. For example, an e-mail message method might come in two versions, one of which accepts an argument for the "from" e-mail address. The other method might look up a default "from" e-mail address instead. Python doesn't permit multiple methods with the same name, but it does provide a different, equally flexible, interface.

We've seen some of the possible ways to send arguments to methods and functions in previous examples, but now we'll cover all the details. The simplest function accepts no arguments. We probably don't need an example, but here's one for completeness:

```
def no_args():
    pass
```

Here's how it's called:

```
no_args()
```

A function that does accept arguments will provide the names of those arguments in a comma-separated list. Only the name of each argument needs to be supplied.

When calling the function, these positional arguments must be specified in order, and none can be missed or skipped. This is the most common way we've specified arguments in our previous examples:

```
def mandatory_args(x, y, z):
    pass
```

To call it:

```
mandatory_args("a string", a_variable, 5)
```

Any type of object can be passed as an argument: an object, a container, a primitive, even functions and classes. The preceding call shows a hardcoded string, an unknown variable, and an integer passed into the function.

Default arguments

If we want to make an argument optional, rather than creating a second method with a different set of arguments, we can specify a default value in a single method, using an equals sign. If the calling code does not supply this argument, it will be assigned a default value. However, the calling code can still choose to override the default by passing in a different value. Often, a default value of None, or an empty string or list is suitable.

Here's a function definition with default arguments:

```
def default_arguments(x, y, z, a="Some String", b=False):
    pass
```

The first three arguments are still mandatory and must be passed by the calling code. The last two parameters have default arguments supplied.

There are several ways we can call this function. We can supply all arguments in order as though all the arguments were positional arguments:

```
default_arguments("a string", variable, 8, "", True)
```

Alternatively, we can supply just the mandatory arguments in order, leaving the keyword arguments to be assigned their default values:

```
default_arguments("a longer string", some_variable, 14)
```

We can also use the equals sign syntax when calling a function to provide values in a different order, or to skip default values that we aren't interested in. For example, we can skip the first keyword arguments and supply the second one:

```
default_arguments("a string", variable, 14, b=True)
```

Surprisingly, we can even use the equals sign syntax to mix up the order of positional arguments, so long as all of them are supplied:

```
>>> default_arguments(y=1,z=2,x=3,a="hi")
3 1 2 hi False
```

With so many options, it may seem hard to pick one, but if you think of the positional arguments as an ordered list, and keyword arguments as sort of like a dictionary, you'll find that the correct layout tends to fall into place. If you need to require the caller to specify an argument, make it mandatory; if you have a sensible default, then make it a keyword argument. Choosing how to call the method normally takes care of itself, depending on which values need to be supplied, and which can be left at their defaults.

One thing to take note of with keyword arguments is that anything we provide as a default argument is evaluated when the function is first interpreted, not when it is called. This means we can't have dynamically generated default values. For example, the following code won't behave quite as expected:

```
number = 5
def funky_function(number=number):
    print(number)

number=6
funky_function(8)
funky_function()
print(number)
```

If we run this code, it outputs the number 8 first, but then it outputs the number 5 for the call with no arguments. We had set the variable to the number 6, as evidenced by the last line of output, but when the function is called, the number 5 is printed; the default value was calculated when the function was defined, not when it was called.

This is tricky with empty containers such as lists, sets, and dictionaries. For example, it is common to ask calling code to supply a list that our function is going to manipulate, but the list is optional. We'd like to make an empty list as a default argument. We can't do this; it will create only one list, when the code is first constructed:

```
>>> def hello(b=[]):
...     b.append('a')
...     print(b)
...
```

```
>>> hello()
['a']
>>> hello()
['a', 'a']
```

Whoops, that's not quite what we expected! The usual way to get around this is to make the default value `None`, and then use the idiom `iargument = argument if argument else []` inside the method. Pay close attention!

Variable argument lists

Default values alone do not allow us all the flexible benefits of method overloading. The thing that makes Python really slick is the ability to write methods that accept an arbitrary number of positional or keyword arguments without explicitly naming them. We can also pass arbitrary lists and dictionaries into such functions.

For example, a function to accept a link or list of links and download the web pages could use such variadic arguments, or **varargs**. Instead of accepting a single value that is expected to be a list of links, we can accept an arbitrary number of arguments, where each argument is a different link. We do this by specifying the * operator in the function definition:

```
def get_pages(*links):
    for link in links:
        #download the link with urllib
        print(link)
```

The `*links` parameter says "I'll accept any number of arguments and put them all in a list named `links`". If we supply only one argument, it'll be a list with one element; if we supply no arguments, it'll be an empty list. Thus, all these function calls are valid:

```
get_pages()
get_pages('http://www.archlinux.org')
get_pages('http://www.archlinux.org',
        'http://ccphillips.net/')
```

We can also accept arbitrary keyword arguments. These arrive into the function as a dictionary. They are specified with two asterisks (as in `**kwargs`) in the function declaration. This tool is commonly used in configuration setups. The following class allows us to specify a set of options with default values:

```
class Options:
    default_options = {
```

```
            'port': 21,
            'host': 'localhost',
            'username': None,
            'password': None,
            'debug': False,
            }
    def __init__(self, **kwargs):
        self.options = dict(Options.default_options)
        self.options.update(kwargs)

    def __getitem__(self, key):
        return self.options[key]
```

All the interesting stuff in this class happens in the __init__ method. We have a dictionary of default options and values at the class level. The first thing the __init__ method does is make a copy of this dictionary. We do that instead of modifying the dictionary directly in case we instantiate two separate sets of options. (Remember, class-level variables are shared between instances of the class.) Then, __init__ uses the update method on the new dictionary to change any non-default values to those supplied as keyword arguments. The __getitem__ method simply allows us to use the new class using indexing syntax. Here's a session demonstrating the class in action:

```
>>> options = Options(username="dusty", password="drowssap",
        debug=True)
>>> options['debug']
True
>>> options['port']
21
>>> options['username']
'dusty'
```

We're able to access our options instance using dictionary indexing syntax, and the dictionary includes both default values and the ones we set using keyword arguments.

The keyword argument syntax can be dangerous, as it may break the "explicit is better than implicit" rule. In the preceding example, it's possible to pass arbitrary keyword arguments to the Options initializer to represent options that don't exist in the default dictionary. This may not be a bad thing, depending on the purpose of the class, but it makes it hard for someone using the class to discover what valid options are available. It also makes it easy to enter a confusing typo ("Debug" instead of "debug", for example) that adds two options where only one should have existed.

Keyword arguments are also very useful when we need to accept arbitrary arguments to pass to a second function, but we don't know what those arguments will be. We saw this in action in *Chapter 3, When Objects Are Alike,* when we were building support for multiple inheritance. We can, of course, combine the variable argument and variable keyword argument syntax in one function call, and we can use normal positional and default arguments as well. The following example is somewhat contrived, but demonstrates the four types in action:

```python
import shutil
import os.path
def augmented_move(target_folder, *filenames,
        verbose=False, **specific):
    '''Move all filenames into the target_folder, allowing
    specific treatment of certain files.'''

    def print_verbose(message, filename):
        '''print the message only if verbose is enabled'''
        if verbose:
            print(message.format(filename))

    for filename in filenames:
        target_path = os.path.join(target_folder, filename)
        if filename in specific:
            if specific[filename] == 'ignore':
                print_verbose("Ignoring {0}", filename)
            elif specific[filename] == 'copy':
                print_verbose("Copying {0}", filename)
                shutil.copyfile(filename, target_path)
        else:
            print_verbose("Moving {0}", filename)
            shutil.move(filename, target_path)
```

This example will process an arbitrary list of files. The first argument is a target folder, and the default behavior is to move all remaining non-keyword argument files into that folder. Then there is a keyword-only argument, verbose, which tells us whether to print information on each file processed. Finally, we can supply a dictionary containing actions to perform on specific filenames; the default behavior is to move the file, but if a valid string action has been specified in the keyword arguments, it can be ignored or copied instead. Notice the ordering of the parameters in the function; first the positional argument is specified, then the *filenames list, then any specific keyword-only arguments, and finally, a **specific dictionary to hold remaining keyword arguments.

We create an inner helper function, `print_verbose`, which will print messages only if the `verbose` key has been set. This function keeps code readable by encapsulating this functionality into a single location.

In common cases, assuming the files in question exist, this function could be called as:

```
>>> augmented_move("move_here", "one", "two")
```

This command would move the files `one` and `two` into the `move_here` directory, assuming they exist (there's no error checking or exception handling in the function, so it would fail spectacularly if the files or target directory didn't exist). The move would occur without any output, since `verbose` is `False` by default.

If we want to see the output, we can call it with:

```
>>> augmented_move("move_here", "three", verbose=True)
Moving three
```

This moves one file named `three`, and tells us what it's doing. Notice that it is impossible to specify `verbose` as a positional argument in this example; we must pass a keyword argument. Otherwise, Python would think it was another filename in the `*filenames` list.

If we want to copy or ignore some of the files in the list, instead of moving them, we can pass additional keyword arguments:

```
>>> augmented_move("move_here", "four", "five", "six",
        four="copy", five="ignore")
```

This will move the sixth file and copy the fourth, but won't display any output, since we didn't specify `verbose`. Of course, we can do that too, and keyword arguments can be supplied in any order:

```
>>> augmented_move("move_here", "seven", "eight", "nine",
        seven="copy", verbose=True, eight="ignore")
Copying seven
Ignoring eight
Moving nine
```

Unpacking arguments

There's one more nifty trick involving variable arguments and keyword arguments. We've used it in some of our previous examples, but it's never too late for an explanation. Given a list or dictionary of values, we can pass those values into a function as if they were normal positional or keyword arguments. Have a look at this code:

```python
def show_args(arg1, arg2, arg3="THREE"):
    print(arg1, arg2, arg3)

some_args = range(3)
more_args = {
        "arg1": "ONE",
        "arg2": "TWO"}

print("Unpacking a sequence:", end=" ")

show_args(*some_args)
print("Unpacking a dict:", end=" ")

show_args(**more_args)
```

Here's what it looks like when we run it:

Unpacking a sequence: 0 1 2

Unpacking a dict: ONE TWO THREE

The function accepts three arguments, one of which has a default value. But when we have a list of three arguments, we can use the * operator inside a function call to unpack it into the three arguments. If we have a dictionary of arguments, we can use the ** syntax to unpack it as a collection of keyword arguments.

This is most often useful when mapping information that has been collected from user input or from an outside source (for example, an Internet page or a text file) to a function or method call.

Remember our earlier example that used headers and lines in a text file to create a list of dictionaries with contact information? Instead of just adding the dictionaries to a list, we could use keyword unpacking to pass the arguments to the __init__ method on a specially built Contact object that accepts the same set of arguments. See if you can adapt the example to make this work.

Functions are objects too

Programming languages that overemphasize object-oriented principles tend to frown on functions that are not methods. In such languages, you're expected to create an object to sort of wrap the single method involved. There are numerous situations where we'd like to pass around a small object that is simply called to perform an action. This is most frequently done in event-driven programming, such as graphical toolkits or asynchronous servers; we'll see some design patterns that use it in *Chapter 10, Python Design Patterns I* and *Chapter 11, Python Design Patterns II*.

In Python, we don't need to wrap such methods in an object, because functions already are objects! We can set attributes on functions (though this isn't a common activity), and we can pass them around to be called at a later date. They even have a few special properties that can be accessed directly. Here's yet another contrived example:

```python
def my_function():
    print("The Function Was Called")
my_function.description = "A silly function"

def second_function():
    print("The second was called")
second_function.description = "A sillier function."

def another_function(function):
    print("The description:", end=" ")
    print(function.description)
    print("The name:", end=" ")
    print(function.__name__)
    print("The class:", end=" ")
    print(function.__class__)
    print("Now I'll call the function passed in")
    function()

another_function(my_function)
another_function(second_function)
```

If we run this code, we can see that we were able to pass two different functions into our third function, and get different output for each one:

```
The description: A silly function
The name: my_function
The class: <class 'function'>
Now I'll call the function passed in
```

```
The Function Was Called
The description: A sillier function.
The name: second_function
The class: <class 'function'>
Now I'll call the function passed in
The second was called
```

We set an attribute on the function, named `description` (not very good descriptions, admittedly). We were also able to see the function's `__name__` attribute, and to access its class, demonstrating that the function really is an object with attributes. Then we called the function by using the callable syntax (the parentheses).

The fact that functions are top-level objects is most often used to pass them around to be executed at a later date, for example, when a certain condition has been satisfied. Let's build an event-driven timer that does just this:

```python
import datetime
import time

class TimedEvent:
    def __init__(self, endtime, callback):
        self.endtime = endtime
        self.callback = callback

    def ready(self):
        return self.endtime <= datetime.datetime.now()

class Timer:
    def __init__(self):
        self.events = []

    def call_after(self, delay, callback):
        end_time = datetime.datetime.now() + \
                datetime.timedelta(seconds=delay)

        self.events.append(TimedEvent(end_time, callback))

    def run(self):
        while True:
            ready_events = (e for e in self.events if e.ready())
            for event in ready_events:
                event.callback(self)
                self.events.remove(event)
            time.sleep(0.5)
```

In production, this code should definitely have extra documentation using docstrings! The `call_after` method should at least mention that the `delay` parameter is in seconds, and that the `callback` function should accept one argument: the timer doing the calling.

We have two classes here. The `TimedEvent` class is not really meant to be accessed by other classes; all it does is store `endtime` and `callback`. We could even use a `tuple` or `namedtuple` here, but as it is convenient to give the object a behavior that tells us whether or not the event is ready to run, we use a class instead.

The `Timer` class simply stores a list of upcoming events. It has a `call_after` method to add a new event. This method accepts a `delay` parameter representing the number of seconds to wait before executing the callback, and the `callback` function itself: a function to be executed at the correct time. This `callback` function should accept one argument.

The `run` method is very simple; it uses a generator expression to filter out any events whose time has come, and executes them in order. The timer loop then continues indefinitely, so it has to be interrupted with a keyboard interrupt (*Ctrl + C* or *Ctrl + Break*). We sleep for half a second after each iteration so as to not grind the system to a halt.

The important things to note here are the lines that touch callback functions. The function is passed around like any other object and the timer never knows or cares what the original name of the function is or where it was defined. When it's time to call the function, the timer simply applies the parenthesis syntax to the stored variable.

Here's a set of callbacks that test the timer:

```
from timer import Timer
import datetime

def format_time(message, *args):
    now = datetime.datetime.now().strftime("%I:%M:%S")
    print(message.format(*args, now=now))

def one(timer):
    format_time("{now}: Called One")

def two(timer):
    format_time("{now}: Called Two")

def three(timer):
```

```
        format_time("{now}: Called Three")

    class Repeater:
        def __init__(self):
            self.count = 0
        def repeater(self, timer):
            format_time("{now}: repeat {0}", self.count)
            self.count += 1
            timer.call_after(5, self.repeater)

timer = Timer()
timer.call_after(1, one)
timer.call_after(2, one)
timer.call_after(2, two)
timer.call_after(4, two)
timer.call_after(3, three)
timer.call_after(6, three)
repeater = Repeater()
timer.call_after(5, repeater.repeater)
format_time("{now}: Starting")
timer.run()
```

This example allows us to see how multiple callbacks interact with the timer. The first function is the format_time function. It uses the string format method to add the current time to the message, and illustrates variable arguments in action. The format_time method will accept any number of positional arguments, using variable argument syntax, which are then forwarded as positional arguments to the string's format method. After this, we create three simple callback methods that simply output the current time and a short message telling us which callback has been fired.

The Repeater class demonstrates that methods can be used as callbacks too, since they are really just functions. It also shows why the timer argument to the callback functions is useful: we can add a new timed event to the timer from inside a presently running callback. We then create a timer and add several events to it that are called after different amounts of time. Finally, we start the timer running; the output shows that events are run in the expected order:

```
02:53:35: Starting
02:53:36: Called One
02:53:37: Called One
02:53:37: Called Two
02:53:38: Called Three
02:53:39: Called Two
02:53:40: repeat 0
```

```
02:53:41: Called Three
02:53:45: repeat 1
02:53:50: repeat 2
02:53:55: repeat 3
02:54:00: repeat 4
```

Python 3.4 introduces a generic event-loop architecture similar to this. We'll be discussing it later in *Chapter 13, Concurrency*.

Using functions as attributes

One of the interesting effects of functions being objects is that they can be set as callable attributes on other objects. It is possible to add or change a function to an instantiated object:

```python
class A:
    def print(self):
        print("my class is A")

def fake_print():
    print("my class is not A")

a = A()
a.print()
a.print = fake_print
a.print()
```

This code creates a very simple class with a `print` method that doesn't tell us anything we didn't know. Then we create a new function that tells us something we don't believe.

When we call `print` on an instance of the `A` class, it behaves as expected. If we then set the `print` method to point at a new function, it tells us something different:

```
my class is A
my class is not A
```

It is also possible to replace methods on classes instead of objects, although in that case we have to add the `self` argument to the parameter list. This will change the method for all instances of that object, even ones that have already been instantiated. Obviously, replacing methods like this can be both dangerous and confusing to maintain. Somebody reading the code will see that a method has been called and look up that method on the original class. But the method on the original class is not the one that was called. Figuring out what really happened can become a tricky, frustrating debugging session.

It does have its uses though. Often, replacing or adding methods at run time (called **monkey-patching**) is used in automated testing. If testing a client-server application, we may not want to actually connect to the server while testing the client; this may result in accidental transfers of funds or embarrassing test e-mails being sent to real people. Instead, we can set up our test code to replace some of the key methods on the object that sends requests to the server, so it only records that the methods have been called.

Monkey-patching can also be used to fix bugs or add features in third-party code that we are interacting with, and does not behave quite the way we need it to. It should, however, be applied sparingly; it's almost always a "messy hack". Sometimes, though, it is the only way to adapt an existing library to suit our needs.

Callable objects

Just as functions are objects that can have attributes set on them, it is possible to create an object that can be called as though it were a function.

Any object can be made callable by simply giving it a __call__ method that accepts the required arguments. Let's make our Repeater class, from the timer example, a little easier to use by making it a callable:

```
class Repeater:
    def __init__(self):
        self.count = 0


    def __call__(self, timer):
        format_time("{now}: repeat {0}", self.count)
        self.count += 1

        timer.call_after(5, self)

timer = Timer()

timer.call_after(5, Repeater())
format_time("{now}: Starting")
timer.run()
```

This example isn't much different from the earlier class; all we did was change the name of the `repeater` function to `__call__` and pass the object itself as a callable. Note that when we make the `call_after` call, we pass the argument `Repeater()`. Those two parentheses are creating a new instance of the class; they are not explicitly calling the class. This happens later, inside the timer. If we want to execute the `__call__` method on a newly instantiated object, we'd use a rather odd syntax: `Repeater()()`. The first set of parentheses constructs the object; the second set executes the `__call__` method. If we find ourselves doing this, we may not be using the correct abstraction. Only implement the `__call__` function on an object if the object is meant to be treated like a function.

Case study

To tie together some of the principles presented in this chapter, let's build a mailing list manager. The manager will keep track of e-mail addresses categorized into named groups. When it's time to send a message, we can pick a group and send the message to all e-mail addresses assigned to that group.

Now, before we start working on this project, we ought to have a safe way to test it, without sending e-mails to a bunch of real people. Luckily, Python has our back here; like the test HTTP server, it has a built-in **Simple Mail Transfer Protocol (SMTP)** server that we can instruct to capture any messages we send without actually sending them. We can run the server with the following command:

```
python -m smtpd -n -c DebuggingServer localhost:1025
```

Running this command at a command prompt will start an SMTP server running on port 1025 on the local machine. But we've instructed it to use the `DebuggingServer` class (it comes with the built-in SMTP module), which, instead of sending mails to the intended recipients, simply prints them on the terminal screen as it receives them. Neat, eh?

Now, before writing our mailing list, let's write some code that actually sends mail. Of course, Python supports this in the standard library, too, but it's a bit of an odd interface, so we'll write a new function to wrap it all cleanly:

```
import smtplib
from email.mime.text import MIMEText

def send_email(subject, message, from_addr, *to_addrs,
```

```
              host="localhost", port=1025, **headers):

    email = MIMEText(message)
    email['Subject'] = subject
    email['From'] = from_addr
    for header, value in headers.items():
        email[header] = value

    sender = smtplib.SMTP(host, port)
    for addr in to_addrs:
        del email['To']
        email['To'] = addr
        sender.sendmail(from_addr, addr, email.as_string())
    sender.quit()
```

We won't cover the code inside this method too thoroughly; the documentation in the standard library can give you all the information you need to use the smtplib and email modules effectively.

We've used both variable argument and keyword argument syntax in the function call. The variable argument list allows us to supply a single string in the default case of having a single to address, as well as permitting multiple addresses to be supplied if required. Any extra keyword arguments are mapped to e-mail headers. This is an exciting use of variable arguments and keyword arguments, but it's not really a great interface for the person calling the function. In fact, it makes many things the programmer will want to do impossible.

The headers passed into the function represent auxiliary headers that can be attached to a method. Such headers might include Reply-To, Return-Path, or *X-pretty-much-anything*. But in order to be a valid identifier in Python, a name cannot include the - character. In general, that character represents subtraction. So, it's not possible to call a function with Reply-To = my@email.com. It appears we were too eager to use keyword arguments because they are a new tool we just learned about in this chapter.

We'll have to change the argument to a normal dictionary; this will work because any string can be used as a key in a dictionary. By default, we'd want this dictionary to be empty, but we can't make the default parameter an empty dictionary. So, we'll have to make the default argument None, and then set up the dictionary at the beginning of the method:

```
def send_email(subject, message, from_addr, *to_addrs,
```

```
        host="localhost", port=1025, headers=None):

    headers = {} if headers is None else headers
```

If we have our debugging SMTP server running in one terminal, we can test this code in a Python interpreter:

```
>>> send_email("A model subject", "The message contents",
 "from@example.com", "to1@example.com", "to2@example.com")
```

Then, if we check the output from the debugging SMTP server, we get the following:

```
---------- MESSAGE FOLLOWS ----------
Content-Type: text/plain; charset="us-ascii"
MIME-Version: 1.0
Content-Transfer-Encoding: 7bit
Subject: A model subject
From: from@example.com
To: to1@example.com
X-Peer: 127.0.0.1


The message contents
------------ END MESSAGE ------------
---------- MESSAGE FOLLOWS ----------
Content-Type: text/plain; charset="us-ascii"
MIME-Version: 1.0
Content-Transfer-Encoding: 7bit
Subject: A model subject
From: from@example.com
To: to2@example.com
X-Peer: 127.0.0.1


The message contents
------------ END MESSAGE ------------
```

Excellent, it has "sent" our e-mail to the two expected addresses with subject and message contents included. Now that we can send messages, let's work on the e-mail group management system. We'll need an object that somehow matches e-mail addresses with the groups they are in. Since this is a many-to-many relationship (any one e-mail address can be in multiple groups; any one group can be associated with multiple e-mail addresses), none of the data structures we've studied seems quite ideal. We could try a dictionary of group-names matched to a list of associated e-mail addresses, but that would duplicate e-mail addresses. We could also try a dictionary of e-mail addresses matched to groups, resulting in a duplication of groups. Neither seems optimal. Let's try this latter version, even though intuition tells me the groups to e-mail address solution would be more straightforward.

Since the values in our dictionary will always be collections of unique e-mail addresses, we should probably store them in a `set` container. We can use `defaultdict` to ensure that there is always a `set` container available for each key:

```python
from collections import defaultdict
class MailingList:
    '''Manage groups of e-mail addresses for sending e-mails.'''
    def __init__(self):
        self.email_map = defaultdict(set)

    def add_to_group(self, email, group):
        self.email_map[email].add(group)
```

Now, let's add a method that allows us to collect all the e-mail addresses in one or more groups. This can be done by converting the list of groups to a set:

```python
def emails_in_groups(self, *groups):
    groups = set(groups)
    emails = set()
    for e, g in self.email_map.items():
        if g & groups:
            emails.add(e)
    return emails
```

First, look at what we're iterating over: `self.email_map.items()`. This method, of course, returns a tuple of key-value pairs for each item in the dictionary. The values are sets of strings representing the groups. We split these into two variables named `e` and `g`, short for e-mail and groups. We add the e-mail address to the set of return values only if the passed in groups intersect with the e-mail address groups. The `g & groups` syntax is a shortcut for `g.intersection(groups)`; the `set` class does this by implementing the special `__and__` method to call `intersection`.

This code could be made a wee bit more concise using a set comprehension, which we'll discuss in *Chapter 9, The Iterator Pattern.*

Now, with these building blocks, we can trivially add a method to our `MailingList` class that sends messages to specific groups:

```
def send_mailing(self, subject, message, from_addr,
        *groups, headers=None):
    emails = self.emails_in_groups(*groups)
    send_email(subject, message, from_addr,
            *emails, headers=headers)
```

This function relies on variable argument lists. As input, it takes a list of groups as variable arguments. It gets the list of e-mails for the specified groups and passes those as variable arguments into `send_email`, along with other arguments that were passed into this method.

The program can be tested by ensuring the SMTP debugging server is running in one command prompt, and, in a second prompt, loading the code using:

```
python -i mailing_list.py
```

Create a `MailingList` object with:

```
>>> m = MailingList()
```

Then create a few fake e-mail addresses and groups, along the lines of:

```
>>> m.add_to_group("friend1@example.com", "friends")
>>> m.add_to_group("friend2@example.com", "friends")
>>> m.add_to_group("family1@example.com", "family")
>>> m.add_to_group("pro1@example.com", "professional")
```

Finally, use a command like this to send e-mails to specific groups:

```
>>> m.send_mailing("A Party",
"Friends and family only: a party", "me@example.com", "friends",
"family", headers={"Reply-To": "me2@example.com"})
```

E-mails to each of the addresses in the specified groups should show up in the console on the SMTP server.

The mailing list works fine as it is, but it's kind of useless; as soon as we exit the program, our database of information is lost. Let's modify it to add a couple of methods to load and save the list of e-mail groups from and to a file.

In general, when storing structured data on disk, it is a good idea to put a lot of thought into how it is stored. One of the reasons myriad database systems exist is that if someone else has put this thought into how data is stored, you don't have to. We'll be looking at some data serialization mechanisms in the next chapter, but for this example, let's keep it simple and go with the first solution that could possibly work.

The data format I have in mind is to store each e-mail address followed by a space, followed by a comma-separated list of groups. This format seems reasonable, and we're going to go with it because data formatting isn't the topic of this chapter. However, to illustrate just why you need to think hard about how you format data on disk, let's highlight a few problems with the format.

First, the space character is technically legal in e-mail addresses. Most e-mail providers prohibit it (with good reason), but the specification defining e-mail addresses says an e-mail can contain a space if it is in quotation marks. If we are to use a space as a sentinel in our data format, we should technically be able to differentiate between that space and a space that is part of an e-mail. We're going to pretend this isn't true, for simplicity's sake, but real-life data encoding is full of stupid issues like this. Second, consider the comma-separated list of groups. What happens if someone decides to put a comma in a group name? If we decide to make commas illegal in group names, we should add validation to ensure this to our add_to_group method. For pedagogical clarity, we'll ignore this problem too. Finally, there are many security implications we need to consider: can someone get themselves into the wrong group by putting a fake comma in their e-mail address? What does the parser do if it encounters an invalid file?

The takeaway from this discussion is to try to use a data-storage method that has been field tested, rather than designing your own data serialization protocol. There are a ton of bizarre edge cases you might overlook, and it's better to use code that has already encountered and fixed those edge cases.

But forget that, let's just write some basic code that uses an unhealthy dose of wishful thinking to pretend this simple data format is safe:

```
email1@mydomain.com group1,group2
email2@mydomain.com group2,group3
```

The code to do this is as follows:

```
def save(self):
    with open(self.data_file, 'w') as file:
        for email, groups in self.email_map.items():
            file.write(
```

```
                        '{} {}\n'.format(email, ','.join(groups))
                    )

    def load(self):
        self.email_map = defaultdict(set)
        try:
            with open(self.data_file) as file:
                for line in file:
                    email, groups = line.strip().split(' ')
                    groups = set(groups.split(','))
                    self.email_map[email] = groups
        except IOError:
            pass
```

In the `save` method, we open the file in a context manager and write the file as a formatted string. Remember the newline character; Python doesn't add that for us. The `load` method first resets the dictionary (in case it contains data from a previous call to `load`) uses the `for...in` syntax, which loops over each line in the file. Again, the newline character is included in the line variable, so we have to call `.strip()` to take it off. We'll learn more about such string manipulation in the next chapter.

Before using these methods, we need to make sure the object has a `self.data_file` attribute, which can be done by modifying `__init__`:

```
    def __init__(self, data_file):
        self.data_file = data_file
        self.email_map = defaultdict(set)
```

We can test these two methods in the interpreter as follows:

```
>>> m = MailingList('addresses.db')
>>> m.add_to_group('friend1@example.com', 'friends')
>>> m.add_to_group('family1@example.com', 'friends')
>>> m.add_to_group('family1@example.com', 'family')
>>> m.save()
```

The resulting `addresses.db` file contains the following lines, as expected:

```
friend1@example.com friends
family1@example.com friends,family
```

We can also load this data back into a `MailingList` object successfully:

```
>>> m = MailingList('addresses.db')
>>> m.email_map
defaultdict(<class 'set'>, {})
>>> m.load()
>>> m.email_map
defaultdict(<class 'set'>, {'friend2@example.com': {'friends\n'},
'family1@example.com': {'family\n'}, 'friend1@example.com':
{'friends\n'}})
```

As you can see, I forgot to do the `load` command, and it might be easy to forget the `save` command as well. To make this a little easier for anyone who wants to use our `MailingList` API in their own code, let's provide the methods to support a context manager:

```
    def __enter__(self):
        self.load()
        return self

    def __exit__(self, type, value, tb):
        self.save()
```

These simple methods just delegate their work to load and save, but we can now write code like this in the interactive interpreter and know that all the previously stored addresses were loaded on our behalf, and that the whole list will be saved to the file when we are done:

```
>>> with MailingList('addresses.db') as ml:
...     ml.add_to_group('friend2@example.com', 'friends')
...     ml.send_mailing("What's up", "hey friends, how's it going", 'me@
example.com', 'friends')
```

Exercises

If you haven't encountered the `with` statements and context managers before, I encourage you, as usual, to go through your old code and find all the places you were opening files, and make sure they are safely closed using the `with` statement. Look for places that you could write your own context managers as well. Ugly or repetitive `try...finally` clauses are a good place to start, but you may find them useful any time you need to do before and/or after tasks in context.

You've probably used many of the basic built-in functions before now. We covered several of them, but didn't go into a great deal of detail. Play with `enumerate`, `zip`, `reversed`, `any` and `all`, until you know you'll remember to use them when they are the right tool for the job. The `enumerate` function is especially important; because not using it results in some pretty ugly code.

Also explore some applications that pass functions around as callable objects, as well as using the `__call__` method to make your own objects callable. You can get the same effect by attaching attributes to functions or by creating a `__call__` method on an object. In which case would you use one syntax, and when would it be more suitable to use the other?

Our mailing list object could overwhelm an e-mail server if there is a massive number of e-mails to be sent out. Try refactoring it so that you can use different `send_email` functions for different purposes. One such function could be the version we used here. A different version might put the e-mails in a queue to be sent by a server in a different thread or process. A third version could just output the data to the terminal, obviating the need for a dummy SMTP server. Can you construct the mailing list with a callback such that the `send_mailing` function uses whatever is passed in? It would default to the current version if no callback is supplied.

The relationship between arguments, keyword arguments, variable arguments, and variable keyword arguments can be a bit confusing. We saw how painfully they can interact when we covered multiple inheritance. Devise some other examples to see how they can work well together, as well as to understand when they don't.

Summary

We covered a grab bag of topics in this chapter. Each represented an important non-object-oriented feature that is popular in Python. Just because we can use object-oriented principles does not always mean we should!

However, we also saw that Python typically implements such features by providing a syntax shortcut to traditional object-oriented syntax. Knowing the object-oriented principles underlying these tools allows us to use them more effectively in our own classes.

We discussed a series of built-in functions and file I/O operations. There are a whole bunch of different syntaxes available to us when calling functions with arguments, keyword arguments, and variable argument lists. Context managers are useful for the common pattern of sandwiching a piece of code between two method calls. Even functions are objects, and, conversely, any normal object can be made callable.

In the next chapter, we'll learn more about string and file manipulation, and even spend some time with one of the least object-oriented topics in the standard library: regular expressions.

8
Strings and Serialization

Before we get involved with higher level design patterns, let's take a deep dive into one of Python's most common objects: the string. We'll see that there is a lot more to the string than meets the eye, and also cover searching strings for patterns and serializing data for storage or transmission.

In particular, we'll visit:

- The complexities of strings, bytes, and byte arrays
- The ins and outs of string formatting
- A few ways to serialize data
- The mysterious regular expression

Strings

Strings are a basic primitive in Python; we've used them in nearly every example we've discussed so far. All they do is represent an immutable sequence of characters. However, though you may not have considered it before, "character" is a bit of an ambiguous word; can Python strings represent sequences of accented characters? Chinese characters? What about Greek, Cyrillic, or Farsi?

In Python 3, the answer is yes. Python strings are all represented in Unicode, a character definition standard that can represent virtually any character in any language on the planet (and some made-up languages and random characters as well). This is done seamlessly, for the most part. So, let's think of Python 3 strings as an immutable sequence of Unicode characters. So what can we do with this immutable sequence? We've touched on many of the ways strings can be manipulated in previous examples, but let's quickly cover it all in one place: a crash course in string theory!

String manipulation

As you know, strings can be created in Python by wrapping a sequence of characters in single or double quotes. Multiline strings can easily be created using three quote characters, and multiple hardcoded strings can be concatenated together by placing them side by side. Here are some examples:

```
a = "hello"
b = 'world'
c = '''a multiple
line string'''
d = """More
multiple"""
e = ("Three " "Strings "
        "Together")
```

That last string is automatically composed into a single string by the interpreter. It is also possible to concatenate strings using the + operator (as in `"hello " + "world"`). Of course, strings don't have to be hardcoded. They can also come from various outside sources such as text files, user input, or encoded on the network.

> The automatic concatenation of adjacent strings can make for some hilarious bugs when a comma is missed. It is, however, extremely useful when a long string needs to be placed inside a function call without exceeding the 79 character line-length limit suggested by the Python style guide.

Like other sequences, strings can be iterated over (character by character), indexed, sliced, or concatenated. The syntax is the same as for lists.

The `str` class has numerous methods on it to make manipulating strings easier. The `dir` and `help` commands in the Python interpreter can tell us how to use all of them; we'll consider some of the more common ones directly.

Several Boolean convenience methods help us identify whether or not the characters in a string match a certain pattern. Here is a summary of these methods. Most of these, such as `isalpha`, `isupper`/`islower`, and `startswith`/`endswith` have obvious interpretations. The `isspace` method is also fairly obvious, but remember that all whitespace characters (including tab, newline) are considered, not just the space character.

The `istitle` method returns `True` if the first character of each word is capitalized and all other characters are lowercase. Note that it does not strictly enforce the English grammatical definition of title formatting. For example, Leigh Hunt's poem "The Glove and the Lions" should be a valid title, even though not all words are capitalized. Robert Service's "The Cremation of Sam McGee" should also be a valid title, even though there is an uppercase letter in the middle of the last word.

Be careful with the `isdigit`, `isdecimal`, and `isnumeric` methods, as they are more nuanced than you would expect. Many Unicode characters are considered numbers besides the ten digits we are used to. Worse, the period character that we use to construct floats from strings is not considered a decimal character, so `'45.2'.isdecimal()` returns `False`. The real decimal character is represented by Unicode value 0660, as in 45.2, (or `45\u06602`). Further, these methods do not verify whether the strings are valid numbers; "127.0.0.1" returns `True` for all three methods. We might think we should use that decimal character instead of a period for all numeric quantities, but passing that character into the `float()` or `int()` constructor converts that decimal character to a zero:

```
>>> float('45\u06602')
4502.0
```

Other methods useful for pattern matching do not return Booleans. The `count` method tells us how many times a given substring shows up in the string, while `find`, `index`, `rfind`, and `rindex` tell us the position of a given substring within the original string. The two 'r' (for 'right' or 'reverse') methods start searching from the end of the string. The `find` methods return -1 if the substring can't be found, while `index` raises a `ValueError` in this situation. Have a look at some of these methods in action:

```
>>> s = "hello world"
>>> s.count('l')
3
>>> s.find('l')
2
>>> s.rindex('m')
Traceback (most recent call last):
  File "<stdin>", line 1, in <module>
ValueError: substring not found
```

Most of the remaining string methods return transformations of the string. The `upper`, `lower`, `capitalize`, and `title` methods create new strings with all alphabetic characters in the given format. The `translate` method can use a dictionary to map arbitrary input characters to specified output characters.

For all of these methods, note that the input string remains unmodified; a brand new `str` instance is returned instead. If we need to manipulate the resultant string, we should assign it to a new variable, as in `new_value = value.capitalize()`. Often, once we've performed the transformation, we don't need the old value anymore, so a common idiom is to assign it to the same variable, as in `value = value.title()`.

Finally, a couple of string methods return or operate on lists. The `split` method accepts a substring and splits the string into a list of strings wherever that substring occurs. You can pass a number as a second parameter to limit the number of resultant strings. The `rsplit` behaves identically to `split` if you don't limit the number of strings, but if you do supply a limit, it starts splitting from the end of the string. The `partition` and `rpartition` methods split the string at only the first or last occurrence of the substring, and return a tuple of three values: characters before the substring, the substring itself, and the characters after the substring.

As the inverse of `split`, the `join` method accepts a list of strings, and returns all of those strings combined together by placing the original string between them. The `replace` method accepts two arguments, and returns a string where each instance of the first argument has been replaced with the second. Here are some of these methods in action:

```
>>> s = "hello world, how are you"
>>> s2 = s.split(' ')
>>> s2
['hello', 'world,', 'how', 'are', 'you']
>>> '#'.join(s2)
'hello#world,#how#are#you'
>>> s.replace(' ', '**')
'hello**world,**how**are**you'
>>> s.partition(' ')
('hello', ' ', 'world, how are you')
```

There you have it, a whirlwind tour of the most common methods on the `str` class! Now, let's look at Python 3's method for composing strings and variables to create new strings.

String formatting

Python 3 has a powerful string formatting and templating mechanism that allows us to construct strings comprised of hardcoded text and interspersed variables. We've used it in many previous examples, but it is much more versatile than the simple formatting specifiers we've used.

Any string can be turned into a format string by calling the `format()` method on it. This method returns a new string where specific characters in the input string have been replaced with values provided as arguments and keyword arguments passed into the function. The `format` method does not require a fixed set of arguments; internally, it uses the `*args` and `**kwargs` syntax that we discussed in *Chapter 7, Python Object-oriented Shortcuts*.

The special characters that are replaced in formatted strings are the opening and closing brace characters: { and }. We can insert pairs of these in a string and they will be replaced, in order, by any positional arguments passed to the `str.format` method:

```
template = "Hello {}, you are currently {}."
print(template.format('Dusty', 'writing'))
```

If we run these statements, it replaces the braces with variables, in order:

Hello Dusty, you are currently writing.

This basic syntax is not terribly useful if we want to reuse variables within one string or decide to use them in a different position. We can place zero-indexed integers inside the curly braces to tell the formatter which positional variable gets inserted at a given position in the string. Let's repeat the name:

```
template = "Hello {0}, you are {1}. Your name is {0}."
print(template.format('Dusty', 'writing'))
```

If we use these integer indexes, we have to use them in all the variables. We can't mix empty braces with positional indexes. For example, this code fails with an appropriate `ValueError` exception:

```
template = "Hello {}, you are {}. Your name is {0}."
print(template.format('Dusty', 'writing'))
```

Escaping braces

Brace characters are often useful in strings, aside from formatting. We need a way to escape them in situations where we want them to be displayed as themselves, rather than being replaced. This can be done by doubling the braces. For example, we can use Python to format a basic Java program:

```
template = """
public class {0} {{
    public static void main(String[] args) {{
        System.out.println("{1}");
    }}
}}"""

print(template.format("MyClass", "print('hello world')"));
```

Wherever we see the {{ or }} sequence in the template, that is, the braces enclosing the Java class and method definition, we know the `format` method will replace them with single braces, rather than some argument passed into the `format` method. Here's the output:

```
public class MyClass {
    public static void main(String[] args) {
        System.out.println("print('hello world')");
    }
}
```

The class name and contents of the output have been replaced with two parameters, while the double braces have been replaced with single braces, giving us a valid Java file. Turns out, this is about the simplest possible Python program to print the simplest possible Java program that can print the simplest possible Python program!

Keyword arguments

If we're formatting complex strings, it can become tedious to remember the order of the arguments or to update the template if we choose to insert a new argument. The `format` method therefore allows us to specify names inside the braces instead of numbers. The named variables are then passed to the `format` method as keyword arguments:

```
template = """
From: <{from_email}>
To: <{to_email}>
Subject: {subject}

{message}"""
print(template.format(
    from_email = "a@example.com",
    to_email = "b@example.com",
    message = "Here's some mail for you. "
    " Hope you enjoy the message!",
    subject = "You have mail!"
    ))
```

We can also mix index and keyword arguments (as with all Python function calls, the keyword arguments must follow the positional ones). We can even mix unlabeled positional braces with keyword arguments:

```
print("{} {label} {}".format("x", "y", label="z"))
```

As expected, this code outputs:

```
x z y
```

Container lookups

We aren't restricted to passing simple string variables into the `format` method. Any primitive, such as integers or floats can be printed. More interestingly, complex objects, including lists, tuples, dictionaries, and arbitrary objects can be used, and we can access indexes and variables (but not methods) on those objects from within the `format` string.

For example, if our e-mail message had grouped the from and to e-mail addresses into a tuple, and placed the subject and message in a dictionary, for some reason (perhaps because that's the input required for an existing `send_mail` function we want to use), we can format it like this:

```
emails = ("a@example.com", "b@example.com")
message = {
        'subject': "You Have Mail!",
        'message': "Here's some mail for you!"
        }
template = """
From: <{0[0]}>
To: <{0[1]}>
Subject: {message[subject]}
{message[message]}"""
print(template.format(emails, message=message))
```

The variables inside the braces in the template string look a little weird, so let's look at what they're doing. We have passed one argument as a position-based parameter and one as a keyword argument. The two e-mail addresses are looked up by `0[x]`, where x is either `0` or `1`. The initial zero represents, as with other position-based arguments, the first positional argument passed to `format` (the `emails` tuple, in this case).

The square brackets with a number inside are the same kind of index lookup we see in regular Python code, so `0[0]` maps to `emails[0]`, in the `emails` tuple. The indexing syntax works with any indexable object, so we see similar behavior when we access `message[subject]`, except this time we are looking up a string key in a dictionary. Notice that unlike in Python code, we do not need to put quotes around the string in the dictionary lookup.

We can even do multiple levels of lookup if we have nested data structures. I would recommend against doing this often, as template strings rapidly become difficult to understand. If we have a dictionary that contains a tuple, we can do this:

```
emails = ("a@example.com", "b@example.com")
message = {
        'emails': emails,
        'subject': "You Have Mail!",
        'message': "Here's some mail for you!"
        }
template = """
From: <{0[emails][0]}>
To: <{0[emails][1]}>
Subject: {0[subject]}
{0[message]}"""
print(template.format(message))
```

Object lookups

Indexing makes `format` lookup powerful, but we're not done yet! We can also pass arbitrary objects as parameters, and use the dot notation to look up attributes on those objects. Let's change our e-mail message data once again, this time to a class:

```
class EMail:
    def __init__(self, from_addr, to_addr, subject, message):
        self.from_addr = from_addr
        self.to_addr = to_addr
        self.subject = subject
        self.message = message

email = EMail("a@example.com", "b@example.com",
        "You Have Mail!",
         "Here's some mail for you!")

template = """
From: <{0.from_addr}>
To: <{0.to_addr}>
Subject: {0.subject}

{0.message}"""
print(template.format(email))
```

The template in this example may be more readable than the previous examples, but the overhead of creating an e-mail class adds complexity to the Python code. It would be foolish to create a class for the express purpose of including the object in a template. Typically, we'd use this sort of lookup if the object we are trying to format already exists. This is true of all the examples; if we have a tuple, list, or dictionary, we'll pass it into the template directly. Otherwise, we'd just create a simple set of positional and keyword arguments.

Making it look right

It's nice to be able to include variables in template strings, but sometimes the variables need a bit of coercion to make them look right in the output. For example, if we are doing calculations with currency, we may end up with a long decimal that we don't want to show up in our template:

```
subtotal = 12.32
tax = subtotal * 0.07
total = subtotal + tax

print("Sub: ${0} Tax: ${1} Total: ${total}".format(
    subtotal, tax, total=total))
```

If we run this formatting code, the output doesn't quite look like proper currency:

Sub: $12.32 Tax: $0.8624 Total: $13.182400000000001

 Technically, we should never use floating-point numbers in currency calculations like this; we should construct `decimal.Decimal()` objects instead. Floats are dangerous because their calculations are inherently inaccurate beyond a specific level of precision. But we're looking at strings, not floats, and currency is a great example for formatting!

To fix the preceding `format` string, we can include some additional information inside the curly braces to adjust the formatting of the parameters. There are tons of things we can customize, but the basic syntax inside the braces is the same; first, we use whichever of the earlier layouts (positional, keyword, index, attribute access) is suitable to specify the variable that we want to place in the template string. We follow this with a colon, and then the specific syntax for the formatting. Here's an improved version:

```
print("Sub: ${0:0.2f} Tax: ${1:0.2f} "
        "Total: ${total:0.2f}".format(
            subtotal, tax, total=total))
```

The `0.2f` format specifier after the colons basically says, from left to right: for values lower than one, make sure a zero is displayed on the left side of the decimal point; show two places after the decimal; format the input value as a float.

We can also specify that each number should take up a particular number of characters on the screen by placing a value before the period in the precision. This can be useful for outputting tabular data, for example:

```
orders = [('burger', 2, 5),
          ('fries', 3.5, 1),
          ('cola', 1.75, 3)]

print("PRODUCT    QUANTITY    PRICE    SUBTOTAL")
for product, price, quantity in orders:
    subtotal = price * quantity
    print("{0:10s}{1: ^9d}    ${2: <8.2f}${3: >7.2f}".format(
        product, quantity, price, subtotal))
```

Ok, that's a pretty scary looking format string, so let's see how it works before we break it down into understandable parts:

```
PRODUCT     QUANTITY     PRICE     SUBTOTAL
burger         5         $2.00     $   10.00
fries          1         $3.50     $    3.50
cola           3         $1.75     $    5.25
```

Nifty! So, how is this actually happening? We have four variables we are formatting, in each line in the `for` loop. The first variable is a string and is formatted with `{0:10s}`. The s means it is a string variable, and the 10 means it should take up ten characters. By default, with strings, if the string is shorter than the specified number of characters, it appends spaces to the right side of the string to make it long enough (beware, however: if the original string is too long, it won't be truncated!). We can change this behavior (to fill with other characters or change the alignment in the format string), as we do for the next value, `quantity`.

The formatter for the `quantity` value is `{1: ^9d}`. The d represents an integer value. The 9 tells us the value should take up nine characters. But with integers, instead of spaces, the extra characters are zeros, by default. That looks kind of weird. So we explicitly specify a space (immediately after the colon) as a padding character. The caret character ^ tells us that the number should be aligned in the center of this available padding; this makes the column look a bit more professional. The specifiers have to be in the right order, although all are optional: fill first, then align, then the size, and finally, the type.

We do similar things with the specifiers for price and subtotal. For `price`, we use `{2: <8.2f}` and for `subtotal`, `{3: >7.2f}`. In both cases, we're specifying a space as the fill character, but we use the `<` and `>` symbols, respectively, to represent that the numbers should be aligned to the left or right within the minimum space of eight or seven characters. Further, each float should be formatted to two decimal places.

The "type" character for different types can affect formatting output as well. We've seen the `s`, `d`, and `f` types, for strings, integers, and floats. Most of the other format specifiers are alternative versions of these; for example, `o` represents octal format and `x` represents hexadecimal for integers. The `n` type specifier can be useful for formatting integer separators in the current locale's format. For floating-point numbers, the `%` type will multiply by 100 and format a float as a percentage.

While these standard formatters apply to most built-in objects, it is also possible for other objects to define nonstandard specifiers. For example, if we pass a `datetime` object into `format`, we can use the specifiers used in the `datetime.strftime` function, as follows:

```
import datetime
print("{0:%Y-%m-%d %I:%M%p }".format(
    datetime.datetime.now()))
```

It is even possible to write custom formatters for objects we create ourselves, but that is beyond the scope of this book. Look into overriding the `__format__` special method if you need to do this in your code. The most comprehensive instructions can be found in PEP 3101 at `http://www.python.org/dev/peps/pep-3101/`, although the details are a bit dry. You can find more digestible tutorials using a web search.

The Python formatting syntax is quite flexible but it is a difficult mini-language to remember. I use it every day and still occasionally have to look up forgotten concepts in the documentation. It also isn't powerful enough for serious templating needs, such as generating web pages. There are several third-party templating libraries you can look into if you need to do more than basic formatting of a few strings.

Strings are Unicode

At the beginning of this section, we defined strings as collections of immutable Unicode characters. This actually makes things very complicated at times, because Unicode isn't really a storage format. If you get a string of bytes from a file or a socket, for example, they won't be in Unicode. They will, in fact, be the built-in type `bytes`. Bytes are immutable sequences of... well, bytes. Bytes are the lowest-level storage format in computing. They represent 8 bits, usually described as an integer between 0 and 255, or a hexadecimal equivalent between 0 and FF. Bytes don't represent anything specific; a sequence of bytes may store characters of an encoded string, or pixels in an image.

If we print a byte object, any bytes that map to ASCII representations will be printed as their original character, while non-ASCII bytes (whether they are binary data or other characters) are printed as hex codes escaped by the \x escape sequence. You may find it odd that a byte, represented as an integer, can map to an ASCII character. But ASCII is really just a code where each letter is represented by a different byte pattern, and therefore, a different integer. The character "a" is represented by the same byte as the integer 97, which is the hexadecimal number 0x61. Specifically, all of these are an interpretation of the binary pattern 01100001.

Many I/O operations only know how to deal with bytes, even if the bytes object refers to textual data. It is therefore vital to know how to convert between bytes and Unicode.

The problem is that there are many ways to map bytes to Unicode text. Bytes are machine-readable values, while text is a human-readable format. Sitting in between is an encoding that maps a given sequence of bytes to a given sequence of text characters.

However, there are multiple such encodings (ASCII is only one of them). The same sequence of bytes represents completely different text characters when mapped using different encodings! So, bytes must be decoded using the same character set with which they were encoded. It's not possible to get text from bytes without knowing how the bytes should be decoded. If we receive unknown bytes without a specified encoding, the best we can do is guess what format they are encoded in, and we may be wrong.

Converting bytes to text

If we have an array of bytes from somewhere, we can convert it to Unicode using the .decode method on the bytes class. This method accepts a string for the name of the character encoding. There are many such names; common ones for Western languages include ASCII, UTF-8, and latin-1.

The sequence of bytes (in hex), 63 6c 69 63 68 e9, actually represents the characters of the word cliché in the latin-1 encoding. The following example will encode this sequence of bytes and convert it to a Unicode string using the latin-1 encoding:

```
characters = b'\x63\x6c\x69\x63\x68\xe9'
print(characters)
print(characters.decode("latin-1"))
```

The first line creates a `bytes` object; the `b` character immediately before the string tells us that we are defining a `bytes` object instead of a normal Unicode string. Within the string, each byte is specified using—in this case—a hexadecimal number. The \x character escapes within the byte string, and each say, "the next two characters represent a byte using hexadecimal digits."

Provided we are using a shell that understands the latin-1 encoding, the two `print` calls will output the following strings:

b'clich\xe9'

cliché

The first `print` statement renders the bytes for ASCII characters as themselves. The unknown (unknown to ASCII, that is) character stays in its escaped hex format. The output includes a `b` character at the beginning of the line to remind us that it is a `bytes` representation, not a string.

The next call decodes the string using latin-1 encoding. The `decode` method returns a normal (Unicode) string with the correct characters. However, if we had decoded this same string using the Cyrillic "iso8859-5" encoding, we'd have ended up with the string 'clichщ'! This is because the \xe9 byte maps to different characters in the two encodings.

Converting text to bytes

If we need to convert incoming bytes into Unicode, clearly we're also going to have situations where we convert outgoing Unicode into byte sequences. This is done with the `encode` method on the `str` class, which, like the `decode` method, requires a character set. The following code creates a Unicode string and encodes it in different character sets:

```
characters = "cliché"
print(characters.encode("UTF-8"))
print(characters.encode("latin-1"))
print(characters.encode("CP437"))
print(characters.encode("ascii"))
```

The first three encodings create a different set of bytes for the accented character. The fourth one can't even handle that byte:

b'clich\xc3\xa9'

b'clich\xe9'

b'clich\x82'

Traceback (most recent call last):

```
   File "1261_10_16_decode_unicode.py", line 5, in <module>
     print(characters.encode("ascii"))
```

UnicodeEncodeError: 'ascii' codec can't encode character '\xe9' in
position 5: ordinal not in range(128)

Do you understand the importance of encoding now? The accented character is
represented as a different byte for each encoding; if we use the wrong one when
we are decoding bytes to text, we get the wrong character.

The exception in the last case is not always the desired behavior; there may be cases
where we want the unknown characters to be handled in a different way. The encode
method takes an optional string argument named errors that can define how such
characters should be handled. This string can be one of the following:

- strict
- replace
- ignore
- xmlcharrefreplace

The strict replacement strategy is the default we just saw. When a byte sequence
is encountered that does not have a valid representation in the requested encoding,
an exception is raised. When the replace strategy is used, the character is replaced
with a different character; in ASCII, it is a question mark; other encodings may
use different symbols, such as an empty box. The ignore strategy simply discards
any bytes it doesn't understand, while the xmlcharrefreplace strategy creates an
xml entity representing the Unicode character. This can be useful when converting
unknown strings for use in an XML document. Here's how each of the strategies
affects our sample word:

Strategy	"cliché".encode("ascii", strategy)
replace	b'clich?'
ignore	b'clich'
xmlcharrefreplace	b'cliché'

It is possible to call the str.encode and bytes.decode methods without passing
an encoding string. The encoding will be set to the default encoding for the current
platform. This will depend on the current operating system and locale or regional
settings; you can look it up using the sys.getdefaultencoding() function. It is
usually a good idea to specify the encoding explicitly, though, since the default
encoding for a platform may change, or the program may one day be extended to
work on text from a wider variety of sources.

If you are encoding text and don't know which encoding to use, it is best to use the UTF-8 encoding. UTF-8 is able to represent any Unicode character. In modern software, it is a de facto standard encoding to ensure documents in any language—or even multiple languages—can be exchanged. The various other possible encodings are useful for legacy documents or in regions that still use different character sets by default.

The UTF-8 encoding uses one byte to represent ASCII and other common characters, and up to four bytes for more complex characters. UTF-8 is special because it is backwards-compatible with ASCII; any ASCII document encoded using UTF-8 will be identical to the original ASCII document.

I can never remember whether to use `encode` or `decode` to convert from binary bytes to Unicode. I always wished these methods were named "to_binary" and "from_binary" instead. If you have the same problem, try mentally replacing the word "code" with "binary"; "enbinary" and "debinary" are pretty close to "to_binary" and "from_binary". I have saved a lot of time by not looking up the method help files since devising this mnemonic.

Mutable byte strings

The `bytes` type, like `str`, is immutable. We can use index and slice notation on a `bytes` object and search for a particular sequence of bytes, but we can't extend or modify them. This can be very inconvenient when dealing with I/O, as it is often necessary to buffer incoming or outgoing bytes until they are ready to be sent. For example, if we are receiving data from a socket, it may take several `recv` calls before we have received an entire message.

This is where the `bytearray` built-in comes in. This type behaves something like a list, except it only holds bytes. The constructor for the class can accept a `bytes` object to initialize it. The `extend` method can be used to append another `bytes` object to the existing array (for example, when more data comes from a socket or other I/O channel).

Slice notation can be used on `bytearray` to modify the item inline. For example, this code constructs a `bytearray` from a `bytes` object and then replaces two bytes:

```
b = bytearray(b"abcdefgh")
b[4:6] = b"\x15\xa3"
print(b)
```

The output looks like this:

```
bytearray(b'abcd\x15\xa3gh')
```

Be careful; if we want to manipulate a single element in the `bytearray`, it will expect us to pass an integer between 0 and 255 inclusive as the value. This integer represents a specific `bytes` pattern. If we try to pass a character or `bytes` object, it will raise an exception.

A single byte character can be converted to an integer using the `ord` (short for ordinal) function. This function returns the integer representation of a single character:

```
b = bytearray(b'abcdef')
b[3] = ord(b'g')
b[4] = 68
print(b)
```

The output looks like this:

`bytearray(b'abcgDf')`

After constructing the array, we replace the character at index 3 (the fourth character, as indexing starts at 0, as with lists) with byte 103. This integer was returned by the `ord` function and is the ASCII character for the lowercase g. For illustration, we also replaced the next character up with the byte number 68, which maps to the ASCII character for the uppercase D.

The `bytearray` type has methods that allow it to behave like a list (we can append integer bytes to it, for example), but also like a `bytes` object; we can use methods like `count` and `find` the same way they would behave on a `bytes` or `str` object. The difference is that `bytearray` is a mutable type, which can be useful for building up complex sequences of bytes from a specific input source.

Regular expressions

You know what's really hard to do using object-oriented principles? Parsing strings to match arbitrary patterns, that's what. There have been a fair number of academic papers written in which object-oriented design is used to set up string parsing, but the result is always very verbose and hard to read, and they are not widely used in practice.

In the real world, string parsing in most programming languages is handled by regular expressions. These are not verbose, but, boy, are they ever hard to read, at least until you learn the syntax. Even though regular expressions are not object oriented, the Python regular expression library provides a few classes and objects that you can use to construct and run regular expressions.

Regular expressions are used to solve a common problem: Given a string, determine whether that string matches a given pattern and, optionally, collect substrings that contain relevant information. They can be used to answer questions like:

- Is this string a valid URL?
- What is the date and time of all warning messages in a log file?
- Which users in /etc/passwd are in a given group?
- What username and document were requested by the URL a visitor typed?

There are many similar scenarios where regular expressions are the correct answer. Many programmers have made the mistake of implementing complicated and fragile string parsing libraries because they didn't know or wouldn't learn regular expressions. In this section, we'll gain enough knowledge of regular expressions to not make such mistakes!

Matching patterns

Regular expressions are a complicated mini-language. They rely on special characters to match unknown strings, but let's start with literal characters, such as letters, numbers, and the space character, which always match themselves. Let's see a basic example:

```
import re

search_string = "hello world"
pattern = "hello world"

match = re.match(pattern, search_string)

if match:
    print("regex matches")
```

The Python Standard Library module for regular expressions is called re. We import it and set up a search string and pattern to search for; in this case, they are the same string. Since the search string matches the given pattern, the conditional passes and the print statement executes.

Bear in mind that the match function matches the pattern to the beginning of the string. Thus, if the pattern were "ello world", no match would be found. With confusing asymmetry, the parser stops searching as soon as it finds a match, so the pattern "hello wo" matches successfully. Let's build a small example program to demonstrate these differences and help us learn other regular expression syntax:

```
import sys
```

```
import re

pattern = sys.argv[1]
search_string = sys.argv[2]
match = re.match(pattern, search_string)

if match:
    template = "'{}' matches pattern '{}'"
else:
    template = "'{}' does not match pattern '{}'"

print(template.format(search_string, pattern))
```

This is just a generic version of the earlier example that accepts the pattern and search string from the command line. We can see how the start of the pattern must match, but a value is returned as soon as a match is found in the following command-line interaction:

```
$ python regex_generic.py "hello worl" "hello world"
'hello world' matches pattern 'hello worl'
$ python regex_generic.py "ello world" "hello world"
'hello world' does not match pattern 'ello world'
```

We'll be using this script throughout the next few sections. While the script is always invoked with the command line `python regex_generic.py "<pattern>" "<string>"`, we'll only see the output in the following examples, to conserve space.

If you need control over whether items happen at the beginning or end of a line (or if there are no newlines in the string, at the beginning and end of the string), you can use the ^ and $ characters to represent the start and end of the string respectively. If you want a pattern to match an entire string, it's a good idea to include both of these:

```
'hello world' matches pattern '^hello world$'
'hello worl' does not match pattern '^hello world$'
```

Matching a selection of characters

Let's start with matching an arbitrary character. The period character, when used in a regular expression pattern, can match any single character. Using a period in the string means you don't care what the character is, just that there is a character there. For example:

```
'hello world' matches pattern 'hel.o world'
'helpo world' matches pattern 'hel.o world'
```

```
'hel o world' matches pattern 'hel.o world'
'helo world' does not match pattern 'hel.o world'
```

Notice how the last example does not match because there is no character at the period's position in the pattern.

That's all well and good, but what if we only want a few specific characters to match? We can put a set of characters inside square brackets to match any one of those characters. So if we encounter the string [abc] in a regular expression pattern, we know that those five (including the two square brackets) characters will only match one character in the string being searched, and further, that this one character will be either an a, a b, or a c. See a few examples:

```
'hello world' matches pattern 'hel[lp]o world'
'helpo world' matches pattern 'hel[lp]o world'
'helPo world' does not match pattern 'hel[lp]o world'
```

These square bracket sets should be named character sets, but they are more often referred to as **character classes**. Often, we want to include a large range of characters inside these sets, and typing them all out can be monotonous and error-prone. Fortunately, the regular expression designers thought of this and gave us a shortcut. The dash character, in a character set, will create a range. This is especially useful if you want to match "all lower case letters", "all letters", or "all numbers" as follows:

```
'hello   world' does not match pattern 'hello [a-z] world'
'hello b world' matches pattern 'hello [a-z] world'
'hello B world' matches pattern 'hello [a-zA-Z] world'
'hello 2 world' matches pattern 'hello [a-zA-Z0-9] world'
```

There are other ways to match or exclude individual characters, but you'll need to find a more comprehensive tutorial via a web search if you want to find out what they are!

Escaping characters

If putting a period character in a pattern matches any arbitrary character, how do we match just a period in a string? One way might be to put the period inside square brackets to make a character class, but a more generic method is to use backslashes to escape it. Here's a regular expression to match two digit decimal numbers between 0.00 and 0.99:

```
'0.05' matches pattern '0\.[0-9][0-9]'
'005' does not match pattern '0\.[0-9][0-9]'
'0,05' does not match pattern '0\.[0-9][0-9]'
```

For this pattern, the two characters \. match the single . character. If the period character is missing or is a different character, it does not match.

This backslash escape sequence is used for a variety of special characters in regular expressions. You can use \[to insert a square bracket without starting a character class, and \(to insert a parenthesis, which we'll later see is also a special character.

More interestingly, we can also use the escape symbol followed by a character to represent special characters such as newlines (\n), and tabs (\t). Further, some character classes can be represented more succinctly using escape strings; \s represents whitespace characters, \w represents letters, numbers, and underscore, and \d represents a digit:

```
'(abc]' matches pattern '\(abc\]'
' 1a' matches pattern '\s\d\w'
'\t5n' does not match pattern '\s\d\w'
'5n' matches pattern '\s\d\w'
```

Matching multiple characters

With this information, we can match most strings of a known length, but most of the time we don't know how many characters to match inside a pattern. Regular expressions can take care of this, too. We can modify a pattern by appending one of several hard-to-remember punctuation symbols to match multiple characters.

The asterisk (*) character says that the previous pattern can be matched zero or more times. This probably sounds silly, but it's one of the most useful repetition characters. Before we explore why, consider some silly examples to make sure we understand what it does:

```
'hello' matches pattern 'hel*o'
'heo' matches pattern 'hel*o'
'helllllo' matches pattern 'hel*o'
```

So, the * character in the pattern says that the previous pattern (the l character) is optional, and if present, can be repeated as many times as possible to match the pattern. The rest of the characters (h, e, and o) have to appear exactly once.

It's pretty rare to want to match a single letter multiple times, but it gets more interesting if we combine the asterisk with patterns that match multiple characters. .*, for example, will match any string, whereas [a-z]* matches any collection of lowercase words, including the empty string.

For example:

```
'A string.' matches pattern '[A-Z][a-z]* [a-z]*\.'
'No .' matches pattern '[A-Z][a-z]* [a-z]*\.'
'' matches pattern '[a-z]*.*'
```

The plus (+) sign in a pattern behaves similarly to an asterisk; it states that the previous pattern can be repeated one or more times, but, unlike the asterisk is not optional. The question mark (?) ensures a pattern shows up exactly zero or one times, but not more. Let's explore some of these by playing with numbers (remember that \d matches the same character class as [0-9]:

```
'0.4' matches pattern '\d+\.\d+'
'1.002' matches pattern '\d+\.\d+'
'1.' does not match pattern '\d+\.\d+'
'1%' matches pattern '\d?\d%'
'99%' matches pattern '\d?\d%'
'999%' does not match pattern '\d?\d%'
```

Grouping patterns together

So far we've seen how we can repeat a pattern multiple times, but we are restricted in what patterns we can repeat. If we want to repeat individual characters, we're covered, but what if we want a repeating sequence of characters? Enclosing any set of patterns in parenthesis allows them to be treated as a single pattern when applying repetition operations. Compare these patterns:

```
'abccc' matches pattern 'abc{3}'
'abccc' does not match pattern '(abc){3}'
'abcabcabc' matches pattern '(abc){3}'
```

Combined with complex patterns, this grouping feature greatly expands our pattern-matching repertoire. Here's a regular expression that matches simple English sentences:

```
'Eat.' matches pattern '[A-Z][a-z]*( [a-z]+)*\.$'
'Eat more good food.' matches pattern '[A-Z][a-z]*( [a-z]+)*\.$'
'A good meal.' matches pattern '[A-Z][a-z]*( [a-z]+)*\.$'
```

The first word starts with a capital, followed by zero or more lowercase letters. Then, we enter a parenthetical that matches a single space followed by a word of one or more lowercase letters. This entire parenthetical is repeated zero or more times, and the pattern is terminated with a period. There cannot be any other characters after the period, as indicated by the $ matching the end of string.

We've seen many of the most basic patterns, but the regular expression language supports many more. I spent my first few years using regular expressions looking up the syntax every time I needed to do something. It is worth bookmarking Python's documentation for the `re` module and reviewing it frequently. There are very few things that regular expressions cannot match, and they should be the first tool you reach for when parsing strings.

Getting information from regular expressions

Let's now focus on the Python side of things. The regular expression syntax is the furthest thing from object-oriented programming. However, Python's `re` module provides an object-oriented interface to enter the regular expression engine.

We've been checking whether the `re.match` function returns a valid object or not. If a pattern does not match, that function returns `None`. If it does match, however, it returns a useful object that we can introspect for information about the pattern.

So far, our regular expressions have answered questions such as "Does this string match this pattern?" Matching patterns is useful, but in many cases, a more interesting question is, "If this string matches this pattern, what is the value of a relevant substring?" If you use groups to identify parts of the pattern that you want to reference later, you can get them out of the match return value as illustrated in the next example:

```
pattern = "^[a-zA-Z.]+@([a-z.]*\.[a-z]+)$"
search_string = "some.user@example.com"
match = re.match(pattern, search_string)

if match:
    domain = match.groups()[0]
    print(domain)
```

The specification describing valid e-mail addresses is extremely complicated, and the regular expression that accurately matches all possibilities is obscenely long. So we cheated and made a simple regular expression that matches some common e-mail addresses; the point is that we want to access the domain name (after the @ sign) so we can connect to that address. This is done easily by wrapping that part of the pattern in parenthesis and calling the `groups()` method on the object returned by match.

The `groups` method returns a tuple of all the groups matched inside the pattern, which you can index to access a specific value. The groups are ordered from left to right. However, bear in mind that groups can be nested, meaning you can have one or more groups inside another group. In this case, the groups are returned in the order of their left-most brackets, so the outermost group will be returned before its inner matching groups.

In addition to the match function, the re module provides a couple other useful functions, search, and findall. The search function finds the first instance of a matching pattern, relaxing the restriction that the pattern start at the first letter of the string. Note that you can get a similar effect by using match and putting a ^. * character at the front of the pattern to match any characters between the start of the string and the pattern you are looking for.

The findall function behaves similarly to search, except that it finds all non-overlapping instances of the matching pattern, not just the first one. Basically, it finds the first match, then it resets the search to the end of that matching string and finds the next one.

Instead of returning a list of match objects, as you would expect, it returns a list of matching strings. Or tuples. Sometimes it's strings, sometimes it's tuples. It's not a very good API at all! As with all bad APIs, you'll have to memorize the differences and not rely on intuition. The type of the return value depends on the number of bracketed groups inside the regular expression:

- If there are no groups in the pattern, re.findall will return a list of strings, where each value is a complete substring from the source string that matches the pattern

- If there is exactly one group in the pattern, re.findall will return a list of strings where each value is the contents of that group

- If there are multiple groups in the pattern, then re.findall will return a list of tuples where each tuple contains a value from a matching group, in order

When you are designing function calls in your own Python libraries, try to make the function always return a consistent data structure. It is often good to design functions that can take arbitrary inputs and process them, but the return value should not switch from single value to a list, or a list of values to a list of tuples depending on the input. Let re.findall be a lesson!

The examples in the following interactive session will hopefully clarify the differences:

```
>>> import re
>>> re.findall('a.', 'abacadefagah')
['ab', 'ac', 'ad', 'ag', 'ah']
>>> re.findall('a(.)', 'abacadefagah')
['b', 'c', 'd', 'g', 'h']
>>> re.findall('(a)(.)', 'abacadefagah')
```

```
[('a', 'b'), ('a', 'c'), ('a', 'd'), ('a', 'g'), ('a', 'h')]
>>> re.findall('((a)(.))', 'abacadefagah')
[('ab', 'a', 'b'), ('ac', 'a', 'c'), ('ad', 'a', 'd'), ('ag', 'a', 'g'),
('ah', 'a', 'h')]
```

Making repeated regular expressions efficient

Whenever you call one of the regular expression methods, the engine has to convert the pattern string into an internal structure that makes searching strings fast. This conversion takes a non-trivial amount of time. If a regular expression pattern is going to be reused multiple times (for example, inside a `for` or `while` loop), it would be better if this conversion step could be done only once.

This is possible with the `re.compile` method. It returns an object-oriented version of the regular expression that has been compiled down and has the methods we've explored (`match`, `search`, `findall`) already, among others. We'll see examples of this in the case study.

This has definitely been a condensed introduction to regular expressions. At this point, we have a good feel for the basics and will recognize when we need to do further research. If we have a string pattern matching problem, regular expressions will almost certainly be able to solve them for us. However, we may need to look up new syntaxes in a more comprehensive coverage of the topic. But now we know what to look for! Let's move on to a completely different topic: serializing data for storage.

Serializing objects

Nowadays, we take the ability to write data to a file and retrieve it at an arbitrary later date for granted. As convenient as this is (imagine the state of computing if we couldn't store anything!), we often find ourselves converting data we have stored in a nice object or design pattern in memory into some kind of clunky text or binary format for storage, transfer over the network, or remote invocation on a distant server.

The Python `pickle` module is an object-oriented way to store objects directly in a special storage format. It essentially converts an object (and all the objects it holds as attributes) into a sequence of bytes that can be stored or transported however we see fit.

For basic work, the `pickle` module has an extremely simple interface. It is comprised of four basic functions for storing and loading data; two for manipulating file-like objects, and two for manipulating `bytes` objects (the latter are just shortcuts to the file-like interface, so we don't have to create a `BytesIO` file-like object ourselves).

The dump method accepts an object to be written and a file-like object to write the serialized bytes to. This object must have a write method (or it wouldn't be file-like), and that method must know how to handle a bytes argument (so a file opened for text output wouldn't work).

The load method does exactly the opposite; it reads a serialized object from a file-like object. This object must have the proper file-like read and readline arguments, each of which must, of course, return bytes. The pickle module will load the object from these bytes and the load method will return the fully reconstructed object. Here's an example that stores and then loads some data in a list object:

```
import pickle

some_data = ["a list", "containing", 5,
        "values including another list",
        ["inner", "list"]]

with open("pickled_list", 'wb') as file:
    pickle.dump(some_data, file)

with open("pickled_list", 'rb') as file:
    loaded_data = pickle.load(file)

print(loaded_data)
assert loaded_data == some_data
```

This code works as advertised: the objects are stored in the file and then loaded from the same file. In each case, we open the file using a with statement so that it is automatically closed. The file is first opened for writing and then a second time for reading, depending on whether we are storing or loading data.

The assert statement at the end would raise an error if the newly loaded object is not equal to the original object. Equality does not imply that they are the same object. Indeed, if we print the id() of both objects, we would discover they are different. However, because they are both lists whose contents are equal, the two lists are also considered equal.

The dumps and loads functions behave much like their file-like counterparts, except they return or accept bytes instead of file-like objects. The dumps function requires only one argument, the object to be stored, and it returns a serialized bytes object. The loads function requires a bytes object and returns the restored object. The 's' character in the method names is short for string; it's a legacy name from ancient versions of Python, where str objects were used instead of bytes.

Both `dump` methods accept an optional `protocol` argument. If we are saving and loading pickled objects that are only going to be used in Python 3 programs, we don't need to supply this argument. Unfortunately, if we are storing objects that may be loaded by older versions of Python, we have to use an older and less efficient protocol. This should not normally be an issue. Usually, the only program that would load a pickled object would be the same one that stored it. Pickle is an unsafe format, so we don't want to be sending it unsecured over the Internet to unknown interpreters.

The argument supplied is an integer version number. The default version is number 3, representing the current highly efficient storage system used by Python 3 pickling. The number 2 is the older version, which will store an object that can be loaded on all interpreters back to Python 2.3. As 2.6 is the oldest of Python that is still widely used in the wild, version 2 pickling is normally sufficient. Versions 0 and 1 are supported on older interpreters; 0 is an ASCII format, while 1 is a binary format. There is also an optimized version 4 that may one day become the default.

As a rule of thumb, then, if you know that the objects you are pickling will only be loaded by a Python 3 program (for example, only your program will be loading them), use the default pickling protocol. If they may be loaded by unknown interpreters, pass a protocol value of 2, unless you really believe they may need to be loaded by an archaic version of Python.

If we do pass a protocol to `dump` or `dumps`, we should use a keyword argument to specify it: `pickle.dumps(my_object, protocol=2)`. This is not strictly necessary, as the method only accepts two arguments, but typing out the full keyword argument reminds readers of our code what the purpose of the number is. Having a random integer in the method call would be hard to read. Two what? Store two copies of the object, maybe? Remember, code should always be readable. In Python, less code is often more readable than longer code, but not always. Be explicit.

It is possible to call `dump` or `load` on a single open file more than once. Each call to `dump` will store a single object (plus any objects it is composed of or contains), while a call to `load` will load and return just one object. So for a single file, each separate call to `dump` when storing the object should have an associated call to `load` when restoring at a later date.

Customizing pickles

With most common Python objects, pickling "just works". Basic primitives such as integers, floats, and strings can be pickled, as can any container object, such as lists or dictionaries, provided the contents of those containers are also picklable. Further, and importantly, any object can be pickled, so long as all of its attributes are also picklable.

So what makes an attribute unpicklable? Usually, it has something to do with time-sensitive attributes that it would not make sense to load in the future. For example, if we have an open network socket, open file, running thread, or database connection stored as an attribute on an object, it would not make sense to pickle these objects; a lot of operating system state would simply be gone when we attempted to reload them later. We can't just pretend a thread or socket connection exists and make it appear! No, we need to somehow customize how such transient data is stored and restored.

Here's a class that loads the contents of a web page every hour to ensure that they stay up to date. It uses the `threading.Timer` class to schedule the next update:

```python
from threading import Timer
import datetime
from urllib.request import urlopen

class UpdatedURL:
    def __init__(self, url):
        self.url = url
        self.contents = ''
        self.last_updated = None
        self.update()

    def update(self):
        self.contents = urlopen(self.url).read()
        self.last_updated = datetime.datetime.now()
        self.schedule()

    def schedule(self):
        self.timer = Timer(3600, self.update)
        self.timer.setDaemon(True)
        self.timer.start()
```

The `url`, `contents`, and `last_updated` are all pickleable, but if we try to pickle an instance of this class, things go a little nutty on the `self.timer` instance:

```python
>>> u = UpdatedURL("http://news.yahoo.com/")
>>> import pickle
>>> serialized = pickle.dumps(u)
Traceback (most recent call last):
  File "<pyshell#3>", line 1, in <module>
    serialized = pickle.dumps(u)
_pickle.PicklingError: Can't pickle <class '_thread.lock'>: attribute
lookup lock on _thread failed
```

That's not a very useful error, but it looks like we're trying to pickle something we shouldn't be. That would be the `Timer` instance; we're storing a reference to `self.timer` in the schedule method, and that attribute cannot be serialized.

When `pickle` tries to serialize an object, it simply tries to store the object's `__dict__` attribute; `__dict__` is a dictionary mapping all the attribute names on the object to their values. Luckily, before checking `__dict__`, `pickle` checks to see whether a `__getstate__` method exists. If it does, it will store the return value of that method instead of the `__dict__`.

Let's add a `__getstate__` method to our `UpdatedURL` class that simply returns a copy of the `__dict__` without a timer:

```
def __getstate__(self):
    new_state = self.__dict__.copy()
    if 'timer' in new_state:
        del new_state['timer']
    return new_state
```

If we pickle the object now, it will no longer fail. And we can even successfully restore that object using `loads`. However, the restored object doesn't have a timer attribute, so it will not be refreshing the content like it is designed to do. We need to somehow create a new timer (to replace the missing one) when the object is unpickled.

As we might expect, there is a complementary `__setstate__` method that can be implemented to customize unpickling. This method accepts a single argument, which is the object returned by `__getstate__`. If we implement both methods, `__getstate__` is not required to return a dictionary, since `__setstate__` will know what to do with whatever object `__getstate__` chooses to return. In our case, we simply want to restore the `__dict__`, and then create a new timer:

```
def __setstate__(self, data):
    self.__dict__ = data
    self.schedule()
```

The `pickle` module is very flexible and provides other tools to further customize the pickling process if you need them. However, these are beyond the scope of this book. The tools we've covered are sufficient for many basic pickling tasks. Objects to be pickled are normally relatively simple data objects; we would not likely pickle an entire running program or complicated design pattern, for example.

Serializing web objects

It is not a good idea to load a pickled object from an unknown or untrusted source. It is possible to inject arbitrary code into a pickled file to maliciously attack a computer via the pickle. Another disadvantage of pickles is that they can only be loaded by other Python programs, and cannot be easily shared with services written in other languages.

There are many formats that have been used for this purpose over the years. XML (Extensible Markup Language) used to be very popular, especially with Java developers. YAML (Yet Another Markup Language) is another format that you may see referenced occasionally. Tabular data is frequently exchanged in the CSV (Comma Separated Value) format. Many of these are fading into obscurity and there are many more that you will encounter over time. Python has solid standard or third-party libraries for all of them.

Before using such libraries on untrusted data, make sure to investigate security concerns with each of them. XML and YAML, for example, both have obscure features that, used maliciously, can allow arbitrary commands to be executed on the host machine. These features may not be turned off by default. Do your research.

JavaScript Object Notation (JSON) is a human readable format for exchanging primitive data. JSON is a standard format that can be interpreted by a wide array of heterogeneous client systems. Hence, JSON is extremely useful for transmitting data between completely decoupled systems. Further, JSON does not have any support for executable code, only data can be serialized; thus, it is more difficult to inject malicious statements into it.

Because JSON can be easily interpreted by JavaScript engines, it is often used for transmitting data from a web server to a JavaScript-capable web browser. If the web application serving the data is written in Python, it needs a way to convert internal data into the JSON format.

There is a module to do this, predictably named `json`. This module provides a similar interface to the `pickle` module, with `dump`, `load`, `dumps`, and `loads` functions. The default calls to these functions are nearly identical to those in `pickle`, so let us not repeat the details. There are a couple differences; obviously, the output of these calls is valid JSON notation, rather than a pickled object. In addition, the `json` functions operate on `str` objects, rather than `bytes`. Therefore, when dumping to or loading from a file, we need to create text files rather than binary ones.

The JSON serializer is not as robust as the `pickle` module; it can only serialize basic types such as integers, floats, and strings, and simple containers such as dictionaries and lists. Each of these has a direct mapping to a JSON representation, but JSON is unable to represent classes, methods, or functions. It is not possible to transmit complete objects in this format. Because the receiver of an object we have dumped to JSON format is normally not a Python object, it would not be able to understand classes or methods in the same way that Python does, anyway. In spite of the O for Object in its name, JSON is a **data** notation; objects, as you recall, are composed of both data and behavior.

If we do have objects for which we want to serialize only the data, we can always serialize the object's __dict__ attribute. Or we can semiautomate this task by supplying custom code to create or parse a JSON serializable dictionary from certain types of objects.

In the json module, both the object storing and loading functions accept optional arguments to customize the behavior. The dump and dumps methods accept a poorly named cls (short for class, which is a reserved keyword) keyword argument. If passed, this should be a subclass of the JSONEncoder class, with the default method overridden. This method accepts an arbitrary object and converts it to a dictionary that json can digest. If it doesn't know how to process the object, we should call the super() method, so that it can take care of serializing basic types in the normal way.

The load and loads methods also accept such a cls argument that can be a subclass of the inverse class, JSONDecoder. However, it is normally sufficient to pass a function into these methods using the object_hook keyword argument. This function accepts a dictionary and returns an object; if it doesn't know what to do with the input dictionary, it can return it unmodified.

Let's look at an example. Imagine we have the following simple contact class that we want to serialize:

```
class Contact:
    def __init__(self, first, last):
        self.first = first
        self.last = last

    @property
    def full_name(self):
        return("{} {}".format(self.first, self.last))
```

We could just serialize the __dict__ attribute:

```
>>> c = Contact("John", "Smith")
>>> json.dumps(c.__dict__)
'{"last": "Smith", "first": "John"}'
```

But accessing special (double-underscore) attributes in this fashion is kind of crude. Also, what if the receiving code (perhaps some JavaScript on a web page) wanted that full_name property to be supplied? Of course, we could construct the dictionary by hand, but let's create a custom encoder instead:

```
import json
class ContactEncoder(json.JSONEncoder):
    def default(self, obj):
        if isinstance(obj, Contact):
            return {'is_contact': True,
                    'first': obj.first,
                    'last': obj.last,
                    'full': obj.full_name}
        return super().default(obj)
```

The default method basically checks to see what kind of object we're trying to serialize; if it's a contact, we convert it to a dictionary manually; otherwise, we let the parent class handle serialization (by assuming that it is a basic type, which json knows how to handle). Notice that we pass an extra attribute to identify this object as a contact, since there would be no way to tell upon loading it. This is just a convention; for a more generic serialization mechanism, it might make more sense to store a string type in the dictionary, or possibly even the full class name, including package and module. Remember that the format of the dictionary depends on the code at the receiving end; there has to be an agreement as to how the data is going to be specified.

We can use this class to encode a contact by passing the class (not an instantiated object) to the dump or dumps function:

```
>>> c = Contact("John", "Smith")
>>> json.dumps(c, cls=ContactEncoder)
'{"is_contact": true, "last": "Smith", "full": "John Smith",
"first": "John"}'
```

For decoding, we can write a function that accepts a dictionary and checks the existence of the is_contact variable to decide whether to convert it to a contact:

```
def decode_contact(dic):
        if dic.get('is_contact'):
            return Contact(dic['first'], dic['last'])
        else:
            return dic
```

We can pass this function to the load or loads function using the object_hook keyword argument:

```
>>> data = ('{"is_contact": true, "last": "smith",'
    '"full": "john smith", "first": "john"}')

>>> c = json.loads(data, object_hook=decode_contact)
>>> c
<__main__.Contact object at 0xa02918c>
>>> c.full_name
'john smith'
```

Case study

Let's build a basic regular expression-powered templating engine in Python. This engine will parse a text file (such as an HTML page) and replace certain directives with text calculated from the input to those directives. This is about the most complicated task we would want to do with regular expressions; indeed, a full-fledged version of this would likely utilize a proper language parsing mechanism.

Consider the following input file:

```
/** include header.html **/
<h1>This is the title of the front page</h1>
/** include menu.html **/
<p>My name is /** variable name **/.
This is the content of my front page. It goes below the menu.</p>
<table>
<tr><th>Favourite Books</th></tr>
/** loopover book_list **/
<tr><td>/** loopvar **/</td></tr>

/** endloop **/
</table>
/** include footer.html **/
Copyright &copy; Today
```

This file contains "tags" of the form /** <directive> <data> **/ where the data is an optional single word and the directives are:

- `include`: Copy the contents of another file here
- `variable`: Insert the contents of a variable here
- `loopover`: Repeat the contents of the loop for a variable that is a list
- `endloop`: Signal the end of looped text
- `loopvar`: Insert a single value from the list being looped over

This template will render a different page depending which variables are passed into it. These variables will be passed in from a so-called context file. This will be encoded as a `json` object with keys representing the variables in question. My context file might look like this, but you would derive your own:

```
{
    "name": "Dusty",
    "book_list": [
        "Thief Of Time",
        "The Thief",
        "Snow Crash",
        "Lathe Of Heaven"
    ]
}
```

Before we get into the actual string processing, let's throw together some object-oriented boilerplate code for processing files and grabbing data from the command line:

```
import re
import sys
import json
from pathlib import Path


DIRECTIVE_RE = re.compile(
    r'/\*\*\s*(include|variable|loopover|endloop|loopvar)'
    r'\s*([^ ]*)\s*\*\*/')


class TemplateEngine:
    def __init__(self, infilename, outfilename, contextfilename):
        self.template = open(infilename).read()
        self.working_dir = Path(infilename).absolute().parent
        self.pos = 0
        self.outfile = open(outfilename, 'w')
```

```
            with open(contextfilename) as contextfile:
                self.context = json.load(contextfile)

        def process(self):
            print("PROCESSING...")


    if __name__ == '__main__':
        infilename, outfilename, contextfilename = sys.argv[1:]
        engine = TemplateEngine(infilename, outfilename, contextfilename)
        engine.process()
```

This is all pretty basic, we create a class and initialize it with some variables passed in on the command line.

Notice how we try to make the regular expression a little bit more readable by breaking it across two lines? We use raw strings (the r prefix), so we don't have to double escape all our backslashes. This is common in regular expressions, but it's still a mess. (Regular expressions always are, but they're often worth it.)

The `pos` indicates the current character in the content that we are processing; we'll see a lot more of it in a moment.

Now "all that's left" is to implement that process method. There are a few ways to do this. Let's do it in a fairly explicit way.

The process method has to find each directive that matches the regular expression and do the appropriate work with it. However, it also has to take care of outputting the normal text before, after, and between each directive to the output file, unmodified.

One good feature of the compiled version of regular expressions is that we can tell the `search` method to start searching at a specific position by passing the `pos` keyword argument. If we temporarily define doing the appropriate work with a directive as "ignore the directive and delete it from the output file", our process loop looks quite simple:

```
    def process(self):
        match = DIRECTIVE_RE.search(self.template, pos=self.pos)
        while match:
            self.outfile.write(self.template[self.pos:match.start()])
            self.pos = match.end()
            match = DIRECTIVE_RE.search(self.template, pos=self.pos)
        self.outfile.write(self.template[self.pos:])
```

In English, this function finds the first string in the text that matches the regular expression, outputs everything from the current position to the start of that match, and then advances the position to the end of aforesaid match. Once it's out of matches, it outputs everything since the last position.

Of course, ignoring the directive is pretty useless in a templating engine, so let's set up replace that position advancing line with code that delegates to a different method on the class depending on the directive:

```
def process(self):
    match = DIRECTIVE_RE.search(self.template, pos=self.pos)
    while match:
        self.outfile.write(self.template[self.pos:match.start()])
        directive, argument = match.groups()
        method_name = 'process_{}'.format(directive)
        getattr(self, method_name)(match, argument)
        match = DIRECTIVE_RE.search(self.template, pos=self.pos)
    self.outfile.write(self.template[self.pos:])
```

So we grab the directive and the single argument from the regular expression. The directive becomes a method name and we dynamically look up that method name on the self object (a little error processing here in case the template writer provides an invalid directive would be better). We pass the match object and argument into that method and assume that method will deal with everything appropriately, including moving the pos pointer.

Now that we've got our object-oriented architecture this far, it's actually pretty simple to implement the methods that are delegated to. The include and variable directives are totally straightforward:

```
def process_include(self, match, argument):
    with (self.working_dir / argument).open() as includefile:
        self.outfile.write(includefile.read())
        self.pos = match.end()

def process_variable(self, match, argument):
    self.outfile.write(self.context.get(argument, ''))
    self.pos = match.end()
```

The first simply looks up the included file and inserts the file contents, while the second looks up the variable name in the context dictionary (which was loaded from json in the __init__ method), defaulting to an empty string if it doesn't exist.

The three methods that deal with looping are a bit more intense, as they have to share state between the three of them. For simplicity (I'm sure you're eager to see the end of this long chapter, we're almost there!), we'll handle this as instance variables on the class itself. As an exercise, you might want to consider better ways to architect this, especially after reading the next three chapters.

```python
def process_loopover(self, match, argument):
    self.loop_index = 0
    self.loop_list = self.context.get(argument, [])
    self.pos = self.loop_pos = match.end()

def process_loopvar(self, match, argument):
    self.outfile.write(self.loop_list[self.loop_index])
    self.pos = match.end()

def process_endloop(self, match, argument):
    self.loop_index += 1
    if self.loop_index >= len(self.loop_list):
        self.pos = match.end()
        del self.loop_index
        del self.loop_list
        del self.loop_pos
    else:
        self.pos = self.loop_pos
```

When we encounter the `loopover` directive, we don't have to output anything, but we do have to set the initial state on three variables. The `loop_list` variable is assumed to be a list pulled from the context dictionary. The `loop_index` variable indicates what position in that list should be output in this iteration of the loop, while `loop_pos` is stored so we know where to jump back to when we get to the end of the loop.

The `loopvar` directive outputs the value at the current position in the `loop_list` variable and skips to the end of the directive. Note that it doesn't increment the loop index because the `loopvar` directive could be called multiple times inside a loop.

The `endloop` directive is more complicated. It determines whether there are more elements in the `loop_list`; if there are, it just jumps back to the start of the loop, incrementing the index. Otherwise, it resets all the variables that were being used to process the loop and jumps to the end of the directive so the engine can carry on with the next match.

Note that this particular looping mechanism is very fragile; if a template designer were to try nesting loops or forget an `endloop` call, it would go poorly for them. We would need a lot more error checking and probably want to store more loop state to make this a production platform. But I promised that the end of the chapter was nigh, so let's just head to the exercises, after seeing how our sample template is rendered with its context:

```
<html>
    <body>

<h1>This is the title of the front page</h1>
<a href="link1.html">First Link</a>
<a href="link2.html">Second Link</a>

<p>My name is Dusty.
This is the content of my front page. It goes below the menu.</p>
<table>
<tr><th>Favourite Books</th></tr>

<tr><td>Thief Of Time</td></tr>

<tr><td>The Thief</td></tr>

<tr><td>Snow Crash</td></tr>

<tr><td>Lathe Of Heaven</td></tr>

</table>
    </body>
</html>

Copyright &copy; Today
```

There are some weird newline effects due to the way we planned our template, but it works as expected.

Exercises

We've covered a wide variety of topics in this chapter, from strings to regular expressions, to object serialization, and back again. Now it's time to consider how these ideas can be applied to your own code.

Python strings are very flexible, and Python is an extremely powerful tool for string-based manipulations. If you don't do a lot of string processing in your daily work, try designing a tool that is exclusively intended for manipulating strings. Try to come up with something innovative, but if you're stuck, consider writing a web log analyzer (how many requests per hour? How many people visit more than five pages?) or a template tool that replaces certain variable names with the contents of other files.

Spend a lot of time toying with the string formatting operators until you've got the syntax memorized. Write a bunch of template strings and objects to pass into the format function, and see what kind of output you get. Try the exotic formatting operators, such as percentage or hexadecimal notation. Try out the fill and alignment operators, and see how they behave differently for integers, strings, and floats. Consider writing a class of your own that has a __format__ method; we didn't discuss this in detail, but explore just how much you can customize formatting.

Make sure you understand the difference between bytes and str objects. The distinction is very complicated in older versions of Python (there was no bytes, and str acted like both bytes and str unless we needed non-ASCII characters in which case there was a separate unicode object, which was similar to Python 3's str class. It's even more confusing than it sounds!). It's clearer nowadays; bytes is for binary data, and str is for character data. The only tricky part is knowing how and when to convert between the two. For practice, try writing text data to a file opened for writing bytes (you'll have to encode the text yourself), and then reading from the same file.

Do some experimenting with bytearray; see how it can act both like a bytes object and a list or container object at the same time. Try writing to a buffer that holds data in the bytes array until it is a certain length before returning it. You can simulate the code that puts data into the buffer by using time.sleep calls to ensure data doesn't arrive too quickly.

Study regular expressions online. Study them some more. Especially learn about named groups greedy versus lazy matching, and regex flags, three features that we didn't cover in this chapter. Make conscious decisions about when not to use them. Many people have very strong opinions about regular expressions and either overuse them or refuse to use them at all. Try to convince yourself to use them only when appropriate, and figure out when that is.

If you've ever written an adapter to load small amounts of data from a file or database and convert it to an object, consider using a pickle instead. Pickles are not efficient for storing massive amounts of data, but they can be useful for loading configuration or other simple objects. Try coding it multiple ways: using a pickle, a text file, or a small database. Which do you find easiest to work with?

Try experimenting with pickling data, then modifying the class that holds the data, and loading the pickle into the new class. What works? What doesn't? Is there a way to make drastic changes to a class, such as renaming an attribute or splitting it into two new attributes and still get the data out of an older pickle? (Hint: try placing a private pickle version number on each object and update it each time you change the class; you can then put a migration path in `__setstate__`.)

If you do any web development at all, do some experimenting with the JSON serializer. Personally, I prefer to serialize only standard JSON serializable objects, rather than writing custom encoders or `object_hooks`, but the desired effect really depends on the interaction between the frontend (JavaScript, typically) and backend code.

Create some new directives in the templating engine that take more than one or an arbitrary number of arguments. You might need to modify the regular expression or add new ones. Have a look at the Django project's online documentation, and see if there are any other template tags you'd like to work with. Try mimicking their filter syntax instead of using the variable tag. Revisit this chapter when you've studied iteration and coroutines and see if you can come up with a more compact way of representing the state between related directives, such as the loop.

Summary

We've covered string manipulation, regular expressions, and object serialization in this chapter. Hardcoded strings and program variables can be combined into outputtable strings using the powerful string formatting system. It is important to distinguish between binary and textual data and `bytes` and `str` have specific purposes that must be understood. Both are immutable, but the `bytearray` type can be used when manipulating bytes.

Regular expressions are a complex topic, but we scratched the surface. There are many ways to serialize Python data; pickles and JSON are two of the most popular.

In the next chapter, we'll look at a design pattern that is so fundamental to Python programming that it has been given special syntax support: the iterator pattern.

9
The Iterator Pattern

We've discussed how many of Python's built-ins and idioms that seem, at first blush, to be non-object-oriented are actually providing access to major objects under the hood. In this chapter, we'll discuss how the `for` loop that seems so structured is actually a lightweight wrapper around a set of object-oriented principles. We'll also see a variety of extensions to this syntax that automatically create even more types of object. We will cover:

- What design patterns are
- The iterator protocol — one of the most powerful design patterns
- List, set, and dictionary comprehensions
- Generators and coroutines

Design patterns in brief

When engineers and architects decide to build a bridge, or a tower, or a building, they follow certain principles to ensure structural integrity. There are various possible designs for bridges (suspension or cantilever, for example), but if the engineer doesn't use one of the standard designs, and doesn't have a brilliant new design, it is likely the bridge he/she designs will collapse.

Design patterns are an attempt to bring this same formal definition for correctly designed structures to software engineering. There are many different design patterns to solve different general problems. People who create design patterns first identify a common problem faced by developers in a wide variety of situations. They then suggest what might be considered the ideal solution for that problem, in terms of object-oriented design.

Knowing a design pattern and choosing to use it in our software does not, however, guarantee that we are creating a "correct" solution. In 1907, the Québec Bridge (to this day, the longest cantilever bridge in the world) collapsed before construction was completed, because the engineers who designed it grossly underestimated the weight of the steel used to construct it. Similarly, in software development, we may incorrectly choose or apply a design pattern, and create software that "collapses" under normal operating situations or when stressed beyond its original design limits.

Any one design pattern proposes a set of objects interacting in a specific way to solve a general problem. The job of the programmer is to recognize when they are facing a specific version of that problem, and to adapt the general design in their solution.

In this chapter, we'll be covering the iterator design pattern. This pattern is so powerful and pervasive that the Python developers have provided multiple syntaxes to access the object-oriented principles underlying the pattern. We will be covering other design patterns in the next two chapters. Some of them have language support and some don't, but none of them is as intrinsically a part of the Python coder's daily life as the iterator pattern.

Iterators

In typical design pattern parlance, an iterator is an object with a `next()` method and a `done()` method; the latter returns `True` if there are no items left in the sequence. In a programming language without built-in support for iterators, the iterator would be looped over like this:

```
while not iterator.done():
    item = iterator.next()
    # do something with the item
```

In Python, iteration is a special feature, so the method gets a special name, `__next__`. This method can be accessed using the `next(iterator)` built-in. Rather than a `done` method, the iterator protocol raises `StopIteration` to notify the loop that it has completed. Finally, we have the much more readable `for item in iterator` syntax to actually access items in an iterator instead of messing around with a `while` loop. Let's look at these in more detail.

The iterator protocol

The abstract base class `Iterator`, in the `collections.abc` module, defines the iterator protocol in Python. As mentioned, it must have a __next__ method that the `for` loop (and other features that support iteration) can call to get a new element from the sequence. In addition, every iterator must also fulfill the `Iterable` interface. Any class that provides an __iter__ method is iterable; that method must return an `Iterator` instance that will cover all the elements in that class. Since an iterator is already looping over elements, its __iter__ function traditionally returns itself.

This might sound a bit confusing, so have a look at the following example, but note that this is a very verbose way to solve this problem. It clearly explains iteration and the two protocols in question, but we'll be looking at several more readable ways to get this effect later in this chapter:

```python
class CapitalIterable:
    def __init__(self, string):
        self.string = string

    def __iter__(self):
        return CapitalIterator(self.string)


class CapitalIterator:
    def __init__(self, string):
        self.words = [w.capitalize() for w in string.split()]
        self.index = 0

    def __next__(self):
        if self.index == len(self.words):
            raise StopIteration()

        word = self.words[self.index]
        self.index += 1
        return word

    def __iter__(self):
        return self
```

This example defines an `CapitalIterable` class whose job is to loop over each of the words in a string and output them with the first letter capitalized. Most of the work of that iterable is passed to the `CapitalIterator` implementation. The canonical way to interact with this iterator is as follows:

```
>>> iterable = CapitalIterable('the quick brown fox jumps over the lazy
dog')
>>> iterator = iter(iterable)
>>> while True:
...     try:
...         print(next(iterator))
...     except StopIteration:
...         break
...
The
Quick
Brown
Fox
Jumps
Over
The
Lazy
Dog
```

This example first constructs an iterable and retrieves an iterator from it. The distinction may need explanation; the iterable is an object with elements that can be looped over. Normally, these elements can be looped over multiple times, maybe even at the same time or in overlapping code. The iterator, on the other hand, represents a specific location in that iterable; some of the items have been consumed and some have not. Two different iterators might be at different places in the list of words, but any one iterator can mark only one place.

Each time `next()` is called on the iterator, it returns another token from the iterable, in order. Eventually, the iterator will be exhausted (won't have any more elements to return), in which case `StopIteration` is raised, and we break out of the loop.

Of course, we already know a much simpler syntax for constructing an iterator from an iterable:

```
>>> for i in iterable:
...     print(i)
...
The
Quick
Brown
Fox
Jumps
Over
The
Lazy
Dog
```

As you can see, the for statement, in spite of not looking terribly object-oriented, is actually a shortcut to some obviously object-oriented design principles. Keep this in mind as we discuss comprehensions, as they, too, appear to be the polar opposite of an object-oriented tool. Yet, they use the exact same iteration protocol as for loops and are just another kind of shortcut.

Comprehensions

Comprehensions are simple, but powerful, syntaxes that allow us to transform or filter an iterable object in as little as one line of code. The resultant object can be a perfectly normal list, set, or dictionary, or it can be a generator expression that can be efficiently consumed in one go.

List comprehensions

List comprehensions are one of the most powerful tools in Python, so people tend to think of them as advanced. They're not. Indeed, I've taken the liberty of littering previous examples with comprehensions and assuming you'd understand them. While it's true that advanced programmers use comprehensions a lot, it's not because they're advanced, it's because they're trivial, and handle some of the most common operations in software development.

Let's have a look at one of those common operations; namely, converting a list of items into a list of related items. Specifically, let's assume we just read a list of strings from a file, and now we want to convert it to a list of integers. We know every item in the list is an integer, and we want to do some activity (say, calculate an average) on those numbers. Here's one simple way to approach it:

```
input_strings = ['1', '5', '28', '131', '3']

output_integers = []
for num in input_strings:
    output_integers.append(int(num))
```

This works fine and it's only three lines of code. If you aren't used to comprehensions, you may not even think it looks ugly! Now, look at the same code using a list comprehension:

```
input_strings = ['1', '5', '28', '131', '3']output_integers =
[int(num) for num in input_strings]
```

We're down to one line and, importantly for performance, we've dropped an `append` method call for each item in the list. Overall, it's pretty easy to tell what's going on, even if you're not used to comprehension syntax.

The square brackets indicate, as always, that we're creating a list. Inside this list is a `for` loop that iterates over each item in the input sequence. The only thing that may be confusing is what's happening between the list's opening brace and the start of the `for` loop. Whatever happens here is applied to *each* of the items in the input list. The item in question is referenced by the `num` variable from the loop. So, it's converting each individual element to an `int` data type.

That's all there is to a basic list comprehension. They are not so advanced after all. Comprehensions are highly optimized C code; list comprehensions are far faster than `for` loops when looping over a huge number of items. If readability alone isn't a convincing reason to use them as much as possible, speed should be.

Converting one list of items into a related list isn't the only thing we can do with a list comprehension. We can also choose to exclude certain values by adding an `if` statement inside the comprehension. Have a look:

```
output_ints = [int(n) for n in input_strings if len(n) < 3]
```

I shortened the name of the variable from `num` to `n` and the result variable to `output_ints` so it would still fit on one line. Other than this, all that's different between this example and the previous one is the `if len(n) < 3` part. This extra code excludes any strings with more than two characters. The `if` statement is applied before the `int` function, so it's testing the length of a string. Since our input strings are all integers at heart, it excludes any number over 99. Now that is all there is to list comprehensions! We use them to map input values to output values, applying a filter along the way to include or exclude any values that meet a specific condition.

Any iterable can be the input to a list comprehension; anything we can wrap in a `for` loop can also be placed inside a comprehension. For example, text files are iterable; each call to `__next__` on the file's iterator will return one line of the file. We could load a tab delimited file where the first line is a header row into a dictionary using the `zip` function:

```
import sys
filename = sys.argv[1]

with open(filename) as file:
    header = file.readline().strip().split('\t')
    contacts = [
            dict(
                zip(header, line.strip().split('\t'))
                ) for line in file
            ]

for contact in contacts:
    print("email: {email} -- {last}, {first}".format(
        **contact))
```

This time, I've added some whitespace to make it somewhat more readable (list comprehensions don't *have* to fit on one line). This example creates a list of dictionaries from the zipped header and split lines for each line in the file.

Er, what? Don't worry if that code or explanation doesn't make sense; it's a bit confusing. One list comprehension is doing a pile of work here, and the code is hard to understand, read, and ultimately, maintain. This example shows that list comprehensions aren't always the best solution; most programmers would agree that a `for` loop would be more readable than this version.

Remember: the tools we are provided with should not be abused! Always pick the right tool for the job, which is always to write maintainable code.

Set and dictionary comprehensions

Comprehensions aren't restricted to lists. We can use a similar syntax with braces to create sets and dictionaries as well. Let's start with sets. One way to create a set is to wrap a list comprehension in the `set()` constructor, which converts it to a set. But why waste memory on an intermediate list that gets discarded, when we can create a set directly?

Here's an example that uses a named tuple to model author/title/genre triads, and then retrieves a set of all the authors that write in a specific genre:

```python
from collections import namedtuple

Book = namedtuple("Book", "author title genre")
books = [
        Book("Pratchett", "Nightwatch", "fantasy"),
        Book("Pratchett", "Thief Of Time", "fantasy"),
        Book("Le Guin", "The Dispossessed", "scifi"),
        Book("Le Guin", "A Wizard Of Earthsea", "fantasy"),
        Book("Turner", "The Thief", "fantasy"),
        Book("Phillips", "Preston Diamond", "western"),
        Book("Phillips", "Twice Upon A Time", "scifi"),
        ]

fantasy_authors = {
        b.author for b in books if b.genre == 'fantasy'}
```

The highlighted set comprehension sure is short in comparison to the demo-data setup! If we were to use a list comprehension, of course, Terry Pratchett would have been listed twice.. As it is, the nature of sets removes the duplicates, and we end up with:

```python
>>> fantasy_authors
{'Turner', 'Pratchett', 'Le Guin'}
```

We can introduce a colon to create a dictionary comprehension. This converts a sequence into a dictionary using *key: value* pairs. For example, it may be useful to quickly look up the author or genre in a dictionary if we know the title. We can use a dictionary comprehension to map titles to book objects:

```python
fantasy_titles = {
        b.title: b for b in books if b.genre == 'fantasy'}
```

Now, we have a dictionary, and can look up books by title using the normal syntax.

In summary, comprehensions are not advanced Python, nor are they "non-object-oriented" tools that should be avoided. They are simply a more concise and optimized syntax for creating a list, set, or dictionary from an existing sequence.

Generator expressions

Sometimes we want to process a new sequence without placing a new list, set, or dictionary into system memory. If we're just looping over items one at a time, and don't actually care about having a final container object created, creating that container is a waste of memory. When processing one item at a time, we only need the current object stored in memory at any one moment. But when we create a container, all the objects have to be stored in that container before we start processing them.

For example, consider a program that processes log files. A very simple log might contain information in this format:

```
Jan 26, 2015 11:25:25    DEBUG      This is a debugging message.
Jan 26, 2015 11:25:36    INFO       This is an information method.
Jan 26, 2015 11:25:46    WARNING    This is a warning. It could be
serious.
Jan 26, 2015 11:25:52    WARNING    Another warning sent.
Jan 26, 2015 11:25:59    INFO       Here's some information.
Jan 26, 2015 11:26:13    DEBUG      Debug messages are only useful
if you want to figure something out.
Jan 26, 2015 11:26:32    INFO       Information is usually harmless,
but helpful.
Jan 26, 2015 11:26:40    WARNING    Warnings should be heeded.
Jan 26, 2015 11:26:54    WARNING    Watch for warnings.
```

Log files for popular web servers, databases, or e-mail servers can contain many gigabytes of data (I recently had to clean nearly 2 terabytes of logs off a misbehaving system). If we want to process each line in the log, we can't use a list comprehension; it would create a list containing every line in the file. This probably wouldn't fit in RAM and could bring the computer to its knees, depending on the operating system.

If we used a `for` loop on the log file, we could process one line at a time before reading the next one into memory. Wouldn't be nice if we could use comprehension syntax to get the same effect?

This is where generator expressions come in. They use the same syntax as comprehensions, but they don't create a final container object. To create a generator expression, wrap the comprehension in () instead of [] or {}.

The following code parses a log file in the previously presented format, and outputs a new log file that contains only the WARNING lines:

```
import sys

inname = sys.argv[1]
outname = sys.argv[2]

with open(inname) as infile:
    with open(outname, "w") as outfile:
        warnings = (l for l in infile if 'WARNING' in l)
        for l in warnings:
            outfile.write(l)
```

This program takes the two filenames on the command line, uses a generator expression to filter out the warnings (in this case, it uses the if syntax, and leaves the line unmodified), and then outputs the warnings to another file. If we run it on our sample file, the output looks like this:

```
Jan 26, 2015 11:25:46    WARNING    This is a warning. It could be
serious.
Jan 26, 2015 11:25:52    WARNING    Another warning sent.
Jan 26, 2015 11:26:40    WARNING    Warnings should be heeded.
Jan 26, 2015 11:26:54    WARNING    Watch for warnings.
```

Of course, with such a short input file, we could have safely used a list comprehension, but if the file is millions of lines long, the generator expression will have a huge impact on both memory and speed.

Generator expressions are frequently most useful inside function calls. For example, we can call sum, min, or max, on a generator expression instead of a list, since these functions process one object at a time. We're only interested in the result, not any intermediate container.

In general, a generator expression should be used whenever possible. If we don't actually need a list, set, or dictionary, but simply need to filter or convert items in a sequence, a generator expression will be most efficient. If we need to know the length of a list, or sort the result, remove duplicates, or create a dictionary, we'll have to use the comprehension syntax.

Generators

Generator expressions are actually a sort of comprehension too; they compress the more advanced (this time it really is more advanced!) generator syntax into one line. The greater generator syntax looks even less object-oriented than anything we've seen, but we'll discover that once again, it is a simple syntax shortcut to create a kind of object.

Let's take the log file example a little further. If we want to delete the WARNING column from our output file (since it's redundant: this file contains only warnings), we have several options, at various levels of readability. We can do it with a generator expression:

```
import sys
inname, outname = sys.argv[1:3]

with open(inname) as infile:
    with open(outname, "w") as outfile:
        warnings = (l.replace('\tWARNING', '')
                for l in infile if 'WARNING' in l)
        for l in warnings:
            outfile.write(l)
```

That's perfectly readable, though I wouldn't want to make the expression much more complicated than that. We could also do it with a normal `for` loop:

```
import sys
inname, outname = sys.argv[1:3]

with open(inname) as infile:
    with open(outname, "w") as outfile:
        for l in infile:
            if 'WARNING' in l:
                outfile.write(l.replace('\tWARNING', ''))
```

That's maintainable, but so many levels of indent in so few lines is kind of ugly. More alarmingly, if we wanted to do something different with the lines, rather than just printing them out, we'd have to duplicate the looping and conditional code, too. Now let's consider a truly object-oriented solution, without any shortcuts:

```
import sys
inname, outname = sys.argv[1:3]

class WarningFilter:
    def __init__(self, insequence):
```

```
            self.insequence = insequence
    def __iter__(self):
        return self
    def __next__(self):
        l = self.insequence.readline()
        while l and 'WARNING' not in l:
            l = self.insequence.readline()
        if not l:
            raise StopIteration
        return l.replace('\tWARNING', '')

with open(inname) as infile:
    with open(outname, "w") as outfile:
        filter = WarningFilter(infile)
        for l in filter:
            outfile.write(l)
```

No doubt about it: that is so ugly and difficult to read that
you may not even be able to tell what's going on. We created an object that takes
a file object as input, and provides a __next__ method like any iterator.

This __next__ method reads lines from the file, discarding them if they are not
WARNING lines. When it encounters a WARNING line, it returns it. Then the for loop
will call __next__ again to process the next WARNING line. When we run out of lines,
we raise StopIteration to tell the loop we're finished iterating. It's pretty ugly
compared to the other examples, but it's also powerful; now that we have a class
in our hands, we can do whatever we want with it.

With that background behind us, we finally get to see generators in action. This
next example does *exactly* the same thing as the previous one: it creates an object
with a __next__ method that raises StopIteration when it's out of inputs:

```
import sys
inname, outname = sys.argv[1:3]


def warnings_filter(insequence):
    for l in insequence:
        if 'WARNING' in l:
            yield l.replace('\tWARNING', '')


with open(inname) as infile:
    with open(outname, "w") as outfile:
```

```
filter = warnings_filter(infile)
for l in filter:
    outfile.write(l)
```

OK, that's pretty readable, maybe... at least it's short. But what on earth is going on here, it makes no sense whatsoever. And what is `yield`, anyway?

In fact, `yield` is the key to generators. When Python sees `yield` in a function, it takes that function and wraps it up in an object not unlike the one in our previous example. Think of the `yield` statement as similar to the `return` statement; it exits the function and returns a line. Unlike `return`, however, when the function is called again (via `next()`), it will start where it left off—on the line after the `yield` statement—instead of at the beginning of the function. In this example, there is no line "after" the `yield` statement, so it jumps to the next iteration of the `for` loop. Since the `yield` statement is inside an `if` statement, it only yields lines that contain WARNING.

While it looks like this is just a function looping over the lines, it is actually creating a special type of object, a generator object:

```
>>> print(warnings_filter([]))
<generator object warnings_filter at 0xb728c6bc>
```

I passed an empty list into the function to act as an iterator. All the function does is create and return a generator object. That object has __iter__ and __next__ methods on it, just like the one we created in the previous example. Whenever __next__ is called, the generator runs the function until it finds a `yield` statement. it then returns the value from `yield`, and the next time __next__ is called, it picks up where it left off.

This use of generators isn't that advanced, but if you don't realize the function is creating an object, it can seem like magic. This example was quite simple, but you can get really powerful effects by making multiple calls to `yield` in a single function; the generator will simply pick up at the most recent `yield` and continue to the next one.

Yield items from another iterable

Often, when we build a generator function, we end up in a situation where we want to yield data from another iterable object, possibly a list comprehension or generator expression we constructed inside the generator, or perhaps some external items that were passed into the function. This has always been possible by looping over the iterable and individually yielding each item. However, in Python version 3.3, the Python developers introduced a new syntax to make this a little more elegant.

Let's adapt the generator example a bit so that instead of accepting a sequence of lines, it accepts a filename. This would normally be frowned upon as it ties the object to a particular paradigm. When possible we should operate on iterators as input; this way the same function could be used regardless of whether the log lines came from a file, memory, or a web-based log aggregator. So the following example is contrived for pedagogical reasons.

This version of the code illustrates that your generator can do some basic setup before yielding information from another iterable (in this case, a generator expression):

```
import sys
inname, outname = sys.argv[1:3]


def warnings_filter(infilename):
    with open(infilename) as infile:
        yield from (
            l.replace('\tWARNING', '')
            for l in infile
            if 'WARNING' in l
        )

filter = warnings_filter(inname)
with open(outname, "w") as outfile:
    for l in filter:
        outfile.write(l)
```

This code combines the `for` loop from the previous example into a generator expression. Notice how I put the three clauses of the generator expression (the transformation, the loop, and the filter) on separate lines to make them more readable. Notice also that this transformation didn't help enough; the previous example with a `for` loop was more readable.

So let's consider an example that is more readable than its alternative. It can be useful to construct a generator that yields data from multiple other generators. The `itertools.chain` function, for example, yields data from iterables in sequence until they have all been exhausted. This can be implemented far too easily using the `yield from` syntax, so let's consider a classic computer science problem: walking a general tree.

A common implementation of the general tree data structure is a computer's filesystem. Let's model a few folders and files in a Unix filesystem so we can use `yield from` to walk them effectively:

```
class File:
    def __init__(self, name):
```

```
        self.name = name

class Folder(File):
    def __init__(self, name):
        super().__init__(name)
        self.children = []

root = Folder('')
etc = Folder('etc')
root.children.append(etc)
etc.children.append(File('passwd'))
etc.children.append(File('groups'))
httpd = Folder('httpd')
etc.children.append(httpd)
httpd.children.append(File('http.conf'))
var = Folder('var')
root.children.append(var)
log = Folder('log')
var.children.append(log)
log.children.append(File('messages'))
log.children.append(File('kernel'))
```

This setup code looks like a lot of work, but in a real filesystem, it would be even more involved. We'd have to read data from the hard drive and structure it into the tree. Once in memory, however, the code that outputs every file in the filesystem is quite elegant:

```
def walk(file):
    if isinstance(file, Folder):
        yield file.name + '/'
        for f in file.children:
            yield from walk(f)
    else:
        yield file.name
```

If this code encounters a directory, it recursively asks `walk()` to generate a list of all files subordinate to each of its children, and then yields all that data plus its own filename. In the simple case that it has encountered a normal file, it just yields that name.

As an aside, solving the preceding problem without using a generator is tricky enough that this problem is a common interview question. If you answer it as shown like this, be prepared for your interviewer to be both impressed and somewhat irritated that you answered it so easily. They will likely demand that you explain exactly what is going on. Of course, armed with the principles you've leaned in this chapter, you won't have any problem.

The `yield from` syntax is a useful shortcut when writing chained generators, but it is more commonly used for a different purpose: piping data through coroutines. We'll see many examples of this in *Chapter 13, Concurrency*, but for now, let's discover what a coroutine is.

Coroutines

Coroutines are extremely powerful constructs that are often confused with generators. Many authors inappropriately describe coroutines as "generators with a bit of extra syntax." This is an easy mistake to make, as, way back in Python 2.5, when coroutines were introduced, they were presented as "we added a `send` method to the generator syntax." This is further complicated by the fact that when you create a coroutine in Python, the object returned is a generator. The difference is actually a lot more nuanced and will make more sense after you've seen a few examples.

> While coroutines in Python are currently tightly coupled to the generator syntax, they are only superficially related to the iterator protocol we have been discussing. The upcoming (as this is published) Python 3.5 release makes coroutines a truly standalone object and will provide a new syntax to work with them.

The other thing to bear in mind is that coroutines are pretty hard to understand. They are not used all that often in the wild, and you could likely skip this section and happily develop in Python for years without missing or even encountering them. There are a couple libraries that use coroutines extensively (mostly for concurrent or asynchronous programming), but they are normally written such that you can use coroutines without actually understanding how they work! So if you get lost in this section, don't despair.

But you won't get lost, having studied the following examples. Here's one of the simplest possible coroutines; it allows us to keep a running tally that can be increased by arbitrary values:

```
def tally():
    score = 0
```

```
    while True:
        increment = yield score
        score += increment
```

This code looks like black magic that couldn't possibly work, so we'll see it working before going into a line-by-line description. This simple object could be used by a scoring application for a baseball team. Separate tallies could be kept for each team, and their score could be incremented by the number of runs accumulated at the end of every half-inning. Look at this interactive session:

```
>>> white_sox = tally()
>>> blue_jays = tally()
>>> next(white_sox)
0
>>> next(blue_jays)
0
>>> white_sox.send(3)
3
>>> blue_jays.send(2)
2
>>> white_sox.send(2)
5
>>> blue_jays.send(4)
6
```

First we construct two `tally` objects, one for each team. Yes, they look like functions, but as with the generator objects in the previous section, the fact that there is a `yield` statement inside the function tells Python to put a great deal of effort into turning the simple function into an object.

We then call `next()` on each of the coroutine objects. This does the same thing as calling next on any generator, which is to say, it executes each line of code until it encounters a `yield` statement, returns the value at that point, and then *pauses* until the next `next()` call.

So far, then, there's nothing new. But look back at the `yield` statement in our coroutine:

```
    increment = yield score
```

Unlike with generators, this yield function looks like it's supposed to return a value and assign it to a variable. This is, in fact, exactly what's happening. The coroutine is still paused at the `yield` statement and waiting to be activated again by another call to `next()`.

Or rather, as you see in the interactive session, a call to a method called `send()`. The `send()` method does *exactly* the same thing as `next()` except that in addition to advancing the generator to the next `yield` statement. It also allows you to pass in a value from outside the generator. This value is assigned to the left side of the `yield` statement.

The thing that is really confusing for many people is the order in which this happens:

- `yield` occurs and the generator pauses
- `send()` occurs from outside the function and the generator wakes up
- The value sent in is assigned to the left side of the `yield` statement
- The generator continues processing until it encounters another `yield` statement

So, in this particular example, after we construct the coroutine and advance it to the `yield` statement with a call to `next()`, each successive call to `send()` passes a value into the coroutine, which adds this value to its score, goes back to the top of the `while` loop, and keeps processing until it hits the `yield` statement. The `yield` statement returns a value, and this value becomes the return value of the most recent call to `send`. Don't miss that: the `send()` method does not just submit a value to the generator, it also returns the value from the upcoming `yield` statement, just like `next()`. This is how we define the difference between a generator and a coroutine: a generator only produces values, while a coroutine can also consume them.

The behavior and syntax of `next(i)`, `i.__next__()`, and `i.send(value)` are rather unintuitive and frustrating. The first is a normal function, the second is a special method, and the last is a normal method. But all three do the same thing: advance the generator until it yields a value and pause. Further, the `next()` function and associated method can be replicated by calling `i.send(None)`. There is value to having two different method names here, since it helps the reader of our code easily see whether they are interacting with a coroutine or a generator. I just find the fact that in one case it's a function call and in the other it's a normal method somewhat irritating.

Back to log parsing

Of course, the previous example could easily have been coded using a couple integer variables and calling x += increment on them. Let's look at a second example where coroutines actually save us some code. This example is a somewhat simplified (for pedagogical reasons) version of a problem I had to solve in my real job. The fact that it logically follows from the earlier discussions about processing a log file is completely serendipitous; those examples were written for the first edition of this book, whereas this problem came up four years later!

The Linux kernel log contains lines that look somewhat, but not quite completely, unlike this:

```
unrelated log messages
sd 0:0:0:0 Attached Disk Drive
unrelated log messages
sd 0:0:0:0 (SERIAL=ZZ12345)
unrelated log messages
sd 0:0:0:0 [sda] Options
unrelated log messages
XFS ERROR [sda]
unrelated log messages
sd 2:0:0:1 Attached Disk Drive
unrelated log messages
sd 2:0:0:1 (SERIAL=ZZ67890)
unrelated log messages
sd 2:0:0:1 [sdb] Options
unrelated log messages
sd 3:0:1:8 Attached Disk Drive
unrelated log messages
sd 3:0:1:8 (SERIAL=WW11111)
unrelated log messages
sd 3:0:1:8 [sdc] Options
unrelated log messages
XFS ERROR [sdc]
unrelated log messages
```

There are a whole bunch of interspersed kernel log messages, some of which pertain to hard disks. The hard disk messages might be interspersed with other messages, but they occur in a predictable format and order, in which a specific drive with a known serial number is associated with a bus identifier (such as 0:0:0:0), and a block device identifier (such as sda) is associated with that bus. Finally, if the drive has a corrupt filesystem, it might fail with an XFS error.

Now, given the preceding log file, the problem we need to solve is how to obtain the serial number of any drives that have XFS errors on them. This serial number might later be used by a data center technician to identify and replace the drive.

We know we can identify the individual lines using regular expressions, but we'll have to change the regular expressions as we loop through the lines, since we'll be looking for different things depending on what we found previously. The other difficult bit is that if we find an error string, the information about which bus contains that string, and what serial number is attached to the drive on that bus has already been processed. This can easily be solved by iterating through the lines of the file in reverse order.

Before you look at this example, be warned — the amount of code required for a coroutine-based solution is scarily small:

```python
import re

def match_regex(filename, regex):
    with open(filename) as file:
        lines = file.readlines()
    for line in reversed(lines):
        match = re.match(regex, line)
        if match:
            regex = yield match.groups()[0]


def get_serials(filename):
    ERROR_RE = 'XFS ERROR (\[sd[a-z]\])'
    matcher = match_regex(filename, ERROR_RE)
    device = next(matcher)
    while True:
        bus = matcher.send(
            '(sd \S+) {}.*'.format(re.escape(device)))
        serial = matcher.send('{} \(SERIAL=([^)]*)\)'.format(bus))
        yield serial
        device = matcher.send(ERROR_RE)

for serial_number in get_serials('EXAMPLE_LOG.log'):
    print(serial_number)
```

This code neatly divides the job into two separate tasks. The first task is to loop over all the lines and spit out any lines that match a given regular expression. The second task is to interact with the first task and give it guidance as to what regular expression it is supposed to be searching for at any given time.

Look at the `match_regex` coroutine first. Remember, it doesn't execute any code when it is constructed; rather, it just creates a coroutine object. Once constructed, someone outside the coroutine will eventually call `next()` to start the code running, at which point it stores the state of two variables, `filename` and `regex`. It then reads all the lines in the file and iterates over them in reverse. Each line is compared to the regular expression that was passed in until it finds a match. When the match is found, the coroutine yields the first group from the regular expression and waits.

At some point in the future, other code will send in a new regular expression to search for. Note that the coroutine never cares what regular expression it is trying to match; it's just looping over lines and comparing them to a regular expression. It's somebody else's responsibility to decide what regular expression to supply.

In this case, that somebody else is the `get_serials` generator. It doesn't care about the lines in the file, in fact it isn't even aware of them. The first thing it does is create a `matcher` object from the `match_regex` coroutine constructor, giving it a default regular expression to search for. It advances the coroutine to its first `yield` and stores the value it returns. It then goes into a loop that instructs the matcher object to search for a bus ID based on the stored device ID, and then a serial number based on that bus ID.

It idly yields that serial number to the outside `for` loop before instructing the matcher to find another device ID and repeat the cycle.

Basically, the coroutine's (`match_regex`, as it uses the `regex = yield` syntax) job is to search for the next important line in the file, while the generator's (`get_serial`, which uses the `yield` syntax without assignment) job is to decide which line is important. The generator has information about this particular problem, such as what order lines will appear in the file. The coroutine, on the other hand, could be plugged into any problem that required searching a file for given regular expressions.

Closing coroutines and throwing exceptions

Normal generators signal their exit from inside by raising `StopIteration`. If we chain multiple generators together (for example, by iterating over one generator from inside another), the `StopIteration` exception will be propagated outward. Eventually, it will hit a `for` loop that will see the exception and know that it's time to exit the loop.

Coroutines don't normally follow the iteration mechanism; rather than pulling data through one until an exception is encountered, data is usually pushed into it (using `send`). The entity doing the pushing is normally the one in charge of telling the coroutine when it's finished; it does this by calling the `close()` method on the coroutine in question.

When called, the `close()` method will raise a `GeneratorExit` exception at the point the coroutine was waiting for a value to be sent in. It is normally good policy for coroutines to wrap their `yield` statements in a `try...finally` block so that any cleanup tasks (such as closing associated files or sockets) can be performed.

If we need to raise an exception inside a coroutine, we can use the `throw()` method in a similar way. It accepts an exception type with optional `value` and `traceback` arguments. The latter is useful when we encounter an exception in one coroutine and want to cause an exception to occur in an adjacent coroutine while maintaining the traceback.

Both of these features are vital if you're building robust coroutine-based libraries, but we are unlikely to encounter them in our day-to-day coding lives.

The relationship between coroutines, generators, and functions

We've seen coroutines in action, so now let's go back to that discussion of how they are related to generators. In Python, as is so often the case, the distinction is quite blurry. In fact, all coroutines are generator objects, and authors often use the two terms interchangeably. Sometimes, they describe coroutines as a subset of generators (only generators that return values from yield are considered coroutines). This is technically true in Python, as we've seen in the previous sections.

However, in the greater sphere of theoretical computer science, coroutines are considered the more general principles, and generators are a specific type of coroutine. Further, normal functions are yet another distinct subset of coroutines.

A coroutine is a routine that can have data passed in at one or more points and get it out at one or more points. In Python, the point where data is passed in and out is the `yield` statement.

A function, or subroutine, is the simplest type of coroutine. You can pass data in at one point, and get data out at one other point when the function returns. While a function can have multiple `return` statements, only one of them can be called for any given invocation of the function.

Finally, a generator is a type of coroutine that can have data passed in at one point, but can pass data out at multiple points. In Python, the data would be passed out at a `yield` statement, but you can't pass data back in. If you called `send`, the data would be silently discarded.

So in theory, generators are types of coroutines, functions are types of coroutines, and there are coroutines that are neither functions nor generators. That's simple enough, eh? So why does it feel more complicated in Python?

In Python, generators and coroutines are both constructed using a syntax that looks like we are constructing a function. But the resulting object is not a function at all; it's a totally different kind of object. Functions are, of course, also objects. But they have a different interface; functions are callable and return values, generators have data pulled out using `next()`, and coroutines have data pushed in using `send`.

Case study

One of the fields in which Python is the most popular these days is data science. Let's implement a basic machine learning algorithm! Machine learning is a huge topic, but the general idea is to make predictions or classifications about future data by using knowledge gained from past data. Uses of such algorithms abound, and data scientists are finding new ways to apply machine learning every day. Some important machine learning applications include computer vision (such as image classification or facial recognition), product recommendation, identifying spam, and speech recognition. We'll look at a simpler problem: given an RGB color definition, what name would humans identify that color as?

There are more than 16 million colors in the standard RGB color space, and humans have come up with names for only a fraction of them. While there are thousands of names (some quite ridiculous; just go to any car dealership or makeup store), let's build a classifier that attempts to divide the RGB space into the basic colors:

- Red
- Purple
- Blue
- Green
- Yellow
- Orange
- Grey
- White
- Pink

The first thing we need is a dataset to train our algorithm on. In a production system, you might scrape a *list of colors* website or survey thousands of people. Instead, I created a simple application that renders a random color and asks the user to select one of the preceding nine options to classify it. This application is included with the example code for this chapter in the `kivy_color_classifier` directory, but we won't be going into the details of this code as its only purpose here is to generate sample data.

 Kivy has an incredibly well-engineered object-oriented API that you may want to explore on your own time. If you would like to develop graphical programs that run on many systems, from your laptop to your cell phone, you might want to check out my book, *Creating Apps In Kivy, O'Reilly*.

For the purposes of this case study, the important thing about that application is the output, which is a **comma-separated value (CSV)** file that contains four values per row: the red, green, and blue values (represented as a floating-point number between zero and one), and one of the preceding nine names that the user assigned to that color. The dataset looks something like this:

```
0.30928279150905513,0.7536768153744394,0.3244011790604804,Green
0.4991001855115986,0.6394567277907686,0.6340502030888825,Grey
0.21132621004927998,0.3307376167520666,0.704037576789711,Blue
0.7260420945787928,0.4025279573860123,0.49781705131696363,Pink
0.706469868610228,0.28530423638868196,0.7880240251003464,Purple
0.692243900051664,0.7053550777777416,0.1845069151913028,Yellow
0.3628979381122397,0.11079495501215897,0.26924540840045075,Purple
0.611273677646518,0.48798521783547677,0.5346130557761224,Purple
 .
 .
 .
0.4014121109376566,0.42176706818252674,0.9601866228083298,Blue
0.17750449496124632,0.8008214961070862,0.5073944321437429,Green
```

I made 200 datapoints (a very few of them untrue) before I got bored and decided it was time to start machine learning on this dataset. These datapoints are shipped with the examples for this chapter if you would like to use my data (nobody's ever told me I'm color-blind, so it should be somewhat reasonable).

We'll be implementing one of the simpler machine-learning algorithms, referred to as k-nearest neighbor. This algorithm relies on some kind of "distance" calculation between points in the dataset (in our case, we can use a three-dimensional version of the Pythagorean theorem). Given a new datapoint, it finds a certain number (referred to as k, as in k-nearest neighbors) of datapoints that are closest to it when measured by that distance calculation. Then it combines those datapoints in some way (an average might work for linear calculations; for our classification problem, we'll use the mode), and returns the result.

We won't go into too much detail about what the algorithm does; rather, we'll focus on some of the ways we can apply the iterator pattern or iterator protocol to this problem.

Let's now write a program that performs the following steps in order:

1. Load the sample data from the file and construct a model from it.
2. Generate 100 random colors.
3. Classify each color and output it to a file in the same format as the input.

Once we have this second CSV file, another Kivy program can load the file and render each color, asking a human user to confirm or deny the accuracy of the prediction, thus informing us of how accurate our algorithm and initial data set are.

The first step is a fairly simple generator that loads CSV data and converts it into a format that is amenable to our needs:

```
import csv

dataset_filename = 'colors.csv'

def load_colors(filename):
    with open(filename) as dataset_file:
        lines = csv.reader(dataset_file)
        for line in lines:
            yield tuple(float(y) for y in line[0:3]), line[3]
```

We haven't seen the `csv.reader` function before. It returns an iterator over the lines in the file. Each value returned by the iterator is a list of strings. In our case, we could have just split on commas and been fine, but `csv.reader` also takes care of managing quotation marks and various other nuances of the comma-separated value format.

We then loop over these lines and convert them to a tuple of color and name, where the color is a tuple of three floating value integers. This tuple is constructed using a generator expression. There might be more readable ways to construct this tuple; do you think the code brevity and the speed of a generator expression is worth the obfuscation? Instead of returning a list of color tuples, it yields them one at a time, thus constructing a generator object.

Now, we need a hundred random colors. There are so many ways this can be done:

- A list comprehension with a nested generator expression: `[tuple(random() for r in range(3)) for r in range(100)]`
- A basic generator function
- A class that implements the `__iter__` and `__next__` protocols

- Push the data through a pipeline of coroutines
- Even just a basic `for` loop

The generator version seems to be most readable, so let's add that function to our program:

```python
from random import random


def generate_colors(count=100):
    for i in range(count):
        yield (random(), random(), random())
```

Notice how we parameterize the number of colors to generate. We can now reuse this function for other color-generating tasks in the future.

Now, before we do the classification step, we need a function to calculate the "distance" between two colors. Since it's possible to think of colors as being three dimensional (red, green, and blue could map to x, y, and z axes, for example), let's use a little basic math:

```python
import math

def color_distance(color1, color2):
    channels = zip(color1, color2)
    sum_distance_squared = 0
    for c1, c2 in channels:
        sum_distance_squared += (c1 - c2) ** 2
    return math.sqrt(sum_distance_squared)
```

This is a pretty basic-looking function; it doesn't look like it's even using the iterator protocol. There's no `yield` function, no comprehensions. However, there is a `for` loop, and that call to the `zip` function is doing some real iteration as well (remember that `zip` yields tuples containing one element from each input iterator).

Note, however, that this function is going to be called a lot of times inside our k-nearest neighbors algorithm. If our code ran too slow and we were able to identify this function as a bottleneck, we might want to replace it with a less readable, but more optimized, generator expression:

```python
def color_distance(color1, color2):
    return math.sqrt(sum((x[0] - x[1]) ** 2 for x in zip(
    color1, color2)))
```

However, I strongly recommend not making such optimizations until you have proven that the readable version is too slow.

Now that we have some plumbing in place, let's do the actual k-nearest neighbor implementation. This seems like a good place to use a coroutine. Here it is with some test code to ensure it's yielding sensible values:

```
def nearest_neighbors(model_colors, num_neighbors):
    model = list(model_colors)
    target = yield
    while True:
        distances = sorted(
            ((color_distance(c[0], target), c) for c in model),
        )
        target = yield [
            d[1] for d in distances[0:num_neighbors]
        ]


model_colors = load_colors(dataset_filename)
target_colors = generate_colors(3)
get_neighbors = nearest_neighbors(model_colors, 5)
next(get_neighbors)

for color in target_colors:
    distances = get_neighbors.send(color)
    print(color)
    for d in distances:
        print(color_distance(color, d[0]), d[1])
```

The coroutine accepts two arguments, the list of colors to be used as a model, and the number of neighbors to query. It converts the model to a list because it's going to be iterated over multiple times. In the body of the coroutine, it accepts a tuple of RGB color values using the `yield` syntax. Then it combines a call to `sorted` with an odd generator expression. See if you can figure out what that generator expression is doing.

It returns a tuple of `(distance, color_data)` for each color in the model. Remember, the model itself contains tuples of `(color, name)`, where `color` is a tuple of three RGB values. Therefore, the generator is returning an iterator over a weird data structure that looks like this:

```
(distance, (r, g, b), color_name)
```

The `sorted` call then sorts the results by their first element, which is distance. This is a complicated piece of code and isn't object-oriented at all. You may want to break it down into a normal `for` loop to ensure you understand what the generator expression is doing. It might also be a good exercise to imagine how this code would look if you were to pass a key argument into the sorted function instead of constructing a tuple.

The `yield` statement is a bit less complicated; it pulls the second value from each of the first k (`distance, color_data`) tuples. In more concrete terms, it yields the (`(r, g, b), color_name`) tuple for the k values with the lowest distance. Or, if you prefer more abstract terms, it yields the target's k-nearest neighbors in the given model.

The remaining code is just boilerplate to test this method; it constructs the model and a color generator, primes the coroutine, and prints the results in a `for` loop.

The two remaining tasks are to choose a color based on the nearest neighbors, and to output the results to a CSV file. Let's make two more coroutines to take care of these tasks. Let's do the output first because it can be tested independently:

```
def write_results(filename="output.csv"):
    with open(filename, "w") as file:
        writer = csv.writer(file)
        while True:
            color, name = yield
            writer.writerow(list(color) + [name])

results = write_results()
next(results)
for i in range(3):
    print(i)
    results.send(((i, i, i), i * 10))
```

This coroutine maintains an open file as state and writes lines of code to it as they are sent in using `send()`. The test code ensures the coroutine is working correctly, so now we can connect the two coroutines with a third one.

The second coroutine uses a bit of an odd trick:

```
from collections import Counter
def name_colors(get_neighbors):
    color = yield
    while True:
        near = get_neighbors.send(color)
        name_guess = Counter(
            n[1] for n in near).most_common(1)[0][0]
        color = yield name_guess
```

This coroutine accepts, *as its argument*, an existing coroutine. In this case, it's an instance of `nearest_neighbors`. This code basically proxies all the values sent into it through that `nearest_neighbors` instance. Then it does some processing on the result to get the most common color out of the values that were returned. In this case, it would probably make just as much sense to adapt the original coroutine to return a name, since it isn't being used for anything else. However, there are many cases where it is useful to pass coroutines around; this is how we do it.

Now all we have to do is connect these various coroutines and pipelines together, and kick off the process with a single function call:

```python
def process_colors(dataset_filename="colors.csv"):
    model_colors = load_colors(dataset_filename)
    get_neighbors = nearest_neighbors(model_colors, 5)
    get_color_name = name_colors(get_neighbors)
    output = write_results()
    next(output)
    next(get_neighbors)
    next(get_color_name)

    for color in generate_colors():
        name = get_color_name.send(color)
        output.send((color, name))


process_colors()
```

So, this function, unlike almost every other function we've defined, is a perfectly normal function without any `yield` statements. It doesn't get turned into a coroutine or generator object. It does, however, construct a generator and three coroutines. Notice how the `get_neighbors` coroutine is passed into the constructor for `name_colors`? Pay attention to how all three coroutines are advanced to their first `yield` statements by calls to `next`.

Once all the pipes are created, we use a `for` loop to send each of the generated colors into the `get_color_name` coroutine, and then we pipe each of the values yielded by that coroutine to the output coroutine, which writes it to a file.

And that's it! I created a second Kivy app that loads the resulting CSV file and presents the colors to the user. The user can select either *Yes* or *No* depending on whether they think the choice made by the machine-learning algorithm matches the choice they would have made. This is not scientifically accurate (it's ripe for observation bias), but it's good enough for playing around. Using my eyes, it succeeded about 84 percent of the time, which is better than my grade 12 average. Not bad for our first ever machine learning experience, eh?

You might be wondering, "what does this have to do with object-oriented programming? There isn't even one class in this code!". In some ways, you'd be right; neither coroutines nor generators are commonly considered object-oriented. However, the functions that create them return objects; in fact, you could think of those functions as constructors. The constructed object has appropriate `send()` and `__next__()` methods. Basically, the coroutine/generator syntax is a syntax shortcut for a particular kind of object that would be quite verbose to create without it.

This case study has been an exercise in bottom-up design. We created various low-level objects that did specific tasks and hooked them all together at the end. I find this to be a common practice when developing with coroutines. The alternative, top-down design sometimes results in more monolithic pieces of code instead of unique individual pieces. In general, we want to find a happy medium between methods that are too large and methods that are too small and it's hard to see how they fit together. This is true, of course, regardless of whether the iterator protocol is being used as we did here.

Exercises

If you don't use comprehensions in your daily coding very often, the first thing you should do is search through some existing code and find some `for` loops. See if any of them can be trivially converted to a generator expression or a list, set, or dictionary comprehension.

Test the claim that list comprehensions are faster than `for` loops. This can be done with the built-in `timeit` module. Use the help documentation for the `timeit.timeit` function to find out how to use it. Basically, write two functions that do the same thing, one using a list comprehension, and one using a `for` loop. Pass each function into `timeit.timeit`, and compare the results. If you're feeling adventurous, compare generators and generator expressions as well. Testing code using `timeit` can become addictive, so bear in mind that code does not need to be hyperfast unless it's being executed an immense number of times, such as on a huge input list or file.

Play around with generator functions. Start with basic iterators that require multiple values (mathematical sequences are canonical examples; the Fibonacci sequence is overused if you can't think of anything better). Try some more advanced generators that do things like take multiple input lists and somehow yield values that merge them. Generators can also be used on files; can you write a simple generator that shows those lines that are identical in two files?

Coroutines abuse the iterator protocol but don't actually fulfill the iterator pattern. Can you build a non-coroutine version of the code that gets a serial number from a log file? Take an object-oriented approach so that you can store an additional state on a class. You'll learn a lot about coroutines if you can create an object that is a drop-in replacement for the existing coroutine.

See if you can abstract the coroutines used in the case study so that the k-nearest-neighbor algorithm can be used on a variety of datasets. You'll likely want to construct a coroutine that accepts other coroutines or functions that do the distance and recombination calculations as parameters, and then calls into those functions to find the actual nearest neighbors.

Summary

In this chapter, we learned that design patterns are useful abstractions that provide "best practice" solutions for common programming problems. We covered our first design pattern, the iterator, as well as numerous ways that Python uses and abuses this pattern for its own nefarious purposes. The original iterator pattern is extremely object-oriented, but it is also rather ugly and verbose to code around. However, Python's built-in syntax abstracts the ugliness away, leaving us with a clean interface to these object-oriented constructs.

Comprehensions and generator expressions can combine container construction with iteration in a single line. Generator objects can be constructed using the `yield` syntax. Coroutines look like generators on the outside but serve a much different purpose.

We'll cover several more design patterns in the next two chapters.

10
Python Design Patterns I

In the last chapter, we were briefly introduced to design patterns, and covered the iterator pattern, a pattern so useful and common that it has been abstracted into the core of the programming language itself. In this chapter, we'll be reviewing other common patterns, and how they are implemented in Python. As with iteration, Python often provides an alternative syntax to make working with such problems simpler. We will cover both the "traditional" design, and the Python version for these patterns. In summary, we'll see:

- Numerous specific patterns
- A canonical implementation of each pattern in Python
- Python syntax to replace certain patterns

The decorator pattern

The decorator pattern allows us to "wrap" an object that provides core functionality with other objects that alter this functionality. Any object that uses the decorated object will interact with it in exactly the same way as if it were undecorated (that is, the interface of the decorated object is identical to that of the core object).

There are two primary uses of the decorator pattern:

- Enhancing the response of a component as it sends data to a second component
- Supporting multiple optional behaviors

The second option is often a suitable alternative to multiple inheritance. We can construct a core object, and then create a decorator around that core. Since the decorator object has the same interface as the core object, we can even wrap the new object in other decorators. Here's how it looks in UML:

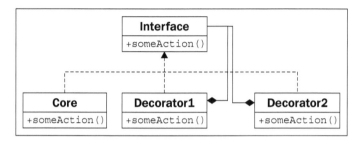

Here, **Core** and all the decorators implement a specific **Interface**. The decorators maintain a reference to another instance of that **Interface** via composition. When called, the decorator does some added processing before or after calling its wrapped interface. The wrapped object may be another decorator, or the core functionality. While multiple decorators may wrap each other, the object in the "center" of all those decorators provides the core functionality.

A decorator example

Let's look at an example from network programming. We'll be using a TCP socket. The `socket.send()` method takes a string of input bytes and outputs them to the receiving socket at the other end. There are plenty of libraries that accept sockets and access this function to send data on the stream. Let's create such an object; it will be an interactive shell that waits for a connection from a client and then prompts the user for a string response:

```python
import socket

def respond(client):
    response = input("Enter a value: ")
    client.send(bytes(response, 'utf8'))
    client.close()

server = socket.socket(socket.AF_INET, socket.SOCK_STREAM)
server.bind(('localhost',2401))
server.listen(1)
try:
    while True:
```

```
        client, addr = server.accept()
        respond(client)
finally:
    server.close()
```

The `respond` function accepts a socket parameter and prompts for data to be sent as a reply, then sends it. To use it, we construct a server socket and tell it to listen on port `2401` (I picked the port randomly) on the local computer. When a client connects, it calls the `respond` function, which requests data interactively and responds appropriately. The important thing to notice is that the `respond` function only cares about two methods of the socket interface: `send` and `close`. To test this, we can write a very simple client that connects to the same port and outputs the response before exiting:

```
import socket

client = socket.socket(socket.AF_INET, socket.SOCK_STREAM)
client.connect(('localhost', 2401))
print("Received: {0}".format(client.recv(1024)))
client.close()
```

To use these programs:

1. Start the server in one terminal.

2. Open a second terminal window and run the client.

3. At the **Enter a value:** prompt in the server window, type a value and press enter.

4. The client will receive what you typed, print it to the console, and exit. Run the client a second time; the server will prompt for a second value.

Now, looking again at our server code, we see two sections. The `respond` function sends data into a socket object. The remaining script is responsible for creating that socket object. We'll create a pair of decorators that customize the socket behavior without having to extend or modify the socket itself.

Let's start with a "logging" decorator. This object outputs any data being sent to the server's console before it sends it to the client:

```
class LogSocket:
    def __init__(self, socket):
        self.socket = socket

    def send(self, data):
```

```
        print("Sending {0} to {1}".format(
            data, self.socket.getpeername()[0]))
        self.socket.send(data)

    def close(self):
        self.socket.close()
```

This class decorates a socket object and presents the `send` and `close` interface to client sockets. A better decorator would also implement (and possibly customize) all of the remaining socket methods. It should properly implement all of the arguments to `send`, (which actually accepts an optional flags argument) as well, but let's keep our example simple! Whenever `send` is called on this object, it logs the output to the screen before sending data to the client using the original socket.

We only have to change one line in our original code to use this decorator. Instead of calling `respond` with the socket, we call it with a decorated socket:

```
respond(LogSocket(client))
```

While that's quite simple, we have to ask ourselves why we didn't just extend the socket class and override the `send` method. We could call `super().send` to do the actual sending, after we logged it. There is nothing wrong with this design either.

When faced with a choice between decorators and inheritance, we should only use decorators if we need to modify the object dynamically, according to some condition. For example, we may only want to enable the logging decorator if the server is currently in debugging mode. Decorators also beat multiple inheritance when we have more than one optional behavior. As an example, we can write a second decorator that compresses data using `gzip` compression whenever `send` is called:

```
import gzip
from io import BytesIO

class GzipSocket:
    def __init__(self, socket):
        self.socket = socket

    def send(self, data):
        buf = BytesIO()
        zipfile = gzip.GzipFile(fileobj=buf, mode="w")
        zipfile.write(data)
        zipfile.close()
        self.socket.send(buf.getvalue())

    def close(self):
        self.socket.close()
```

The `send` method in this version compresses the incoming data before sending it on to the client.

Now that we have these two decorators, we can write code that dynamically switches between them when responding. This example is not complete, but it illustrates the logic we might follow to mix and match decorators:

```
client, addr = server.accept()
if log_send:
    client = LoggingSocket(client)
if client.getpeername()[0] in compress_hosts:
    client = GzipSocket(client)
respond(client)
```

This code checks a hypothetical configuration variable named `log_send`. If it's enabled, it wraps the socket in a `LoggingSocket` decorator. Similarly, it checks whether the client that has connected is in a list of addresses known to accept compressed content. If so, it wraps the client in a `GzipSocket` decorator. Notice that none, either, or both of the decorators may be enabled, depending on the configuration and connecting client. Try writing this using multiple inheritance and see how confused you get!

Decorators in Python

The decorator pattern is useful in Python, but there are other options. For example, we may be able to use monkey-patching, which we discussed in *Chapter 7, Python Object-oriented Shortcuts*, to get a similar effect. Single inheritance, where the "optional" calculations are done in one large method can be an option, and multiple inheritance should not be written off just because it's not suitable for the specific example seen previously!

In Python, it is very common to use this pattern on functions. As we saw in a previous chapter, functions are objects too. In fact, function decoration is so common that Python provides a special syntax to make it easy to apply such decorators to functions.

For example, we can look at the logging example in a more general way. Instead of logging, only send calls on sockets, we may find it helpful to log all calls to certain functions or methods. The following example implements a decorator that does just this:

```
import time

def log_calls(func):
    def wrapper(*args, **kwargs):
        now = time.time()
```

```
        print("Calling {0} with {1} and {2}".format(
            func.__name__, args, kwargs))
        return_value = func(*args, **kwargs)
        print("Executed {0} in {1}ms".format(
            func.__name__, time.time() - now))
        return return_value
    return wrapper

def test1(a,b,c):
    print("\ttest1 called")

def test2(a,b):
    print("\ttest2 called")

def test3(a,b):
    print("\ttest3 called")
    time.sleep(1)

test1 = log_calls(test1)
test2 = log_calls(test2)
test3 = log_calls(test3)

test1(1,2,3)
test2(4,b=5)
test3(6,7)
```

This decorator function is very similar to the example we explored earlier; in those cases, the decorator took a socket-like object and created a socket-like object. This time, our decorator takes a function object and returns a new function object. This code is comprised of three separate tasks:

- A function, log_calls, that accepts another function
- This function defines (internally) a new function, named wrapper, that does some extra work before calling the original function
- This new function is returned

Three sample functions demonstrate the decorator in use. The third one includes a sleep call to demonstrate the timing test. We pass each function into the decorator, which returns a new function. We assign this new function to the original variable name, effectively replacing the original function with a decorated one.

This syntax allows us to build up decorated function objects dynamically, just as we did with the socket example; if we don't replace the name, we can even keep decorated and non-decorated versions for different situations.

Often these decorators are general modifications that are applied permanently to different functions. In this situation, Python supports a special syntax to apply the decorator at the time the function is defined. We've already seen this syntax when we discussed the `property` decorator; now, let's understand how it works.

Instead of applying the decorator function after the method definition, we can use the `@decorator` syntax to do it all at once:

```
@log_calls
def test1(a,b,c):
    print("\ttest1 called")
```

The primary benefit of this syntax is that we can easily see that the function has been decorated at the time it is defined. If the decorator is applied later, someone reading the code may miss that the function has been altered at all. Answering a question like, "Why is my program logging function calls to the console?" can become much more difficult! However, the syntax can only be applied to functions we define, since we don't have access to the source code of other modules. If we need to decorate functions that are part of somebody else's third-party library, we have to use the earlier syntax.

There is more to the decorator syntax than we've seen here. We don't have room to cover the advanced topics here, so check the Python reference manual or other tutorials for more information. Decorators can be created as callable objects, not just functions that return functions. Classes can also be decorated; in that case, the decorator returns a new class instead of a new function. Finally, decorators can take arguments to customize them on a per-function basis.

The observer pattern

The observer pattern is useful for state monitoring and event handling situations. This pattern allows a given object to be monitored by an unknown and dynamic group of "observer" objects.

Whenever a value on the core object changes, it lets all the observer objects know that a change has occurred, by calling an `update()` method. Each observer may be responsible for different tasks whenever the core object changes; the core object doesn't know or care what those tasks are, and the observers don't typically know or care what other observers are doing.

Here, it is in UML:

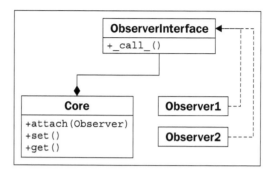

An observer example

The observer pattern might be useful in a redundant backup system. We can write a core object that maintains certain values, and then have one or more observers create serialized copies of that object. These copies might be stored in a database, on a remote host, or in a local file, for example. Let's implement the core object using properties:

```python
class Inventory:
    def __init__(self):
        self.observers = []
        self._product = None
        self._quantity = 0

    def attach(self, observer):
        self.observers.append(observer)

    @property
    def product(self):
        return self._product
    @product.setter
    def product(self, value):
        self._product = value
        self._update_observers()

    @property
    def quantity(self):
        return self._quantity
    @quantity.setter
    def quantity(self, value):
        self._quantity = value
```

```
        self._update_observers()

    def _update_observers(self):
        for observer in self.observers:
            observer()
```

This object has two properties that, when set, call the _update_observers method on itself. All this method does is loop over the available observers and let each one know that something has changed. In this case, we call the observer object directly; the object will have to implement __call__ to process the update. This would not be possible in many object-oriented programming languages, but it's a useful shortcut in Python that can help make our code more readable.

Now let's implement a simple observer object; this one will just print out some state to the console:

```
class ConsoleObserver:
    def __init__(self, inventory):
        self.inventory = inventory

    def __call__(self):
        print(self.inventory.product)
        print(self.inventory.quantity)
```

There's nothing terribly exciting here; the observed object is set up in the initializer, and when the observer is called, we do "something." We can test the observer in an interactive console:

```
>>> i = Inventory()
>>> c = ConsoleObserver(i)
>>> i.attach(c)
>>> i.product = "Widget"
Widget
0
>>> i.quantity = 5
Widget
5
```

After attaching the observer to the inventory object, whenever we change one of the two observed properties, the observer is called and its action is invoked. We can even add two different observer instances:

```
>>> i = Inventory()
>>> c1 = ConsoleObserver(i)
```

```
>>> c2 = ConsoleObserver(i)
>>> i.attach(c1)
>>> i.attach(c2)
>>> i.product = "Gadget"
Gadget
0
Gadget
0
```

This time when we change the product, there are two sets of output, one for each observer. The key idea here is that we can easily add totally different types of observers that back up the data in a file, database, or Internet application at the same time.

The observer pattern detaches the code being observed from the code doing the observing. If we were not using this pattern, we would have had to put code in each of the properties to handle the different cases that might come up; logging to the console, updating a database or file, and so on. The code for each of these tasks would all be mixed in with the observed object. Maintaining it would be a nightmare, and adding new monitoring functionality at a later date would be painful.

The strategy pattern

The strategy pattern is a common demonstration of abstraction in object-oriented programming. The pattern implements different solutions to a single problem, each in a different object. The client code can then choose the most appropriate implementation dynamically at runtime.

Typically, different algorithms have different trade-offs; one might be faster than another, but uses a lot more memory, while a third algorithm may be most suitable when multiple CPUs are present or a distributed system is provided. Here is the strategy pattern in UML:

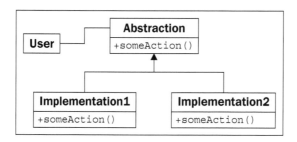

The **User** code connecting to the strategy pattern simply needs to know that it is dealing with the **Abstraction** interface. The actual implementation chosen performs the same task, but in different ways; either way, the interface is identical.

A strategy example

The canonical example of the strategy pattern is sort routines; over the years, numerous algorithms have been invented for sorting a collection of objects; quick sort, merge sort, and heap sort are all fast sort algorithms with different features, each useful in its own right, depending on the size and type of inputs, how out of order they are, and the requirements of the system.

If we have client code that needs to sort a collection, we could pass it to an object with a `sort()` method. This object may be a `QuickSorter` or `MergeSorter` object, but the result will be the same in either case: a sorted list. The strategy used to do the sorting is abstracted from the calling code, making it modular and replaceable.

Of course, in Python, we typically just call the `sorted` function or `list.sort` method and trust that it will do the sorting in a near-optimal fashion. So, we really need to look at a better example.

Let's consider a desktop wallpaper manager. When an image is displayed on a desktop background, it can be adjusted to the screen size in different ways. For example, assuming the image is smaller than the screen, it can be tiled across the screen, centered on it, or scaled to fit. There are other, more complicated, strategies that can be used as well, such as scaling to the maximum height or width, combining it with a solid, semi-transparent, or gradient background color, or other manipulations. While we may want to add these strategies later, let's start with the basic ones.

Our strategy objects takes two inputs; the image to be displayed, and a tuple of the width and height of the screen. They each return a new image the size of the screen, with the image manipulated to fit according to the given strategy. You'll need to install the `pillow` module with `pip3 install pillow` for this example to work:

```
from PIL import Image


class TiledStrategy:
    def make_background(self, img_file, desktop_size):
        in_img = Image.open(img_file)
        out_img = Image.new('RGB', desktop_size)
        num_tiles = [
```

```
                o // i + 1 for o, i in
                zip(out_img.size, in_img.size)
            ]
            for x in range(num_tiles[0]):
                for y in range(num_tiles[1]):
                    out_img.paste(
                        in_img,
                        (
                            in_img.size[0] * x,
                            in_img.size[1] * y,
                            in_img.size[0] * (x+1),
                            in_img.size[1] * (y+1)
                        )
                    )
            return out_img


class CenteredStrategy:
    def make_background(self, img_file, desktop_size):
        in_img = Image.open(img_file)
        out_img = Image.new('RGB', desktop_size)
        left = (out_img.size[0] - in_img.size[0]) // 2
        top = (out_img.size[1] - in_img.size[1]) // 2
        out_img.paste(
            in_img,
            (
                left,
                top,
                left+in_img.size[0],
                top + in_img.size[1]
            )
        )
        return out_img


class ScaledStrategy:
    def make_background(self, img_file, desktop_size):
        in_img = Image.open(img_file)
        out_img = in_img.resize(desktop_size)
        return out_img
```

Here we have three strategies, each using `PIL` to perform their task. Individual strategies have a `make_background` method that accepts the same set of parameters. Once selected, the appropriate strategy can be called to create a correctly sized version of the desktop image. `TiledStrategy` loops over the number of input images that would fit in the width and height of the image and copies it into each location, repeatedly. `CenteredStrategy` figures out how much space needs to be left on the four edges of the image to center it. `ScaledStrategy` forces the image to the output size (ignoring aspect ratio).

Consider how switching between these options would be implemented without the strategy pattern. We'd need to put all the code inside one great big method and use an awkward `if` statement to select the expected one. Every time we wanted to add a new strategy, we'd have to make the method even more ungainly.

Strategy in Python

The preceding canonical implementation of the strategy pattern, while very common in most object-oriented libraries, is rarely seen in Python programming.

These classes each represent objects that do nothing but provide a single function. We could just as easily call that function `__call__` and make the object callable directly. Since there is no other data associated with the object, we need do no more than create a set of top-level functions and pass them around as our strategies instead.

Opponents of design pattern philosophy will therefore say, "because Python has first-class functions, the strategy pattern is unnecessary". In truth, Python's first-class functions allow us to implement the strategy pattern in a more straightforward way. Knowing the pattern exists can still help us choose a correct design for our program, but implement it using a more readable syntax. The strategy pattern, or a top-level function implementation of it, should be used when we need to allow client code or the end user to select from multiple implementations of the same interface.

The state pattern

The state pattern is structurally similar to the strategy pattern, but its intent and purpose are very different. The goal of the state pattern is to represent state-transition systems: systems where it is obvious that an object can be in a specific state, and that certain activities may drive it to a different state.

To make this work, we need a manager, or context class that provides an interface for switching states. Internally, this class contains a pointer to the current state; each state knows what other states it is allowed to be in and will transition to those states depending on actions invoked upon it.

So we have two types of classes, the context class and multiple state classes. The context class maintains the current state, and forwards actions to the state classes. The state classes are typically hidden from any other objects that are calling the context; it acts like a black box that happens to perform state management internally. Here's how it looks in UML:

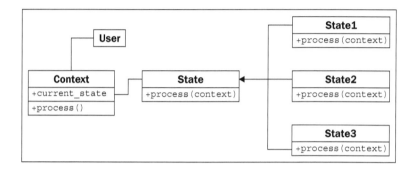

A state example

To illustrate the state pattern, let's build an XML parsing tool. The context class will be the parser itself. It will take a string as input and place the tool in an initial parsing state. The various parsing states will eat characters, looking for a specific value, and when that value is found, change to a different state. The goal is to create a tree of node objects for each tag and its contents. To keep things manageable, we'll parse only a subset of XML - tags and tag names. We won't be able to handle attributes on tags. It will parse text content of tags, but won't attempt to parse "mixed" content, which has tags inside of text. Here is an example "simplified XML" file that we'll be able to parse:

```
<book>
    <author>Dusty Phillips</author>
    <publisher>Packt Publishing</publisher>
    <title>Python 3 Object Oriented Programming</title>
    <content>
        <chapter>
            <number>1</number>
            <title>Object Oriented Design</title>
        </chapter>
        <chapter>
            <number>2</number>
            <title>Objects In Python</title>
        </chapter>
    </content>
</book>
```

Before we look at the states and the parser, let's consider the output of this program. We know we want a tree of Node objects, but what does a Node look like? Well, clearly it'll need to know the name of the tag it is parsing, and since it's a tree, it should probably maintain a pointer to the parent node and a list of the node's children in order. Some nodes have a text value, but not all of them. Let's look at this Node class first:

```
class Node:
    def __init__(self, tag_name, parent=None):
        self.parent = parent
        self.tag_name = tag_name
        self.children = []
        self.text=""

    def __str__(self):
        if self.text:
            return self.tag_name + ": " + self.text
        else:
            return self.tag_name
```

This class sets default attribute values upon initialization. The __str__ method is supplied to help visualize the tree structure when we're finished.

Now, looking at the example document, we need to consider what states our parser can be in. Clearly it's going to start in a state where no nodes have yet been processed. We'll need a state for processing opening tags and closing tags. And when we're inside a tag with text contents, we'll have to process that as a separate state, too.

Switching states can be tricky; how do we know if the next node is an opening tag, a closing tag, or a text node? We could put a little logic in each state to work this out, but it actually makes more sense to create a new state whose sole purpose is figuring out which state we'll be switching to next. If we call this transition state **ChildNode**, we end up with the following states:

- **FirstTag**
- **ChildNode**
- **OpenTag**
- **CloseTag**
- **Text**

The **FirstTag** state will switch to **ChildNode**, which is responsible for deciding which of the other three states to switch to; when those states are finished, they'll switch back to **ChildNode**. The following state-transition diagram shows the available state changes:

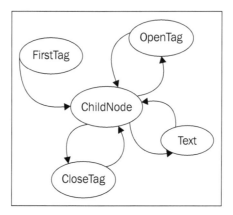

The states are responsible for taking "what's left of the string", processing as much of it as they know what to do with, and then telling the parser to take care of the rest of it. Let's construct the `Parser` class first:

```
class Parser:
    def __init__(self, parse_string):
        self.parse_string = parse_string
        self.root = None
        self.current_node = None

        self.state = FirstTag()

    def process(self, remaining_string):
        remaining = self.state.process(remaining_string, self)
        if remaining:
            self.process(remaining)

    def start(self):
        self.process(self.parse_string)
```

The initializer sets up a few variables on the class that the individual states will access. The `parse_string` instance variable is the text that we are trying to parse. The `root` node is the "top" node in the XML structure. The `current_node` instance variable is the one that we are currently adding children to.

The important feature of this parser is the `process` method, which accepts the remaining string, and passes it off to the current state. The parser (the `self` argument) is also passed into the state's process method so that the state can manipulate it. The state is expected to return the remainder of the unparsed string when it is finished processing. The parser then recursively calls the `process` method on this remaining string to construct the rest of the tree.

Now, let's have a look at the `FirstTag` state:

```
class FirstTag:
    def process(self, remaining_string, parser):
        i_start_tag = remaining_string.find('<')
        i_end_tag = remaining_string.find('>')
        tag_name = remaining_string[i_start_tag+1:i_end_tag]
        root = Node(tag_name)
        parser.root = parser.current_node = root
        parser.state = ChildNode()
        return remaining_string[i_end_tag+1:]
```

This state finds the index (the `i_` stands for index) of the opening and closing angle brackets on the first tag. You may think this state is unnecessary, since XML requires that there be no text before an opening tag. However, there may be whitespace that needs to be consumed; this is why we search for the opening angle bracket instead of assuming it is the first character in the document. Note that this code is assuming a valid input file. A proper implementation would be rigorously testing for invalid input, and would attempt to recover or display an extremely descriptive error message.

The method extracts the name of the tag and assigns it to the root node of the parser. It also assigns it to `current_node`, since that's the one we'll be adding children to next.

Then comes the important part: the method changes the current state on the parser object to a `ChildNode` state. It then returns the remainder of the string (after the opening tag) to allow it to be processed.

The `ChildNode` state, which seems quite complicated, turns out to require nothing but a simple conditional:

```
class ChildNode:
    def process(self, remaining_string, parser):
        stripped = remaining_string.strip()
        if stripped.startswith("</"):
            parser.state = CloseTag()
```

```
        elif stripped.startswith("<"):
            parser.state = OpenTag()
        else:
            parser.state = TextNode()
        return stripped
```

The `strip()` call removes whitespace from the string. Then the parser determines if the next item is an opening or closing tag, or a string of text. Depending on which possibility occurs, it sets the parser to a particular state, and then tells it to parse the remainder of the string.

The `OpenTag` state is similar to the `FirstTag` state, except that it adds the newly created node to the previous `current_node` object's `children` and sets it as the new `current_node`. It places the processor back in the `ChildNode` state before continuing:

```
    class OpenTag:
        def process(self, remaining_string, parser):
            i_start_tag = remaining_string.find('<')
            i_end_tag = remaining_string.find('>')
            tag_name = remaining_string[i_start_tag+1:i_end_tag]
            node = Node(tag_name, parser.current_node)
            parser.current_node.children.append(node)
            parser.current_node = node
            parser.state = ChildNode()
            return remaining_string[i_end_tag+1:]
```

The `CloseTag` state basically does the opposite; it sets the parser's `current_node` back to the parent node so any further children in the outside tag can be added to it:

```
    class CloseTag:
        def process(self, remaining_string, parser):
            i_start_tag = remaining_string.find('<')
            i_end_tag = remaining_string.find('>')
            assert remaining_string[i_start_tag+1] == "/"
            tag_name = remaining_string[i_start_tag+2:i_end_tag]
            assert tag_name == parser.current_node.tag_name
            parser.current_node = parser.current_node.parent
            parser.state = ChildNode()
            return remaining_string[i_end_tag+1:].strip()
```

The two `assert` statements help ensure that the parse strings are consistent. The `if` statement at the end of the method ensures that the processor terminates when it is finished. If the parent of a node is `None`, it means that we are working on the root node.

Finally, the `TextNode` state very simply extracts the text before the next close tag and sets it as a value on the current node:

```
class TextNode:
    def process(self, remaining_string, parser):
        i_start_tag = remaining_string.find('<')
        text = remaining_string[:i_start_tag]
        parser.current_node.text = text
        parser.state = ChildNode()
        return remaining_string[i_start_tag:]
```

Now we just have to set up the initial state on the parser object we created. The initial state is a `FirstTag` object, so just add the following to the `__init__` method:

```
        self.state = FirstTag()
```

To test the class, let's add a main script that opens an file from the command line, parses it, and prints the nodes:

```
if __name__ == "__main__":
    import sys
    with open(sys.argv[1]) as file:
        contents = file.read()
        p = Parser(contents)
        p.start()

        nodes = [p.root]
        while nodes:
            node = nodes.pop(0)
            print(node)
            nodes = node.children + nodes
```

This code opens the file, loads the contents, and parses the result. Then it prints each node and its children in order. The `__str__` method we originally added on the node class takes care of formatting the nodes for printing. If we run the script on the earlier example, it outputs the tree as follows:

```
book
author: Dusty Phillips
publisher: Packt Publishing
title: Python 3 Object Oriented Programming
content
chapter
number: 1
```

```
title: Object Oriented Design
chapter
number: 2
title: Objects In Python
```

Comparing this to the original simplified XML document tells us the parser is working.

State versus strategy

The state pattern looks very similar to the strategy pattern; indeed, the UML diagrams for the two are identical. The implementation, too, is identical; we could even have written our states as first-class functions instead of wrapping them in objects, as was suggested for strategy.

While the two patterns have identical structures, they solve completely different problems. The strategy pattern is used to choose an algorithm at runtime; generally, only one of those algorithms is going to be chosen for a particular use case. The state pattern, on the other hand is designed to allow switching between different states dynamically, as some process evolves. In code, the primary difference is that the strategy pattern is not typically aware of other strategy objects. In the state pattern, either the state or the context needs to know which other states that it can switch to.

State transition as coroutines

The state pattern is the canonical object-oriented solution to state-transition problems. However, the syntax for this pattern is rather verbose. You can get a similar effect by constructing your objects as coroutines. Remember the regular expression log file parser we built in *Chapter 9, The Iterator Pattern*? That was a state-transition problem in disguise. The main difference between that implementation and one that defines all the objects (or functions) used in the state pattern is that the coroutine solution allows us to encode more of the boilerplate in language constructs. There are two implementations, but neither one is inherently better than the other, but you may find that coroutines are more readable, for a given definition of "readable" (you have to understand the syntax of coroutines, first!).

The singleton pattern

The singleton pattern is one of the most controversial patterns; many have accused it of being an "anti-pattern", a pattern that should be avoided, not promoted. In Python, if someone is using the singleton pattern, they're almost certainly doing something wrong, probably because they're coming from a more restrictive programming language.

So why discuss it at all? Singleton is one of the most famous of all design patterns. It is useful in overly object-oriented languages, and is a vital part of traditional object-oriented programming. More relevantly, the idea behind singleton is useful, even if we implement that idea in a totally different way in Python.

The basic idea behind the singleton pattern is to allow exactly one instance of a certain object to exist. Typically, this object is a sort of manager class like those we discussed in *Chapter 5, When to Use Object-oriented Programming*. Such objects often need to be referenced by a wide variety of other objects, and passing references to the manager object around to the methods and constructors that need them can make code hard to read.

Instead, when a singleton is used, the separate objects request the single instance of the manager object from the class, so a reference to it need not to be passed around. The UML diagram doesn't fully describe it, but here it is for completeness:

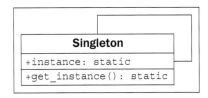

In most programming environments, singletons are enforced by making the constructor private (so no one can create additional instances of it), and then providing a static method to retrieve the single instance. This method creates a new instance the first time it is called, and then returns that same instance each time it is called again.

Singleton implementation

Python doesn't have private constructors, but for this purpose, it has something even better. We can use the __new__ class method to ensure that only one instance is ever created:

```
class OneOnly:
    _singleton = None
    def __new__(cls, *args, **kwargs):
        if not cls._singleton:
            cls._singleton = super(OneOnly, cls
                ).__new__(cls, *args, **kwargs)
        return cls._singleton
```

When __new__ is called, it normally constructs a new instance of that class. When we override it, we first check if our singleton instance has been created; if not, we create it using a super call. Thus, whenever we call the constructor on OneOnly, we always get the exact same instance:

```
>>> o1 = OneOnly()
>>> o2 = OneOnly()
>>> o1 == o2
True
>>> o1
<__main__.OneOnly object at 0xb71c008c>
>>> o2
<__main__.OneOnly object at 0xb71c008c>
```

The two objects are equal and located at the same address; thus, they are the same object. This particular implementation isn't very transparent, since it's not obvious that a singleton object has been created. Whenever we call a constructor, we expect a new instance of that object; in this case, that contract is violated. Perhaps, good docstrings on the class could alleviate this problem if we really think we need a singleton.

But we don't need it. Python coders frown on forcing the users of their code into a specific mindset. We may think only one instance of a class will ever be required, but other programmers may have different ideas. Singletons can interfere with distributed computing, parallel programming, and automated testing, for example. In all those cases, it can be very useful to have multiple or alternative instances of a specific object, even though a "normal' operation may never require one.

Module variables can mimic singletons

Normally, in Python, the singleton pattern can be sufficiently mimicked using module-level variables. It's not as "safe" as a singleton in that people could reassign those variables at any time, but as with the private variables we discussed in *Chapter 2, Objects in Python*, this is acceptable in Python. If someone has a valid reason to change those variables, why should we stop them? It also doesn't stop people from instantiating multiple instances of the object, but again, if they have a valid reason to do so, why interfere?

Ideally, we should give them a mechanism to get access to the "default singleton" value, while also allowing them to create other instances if they need them. While technically not a singleton at all, it provides the most Pythonic mechanism for singleton-like behavior.

To use module-level variables instead of a singleton, we instantiate an instance of the class after we've defined it. We can improve our state pattern to use singletons. Instead of creating a new object every time we change states, we can create a module-level variable that is always accessible:

```python
class FirstTag:
    def process(self, remaining_string, parser):
        i_start_tag = remaining_string.find('<')
        i_end_tag = remaining_string.find('>')
        tag_name = remaining_string[i_start_tag+1:i_end_tag]
        root = Node(tag_name)
        parser.root = parser.current_node = root
        parser.state = child_node
        return remaining_string[i_end_tag+1:]


class ChildNode:
    def process(self, remaining_string, parser):
        stripped = remaining_string.strip()
        if stripped.startswith("</"):
            parser.state = close_tag
        elif stripped.startswith("<"):
            parser.state = open_tag
        else:
            parser.state = text_node
        return stripped


class OpenTag:
    def process(self, remaining_string, parser):
        i_start_tag = remaining_string.find('<')
        i_end_tag = remaining_string.find('>')
        tag_name = remaining_string[i_start_tag+1:i_end_tag]
        node = Node(tag_name, parser.current_node)
        parser.current_node.children.append(node)
        parser.current_node = node
        parser.state = child_node
        return remaining_string[i_end_tag+1:]
class TextNode:
    def process(self, remaining_string, parser):
        i_start_tag = remaining_string.find('<')
        text = remaining_string[:i_start_tag]
        parser.current_node.text = text
        parser.state = child_node
```

```
            return remaining_string[i_start_tag:]

    class CloseTag:
        def process(self, remaining_string, parser):
            i_start_tag = remaining_string.find('<')
            i_end_tag = remaining_string.find('>')
            assert remaining_string[i_start_tag+1] == "/"
            tag_name = remaining_string[i_start_tag+2:i_end_tag]
            assert tag_name == parser.current_node.tag_name
            parser.current_node = parser.current_node.parent
            parser.state = child_node
            return remaining_string[i_end_tag+1:].strip()

    first_tag = FirstTag()
    child_node = ChildNode()
    text_node = TextNode()
    open_tag = OpenTag()
close_tag = CloseTag()
```

All we've done is create instances of the various state classes that can be reused. Notice how we can access these module variables inside the classes, even before the variables have been defined? This is because the code inside the classes is not executed until the method is called, and by this point, the entire module will have been defined.

The difference in this example is that instead of wasting memory creating a bunch of new instances that must be garbage collected, we are reusing a single state object for each state. Even if multiple parsers are running at once, only these state classes need to be used.

When we originally created the state-based parser, you may have wondered why we didn't pass the parser object to __init__ on each individual state, instead of passing it into the process method as we did. The state could then have been referenced as self.parser. This is a perfectly valid implementation of the state pattern, but it would not have allowed leveraging the singleton pattern. If the state objects maintain a reference to the parser, then they cannot be used simultaneously to reference other parsers.

Remember, these are two different patterns with different purposes; the fact that singleton's purpose may be useful for implementing the state pattern does not mean the two patterns are related.

The template pattern

The template pattern is useful for removing duplicate code; it's an implementation to support the **Don't Repeat Yourself** principle we discussed in *Chapter 5, When to Use Object-oriented Programming*. It is designed for situations where we have several different tasks to accomplish that have some, but not all, steps in common. The common steps are implemented in a base class, and the distinct steps are overridden in subclasses to provide custom behavior. In some ways, it's like a generalized strategy pattern, except similar sections of the algorithms are shared using a base class. Here it is in the UML format:

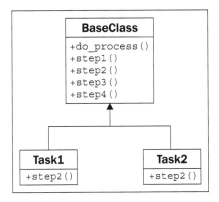

A template example

Let's create a car sales reporter as an example. We can store records of sales in an SQLite database table. SQLite is a simple file-based database engine that allows us to store records using SQL syntax. Python 3 includes SQLite in its standard library, so there are no extra modules required.

We have two common tasks we need to perform:

* Select all sales of new vehicles and output them to the screen in a comma-delimited format
* Output a comma-delimited list of all salespeople with their gross sales and save it to a file that can be imported to a spreadsheet

These seem like quite different tasks, but they have some common features. In both cases, we need to perform the following steps:

1. Connect to the database.
2. Construct a query for new vehicles or gross sales.

3. Issue the query.

4. Format the results into a comma-delimited string.

5. Output the data to a file or e-mail.

The query construction and output steps are different for the two tasks, but the remaining steps are identical. We can use the template pattern to put the common steps in a base class, and the varying steps in two subclasses.

Before we start, let's create a database and put some sample data in it, using a few lines of SQL:

```
import sqlite3

conn = sqlite3.connect("sales.db")

conn.execute("CREATE TABLE Sales (salesperson text, "
        "amt currency, year integer, model text, new boolean)")
conn.execute("INSERT INTO Sales values"
        " ('Tim', 16000, 2010, 'Honda Fit', 'true')")
conn.execute("INSERT INTO Sales values"
        " ('Tim', 9000, 2006, 'Ford Focus', 'false')")
conn.execute("INSERT INTO Sales values"
        " ('Gayle', 8000, 2004, 'Dodge Neon', 'false')")
conn.execute("INSERT INTO Sales values"
        " ('Gayle', 28000, 2009, 'Ford Mustang', 'true')")
conn.execute("INSERT INTO Sales values"
        " ('Gayle', 50000, 2010, 'Lincoln Navigator', 'true')")
conn.execute("INSERT INTO Sales values"
        " ('Don', 20000, 2008, 'Toyota Prius', 'false')")
conn.commit()
conn.close()
```

Hopefully you can see what's going on here even if you don't know SQL; we've created a table to hold the data, and used six insert statements to add sales records. The data is stored in a file named `sales.db`. Now we have a sample we can work with in developing our template pattern.

Since we've already outlined the steps that the template has to perform, we can start by defining the base class that contains the steps. Each step gets its own method (to make it easy to selectively override any one step), and we have one more managerial method that calls the steps in turn. Without any method content, here's how it might look:

```
class QueryTemplate:
    def connect(self):
        pass
```

```
        def construct_query(self):
            pass
        def do_query(self):
            pass
        def format_results(self):
            pass
        def output_results(self):
            pass

        def process_format(self):
            self.connect()
            self.construct_query()
            self.do_query()
            self.format_results()
            self.output_results()
```

The process_format method is the primary method to be called by an outside client. It ensures each step is executed in order, but it does not care if that step is implemented in this class or in a subclass. For our examples, we know that three methods are going to be identical between our two classes:

```
    import sqlite3

    class QueryTemplate:
        def connect(self):
            self.conn = sqlite3.connect("sales.db")

        def construct_query(self):
            raise NotImplementedError()

        def do_query(self):
            results = self.conn.execute(self.query)
            self.results = results.fetchall()

        def format_results(self):
            output = []
            for row in self.results:
                row = [str(i) for i in row]
                output.append(", ".join(row))
            self.formatted_results = "\n".join(output)

        def output_results(self):
            raise NotImplementedError()
```

To help with implementing subclasses, the two methods that are not specified raise `NotImplementedError`. This is a common way to specify abstract interfaces in Python when abstract base classes seem too heavyweight. The methods could have empty implementations (with `pass`), or could be fully unspecified. Raising `NotImplementedError`, however, helps the programmer understand that the class is meant to be subclassed and these methods overridden; empty methods or methods that do not exist are harder to identify as needing to be implemented and to debug if we forget to implement them.

Now we have a template class that takes care of the boring details, but is flexible enough to allow the execution and formatting of a wide variety of queries. The best part is, if we ever want to change our database engine from SQLite to another database engine (such as py-postgresql), we only have to do it here, in this template class, and we don't have to touch the two (or two hundred) subclasses we might have written.

Let's have a look at the concrete classes now:

```python
import datetime
class NewVehiclesQuery(QueryTemplate):
    def construct_query(self):
        self.query = "select * from Sales where new='true'"

    def output_results(self):
        print(self.formatted_results)


class UserGrossQuery(QueryTemplate):
    def construct_query(self):
        self.query = ("select salesperson, sum(amt) " +
        " from Sales group by salesperson")

    def output_results(self):
        filename = "gross_sales_{0}".format(
                datetime.date.today().strftime("%Y%m%d")
                )
        with open(filename, 'w') as outfile:
            outfile.write(self.formatted_results)
```

These two classes are actually pretty short, considering what they're doing: connecting to a database, executing a query, formatting the results, and outputting them. The superclass takes care of the repetitive work, but lets us easily specify those steps that vary between tasks. Further, we can also easily change steps that are provided in the base class. For example, if we wanted to output something other than a comma-delimited string (for example: an HTML report to be uploaded to a website), we can still override `format_results`.

Exercises

While writing this chapter, I discovered that it can be very difficult, and extremely educational, to come up with good examples where specific design patterns should be used. Instead of going over current or old projects to see where you can apply these patterns, as I've suggested in previous chapters, think about the patterns and different situations where they might come up. Try to think outside your own experiences. If your current projects are in the banking business, consider how you'd apply these design patterns in a retail or point-of-sale application. If you normally write web applications, think about using design patterns while writing a compiler.

Look at the decorator pattern and come up with some good examples of when to apply it. Focus on the pattern itself, not the Python syntax we discussed; it's a bit more general than the actual pattern. The special syntax for decorators is, however, something you may want to look for places to apply in existing projects too.

What are some good areas to use the observer pattern? Why? Think about not only how you'd apply the pattern, but how you would implement the same task without using observer? What do you gain, or lose, by choosing to use it?

Consider the difference between the strategy and state patterns. Implementation-wise, they look very similar, yet they have different purposes. Can you think of cases where the patterns could be interchanged? Would it be reasonable to redesign a state-based system to use strategy instead, or vice versa? How different would the design actually be?

The template pattern is such an obvious application of inheritance to reduce duplicate code that you may have used it before, without knowing its name. Try to think of at least half a dozen different scenarios where it would be useful. If you can do this, you'll be finding places for it in your daily coding all the time.

Summary

This chapter discussed several common design patterns in detail, with examples, UML diagrams, and a discussion of the differences between Python and statically typed object-oriented languages. The decorator pattern is often implemented using Python's more generic decorator syntax. The observer pattern is a useful way to decouple events from actions taken on those events. The strategy pattern allows different algorithms to be chosen to accomplish the same task. The state pattern looks similar, but is used instead to represent systems can move between different states using well-defined actions. The singleton pattern, popular in some statically typed languages, is almost always an anti-pattern in Python.

In the next chapter, we'll wrap up our discussion of design patterns.

11
Python Design Patterns II

In this chapter we will be introduced to several more design patterns. Once again, we'll cover the canonical examples as well as any common alternative implementations in Python. We'll be discussing:

- The adapter pattern
- The facade pattern
- Lazy initialization and the flyweight pattern
- The command pattern
- The abstract factory pattern
- The composition pattern

The adapter pattern

Unlike most of the patterns we reviewed in *Chapter 8, Strings and Serialization*, the adapter pattern is designed to interact with existing code. We would not design a brand new set of objects that implement the adapter pattern. Adapters are used to allow two pre-existing objects to work together, even if their interfaces are not compatible. Like the display adapters that allow VGA projectors to be plugged into HDMI ports, an adapter object sits between two different interfaces, translating between them on the fly. The adapter object's sole purpose is to perform this translation job. Adapting may entail a variety of tasks, such as converting arguments to a different format, rearranging the order of arguments, calling a differently named method, or supplying default arguments.

In structure, the adapter pattern is similar to a simplified decorator pattern. Decorators typically provide the same interface that they replace, whereas adapters map between two different interfaces. Here it is in UML form:

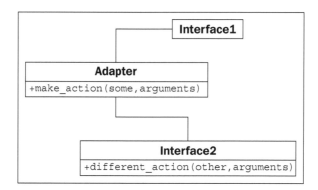

Here, **Interface1** is expecting to call a method called **make_action(some, arguments)**. We already have this perfect **Interface2** class that does everything we want (and to avoid duplication, we don't want to rewrite it!), but it provides a method called **different_action(other, arguments)** instead. The **Adapter** class implements the **make_action** interface and maps the arguments to the existing interface.

The advantage here is that the code that maps from one interface to another is all in one place. The alternative would be really ugly; we'd have to perform the translation in multiple places whenever we need to access this code.

For example, imagine we have the following preexisting class, which takes a string date in the format "YYYY-MM-DD" and calculates a person's age on that day:

```python
class AgeCalculator:
    def __init__(self, birthday):
        self.year, self.month, self.day = (
                int(x) for x in birthday.split('-'))

    def calculate_age(self, date):
        year, month, day = (
                int(x) for x in date.split('-'))
        age = year - self.year
        if (month,day) < (self.month,self.day):
            age -= 1
        return age
```

This is a pretty simple class that does what it's supposed to do. But we have to wonder what the programmer was thinking, using a specifically formatted string instead of using Python's incredibly useful built-in datetime library. As conscientious programmers who reuse code whenever possible, most of the programs we write will interact with datetime objects, not strings.

We have several options to address this scenario; we could rewrite the class to accept datetime objects, which would probably be more accurate anyway. But if this class had been provided by a third party and we don't know or can't change its internal structure, we need to try something else. We could use the class as it is, and whenever we want to calculate the age on a datetime.date object, we could call datetime.date.strftime('%Y-%m-%d') to convert it to the proper format. But that conversion would be happening in a lot of places, and worse, if we mistyped the %m as %M, it would give us the current minute instead of the entered month! Imagine if you wrote that in a dozen different places only to have to go back and change it when you realized your mistake. It's not maintainable code, and it breaks the DRY principle.

Instead, we can write an adapter that allows a normal date to be plugged into a normal AgeCalculator class:

```python
import datetime
class DateAgeAdapter:
    def _str_date(self, date):
        return date.strftime("%Y-%m-%d")

    def __init__(self, birthday):
        birthday = self._str_date(birthday)
        self.calculator = AgeCalculator(birthday)

    def get_age(self, date):
        date = self._str_date(date)
        return self.calculator.calculate_age(date)
```

This adapter converts datetime.date and datetime.time (they have the same interface to strftime) into a string that our original AgeCalculator can use. Now we can use the original code with our new interface. I changed the method signature to get_age to demonstrate that the calling interface may also be looking for a different method name, not just a different type of argument.

Creating a class as an adapter is the usual way to implement this pattern, but, as usual, there are other ways to do it in Python. Inheritance and multiple inheritance can be used to add functionality to a class. For example, we could add an adapter on the date class so that it works with the original AgeCalculator class:

```
import datetime
class AgeableDate(datetime.date):
    def split(self, char):
        return self.year, self.month, self.day
```

It's code like this that makes one wonder if Python should even be legal. We have added a split method to our subclass that takes a single argument (which we ignore) and returns a tuple of year, month, and day. This works flawlessly with the original AgeCalculator class because the code calls strip on a specially formatted string, and strip, in that case, returns a tuple of year, month, and day. The AgeCalculator code only cares if strip exists and returns acceptable values; it doesn't care if we really passed in a string. It really works:

```
>>> bd = AgeableDate(1975, 6, 14)
>>> today = AgeableDate.today()
>>> today
AgeableDate(2015, 8, 4)
>>> a = AgeCalculator(bd)
>>> a.calculate_age(today)
40
```

It works but it's a stupid idea. In this particular instance, such an adapter would be hard to maintain. We'd soon forget why we needed to add a strip method to a date class. The method name is ambiguous. That can be the nature of adapters, but creating an adapter explicitly instead of using inheritance usually clarifies its purpose.

Instead of inheritance, we can sometimes also use monkey-patching to add a method to an existing class. It won't work with the datetime object, as it doesn't allow attributes to be added at runtime, but in normal classes, we can just add a new method that provides the adapted interface that is required by calling code. Alternatively, we could extend or monkey-patch the AgeCalculator itself to replace the calculate_age method with something more amenable to our needs.

Finally, it is often possible to use a function as an adapter; this doesn't obviously fit the actual design of the adapter pattern, but if we recall that functions are essentially objects with a __call__ method, it becomes an obvious adapter adaptation.

The facade pattern

The facade pattern is designed to provide a simple interface to a complex system of components. For complex tasks, we may need to interact with these objects directly, but there is often a "typical" usage for the system for which these complicated interactions aren't necessary. The facade pattern allows us to define a new object that encapsulates this typical usage of the system. Any time we want access to common functionality, we can use the single object's simplified interface. If another part of the project needs access to more complicated functionality, it is still able to interact with the system directly. The UML diagram for the facade pattern is really dependent on the subsystem, but in a cloudy way, it looks like this:

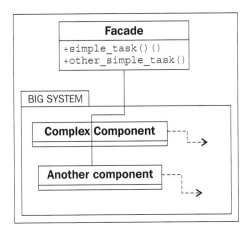

A facade is, in many ways, like an adapter. The primary difference is that the facade is trying to abstract a simpler interface out of a complex one, while the adapter is only trying to map one existing interface to another.

Let's write a simple facade for an e-mail application. The low-level library for sending e-mail in Python, as we saw in *Chapter 7, Python Object-oriented Shortcuts*, is quite complicated. The two libraries for receiving messages are even worse.

It would be nice to have a simple class that allows us to send a single e-mail, and list the e-mails currently in the inbox on an IMAP or POP3 connection. To keep our example short, we'll stick with IMAP and SMTP: two totally different subsystems that happen to deal with e-mail. Our facade performs only two tasks: sending an e-mail to a specific address, and checking the inbox on an IMAP connection. It makes some common assumptions about the connection, such as the host for both SMTP and IMAP is at the same address, that the username and password for both is the same, and that they use standard ports. This covers the case for many e-mail servers, but if a programmer needs more flexibility, they can always bypass the facade and access the two subsystems directly.

The class is initialized with the hostname of the e-mail server, a username, and a password to log in:

```python
import smtplib
import imaplib


class EmailFacade:
    def __init__(self, host, username, password):
        self.host = host
        self.username = username
        self.password = password
```

The `send_email` method formats the e-mail address and message, and sends it using `smtplib`. This isn't a complicated task, but it requires quite a bit of fiddling to massage the "natural" input parameters that are passed into the facade to the correct format to enable `smtplib` to send the message:

```python
def send_email(self, to_email, subject, message):
    if not "@" in self.username:
        from_email = "{0}@{1}".format(
                self.username, self.host)
    else:
        from_email = self.username
    message = ("From: {0}\r\n"
            "To: {1}\r\n"
            "Subject: {2}\r\n\r\n{3}").format(
                from_email,
                to_email,
                subject,
                message)

    smtp = smtplib.SMTP(self.host)
    smtp.login(self.username, self.password)
    smtp.sendmail(from_email, [to_email], message)
```

The `if` statement at the beginning of the method is catching whether or not the `username` is the entire "from" e-mail address or just the part on the left side of the @ symbol; different hosts treat the login details differently.

Finally, the code to get the messages currently in the inbox is a ruddy mess; the IMAP protocol is painfully over-engineered, and the `imaplib` standard library is only a thin layer over the protocol:

```python
def get_inbox(self):
    mailbox = imaplib.IMAP4(self.host)
```

```
mailbox.login(bytes(self.username, 'utf8'),
    bytes(self.password, 'utf8'))
mailbox.select()
x, data = mailbox.search(None, 'ALL')
messages = []
for num in data[0].split():
    x, message = mailbox.fetch(num, '(RFC822)')
    messages.append(message[0][1])
return messages
```

Now, if we add all this together, we have a simple facade class that can send and receive messages in a fairly straightforward manner, much simpler than if we had to interact with these complex libraries directly.

Although it is rarely named in the Python community, the facade pattern is an integral part of the Python ecosystem. Because Python emphasizes language readability, both the language and its libraries tend to provide easy-to-comprehend interfaces to complicated tasks. For example, `for` loops, `list` comprehensions, and generators are all facades into a more complicated iterator protocol. The `defaultdict` implementation is a facade that abstracts away annoying corner cases when a key doesn't exist in a dictionary. The third-party requests library is a powerful facade over less readable libraries for HTTP requests.

The flyweight pattern

The flyweight pattern is a memory optimization pattern. Novice Python programmers tend to ignore memory optimization, assuming the built-in garbage collector will take care of them. This is often perfectly acceptable, but when developing larger applications with many related objects, paying attention to memory concerns can have a huge payoff.

The flyweight pattern basically ensures that objects that share a state can use the same memory for that shared state. It is often implemented only after a program has demonstrated memory problems. It may make sense to design an optimal configuration from the beginning in some situations, but bear in mind that premature optimization is the most effective way to create a program that is too complicated to maintain.

Let's have a look at the UML diagram for the flyweight pattern:

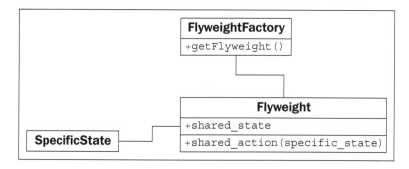

Each **Flyweight** has no specific state; any time it needs to perform an operation on **SpecificState**, that state needs to be passed into the **Flyweight** by the calling code. Traditionally, the factory that returns a flyweight is a separate object; its purpose is to return a flyweight for a given key identifying that flyweight. It works like the singleton pattern we discussed in *Chapter 10, Python Design Patterns I*; if the flyweight exists, we return it; otherwise, we create a new one. In many languages, the factory is implemented, not as a separate object, but as a static method on the `Flyweight` class itself.

Think of an inventory system for car sales. Each individual car has a specific serial number and is a specific color. But most of the details about that car are the same for all cars of a particular model. For example, the Honda Fit DX model is a bare-bones car with few features. The LX model has A/C, tilt, cruise, and power windows and locks. The Sport model has fancy wheels, a USB charger, and a spoiler. Without the flyweight pattern, each individual car object would have to store a long list of which features it did and did not have. Considering the number of cars Honda sells in a year, this would add up to a huge amount of wasted memory. Using the flyweight pattern, we can instead have shared objects for the list of features associated with a model, and then simply reference that model, along with a serial number and color, for individual vehicles. In Python, the flyweight factory is often implemented using that funky __new__ constructor, similar to what we did with the singleton pattern. Unlike singleton, which only needs to return one instance of the class, we need to be able to return different instances depending on the keys. We could store the items in a dictionary and look them up based on the key. This solution is problematic, however, because the item will remain in memory as long as it is in the dictionary. If we sold out of LX model Fits, the Fit flyweight is no longer necessary, yet it will still be in the dictionary. We could, of course, clean this up whenever we sell a car, but isn't that what a garbage collector is for?

We can solve this by taking advantage of Python's `weakref` module. This module provides a `WeakValueDictionary` object, which basically allows us to store items in a dictionary without the garbage collector caring about them. If a value is in a weak referenced dictionary and there are no other references to that object stored anywhere in the application (that is, we sold out of LX models), the garbage collector will eventually clean up for us.

Let's build the factory for our car flyweights first:

```python
import weakref

class CarModel:
    _models = weakref.WeakValueDictionary()

    def __new__(cls, model_name, *args, **kwargs):
        model = cls._models.get(model_name)
        if not model:
            model = super().__new__(cls)
            cls._models[model_name] = model

        return model
```

Basically, whenever we construct a new flyweight with a given name, we first look up that name in the weak referenced dictionary; if it exists, we return that model; if not, we create a new one. Either way, we know the `__init__` method on the flyweight will be called every time, regardless of whether it is a new or existing object. Our `__init__` method can therefore look like this:

```python
    def __init__(self, model_name, air=False, tilt=False,
            cruise_control=False, power_locks=False,
            alloy_wheels=False, usb_charger=False):
        if not hasattr(self, "initted"):
            self.model_name = model_name
            self.air = air
            self.tilt = tilt
            self.cruise_control = cruise_control
            self.power_locks = power_locks
            self.alloy_wheels = alloy_wheels
            self.usb_charger = usb_charger
            self.initted=True
```

The `if` statement ensures that we only initialize the object the first time `__init__` is called. This means we can call the factory later with just the model name and get the same flyweight object back. However, because the flyweight will be garbage-collected if no external references to it exist, we have to be careful not to accidentally create a new flyweight with null values.

Let's add a method to our flyweight that hypothetically looks up a serial number on a specific model of vehicle, and determines if it has been involved in any accidents. This method needs access to the car's serial number, which varies from car to car; it cannot be stored with the flyweight. Therefore, this data must be passed into the method by the calling code:

```python
def check_serial(self, serial_number):
    print("Sorry, we are unable to check "
            "the serial number {0} on the {1} "
            "at this time".format(
                serial_number, self.model_name))
```

We can define a class that stores the additional information, as well as a reference to the flyweight:

```python
class Car:
    def __init__(self, model, color, serial):
        self.model = model
        self.color = color
        self.serial = serial

    def check_serial(self):
        return self.model.check_serial(self.serial)
```

We can also keep track of the available models as well as the individual cars on the lot:

```python
>>> dx = CarModel("FIT DX")
>>> lx = CarModel("FIT LX", air=True, cruise_control=True,
... power_locks=True, tilt=True)
>>> car1 = Car(dx, "blue", "12345")
>>> car2 = Car(dx, "black", "12346")
>>> car3 = Car(lx, "red", "12347")
```

Now, let's demonstrate the weak referencing at work:

```python
>>> id(lx)
3071620300
>>> del lx
>>> del car3
>>> import gc
>>> gc.collect()
0
```

```
>>> lx = CarModel("FIT LX", air=True, cruise_control=True,
... power_locks=True, tilt=True)
>>> id(lx)
3071576140
>>> lx = CarModel("FIT LX")
>>> id(lx)
3071576140
>>> lx.air
True
```

The `id` function tells us the unique identifier for an object. When we call it a second time, after deleting all references to the LX model and forcing garbage collection, we see that the ID has changed. The value in the `CarModel __new__` factory dictionary was deleted and a fresh one created. If we then try to construct a second `CarModel` instance, however, it returns the same object (the IDs are the same), and, even though we did not supply any arguments in the second call, the `air` variable is still set to `True`. This means the object was not initialized the second time, just as we designed.

Obviously, using the flyweight pattern can be more complicated than just storing features on a single car class. When should we choose to use it? The flyweight pattern is designed for conserving memory; if we have hundreds of thousands of similar objects, combining similar properties into a flyweight can have an enormous impact on memory consumption. It is common for programming solutions that optimize CPU, memory, or disk space result in more complicated code than their unoptimized brethren. It is therefore important to weigh up the tradeoffs when deciding between code maintainability and optimization. When choosing optimization, try to use patterns such as flyweight to ensure that the complexity introduced by optimization is confined to a single (well documented) section of the code.

The command pattern

The command pattern adds a level of abstraction between actions that must be done, and the object that invokes those actions, normally at a later time. In the command pattern, client code creates a `Command` object that can be executed at a later date. This object knows about a receiver object that manages its own internal state when the command is executed on it. The `Command` object implements a specific interface (typically it has an `execute` or `do_action` method, and also keeps track of any arguments required to perform the action. Finally, one or more `Invoker` objects execute the command at the correct time.

Here's the UML diagram:

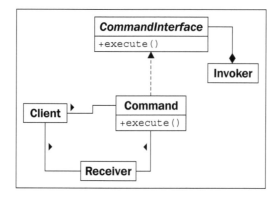

A common example of the command pattern is actions on a graphical window. Often, an action can be invoked by a menu item on the menu bar, a keyboard shortcut, a toolbar icon, or a context menu. These are all examples of Invoker objects. The actions that actually occur, such as Exit, Save, or Copy, are implementations of CommandInterface. A GUI window to receive exit, a document to receive save, and ClipboardManager to receive copy commands, are all examples of possible Receivers.

Let's implement a simple command pattern that provides commands for Save and Exit actions. We'll start with some modest receiver classes:

```python
import sys

class Window:
    def exit(self):
        sys.exit(0)

class Document:
    def __init__(self, filename):
        self.filename = filename
        self.contents = "This file cannot be modified"

    def save(self):
        with open(self.filename, 'w') as file:
            file.write(self.contents)
```

These mock classes model objects that would likely be doing a lot more in a working environment. The window would need to handle mouse movement and keyboard events, and the document would need to handle character insertion, deletion, and selection. But for our example these two classes will do what we need.

Now let's define some invoker classes. These will model toolbar, menu, and keyboard events that can happen; again, they aren't actually hooked up to anything, but we can see how they are decoupled from the command, receiver, and client code:

```
class ToolbarButton:
    def __init__(self, name, iconname):
        self.name = name
        self.iconname = iconname

    def click(self):
        self.command.execute()

class MenuItem:
    def __init__(self, menu_name, menuitem_name):
        self.menu = menu_name
        self.item = menuitem_name

    def click(self):
        self.command.execute()

class KeyboardShortcut:
    def __init__(self, key, modifier):
        self.key = key
        self.modifier = modifier

    def keypress(self):
        self.command.execute()
```

Notice how the various action methods each call the `execute` method on their respective commands? This code doesn't show the `command` attribute being set on each object. They could be passed into the __init__ function, but because they may be changed (for example, with a customizable keybinding editor), it makes more sense to set the attributes on the objects afterwards.

Now, let's hook up the commands themselves:

```
class SaveCommand:
    def __init__(self, document):
        self.document = document

    def execute(self):
        self.document.save()

class ExitCommand:
```

```
    def __init__(self, window):
        self.window = window

    def execute(self):
        self.window.exit()
```

These commands are straightforward; they demonstrate the basic pattern, but it is important to note that we can store state and other information with the command if necessary. For example, if we had a command to insert a character, we could maintain state for the character currently being inserted.

Now all we have to do is hook up some client and test code to make the commands work. For basic testing, we can just include this at the end of the script:

```
window = Window()
document = Document("a_document.txt")
save = SaveCommand(document)
exit = ExitCommand(window)

save_button = ToolbarButton('save', 'save.png')
save_button.command = save
save_keystroke = KeyboardShortcut("s", "ctrl")
save_keystroke.command = save
exit_menu = MenuItem("File", "Exit")
exit_menu.command = exit
```

First we create two receivers and two commands. Then we create several of the available invokers and set the correct command on each of them. To test, we can use `python3 -i filename.py` and run code like `exit_menu.click()`, which will end the program, or `save_keystroke.keystroke()`, which will save the fake file.

Unfortunately, the preceding examples do not feel terribly Pythonic. They have a lot of "boilerplate code" (code that does not accomplish anything, but only provides structure to the pattern), and the Command classes are all eerily similar to each other. Perhaps we could create a generic command object that takes a function as a callback?

In fact, why bother? Can we just use a function or method object for each command? Instead of an object with an `execute()` method, we can write a function and use that as the command directly. This is a common paradigm for the command pattern in Python:

```
import sys

class Window:
```

```
        def exit(self):
            sys.exit(0)

    class MenuItem:
        def click(self):
            self.command()

    window = Window()
    menu_item = MenuItem()
    menu_item.command = window.exit
```

Now that looks a lot more like Python. At first glance, it looks like we've removed the command pattern altogether, and we've tightly connected the `menu_item` and `Window` classes. But if we look closer, we find there is no tight coupling at all. Any callable can be set up as the command on the `MenuItem`, just as before. And the `Window.exit` method can be attached to any invoker. Most of the flexibility of the command pattern has been maintained. We have sacrificed complete decoupling for readability, but this code is, in my opinion, and that of many Python programmers, more maintainable than the fully abstracted version.

Of course, since we can add a `__call__` method to any object, we aren't restricted to functions. The previous example is a useful shortcut when the method being called doesn't have to maintain state, but in more advanced usage, we can use this code as well:

```
    class Document:
        def __init__(self, filename):
            self.filename = filename
            self.contents = "This file cannot be modified"

        def save(self):
            with open(self.filename, 'w') as file:
                file.write(self.contents)

    class KeyboardShortcut:
        def keypress(self):
            self.command()
    class SaveCommand:
        def __init__(self, document):
            self.document = document

        def __call__(self):
```

```
        self.document.save()

document = Document("a_file.txt")
shortcut = KeyboardShortcut()
save_command = SaveCommand(document)
shortcut.command = save_command
```

Here we have something that looks like the first command pattern, but a bit more idiomatic. As you can see, making the invoker call a callable instead of a command object with an execute method has not restricted us in any way. In fact, it's given us more flexibility. We can link to functions directly when that works, yet we can build a complete callable command object when the situation calls for it.

The command pattern is often extended to support undoable commands. For example, a text program may wrap each insertion in a separate command with not only an execute method, but also an undo method that will delete that insertion. A graphics program may wrap each drawing action (rectangle, line, freehand pixels, and so on) in a command that has an undo method that resets the pixels to their original state. In such cases, the decoupling of the command pattern is much more obviously useful, because each action has to maintain enough of its state to undo that action at a later date.

The abstract factory pattern

The abstract factory pattern is normally used when we have multiple possible implementations of a system that depend on some configuration or platform issue. The calling code requests an object from the abstract factory, not knowing exactly what class of object will be returned. The underlying implementation returned may depend on a variety of factors, such as current locale, operating system, or local configuration.

Common examples of the abstract factory pattern include code for operating-system independent toolkits, database backends, and country-specific formatters or calculators. An operating-system-independent GUI toolkit might use an abstract factory pattern that returns a set of WinForm widgets under Windows, Cocoa widgets under Mac, GTK widgets under Gnome, and QT widgets under KDE. Django provides an abstract factory that returns a set of object relational classes for interacting with a specific database backend (MySQL, PostgreSQL, SQLite, and others) depending on a configuration setting for the current site. If the application needs to be deployed in multiple places, each one can use a different database backend by changing only one configuration variable. Different countries have different systems for calculating taxes, subtotals, and totals on retail merchandise; an abstract factory can return a particular tax calculation object.

The UML class diagram for an abstract factory pattern is hard to understand without a specific example, so let's turn things around and create a concrete example first. We'll create a set of formatters that depend on a specific locale and help us format dates and currencies. There will be an abstract factory class that picks the specific factory, as well as a couple example concrete factories, one for France and one for the USA. Each of these will create formatter objects for dates and times, which can be queried to format a specific value. Here's the diagram:

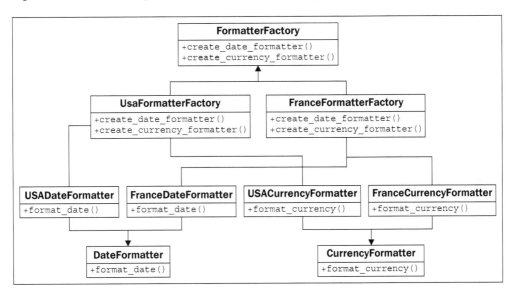

Comparing that image to the earlier simpler text shows that a picture is not always worth a thousand words, especially considering we haven't even allowed for factory selection code here.

Of course, in Python, we don't have to implement any interface classes, so we can discard `DateFormatter`, `CurrencyFormatter`, and `FormatterFactory`. The formatting classes themselves are pretty straightforward, if verbose:

```
class FranceDateFormatter:
    def format_date(self, y, m, d):
        y, m, d = (str(x) for x in (y,m,d))
        y = '20' + y if len(y) == 2 else y
        m = '0' + m if len(m) == 1 else m
        d = '0' + d if len(d) == 1 else d
        return("{0}/{1}/{2}".format(d,m,y))

class USADateFormatter:
```

```
        def format_date(self, y, m, d):
            y, m, d = (str(x) for x in (y,m,d))
            y = '20' + y if len(y) == 2 else y
            m = '0' + m if len(m) == 1 else m
            d = '0' + d if len(d) == 1 else d
            return("{0}-{1}-{2}".format(m,d,y))


    class FranceCurrencyFormatter:
        def format_currency(self, base, cents):
            base, cents = (str(x) for x in (base, cents))
            if len(cents) == 0:
                cents = '00'
            elif len(cents) == 1:
                cents = '0' + cents

            digits = []
            for i,c in enumerate(reversed(base)):
                if i and not i % 3:
                    digits.append(' ')
                digits.append(c)
            base = ''.join(reversed(digits))
            return "{0}€{1}".format(base, cents)


    class USACurrencyFormatter:
        def format_currency(self, base, cents):
            base, cents = (str(x) for x in (base, cents))
            if len(cents) == 0:
                cents = '00'
            elif len(cents) == 1:
                cents = '0' + cents
            digits = []
            for i,c in enumerate(reversed(base)):
                if i and not i % 3:
                    digits.append(',')
                digits.append(c)
            base = ''.join(reversed(digits))
            return "${0}.{1}".format(base, cents)
```

These classes use some basic string manipulation to try to turn a variety of possible inputs (integers, strings of different lengths, and others) into the following formats:

	USA	France
Date	mm-dd-yyyy	dd/mm/yyyy
Currency	$14,500.50	14 500€50

There could obviously be more validation on the input in this code, but let's keep it simple and dumb for this example.

Now that we have the formatters set up, we just need to create the formatter factories:

```
class USAFormatterFactory:
    def create_date_formatter(self):
        return USADateFormatter()
    def create_currency_formatter(self):
        return USACurrencyFormatter()

class FranceFormatterFactory:
    def create_date_formatter(self):
        return FranceDateFormatter()
    def create_currency_formatter(self):
        return FranceCurrencyFormatter()
```

Now we set up the code that picks the appropriate formatter. Since this is the kind of thing that only needs to be set up once, we could make it a singleton—except singletons aren't very useful in Python. Let's just make the current formatter a module-level variable instead:

```
country_code = "US"
factory_map = {
        "US": USAFormatterFactory,
        "FR": FranceFormatterFactory}
formatter_factory = factory_map.get(country_code)()
```

In this example, we hardcode the current country code; in practice, it would likely introspect the locale, the operating system, or a configuration file to choose the code. This example uses a dictionary to associate the country codes with factory classes. Then we grab the correct class from the dictionary and instantiate it.

It is easy to see what needs to be done when we want to add support for more countries: create the new formatter classes and the abstract factory itself. Bear in mind that `Formatter` classes might be reused; for example, Canada formats its currency the same way as the USA, but its date format is more sensible than its Southern neighbor.

Abstract factories often return a singleton object, but this is not required; in our code, it's returning a new instance of each formatter every time it's called. There's no reason the formatters couldn't be stored as instance variables and the same instance returned for each factory.

Looking back at these examples, we see that, once again, there appears to be a lot of boilerplate code for factories that just doesn't feel necessary in Python. Often, the requirements that might call for an abstract factory can be more easily fulfilled by using a separate module for each factory type (for example: the USA and France), and then ensuring that the correct module is being accessed in a factory module. The package structure for such modules might look like this:

```
localize/
    __init__.py
    backends/
        __init__.py
        USA.py
        France.py
        ...
```

The trick is that `__init__.py` in the `localize` package can contain logic that redirects all requests to the correct backend. There is a variety of ways this could be done.

If we know that the backend is never going to change dynamically (that is, without a restart), we can just put some `if` statements in `__init__.py` that check the current country code, and use the usually unacceptable `from .backends.USA import *` syntax to import all variables from the appropriate backend. Or, we could import each of the backends and set a `current_backend` variable to point at a specific module:

```
from .backends import USA, France

if country_code == "US":
    current_backend = USA
```

Depending on which solution we choose, our client code would have to call either `localize.format_date` or `localize.current_backend.format_date` to get a date formatted in the current country's locale. The end result is much more Pythonic than the original abstract factory pattern, and, in typical usage, just as flexible.

The composite pattern

The composite pattern allows complex tree-like structures to be built from simple components. These components, called composite objects, are able to behave sort of like a container and sort of like a variable depending on whether they have child components. Composite objects are container objects, where the content may actually be another composite object.

Traditionally, each component in a composite object must be either a leaf node (that cannot contain other objects) or a composite node. The key is that both composite and leaf nodes can have the same interface. The UML diagram is very simple:

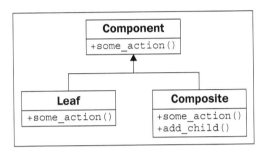

This simple pattern, however, allows us to create complex arrangements of elements, all of which satisfy the interface of the component object. Here is a concrete instance of such a complicated arrangement:

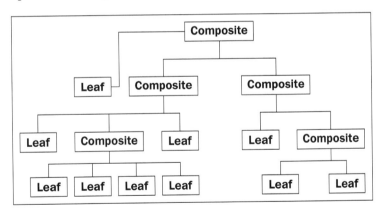

The composite pattern is commonly useful in file/folder-like trees. Regardless of whether a node in the tree is a normal file or a folder, it is still subject to operations such as moving, copying, or deleting the node. We can create a component interface that supports these operations, and then use a composite object to represent folders, and leaf nodes to represent normal files.

Of course, in Python, once again, we can take advantage of duck typing to implicitly provide the interface, so we only need to write two classes. Let's define these interfaces first:

```python
class Folder:
    def __init__(self, name):
        self.name = name
        self.children = {}

    def add_child(self, child):
        pass

    def move(self, new_path):
        pass

    def copy(self, new_path):
        pass

    def delete(self):
        pass


class File:
    def __init__(self, name, contents):
        self.name = name
        self.contents = contents

    def move(self, new_path):
        pass

    def copy(self, new_path):
        pass

    def delete(self):
        pass
```

For each folder (composite) object, we maintain a dictionary of children. Often, a list is sufficient, but in this case, a dictionary will be useful for looking up children by name. Our paths will be specified as node names separated by the / character, similar to paths in a Unix shell.

Thinking about the methods involved, we can see that moving or deleting a node behaves in a similar way, regardless of whether or not it is a file or folder node. Copying, however, has to do a recursive copy for folder nodes, while copying a file node is a trivial operation.

To take advantage of the similar operations, we can extract some of the common methods into a parent class. Let's take that discarded Component interface and change it to a base class:

```python
class Component:
    def __init__(self, name):
        self.name = name

    def move(self, new_path):
        new_folder =get_path(new_path)
        del self.parent.children[self.name]
        new_folder.children[self.name] = self
        self.parent = new_folder

    def delete(self):
        del self.parent.children[self.name]

class Folder(Component):
    def __init__(self, name):
        super().__init__(name)
        self.children = {}

    def add_child(self, child):
        pass

    def copy(self, new_path):
        pass

class File(Component):
    def __init__(self, name, contents):
        super().__init__(name)
        self.contents = contents

    def copy(self, new_path):
        pass

root = Folder('')
def get_path(path):
```

```
        names = path.split('/')[1:]
        node = root
        for name in names:
            node = node.children[name]
        return node
```

We've created the `move` and `delete` methods on the `Component` class. Both of them access a mysterious `parent` variable that we haven't set yet. The `move` method uses a module-level `get_path` function that finds a node from a predefined root node, given a path. All files will be added to this root node or a child of that node. For the `move` method, the target should be a currently existing folder, or we'll get an error. As with many of the examples in technical books, error handling is woefully absent, to help focus on the principles under consideration.

Let's set up that mysterious `parent` variable first; this happens, in the folder's `add_child` method:

```
        def add_child(self, child):
            child.parent = self
            self.children[child.name] = child
```

Well, that was easy enough. Let's see if our composite file hierarchy is working properly:

`$ python3 -i 1261_09_18_add_child.py`

```
>>> folder1 = Folder('folder1')
>>> folder2 = Folder('folder2')
>>> root.add_child(folder1)
>>> root.add_child(folder2)
>>> folder11 = Folder('folder11')
>>> folder1.add_child(folder11)
>>> file111 = File('file111', 'contents')
>>> folder11.add_child(file111)
>>> file21 = File('file21', 'other contents')
>>> folder2.add_child(file21)
>>> folder2.children
{'file21': <__main__.File object at 0xb7220a4c>}
>>> folder2.move('/folder1/folder11')
>>> folder11.children
{'folder2': <__main__.Folder object at 0xb722080c>, 'file111': <__main__.
File object at 0xb72209ec>}
```

```
>>> file21.move('/folder1')
>>> folder1.children
{'file21': <__main__.File object at 0xb7220a4c>, 'folder11': <__main__.
Folder object at 0xb722084c>}
```

Yes, we can create folders, add folders to other folders, add files to folders, and move them around! What more could we ask for in a file hierarchy?

Well, we could ask for copying to be implemented, but to conserve trees, let's leave that as an exercise.

The composite pattern is extremely useful for a variety of tree-like structures, including GUI widget hierarchies, file hierarchies, tree sets, graphs, and HTML DOM. It can be a useful pattern in Python when implemented according to the traditional implementation, as the example earlier demonstrated. Sometimes, if only a shallow tree is being created, we can get away with a list of lists or a dictionary of dictionaries, and do not need to implement custom component, leaf, and composite classes. Other times, we can get away with implementing only one composite class, and treating leaf and composite objects as a single class. Alternatively, Python's duck typing can make it easy to add other objects to a composite hierarchy, as long as they have the correct interface.

Exercises

Before diving into exercises for each design pattern, take a moment to implement the copy method for the File and Folder objects in the previous section. The File method should be quite trivial; just create a new node with the same name and contents, and add it to the new parent folder. The copy method on Folder is quite a bit more complicated, as you first have to duplicate the folder, and then recursively copy each of its children to the new location. You can call the copy() method on the children indiscriminately, regardless of whether each is a file or a folder object. This will drive home just how powerful the composite pattern can be.

Now, as with the previous chapter, look at the patterns we've discussed, and consider ideal places where you might implement them. You may want to apply the adapter pattern to existing code, as it is usually applicable when interfacing with existing libraries, rather than new code. How can you use an adapter to force two interfaces to interact with each other correctly?

Can you think of a system complex enough to justify using the facade pattern? Consider how facades are used in real-life situations, such as the driver-facing interface of a car, or the control panel in a factory. It is similar in software, except the users of the facade interface are other programmers, rather than people trained to use them. Are there complex systems in your latest project that could benefit from the facade pattern?

It's possible you don't have any huge, memory-consuming code that would benefit from the flyweight pattern, but can you think of situations where it might be useful? Anywhere that large amounts of overlapping data need to be processed, a flyweight is waiting to be used. Would it be useful in the banking industry? In web applications? At what point does the flyweight pattern make sense? When is it overkill?

What about the command pattern? Can you think of any common (or better yet, uncommon) examples of places where the decoupling of action from invocation would be useful? Look at the programs you use on a daily basis, and imagine how they are implemented internally. It's likely that many of them use the command pattern for one purpose or another.

The abstract factory pattern, or the somewhat more Pythonic derivatives we discussed, can be very useful for creating one-touch-configurable systems. Can you think of places where such systems are useful?

Finally, consider the composite pattern. There are tree-like structures all around us in programming; some of them, like our file hierarchy example, are blatant; others are fairly subtle. What situations might arise where the composite pattern would be useful? Can you think of places where you can use it in your own code? What if you adapted the pattern slightly; for example, to contain different types of leaf or composite nodes for different types of objects?

Summary

In this chapter, we went into detail on several more design patterns, covering their canonical descriptions as well as alternatives for implementing them in Python, which is often more flexible and versatile than traditional object-oriented languages. The adapter pattern is useful for matching interfaces, while the facade pattern is suited to simplifying them. Flyweight is a complicated pattern and only useful if memory optimization is required. In Python, the command pattern is often more aptly implemented using first class functions as callbacks. Abstract factories allow run-time separation of implementations depending on configuration or system information. The composite pattern is used universally for tree-like structures.

In the next chapter, we'll discuss how important it is to test Python programs, and how to do it.

12
Testing Object-oriented Programs

Skilled Python programmers agree that testing is one of the most important aspects of software development. Even though this chapter is placed near the end of the book, it is not an afterthought; everything we have studied so far will help us when writing tests. We'll be studying:

- The importance of unit testing and test-driven development
- The standard `unittest` module
- The `py.test` automated testing suite
- The `mock` module
- Code coverage
- Cross-platform testing with `tox`

Why test?

A large collection of programmers already know how important it is to test their code. If you're among them, feel free to skim this section. You'll find the next section — where we actually see how to do the tests in Python — much more scintillating. If you're not convinced of the importance of testing, I promise that your code is broken, you just don't know it. Read on!

Some people argue that testing is more important in Python code because of its dynamic nature; compiled languages such as Java and C++ are occasionally thought to be somehow "safer" because they enforce type checking at compile time. However, Python tests rarely check types. They're checking values. They're making sure that the right attributes have been set at the right time or that the sequence has the right length, order, and values. These higher-level things need to be tested in any language. The real reason Python programmers test more than programmers of other languages is that it is so easy to test in Python!

But why test? Do we really need to test? What if we didn't test? To answer those questions, write a tic-tac-toe game from scratch without any testing at all. Don't run it until it is completely written, start to finish. Tic-tac-toe is fairly simple to implement if you make both players human players (no artificial intelligence). You don't even have to try to calculate who the winner is. Now run your program. And fix all the errors. How many were there? I recorded eight on my tic-tac-toe implementation, and I'm not sure I caught them all. Did you?

We need to test our code to make sure it works. Running the program, as we just did, and fixing the errors is one crude form of testing. Python programmers are able to write a few lines of code and run the program to make sure those lines are doing what they expect. But changing a few lines of code can affect parts of the program that the developer hadn't realized will be influenced by the changes, and therefore won't test it. Furthermore, as a program grows, the various paths that the interpreter can take through that code also grow, and it quickly becomes impossible to manually test all of them.

To handle this, we write automated tests. These are programs that automatically run certain inputs through other programs or parts of programs. We can run these test programs in seconds and cover more possible input situations than one programmer would think to test every time they change something.

There are four main reasons to write tests:

- To ensure that code is working the way the developer thinks it should
- To ensure that code continues working when we make changes
- To ensure that the developer understood the requirements
- To ensure that the code we are writing has a maintainable interface

The first point really doesn't justify the time it takes to write a test; we can simply test the code directly in the interactive interpreter. But when we have to perform the same sequence of test actions multiple times, it takes less time to automate those steps once and then run them whenever necessary. It is a good idea to run tests whenever we change code, whether it is during initial development or maintenance releases. When we have a comprehensive set of automated tests, we can run them after code changes and know that we didn't inadvertently break anything that was tested.

The last two points are more interesting. When we write tests for code, it helps us design the API, interface, or pattern that code takes. Thus, if we misunderstood the requirements, writing a test can help highlight that misunderstanding. On the other side, if we're not certain how we want to design a class, we can write a test that interacts with that class so we have an idea what the most natural way to test it would be. In fact, it is often beneficial to write the tests before we write the code we are testing.

Test-driven development

"Write tests first" is the mantra of test-driven development. Test-driven development takes the "untested code is broken code" concept one step further and suggests that only unwritten code should be untested. Do not write any code until you have written the tests for this code. So the first step is to write a test that proves the code would work. Obviously, the test is going to fail, since the code hasn't been written. Then write the code that ensures the test passes. Then write another test for the next segment of code.

Test-driven development is fun. It allows us to build little puzzles to solve. Then we implement the code to solve the puzzles. Then we make a more complicated puzzle, and we write code that solves the new puzzle without unsolving the previous one.

There are two goals to the test-driven methodology. The first is to ensure that tests really get written. It's so very easy, after we have written code, to say: "Hmm, it seems to work. I don't have to write any tests for this. It was just a small change, nothing could have broken." If the test is already written before we write the code, we will know exactly when it works (because the test will pass), and we'll know in the future if it is ever broken by a change we, or someone else has made.

Secondly, writing tests first forces us to consider exactly how the code will be interacted with. It tells us what methods objects need to have and how attributes will be accessed. It helps us break up the initial problem into smaller, testable problems, and then to recombine the tested solutions into larger, also tested, solutions. Writing tests can thus become a part of the design process. Often, if we're writing a test for a new object, we discover anomalies in the design that force us to consider new aspects of the software.

As a concrete example, imagine writing code that uses an object-relational mapper to store object properties in a database. It is common to use an automatically assigned database ID in such objects. Our code might use this ID for various purposes. If we are writing a test for such code, before we write it, we may realize that our design is faulty because objects do not have these IDs until they have been saved to the database. If we want to manipulate an object without saving it in our test, it will highlight this problem before we have written code based on the faulty premise.

Testing makes software better. Writing tests before we release the software makes it better before the end user sees or purchases the buggy version (I have worked for companies that thrive on the "the users can test it" philosophy. It's not a healthy business model!). Writing tests before we write software makes it better the first time it is written.

Unit testing

Let's start our exploration with Python's built-in test library. This library provides a common interface for **unit tests**. Unit tests focus on testing the least amount of code possible in any one test. Each one tests a single unit of the total amount of available code.

The Python library for this is called, unsurprisingly, `unittest`. It provides several tools for creating and running unit tests, the most important being the `TestCase` class. This class provides a set of methods that allow us to compare values, set up tests, and clean up when they have finished.

When we want to write a set of unit tests for a specific task, we create a subclass of `TestCase`, and write individual methods to do the actual testing. These methods must all start with the name `test`. When this convention is followed, the tests automatically run as part of the test process. Normally, the tests set some values on an object and then run a method, and use the built-in comparison methods to ensure that the right results were calculated. Here's a very simple example:

```python
import unittest


class CheckNumbers(unittest.TestCase):
    def test_int_float(self):
        self.assertEqual(1, 1.0)


if __name__ == "__main__":
    unittest.main()
```

This code simply subclasses the `TestCase` class and adds a method that calls the `TestCase.assertEqual` method. This method will either succeed or raise an exception, depending on whether the two parameters are equal. If we run this code, the `main` function from `unittest` will give us the following output:

```
.
----------------------------------------------------------------
Ran 1 test in 0.000s


OK
```

Did you know that floats and integers can compare as equal? Let's add a failing test:

```
    def test_str_float(self):
        self.assertEqual(1, "1")
```

The output of this code is more sinister, as integers and strings are not considered equal:

```
.F
================================================================
FAIL: test_str_float (__main__.CheckNumbers)
----------------------------------------------------------------
Traceback (most recent call last):
  File "simplest_unittest.py", line 8, in test_str_float
    self.assertEqual(1, "1")
AssertionError: 1 != '1'


----------------------------------------------------------------
Ran 2 tests in 0.001s


FAILED (failures=1)
```

The dot on the first line indicates that the first test (the one we wrote before) passed successfully; the letter `F` after it shows that the second test failed. Then, at the end, it gives us some informative output telling us how and where the test failed, along with a summary of the number of failures.

We can have as many test methods on one TestCase class as we like; as long as the method name begins with test, the test runner will execute each one as a separate test. Each test should be completely independent of other tests. Results or calculations from a previous test should have no impact on the current test. The key to writing good unit tests is to keep each test method as short as possible, testing a small unit of code with each test case. If your code does not seem to naturally break up into such testable units, it's probably a sign that your design needs rethinking.

Assertion methods

The general layout of a test case is to set certain variables to known values, run one or more functions, methods, or processes, and then "prove" that correct expected results were returned or calculated by using TestCase assertion methods.

There are a few different assertion methods available to confirm that specific results have been achieved. We just saw assertEqual, which will cause a test failure if the two parameters do not pass an equality check. The inverse, assertNotEqual, will fail if the two parameters do compare as equal. The assertTrue and assertFalse methods each accept a single expression, and fail if the expression does not pass an if test. These tests are not checking for the Boolean values True or False. Rather, they test the same condition as though an if statement were used: False, None, 0, or an empty list, dictionary, string, set, or tuple would pass a call to the assertFalse method, while nonzero numbers, containers with values in them, or the value True would succeed when calling the assertTrue method.

There is an assertRaises method that can be used to ensure a specific function call raises a specific exception or, optionally, it can be used as a context manager to wrap inline code. The test passes if the code inside the with statement raises the proper exception; otherwise, it fails. Here's an example of both versions:

```python
import unittest

def average(seq):
    return sum(seq) / len(seq)

class TestAverage(unittest.TestCase):
    def test_zero(self):
        self.assertRaises(ZeroDivisionError,
            average,
```

```
                    [])

        def test_with_zero(self):
            with self.assertRaises(ZeroDivisionError):
                average([])


    if __name__ == "__main__":
        unittest.main()
```

The context manager allows us to write the code the way we would normally write it (by calling functions or executing code directly), rather than having to wrap the function call in another function call.

There are also several other assertion methods, summarized in the following table:

Methods	Description
assertGreater assertGreaterEqual assertLess assertLessEqual	Accept two comparable objects and ensure the named inequality holds.
assertIn assertNotIn	Ensure an element is (or is not) an element in a container object.
assertIsNone assertIsNotNone	Ensure an element is (or is not) the exact value None (but not another falsey value).
assertSameElements	Ensure two container objects have the same elements, ignoring the order.
assertSequenceEqualassertDictEqual assertSetEqual assertListEqual assertTupleEqual	Ensure two containers have the same elements in the same order. If there's a failure, show a code diff comparing the two lists to see where they differ. The last four methods also test the type of the list.

Each of the assertion methods accepts an optional argument named msg. If supplied, it is included in the error message if the assertion fails. This is useful for clarifying what was expected or explaining where a bug may have occurred to cause the assertion to fail.

Reducing boilerplate and cleaning up

After writing a few small tests, we often find that we have to do the same setup code for several related tests. For example, the following list subclass has three methods for statistical calculations:

```python
from collections import defaultdict

class StatsList(list):
    def mean(self):
        return sum(self) / len(self)

    def median(self):
        if len(self) % 2:
            return self[int(len(self) / 2)]
        else:
            idx = int(len(self) / 2)
            return (self[idx] + self[idx-1]) / 2

    def mode(self):
        freqs = defaultdict(int)
        for item in self:
            freqs[item] += 1
        mode_freq = max(freqs.values())
        modes = []
        for item, value in freqs.items():
            if value == mode_freq:
                modes.append(item)
        return modes
```

Clearly, we're going to want to test situations with each of these three methods that have very similar inputs; we'll want to see what happens with empty lists or with lists containing non-numeric values or with lists containing a normal dataset. We can use the setUp method on the TestCase class to do initialization for each test. This method accepts no arguments, and allows us to do arbitrary setup before each test is run. For example, we can test all three methods on identical lists of integers as follows:

```python
from stats import StatsList
import unittest

class TestValidInputs(unittest.TestCase):
    def setUp(self):
        self.stats = StatsList([1,2,2,3,3,4])

    def test_mean(self):
```

```
        self.assertEqual(self.stats.mean(), 2.5)

    def test_median(self):
        self.assertEqual(self.stats.median(), 2.5)
        self.stats.append(4)
        self.assertEqual(self.stats.median(), 3)

    def test_mode(self):
        self.assertEqual(self.stats.mode(), [2,3])
        self.stats.remove(2)
        self.assertEqual(self.stats.mode(), [3])

if __name__ == "__main__":
    unittest.main()
```

If we run this example, it indicates that all tests pass. Notice first that the `setUp` method is never explicitly called inside the three `test_*` methods. The test suite does this on our behalf. More importantly notice how `test_median` alters the list, by adding an additional 4 to it, yet when `test_mode` is called, the list has returned to the values specified in `setUp` (if it had not, there would be two fours in the list, and the `mode` method would have returned three values). This shows that `setUp` is called individually before each test, to ensure the test class starts with a clean slate. Tests can be executed in any order, and the results of one test should not depend on any other tests.

In addition to the `setUp` method, `TestCase` offers a no-argument `tearDown` method, which can be used for cleaning up after each and every test on the class has run. This is useful if cleanup requires anything other than letting an object be garbage collected. For example, if we are testing code that does file I/O, our tests may create new files as a side effect of testing; the `tearDown` method can remove these files and ensure the system is in the same state it was before the tests ran. Test cases should never have side effects. In general, we group test methods into separate `TestCase` subclasses depending on what setup code they have in common. Several tests that require the same or similar setup will be placed in one class, while tests that require unrelated setup go in another class.

Organizing and running tests

It doesn't take long for a collection of unit tests to grow very large and unwieldy. It quickly becomes complicated to load and run all the tests at once. This is a primary goal of unit testing; it should be trivial to run all tests on our program and get a quick "yes or no" answer to the question, "Did my recent changes break any existing tests?".

Python's `discover` module basically looks for any modules in the current folder or subfolders with names that start with the characters `test`. If it finds any `TestCase` objects in these modules, the tests are executed. It's a painless way to ensure we don't miss running any tests. To use it, ensure your test modules are named `test_<something>.py` and then run the command `python3 -m unittest discover`.

Ignoring broken tests

Sometimes, a test is known to fail, but we don't want the test suite to report the failure. This may be because a broken or unfinished feature has had tests written, but we aren't currently focusing on improving it. More often, it happens because a feature is only available on a certain platform, Python version, or for advanced versions of a specific library. Python provides us with a few decorators to mark tests as expected to fail or to be skipped under known conditions.

The decorators are:

- `expectedFailure()`
- `skip(reason)`
- `skipIf(condition, reason)`
- `skipUnless(condition, reason)`

These are applied using the Python decorator syntax. The first one accepts no arguments, and simply tells the test runner not to record the test as a failure when it fails. The `skip` method goes one step further and doesn't even bother to run the test. It expects a single string argument describing why the test was skipped. The other two decorators accept two arguments, one a Boolean expression that indicates whether or not the test should be run, and a similar description. In use, these three decorators might be applied like this:

```python
import unittest
import sys


class SkipTests(unittest.TestCase):
    @unittest.expectedFailure
    def test_fails(self):
        self.assertEqual(False, True)

    @unittest.skip("Test is useless")
```

```
    def test_skip(self):
        self.assertEqual(False, True)

    @unittest.skipIf(sys.version_info.minor == 4,
            "broken on 3.4")
    def test_skipif(self):
        self.assertEqual(False, True)

    @unittest.skipUnless(sys.platform.startswith('linux'),
            "broken unless on linux")
    def test_skipunless(self):
        self.assertEqual(False, True)

if __name__ == "__main__":
    unittest.main()
```

The first test fails, but it is reported as an expected failure; the second test is never run. The other two tests may or may not be run depending on the current Python version and operating system. On my Linux system running Python 3.4, the output looks like this:

```
xssF
================================================================
FAIL: test_skipunless (__main__.SkipTests)
----------------------------------------------------------------
Traceback (most recent call last):
  File "skipping_tests.py", line 21, in test_skipunless
    self.assertEqual(False, True)
AssertionError: False != True


----------------------------------------------------------------
Ran 4 tests in 0.001s


FAILED (failures=1, skipped=2, expected failures=1)
```

The x on the first line indicates an expected failure; the two s characters represent skipped tests, and the F indicates a real failure, since the conditional to skipUnless was True on my system.

Testing with py.test

The Python `unittest` module requires a lot of boilerplate code to set up and initialize tests. It is based on the very popular JUnit testing framework for Java. It even uses the same method names (you may have noticed they don't conform to the PEP-8 naming standard, which suggests underscores rather than CamelCase to separate words in a method name) and test layout. While this is effective for testing in Java, it's not necessarily the best design for Python testing.

Because Python programmers like their code to be elegant and simple, other test frameworks have been developed, outside the standard library. Two of the more popular ones are `py.test` and `nose`. The former is more robust and has had Python 3 support for much longer, so we'll discuss it here.

Since `py.test` is not part of the standard library, you'll need to download and install it yourself; you can get it from the `py.test` home page at `http://pytest.org/`. The website has comprehensive installation instructions for a variety of interpreters and platforms, but you can usually get away with the more common python package installer, pip. Just type `pip install pytest` on your command line and you'll be good to go.

`py.test` has a substantially different layout from the `unittest` module. It doesn't require test cases to be classes. Instead, it takes advantage of the fact that Python functions are objects, and allows any properly named function to behave like a test. Rather than providing a bunch of custom methods for asserting equality, it uses the `assert` statement to verify results. This makes tests more readable and maintainable. When we run `py.test`, it will start in the current folder and search for any modules in that folder or subpackages whose names start with the characters `test_`. If any functions in this module also start with `test`, they will be executed as individual tests. Furthermore, if there are any classes in the module whose name starts with `Test`, any methods on that class that start with `test_` will also be executed in the test environment.

Let's port the simplest possible `unittest` example we wrote earlier to `py.test`:

```
def test_int_float():
    assert 1 == 1.0
```

For the exact same test, we've written two lines of more readable code, in comparison to the six lines required in our first `unittest` example.

However, we are not forbidden from writing class-based tests. Classes can be useful for grouping related tests together or for tests that need to access related attributes or methods on the class. This example shows an extended class with a passing and a failing test; we'll see that the error output is more comprehensive than that provided by the `unittest` module:

```
class TestNumbers:
    def test_int_float(self):
        assert 1 == 1.0

    def test_int_str(self):
        assert 1 == "1"
```

Notice that the class doesn't have to extend any special objects to be picked up as a test (although `py.test` will run standard `unittest TestCases` just fine). If we run `py.test <filename>`, the output looks like this:

```
=============== test session starts ===============
python: platform linux2 -- Python 3.4.1 -- pytest-2.6.4
test object 1: class_pytest.py


class_pytest.py .F


==================== FAILURES====================
_____ TestNumbers.test_int_str _____


self = <class_pytest.TestNumbers object at 0x85b4fac>


    def test_int_str(self):
>       assert 1 == "1"
E       assert 1 == '1'


class_pytest.py:7: AssertionError
====== 1 failed, 1 passed in 0.10 seconds =======
```

The output starts with some useful information about the platform and interpreter. This can be useful for sharing bugs across disparate systems. The third line tells us the name of the file being tested (if there are multiple test modules picked up, they will all be displayed), followed by the familiar `.F` we saw in the `unittest` module; the `.` character indicates a passing test, while the letter `F` demonstrates a failure.

After all tests have run, the error output for each of them is displayed. It presents a summary of local variables (there is only one in this example: the `self` parameter passed into the function), the source code where the error occurred, and a summary of the error message. In addition, if an exception other than an `AssertionError` is raised, `py.test` will present us with a complete traceback, including source code references.

By default, `py.test` suppresses output from `print` statements if the test is successful. This is useful for test debugging; when a test is failing, we can add `print` statements to the test to check the values of specific variables and attributes as the test runs. If the test fails, these values are output to help with diagnosis. However, once the test is successful, the `print` statement output is not displayed, and they can be easily ignored. We don't have to "clean up" the output by removing `print` statements. If the tests ever fail again, due to future changes, the debugging output will be immediately available.

One way to do setup and cleanup

`py.test` supports setup and teardown methods similar to those used in `unittest`, but it provides even more flexibility. We'll discuss these briefly, since they are familiar, but they are not used as extensively as in the `unittest` module, as `py.test` provides us with a powerful funcargs facility, which we'll discuss in the next section.

If we are writing class-based tests, we can use two methods called `setup_method` and `teardown_method` in basically the same way that `setUp` and `tearDown` are called in `unittest`. They are called before and after each test method in the class to perform setup and cleanup duties. There is one difference from the `unittest` methods though. Both methods accept an argument: the function object representing the method being called.

In addition, `py.test` provides other setup and teardown functions to give us more control over when setup and cleanup code is executed. The `setup_class` and `teardown_class` methods are expected to be class methods; they accept a single argument (there is no `self` argument) representing the class in question.

Finally, we have the `setup_module` and `teardown_module` functions, which are run immediately before and after all tests (in functions or classes) in that module. These can be useful for "one time" setup, such as creating a socket or database connection that will be used by all tests in the module. Be careful with this one, as it can accidentally introduce dependencies between tests if the object being set up stores the state.

That short description doesn't do a great job of explaining exactly when these methods are called, so let's look at an example that illustrates exactly when it happens:

```python
def setup_module(module):
    print("setting up MODULE {0}".format(
        module.__name__))

def teardown_module(module):
    print("tearing down MODULE {0}".format(
        module.__name__))

def test_a_function():
    print("RUNNING TEST FUNCTION")

class BaseTest:
    def setup_class(cls):
        print("setting up CLASS {0}".format(
            cls.__name__))

    def teardown_class(cls):
        print("tearing down CLASS {0}\n".format(
            cls.__name__))

    def setup_method(self, method):
        print("setting up METHOD {0}".format(
            method.__name__))

    def teardown_method(self, method):
        print("tearing down  METHOD {0}".format(
            method.__name__))

class TestClass1(BaseTest):
    def test_method_1(self):
        print("RUNNING METHOD 1-1")

    def test_method_2(self):
```

```
        print("RUNNING METHOD 1-2")

  class TestClass2(BaseTest):
      def test_method_1(self):
          print("RUNNING METHOD 2-1")

      def test_method_2(self):
          print("RUNNING METHOD 2-2")
```

The sole purpose of the BaseTest class is to extract four methods that would be otherwise identical to the test classes, and use inheritance to reduce the amount of duplicate code. So, from the point of view of py.test, the two subclasses have not only two test methods each, but also two setup and two teardown methods (one at the class level, one at the method level).

If we run these tests using py.test with the print function output suppression disabled (by passing the -s or --capture=no flag), they show us when the various functions are called in relation to the tests themselves:

```
py.test setup_teardown.py -s
setup_teardown.py
setting up MODULE setup_teardown
RUNNING TEST FUNCTION
.setting up CLASS TestClass1
setting up METHOD test_method_1
RUNNING METHOD 1-1
.tearing down  METHOD test_method_1
setting up METHOD test_method_2
RUNNING METHOD 1-2
.tearing down  METHOD test_method_2
tearing down CLASS TestClass1
setting up CLASS TestClass2
setting up METHOD test_method_1
RUNNING METHOD 2-1
.tearing down  METHOD test_method_1
setting up METHOD test_method_2
RUNNING METHOD 2-2
.tearing down  METHOD test_method_2
tearing down CLASS TestClass2

tearing down MODULE setup_teardown
```

The setup and teardown methods for the module are executed at the beginning and end of the session. Then the lone module-level test function is run. Next, the setup method for the first class is executed, followed by the two tests for that class. These tests are each individually wrapped in separate `setup_method` and `teardown_method` calls. After the tests have executed, the class teardown method is called. The same sequence happens for the second class, before the `teardown_module` method is finally called, exactly once.

A completely different way to set up variables

One of the most common uses for the various setup and teardown functions is to ensure certain class or module variables are available with a known value before each test method is run.

`py.test` offers a completely different way to do this using what are known as **funcargs**, short for function arguments. Funcargs are basically named variables that are predefined in a test configuration file. This allows us to separate configuration from execution of tests, and allows the funcargs to be used across multiple classes and modules.

To use them, we add parameters to our test function. The names of the parameters are used to look up specific arguments in specially named functions. For example, if we wanted to test the `StatsList` class we used while demonstrating `unittest`, we would again want to repeatedly test a list of valid integers. But we can write our tests like so instead of using a setup method:

```
from stats import StatsList

def pytest_funcarg__valid_stats(request):
    return StatsList([1,2,2,3,3,4])


def test_mean(valid_stats):
    assert valid_stats.mean() == 2.5

def test_median(valid_stats):
    assert valid_stats.median() == 2.5
    valid_stats.append(4)
    assert valid_stats.median() == 3

def test_mode(valid_stats):
    assert valid_stats.mode() == [2,3]
    valid_stats.remove(2)
    assert valid_stats.mode() == [3]
```

Each of the three test methods accepts a parameter named `valid_stats`; this parameter is created by calling the `pytest_funcarg__valid_stats` function defined at the top of the file. It can also be defined in a file called `conftest.py` if the funcarg is needed by multiple modules. The `conftest.py` file is parsed by `py.test` to load any "global" test configuration; it is a sort of catch-all for customizing the `py.test` experience.

As with other `py.test` features, the name of the factory for returning a funcarg is important; funcargs are functions that are named `pytest_funcarg__<identifier>`, where `<identifier>` is a valid variable name that can be used as a parameter in a test function. This function accepts a mysterious `request` parameter, and returns the object to be passed as an argument into the individual test functions. The funcarg is created afresh for each call to an individual test function; this allows us, for example, to change the list in one test and know that it will be reset to its original values in the next test.

Funcargs can do a lot more than return basic variables. That `request` object passed into the funcarg factory provides some extremely useful methods and attributes to modify the funcarg's behavior. The `module`, `cls`, and `function` attributes allow us to see exactly which test is requesting the funcarg. The `config` attribute allows us to check command-line arguments and other configuration data.

More interestingly, the request object provides methods that allow us to do additional cleanup on the funcarg, or to reuse it across tests, activities that would otherwise be relegated to setup and teardown methods of a specific scope.

The `request.addfinalizer` method accepts a callback function that performs cleanup after each test function that uses the funcarg has been called. This provides the equivalent of a teardown method, allowing us to clean up files, close connections, empty lists, or reset queues. For example, the following code tests the `os.mkdir` functionality by creating a temporary directory funcarg:

```python
import tempfile
import shutil
import os.path

def pytest_funcarg__temp_dir(request):
    dir = tempfile.mkdtemp()
    print(dir)

    def cleanup():
        shutil.rmtree(dir)
    request.addfinalizer(cleanup)
```

```
        return dir

    def test_osfiles(temp_dir):
        os.mkdir(os.path.join(temp_dir, 'a'))
        os.mkdir(os.path.join(temp_dir, 'b'))
        dir_contents = os.listdir(temp_dir)
        assert len(dir_contents) == 2
        assert 'a' in dir_contents
        assert 'b' in dir_contents
```

The funcarg creates a new empty temporary directory for files to be created in. Then it adds a finalizer call to remove that directory (using `shutil.rmtree`, which recursively removes a directory and anything inside it) after the test has completed. The filesystem is then left in the same state in which it started.

We can use the `request.cached_setup` method to create function argument variables that last longer than one test. This is useful when setting up an expensive operation that can be reused by multiple tests as long as the resource reuse doesn't break the atomic or unit nature of the tests (so that one test does not rely on and is not impacted by a previous one). For example, if we were to test the following echo server, we may want to run only one instance of the server in a separate process, and then have multiple tests connect to that instance:

```
import socket

s = socket.socket(socket.AF_INET, socket.SOCK_STREAM)
s.setsockopt(socket.SOL_SOCKET, socket.SO_REUSEADDR, 1)
s.bind(('localhost',1028))
s.listen(1)

    while True:
        client, address = s.accept()
        data = client.recv(1024)
        client.send(data)
        client.close()
```

All this code does is listen on a specific port and wait for input from a client socket. When it receives input, it sends the same value back. To test this, we can start the server in a separate process and cache the result for use in multiple tests. Here's how the test code might look:

```
import subprocess
import socket
```

```
import time

def pytest_funcarg__echoserver(request):
    def setup():
        p = subprocess.Popen(
                ['python3', 'echo_server.py'])
        time.sleep(1)
        return p

    def cleanup(p):
        p.terminate()

    return request.cached_setup(
            setup=setup,
            teardown=cleanup,
            scope="session")

def pytest_funcarg__clientsocket(request):
    s = socket.socket(socket.AF_INET, socket.SOCK_STREAM)
    s.connect(('localhost', 1028))
    request.addfinalizer(lambda: s.close())
    return s

def test_echo(echoserver, clientsocket):
    clientsocket.send(b"abc")
    assert clientsocket.recv(3) == b'abc'

def test_echo2(echoserver, clientsocket):
    clientsocket.send(b"def")
    assert clientsocket.recv(3) == b'def'
```

We've created two funcargs here. The first runs the echo server in a separate process, and returns the process object. The second instantiates a new socket object for each test, and closes it when the test has completed, using addfinalizer. The first funcarg is the one we're currently interested in. It looks much like a traditional unit test setup and teardown. We create a setup function that accepts no parameters and returns the correct argument; in this case, a process object that is actually ignored by the tests, since they only care that the server is running. Then, we create a cleanup function (the name of the function is arbitrary since it's just an object we pass into another function), which accepts a single argument: the argument returned by setup. This cleanup code terminates the process.

Instead of returning a funcarg directly, the parent function returns the results of a call to `request.cached_setup`. It accepts two arguments for the `setup` and `teardown` functions (which we just created), and a `scope` argument. This last argument should be one of the three strings "function", "module", or "session"; it determines just how long the argument will be cached. We set it to "session" in this example, so it is cached for the duration of the entire `py.test` run. The process will not be terminated or restarted until all tests have run. The "module" scope, of course, caches it only for tests in that module, and the "function" scope treats the object more like a normal funcarg, in that it is reset after each test function is run.

Skipping tests with py.test

As with the `unittest` module, it is frequently necessary to skip tests in `py.test`, for a variety of reasons: the code being tested hasn't been written yet, the test only runs on certain interpreters or operating systems, or the test is time consuming and should only be run under certain circumstances.

We can skip tests at any point in our code using the `py.test.skip` function. It accepts a single argument: a string describing why it has been skipped. This function can be called anywhere; if we call it inside a test function, the test will be skipped. If we call it at the module level, all the tests in that module will be skipped. If we call it inside a funcarg function, all tests that call that funcarg will be skipped.

Of course, in all these locations, it is often desirable to skip tests only if certain conditions are or are not met. Since we can execute the `skip` function at any place in Python code, we can execute it inside an `if` statement. So we may write a test that looks like this:

```
import sys
import py.test

def test_simple_skip():
    if sys.platform != "fakeos":
        py.test.skip("Test works only on fakeOS")

    fakeos.do_something_fake()
    assert fakeos.did_not_happen
```

That's some pretty silly code, really. There is no Python platform named `fakeos`, so this test will skip on all operating systems. It shows how we can skip conditionally, and since the `if` statement can check any valid conditional, we have a lot of power over when tests are skipped. Often, we check `sys.version_info` to check the Python interpreter version, `sys.platform` to check the operating system, or `some_library.__version__` to check whether we have a recent enough version of a given API.

Since skipping an individual test method or function based on a certain conditional is one of the most common uses of test skipping, py.test provides a convenience decorator that allows us to do this in one line. The decorator accepts a single string, which can contain any executable Python code that evaluates to a Boolean value. For example, the following test will only run on Python 3 or higher:

```
import py.test

@py.test.mark.skipif("sys.version_info <= (3,0)")
def test_python3():
    assert b"hello".decode() == "hello"
```

The py.test.mark.xfail decorator behaves similarly, except that it marks a test as expected to fail, similar to unittest.expectedFailure(). If the test is successful, it will be recorded as a failure; if it fails, it will be reported as expected behavior. In the case of xfail, the conditional argument is optional; if it is not supplied, the test will be marked as expected to fail under all conditions.

Imitating expensive objects

Sometimes, we want to test code that requires an object be supplied that is either expensive or difficult to construct. While this may mean your API needs rethinking to have a more testable interface (which typically means a more usable interface), we sometimes find ourselves writing test code that has a ton of boilerplate to set up objects that are only incidentally related to the code under test.

For example, imagine we have some code that keeps track of flight statuses in a key-value store (such as redis or memcache) such that we can store the timestamp and the most recent status. A basic version of such code might look like this:

```
import datetime
import redis

class FlightStatusTracker:
    ALLOWED_STATUSES = {'CANCELLED', 'DELAYED', 'ON TIME'}

    def __init__(self):
        self.redis = redis.StrictRedis()

    def change_status(self, flight, status):
```

```
        status = status.upper()
        if status not in self.ALLOWED_STATUSES:
            raise ValueError(
                    "{} is not a valid status".format(status))

        key = "flightno:{}".format(flight)
        value = "{}|{}".format(
            datetime.datetime.now().isoformat(), status)
        self.redis.set(key, value)
```

There are a lot of things we ought to test in that `change_status` method. We should check that it raises the appropriate error if a bad status is passed in. We need to ensure that it converts statuses to uppercase. We can see that the key and value have the correct formatting when the `set()` method is called on the `redis` object.

One thing we don't have to check in our unit tests, however, is that the `redis` object is properly storing the data. This is something that absolutely should be tested in integration or application testing, but at the unit test level, we can assume that the py-redis developers have tested their code and that this method does what we want it to. As a rule, unit tests should be self-contained and not rely on the existence of outside resources, such as a running Redis instance.

Instead, we only need to test that the `set()` method was called the appropriate number of times and with the appropriate arguments. We can use `Mock()` objects in our tests to replace the troublesome method with an object we can introspect. The following example illustrates the use of mock:

```
from unittest.mock import Mock
import py.test
def pytest_funcarg__tracker():
    return FlightStatusTracker()

def test_mock_method(tracker):
    tracker.redis.set = Mock()
    with py.test.raises(ValueError) as ex:
        tracker.change_status("AC101", "lost")
    assert ex.value.args[0] == "LOST is not a valid status"
    assert tracker.redis.set.call_count == 0
```

This test, written using py.test syntax, asserts that the correct exception is raised when an inappropriate argument is passed in. In addition, it creates a mock object for the set method and makes sure that it is never called. If it was, it would mean there was a bug in our exception handling code.

Simply replacing the method worked fine in this case, since the object being replaced was destroyed in the end. However, we often want to replace a function or method only for the duration of a test. For example, if we want to test the timestamp formatting in the mock method, we need to know exactly what datetime. datetime.now() is going to return. However, this value changes from run to run. We need some way to pin it to a specific value so we can test it deterministically.

Remember monkey-patching? Temporarily setting a library function to a specific value is an excellent use of it. The mock library provides a patch context manager that allows us to replace attributes on existing libraries with mock objects. When the context manager exits, the original attribute is automatically restored so as not to impact other test cases. Here's an example:

```
from unittest.mock import patch
def test_patch(tracker):
    tracker.redis.set = Mock()
    fake_now = datetime.datetime(2015, 4, 1)
    with patch('datetime.datetime') as dt:
        dt.now.return_value = fake_now
        tracker.change_status("AC102", "on time")
    dt.now.assert_called_once_with()
    tracker.redis.set.assert_called_once_with(
        "flightno:AC102",
        "2015-04-01T00:00:00|ON TIME")
```

In this example, we first construct a value called fake_now, which we will set as the return value of the datetime.datetime.now function. We have to construct this object before we patch datetime.datetime because otherwise we'd be calling the patched now function before we constructed it!

The with statement invites the patch to replace the datetime.datetime module with a mock object, which is returned as the value dt. The neat thing about mock objects is that any time you access an attribute or method on that object, it returns another mock object. Thus when we access dt.now, it gives us a new mock object. We set the return_value of that object to our fake_now object; that way, whenever the datetime.datetime.now function is called, it will return our object instead of a new mock object.

Then, after calling our `change_status` method with known values, we use the mock class's `assert_called_once_with` function to ensure that the `now` function was indeed called exactly once with no arguments. We then call it a second time to prove that the `redis.set` method was called with arguments that were formatted as we expected them to be.

The previous example is a good indication of how writing tests can guide our API design. The `FlightStatusTracker` object looks sensible at first glance; we construct a `redis` connection when the object is constructed, and we call into it when we need it. When we write tests for this code, however, we discover that even if we mock out that `self.redis` variable on a `FlightStatusTracker`, the `redis` connection still has to be constructed. This call actually fails if there is no Redis server running, and our tests also fail.

We could solve this problem by mocking out the `redis.StrictRedis` class to return a mock in a `setUp` method. A better idea, however, might be to rethink our example. Instead of constructing the `redis` instance inside `__init__`, perhaps we should allow the user to pass one in, as in the following example:

```
    def __init__(self, redis_instance=None):
        self.redis = redis_instance if redis_instance else redis.
StrictRedis()
```

This allows us to pass a mock in when we are testing, so the `StrictRedis` method never gets constructed. However, it also allows any client code that talks to `FlightStatusTracker` to pass in their own `redis` instance. There are a variety of reasons they might want to do this. They may have already constructed one for other parts of their code. They may have created an optimized implementation of the `redis` API. Perhaps they have one that logs metrics to their internal monitoring systems. By writing a unit test, we've uncovered a use case that makes our API more flexible from the start, rather than waiting for clients to demand we support their exotic needs.

This has been a brief introduction to the wonders of mocking code. Mocks are part of the standard `unittest` library since Python 3.3, but as you see from these examples, they can also be used with `py.test` and other libraries. Mocks have other more advanced features that you may need to take advantage of as your code gets more complicated. For example, you can use the `spec` argument to invite a mock to imitate an existing class so that it raises an error if code tries to access an attribute that does not exist on the imitated class. You can also construct mock methods that return different arguments each time they are called by passing a list as the `side_effect` argument. The `side_effect` parameter is quite versatile; you can also use it to execute arbitrary functions when the mock is called or to raise an exception.

In general, we should be quite stingy with mocks. If we find ourselves mocking out multiple elements in a given unit test, we may end up testing the mock framework rather than our real code. This serves no useful purpose whatsoever; after all, mocks are well-tested already! If our code is doing a lot of this, it's probably another sign that the API we are testing is poorly designed. Mocks should exist at the boundaries between the code under test and the libraries they interface with. If this isn't happening, we may need to change the API so that the boundaries are redrawn in a different place.

How much testing is enough?

We've already established that untested code is broken code. But how can we tell how well our code is tested? How do we know how much of our code is actually being tested and how much is broken? The first question is the more important one, but it's hard to answer. Even if we know we have tested every line of code in our application, we do not know that we have tested it properly. For example, if we write a stats test that only checks what happens when we provide a list of integers, it may still fail spectacularly if used on a list of floats or strings or self-made objects. The onus of designing complete test suites still lies with the programmer.

The second question—how much of our code is actually being tested—is easy to verify. Code coverage is essentially an estimate of the number of lines of code that are executed by a program. If we know that number and the number of lines that are in the program, we can get an estimate of what percentage of the code was really tested, or covered. If we additionally have an indicator as to which lines were not tested, we can more easily write new tests to ensure those lines are less broken.

The most popular tool for testing code coverage is called, memorably enough, `coverage.py`. It can be installed like most other third-party libraries using the command `pip install coverage`.

We don't have space to cover all the details of the coverage API, so we'll just look at a few typical examples. If we have a Python script that runs all our unit tests for us (for example, using `unittest.main`, a custom test runner or `discover`), we can use the following command to perform a coverage analysis:

```
coverage run coverage_unittest.py
```

This command will exit normally, but it creates a file named `.coverage` that holds the data from the run. We can now use the `coverage report` command to get an analysis of code coverage:

```
>>> coverage report
```

The output is as follows:

```
Name                      Stmts    Exec   Cover
- - - - - - - - - - - - - - - - - - - - - - - - - - - - - - - - - - - - - - - -

coverage_unittest            7       7    100%

stats                       19       6     31%
- - - - - - - - - - - - - - - - - - - - - - - - - - - - - - - - - - - - - - - -

TOTAL                       26      13     50%
```

This basic report lists the files that were executed (our unit test and a module it imported). The number of lines of code in each file, and the number that were executed by the test are also listed. The two numbers are then combined to estimate the amount of code coverage. If we pass the -m option to the report command, it will additionally add a column that looks like this:

```
Missing
- - - - - - - - - - -

8-12, 15-23
```

The ranges of lines listed here identify lines in the stats module that were not executed during the test run.

The example we just ran the code coverage tool on uses the same stats module we created earlier in the chapter. However, it deliberately uses a single test that fails to test a lot of code in the file. Here's the test:

```
from stats import StatsList
import unittest

class TestMean(unittest.TestCase):
    def test_mean(self):
        self.assertEqual(StatsList([1,2,2,3,3,4]).mean(), 2.5)

if __name__ == "__main__":

    unittest.main()
```

This code doesn't test the median or mode functions, which correspond to the line numbers that the coverage output told us were missing.

The textual report is sufficient, but if we use the command coverage html, we can get an even fancier interactive HTML report that we can view in a web browser. The web page even highlights which lines in the source code were and were not tested. Here's how it looks:

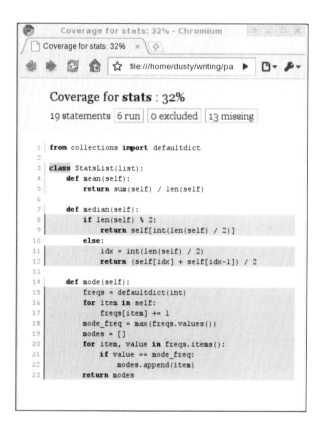

We can use the coverage.py module with py.test as well. We'll need to install the py.test plugin for code coverage, using pip install pytest-coverage. The plugin adds several command-line options to py.test, the most useful being --cover-report, which can be set to html, report, or annotate (the latter actually modifies the source code to highlight any lines that were not covered).

Unfortunately, if we could somehow run a coverage report on this section of the chapter, we'd find that we have not covered most of what there is to know about code coverage! It is possible to use the coverage API to manage code coverage from within our own programs (or test suites), and coverage.py accepts numerous configuration options that we haven't touched on. We also haven't discussed the difference between statement coverage and branch coverage (the latter is much more useful, and the default in recent versions of coverage.py) or other styles of code coverage.

Bear in mind that while 100 percent code coverage is a lofty goal that we should all strive for, 100 percent coverage is not enough! Just because a statement was tested does not mean that it was tested properly for all possible inputs.

Case study

Let's walk through test-driven development by writing a small, tested, cryptography application. Don't worry, you won't need to understand the mathematics behind complicated modern encryption algorithms such as Threefish or RSA. Instead, we'll be implementing a sixteenth-century algorithm known as the Vigenère cipher. The application simply needs to be able to encode and decode a message, given an encoding keyword, using this cipher.

First, we need to understand how the cipher works if we apply it manually (without a computer). We start with a table like this:

```
A B C D E F G H I J K L M N O P Q R S T U V W X Y Z
B C D E F G H I J K L M N O P Q R S T U V W X Y Z A
C D E F G H I J K L M N O P Q R S T U V W X Y Z A B
D E F G H I J K L M N O P Q R S T U V W X Y Z A B C
E F G H I J K L M N O P Q R S T U V W X Y Z A B C D
F G H I J K L M N O P Q R S T U V W X Y Z A B C D E
G H I J K L M N O P Q R S T U V W X Y Z A B C D E F
H I J K L M N O P Q R S T U V W X Y Z A B C D E F G
I J K L M N O P Q R S T U V W X Y Z A B C D E F G H
J K L M N O P Q R S T U V W X Y Z A B C D E F G H I
K L M N O P Q R S T U V W X Y Z A B C D E F G H I J
L M N O P Q R S T U V W X Y Z A B C D E F G H I J K
M N O P Q R S T U V W X Y Z A B C D E F G H I J K L
N O P Q R S T U V W X Y Z A B C D E F G H I J K L M
O P Q R S T U V W X Y Z A B C D E F G H I J K L M N
P Q R S T U V W X Y Z A B C D E F G H I J K L M N O
Q R S T U V W X Y Z A B C D E F G H I J K L M N O P
R S T U V W X Y Z A B C D E F G H I J K L M N O P Q
S T U V W X Y Z A B C D E F G H I J K L M N O P Q R
T U V W X Y Z A B C D E F G H I J K L M N O P Q R S
U V W X Y Z A B C D E F G H I J K L M N O P Q R S T
V W X Y Z A B C D E F G H I J K L M N O P Q R S T U
W X Y Z A B C D E F G H I J K L M N O P Q R S T U V
X Y Z A B C D E F G H I J K L M N O P Q R S T U V W
Y Z A B C D E F G H I J K L M N O P Q R S T U V W X
Z A B C D E F G H I J K L M N O P Q R S T U V W X Y
```

Given a keyword, TRAIN, we can encode the message ENCODED IN PYTHON as follows:

1. Repeat the keyword and message together such that it is easy to map letters from one to the other:

   E N C O D E D I N P Y T H O N   T R A I N T R A I N T R A I N

2. For each letter in the plain text, find the row that begins with that letter in the table.

3. Find the column with the letter associated with the keyword letter for the chosen plaintext letter.

4. The encoded character is at the intersection of this row and column.

For example, the row starting with E intersects the column starting with T at the character X. So, the first letter in the ciphertext is X. The row starting with N intersects the column starting with R at the character E, leading to the ciphertext XE. C intersects A at C, and O intersects I at W. D and N map to Q while E and T map to X. The full encoded message is XECWQXUIVCRKHWA.

Decoding basically follows the opposite procedure. First, find the row with the character for the shared keyword (the T row), then find the location in that row where the encoded character (the X) is located. The plaintext character is at the top of the column for that row (the E).

Implementing it

Our program will need an `encode` method that takes a keyword and plaintext and returns the ciphertext, and a `decode` method that accepts a keyword and ciphertext and returns the original message.

But rather than just writing those methods, let's follow a test-driven development strategy. We'll be using `py.test` for our unit testing. We need an `encode` method, and we know what it has to do; let's write a test for that method first:

```
def test_encode():
    cipher = VigenereCipher("TRAIN")
    encoded = cipher.encode("ENCODEDINPYTHON")
    assert encoded == "XECWQXUIVCRKHWA"
```

This test fails, naturally, because we aren't importing a `VigenereCipher` class anywhere. Let's create a new module to hold that class.

Let's start with the following `VigenereCipher` class:

```
class VigenereCipher:
    def __init__(self, keyword):
        self.keyword = keyword

    def encode(self, plaintext):
        return "XECWQXUIVCRKHWA"
```

If we add a `from vigenere_cipher import VigenereCipher` line to the top of our test class and run `py.test`, the preceding test will pass! We've finished our first test-driven development cycle.

Obviously, returning a hardcoded string is not the most sensible implementation of a cipher class, so let's add a second test:

```
def test_encode_character():
    cipher = VigenereCipher("TRAIN")
    encoded = cipher.encode("E")
    assert encoded == "X"
```

Ah, now that test will fail. It looks like we're going to have to work harder. But I just thought of something: what if someone tries to encode a string with spaces or lowercase characters? Before we start implementing the encoding, let's add some tests for these cases, so we don't we forget them. The expected behavior will be to remove spaces, and to convert lowercase letters to capitals:

```
def test_encode_spaces():
    cipher = VigenereCipher("TRAIN")
    encoded = cipher.encode("ENCODED IN PYTHON")
    assert encoded == "XECWQXUIVCRKHWA"

def test_encode_lowercase():
    cipher = VigenereCipher("TRain")
    encoded = cipher.encode("encoded in Python")
    assert encoded == "XECWQXUIVCRKHWA"
```

If we run the new test suite, we find that the new tests pass (they expect the same hardcoded string). But they ought to fail later if we forget to account for these cases.

Now that we have some test cases, let's think about how to implement our encoding algorithm. Writing code to use a table like we used in the earlier manual algorithm is possible, but seems complicated, considering that each row is just an alphabet rotated by an offset number of characters. It turns out (I asked Wikipedia) that we can use modulo arithmetic to combine the characters instead of doing a table lookup. Given plaintext and keyword characters, if we convert the two letters to their numerical values (with A being 0 and Z being 25), add them together, and take the remainder mod 26, we get the ciphertext character! This is a straightforward calculation, but since it happens on a character-by-character basis, we should probably put it in its own function. And before we do that, we should write a test for the new function:

```
from vigenere_cipher import combine_character
def test_combine_character():
    assert combine_character("E", "T") == "X"
    assert combine_character("N", "R") == "E"
```

Now we can write the code to make this function work. In all honesty, I had to run the test several times before I got this function completely correct; first I returned an integer, and then I forgot to shift the character back up to the normal ASCII scale from the zero-based scale. Having the test available made it easy to test and debug these errors. This is another bonus of test-driven development.

```
def combine_character(plain, keyword):
    plain = plain.upper()
    keyword = keyword.upper()
    plain_num = ord(plain) - ord('A')
    keyword_num = ord(keyword) - ord('A')
    return chr(ord('A') + (plain_num + keyword_num) % 26)
```

Now that `combine_characters` is tested, I thought we'd be ready to implement our `encode` function. However, the first thing we want inside that function is a repeating version of the keyword string that is as long as the plaintext. Let's implement a function for that first. Oops, I mean let's implement the test first!

```
def test_extend_keyword():
    cipher = VigenereCipher("TRAIN")
    extended = cipher.extend_keyword(16)
    assert extended == "TRAINTRAINTRAINT"
```

Before writing this test, I expected to write `extend_keyword` as a standalone function that accepted a keyword and an integer. But as I started drafting the test, I realized it made more sense to use it as a helper method on the `VigenereCipher` class. This shows how test-driven development can help design more sensible APIs. Here's the method implementation:

```
def extend_keyword(self, number):
    repeats = number // len(self.keyword) + 1
    return (self.keyword * repeats)[:number]
```

Once again, this took a few runs of the test to get right. I ended up adding a second versions of the test, one with fifteen and one with sixteen letters, to make sure it works if the integer division has an even number.

Now we're finally ready to write our `encode` method:

```
def encode(self, plaintext):
    cipher = []
    keyword = self.extend_keyword(len(plaintext))
    for p,k in zip(plaintext, keyword):
        cipher.append(combine_character(p,k))
    return "".join(cipher)
```

That looks correct. Our test suite should pass now, right?

Actually, if we run it, we'll find that two tests are still failing. We totally forgot about the spaces and lowercase characters! It is a good thing we wrote those tests to remind us. We'll have to add this line at the beginning of the method:

```
plaintext = plaintext.replace(" ", "").upper()
```

If we have an idea about a corner case in the middle of implementing something, we can create a test describing that idea. We don't even have to implement the test; we can just run `assert False` to remind us to implement it later. The failing test will never let us forget the corner case and it can't be ignored like filing a task can. If it takes a while to get around to fixing the implementation, we can mark the test as an expected failure.

Now all the tests pass successfully. This chapter is pretty long, so we'll condense the examples for decoding. Here are a couple tests:

```
def test_separate_character():
    assert separate_character("X", "T") == "E"
```

```
        assert separate_character("E", "R") == "N"

def test_decode():
    cipher = VigenereCipher("TRAIN")
    decoded = cipher.decode("XECWQXUIVCRKHWA")
    assert decoded == "ENCODEDINPYTHON"
```

Here's the `separate_character` function:

```
def separate_character(cypher, keyword):
    cypher = cypher.upper()
    keyword = keyword.upper()
    cypher_num = ord(cypher) - ord('A')
    keyword_num = ord(keyword) - ord('A')
    return chr(ord('A') + (cypher_num - keyword_num) % 26)
```

And the `decode` method:

```
def decode(self, ciphertext):
    plain = []
    keyword = self.extend_keyword(len(ciphertext))
    for p,k in zip(ciphertext, keyword):
        plain.append(separate_character(p,k))
    return "".join(plain)
```

These methods have a lot of similarity to those used for encoding. The great thing about having all these tests written and passing is that we can now go back and modify our code, knowing it is still safely passing the tests. For example, if we replace our existing `encode` and `decode` methods with these refactored methods, our tests still pass:

```
def _code(self, text, combine_func):
    text = text.replace(" ", "").upper()
    combined = []
    keyword = self.extend_keyword(len(text))
    for p,k in zip(text, keyword):
        combined.append(combine_func(p,k))
    return "".join(combined)

def encode(self, plaintext):
    return self._code(plaintext, combine_character)

def decode(self, ciphertext):
    return self._code(ciphertext, separate_character)
```

This is the final benefit of test-driven development, and the most important. Once the tests are written, we can improve our code as much as we like and be confident that our changes didn't break anything we have been testing for. Furthermore, we know exactly when our refactor is finished: when the tests all pass.

Of course, our tests may not comprehensively test everything we need them to; maintenance or code refactoring can still cause undiagnosed bugs that don't show up in testing. Automated tests are not foolproof. If bugs do occur, however, it is still possible to follow a test-driven plan; step one is to write a test (or multiple tests) that duplicates or "proves" that the bug in question is occurring. This will, of course, fail. Then write the code to make the tests stop failing. If the tests were comprehensive, the bug will be fixed, and we will know if it ever happens again, as soon as we run the test suite.

Finally, we can try to determine how well our tests operate on this code. With the `py.test` coverage plugin installed, `py.test -coverage-report=report` tells us that our test suite has 100 percent code coverage. This is a great statistic, but we shouldn't get too cocky about it. Our code hasn't been tested when encoding messages that have numbers, and its behavior with such inputs is thus undefined.

Exercises

Practice test-driven development. That is your first exercise. It's easier to do this if you're starting a new project, but if you have existing code you need to work on, you can start by writing tests for each new feature you implement. This can become frustrating as you become more enamored with automated tests. The old, untested code will start to feel rigid and tightly coupled, and will become uncomfortable to maintain; you'll start feeling like changes you make are breaking the code and you have no way of knowing, for lack of tests. But if you start small, adding tests will improve, the codebase improves over time.

So to get your feet wet with test-driven development, start a fresh project. Once you've started to appreciate the benefits (you will) and realize that the time spent writing tests is quickly regained in terms of more maintainable code, you'll want to start writing tests for existing code. This is when you should start doing it, not before. Writing tests for code that we "know" works is boring. It is hard to get interested in the project until you realize just how broken the code we thought was working really is.

Try writing the same set of tests using both the built-in `unittest` module and `py.test`. Which do you prefer? `unittest` is more similar to test frameworks in other languages, while `py.test` is arguably more Pythonic. Both allow us to write object-oriented tests and to test object-oriented programs with ease.

We used `py.test` in our case study, but we didn't touch on any features that wouldn't have been easily testable using `unittest`. Try adapting the tests to use test skipping or funcargs. Try the various setup and teardown methods, and compare their use to funcargs. Which feels more natural to you?

In our case study, we have a lot of tests that use a similar `VigenereCipher` object; try reworking this code to use a funcarg. How many lines of code does it save?

Try running a coverage report on the tests you've written. Did you miss testing any lines of code? Even if you have 100 percent coverage, have you tested all the possible inputs? If you're doing test-driven development, 100 percent coverage should follow quite naturally, as you will write a test before the code that satisfies that test. However, if writing tests for existing code, it is more likely that there will be edge conditions that go untested.

Think carefully about the values that are somehow different: empty lists when you expect full ones, zero or one or infinity compared to intermediate integers, floats that don't round to an exact decimal place, strings when you expected numerals, or the ubiquitous `None` value when you expected something meaningful. If your tests cover such edge cases, your code will be in good shape.

Summary

We have finally covered the most important topic in Python programming: automated testing. Test-driven development is considered a best practice. The standard library `unittest` module provides a great out-of-the-box solution for testing, while the `py.test` framework has some more Pythonic syntaxes. Mocks can be used to emulate complex classes in our tests. Code coverage gives us an estimate of how much of our code is being run by our tests, but it does not tell us that we have tested the right things.

In the next chapter, we'll jump into a completely different topic: concurrency.

13
Concurrency

Concurrency is the art of making a computer do (or appear to do) multiple things at once. Historically, this meant inviting the processor to switch between different tasks many times per second. In modern systems, it can also literally mean doing two or more things simultaneously on separate processor cores.

Concurrency is not inherently an object-oriented topic, but Python's concurrent systems are built on top of the object-oriented constructs we've covered throughout the book. This chapter will introduce you to the following topics:

- Threads
- Multiprocessing
- Futures
- AsyncIO

Concurrency is complicated. The basic concepts are fairly simple, but the bugs that can occur are notoriously difficult to track down. However, for many projects, concurrency is the only way to get the performance we need. Imagine if a web server couldn't respond to a user's request until the previous one was completed! We won't be going into all the details of just how hard it is (another full book would be required) but we'll see how to do basic concurrency in Python, and some of the most common pitfalls to avoid.

Threads

Most often, concurrency is created so that work can continue happening while the program is waiting for I/O to happen. For example, a server can start processing a new network request while it waits for data from a previous request to arrive. An interactive program might render an animation or perform a calculation while waiting for the user to press a key. Bear in mind that while a person can type more than 500 characters per minute, a computer can perform billions of instructions per second. Thus, a ton of processing can happen between individual key presses, even when typing quickly.

It's theoretically possible to manage all this switching between activities within your program, but it would be virtually impossible to get right. Instead, we can rely on Python and the operating system to take care of the tricky switching part, while we create objects that appear to be running independently, but simultaneously. These objects are called **threads**; in Python they have a very simple API. Let's take a look at a basic example:

```python
from threading import Thread

class InputReader(Thread):
    def run(self):
        self.line_of_text = input()

print("Enter some text and press enter: ")
thread = InputReader()
thread.start()

count = result = 1
while thread.is_alive():
    result = count * count
    count += 1

print("calculated squares up to {0} * {0} = {1}".format(
    count, result))
print("while you typed '{}'".format(thread.line_of_text))
```

This example runs two threads. Can you see them? Every program has one thread, called the main thread. The code that executes from the beginning is happening in this thread. The second thread, more obviously, exists as the `InputReader` class.

To construct a thread, we must extend the `Thread` class and implement the `run` method. Any code inside the `run` method (or that is called from within that method) is executed in a separate thread.

The new thread doesn't start running until we call the `start()` method on the object. In this case, the thread immediately pauses to wait for input from the keyboard. In the meantime, the original thread continues executing at the point `start` was called. It starts calculating squares inside a `while` loop. The condition in the `while` loop checks if the `InputReader` thread has exited its `run` method yet; once it does, it outputs some summary information to the screen.

If we run the example and type the string "hello world", the output looks as follows:

```
Enter some text and press enter:
hello world
calculated squares up to 1044477 * 1044477 = 1090930114576
while you typed 'hello world'
```

You will, of course, calculate more or less squares while typing the string as the numbers are related to both our relative typing speeds, and to the processor speeds of the computers we are running.

A thread only starts running in concurrent mode when we call the `start` method. If we want to take out the concurrent call to see how it compares, we can call `thread.run()` in the place that we originally called `thread.start()`. The output is telling:

```
Enter some text and press enter:
hello world
calculated squares up to 1 * 1 = 1
while you typed 'hello world'
```

In this case, the thread never becomes alive and the `while` loop never executes. We wasted a lot of CPU power sitting idle while we were typing.

There are a lot of different patterns for using threads effectively. We won't be covering all of them, but we will look at a common one so we can learn about the `join` method. Let's check the current temperature in the capital city of every province in Canada:

```python
from threading import Thread
import json
from urllib.request import urlopen
import time

CITIES = [
    'Edmonton', 'Victoria', 'Winnipeg', 'Fredericton',
    "St. John's", 'Halifax', 'Toronto', 'Charlottetown',
```

```
        'Quebec City', 'Regina'
]

class TempGetter(Thread):
    def __init__(self, city):
        super().__init__()
        self.city = city

    def run(self):
        url_template = (
            'http://api.openweathermap.org/data/2.5/'
            'weather?q={},CA&units=metric')
        response = urlopen(url_template.format(self.city))
        data = json.loads(response.read().decode())
        self.temperature = data['main']['temp']

threads = [TempGetter(c) for c in CITIES]
start = time.time()
for thread in threads:
    thread.start()

for thread in threads:
    thread.join()

for thread in threads:
    print(
        "it is {0.temperature:.0f}°C in {0.city}".format(thread))
print(
    "Got {} temps in {} seconds".format(
    len(threads), time.time() - start))
```

This code constructs 10 threads before starting them. Notice how we can override the
constructor to pass them into the Thread object, remembering to call super to ensure
the Thread is properly initialized. Pay attention to this: the new thread isn't running
yet, so the __init__ method is still executing from inside the main thread. Data we
construct in one thread is accessible from other running threads.

After the 10 threads have been started, we loop over them again, calling the join()
method on each. This method essentially says "wait for the thread to complete before
doing anything". We call this ten times in sequence; the for loop won't exit until all
ten threads have completed.

At this point, we can print the temperature that was stored on each thread object. Notice once again that we can access data that was constructed within the thread from the main thread. In threads, all state is shared by default.

Executing this code on my 100 mbit connection takes about two tenths of a second:

```
it is 5°C in Edmonton

it is 11°C in Victoria

it is 0°C in Winnipeg

it is -10°C in Fredericton

it is -12°C in St. John's

it is -8°C in Halifax

it is -6°C in Toronto

it is -13°C in Charlottetown

it is -12°C in Quebec City

it is 2°C in Regina

    Got 10 temps in 0.18970298767089844 seconds
```

If we run this code in a single thread (by changing the `start()` call to `run()` and commenting out the `join()` call), it takes closer to 2 seconds because each 0.2 second request has to complete before the next one begins. This speedup of 10 times shows just how useful concurrent programming can be.

The many problems with threads

Threads can be useful, especially in other programming languages, but modern Python programmers tend to avoid them for several reasons. As we'll see, there are other ways to do concurrent programming that are receiving more attention from the Python developers. Let's discuss some of these pitfalls before moving on to more salient topics.

Shared memory

The main problem with threads is also their primary advantage. Threads have access to all the memory and thus all the variables in the program. This can too easily cause inconsistencies in the program state. Have you ever encountered a room where a single light has two switches and two different people turn them on at the same time? Each person (thread) expects their action to turn the lamp (a variable) on, but the resulting value (the lamp is off) is inconsistent with those expectations. Now imagine if those two threads were transferring funds between bank accounts or managing the cruise control in a vehicle.

The solution to this problem in threaded programming is to "synchronize" access to any code that reads or writes a shared variable. There are a few different ways to do this, but we won't go into them here so we can focus on more Pythonic constructs. The synchronization solution works, but it is way too easy to forget to apply it. Worse, bugs due to inappropriate use of synchronization are really hard to track down because the order in which threads perform operations is inconsistent. We can't easily reproduce the error. Usually, it is safest to force communication between threads to happen using a lightweight data structure that already uses locks appropriately. Python offers the `queue.Queue` class to do this; it's functionality is basically the same as the `multiprocessing.Queue` that we will discuss in the next section.

In some cases, these disadvantages might be outweighed by the one advantage of allowing shared memory: it's fast. If multiple threads need access to a huge data structure, shared memory can provide that access quickly. However, this advantage is usually nullified by the fact that, in Python, it is impossible for two threads running on different CPU cores to be performing calculations at exactly the same time. This brings us to our second problem with threads.

The global interpreter lock

In order to efficiently manage memory, garbage collection, and calls to machine code in libraries, Python has a utility called the **global interpreter lock**, or **GIL**. It's impossible to turn off, and it means that threads are useless in Python for one thing that they excel at in other languages: parallel processing. The GIL's primary effect, for our purposes is to prevent any two threads from doing work at the exact same time, even if they have work to do. In this case, "doing work" means using the CPU, so it's perfectly ok for multiple threads to access the disk or network; the GIL is released as soon as the thread starts to wait for something.

The GIL is quite highly disparaged, mostly by people who don't understand what it is or all the benefits it brings to Python. It would definitely be nice if our language didn't have this restriction, but the Python reference developers have determined that, for now at least, it brings more value than it costs. It makes the reference implementation easier to maintain and develop, and during the single-core processor days when Python was originally developed, it actually made the interpreter faster. The net result of the GIL, however, is that it limits the benefits that threads bring us, without alleviating the costs.

While the GIL is a problem in the reference implementation of Python that most people use, it has been solved in some of the nonstandard implementations such as IronPython and Jython. Unfortunately, at the time of publication, none of these support Python 3.

Thread overhead

One final limitation of threads as compared to the asynchronous system we will be discussing later is the cost of maintaining the thread. Each thread takes up a certain amount of memory (both in the Python process and the operating system kernel) to record the state of that thread. Switching between the threads also uses a (small) amount of CPU time. This work happens seamlessly without any extra coding (we just have to call `start()` and the rest is taken care of), but the work still has to happen somewhere.

This can be alleviated somewhat by structuring our workload so that threads can be reused to perform multiple jobs. Python provides a `ThreadPool` feature to handle this. It is shipped as part of the multiprocessing library and behaves identically to the `ProcessPool`, that we will discuss shortly, so let's defer discussion until the next section.

Multiprocessing

The multiprocessing API was originally designed to mimic the thread API. However, it has evolved and in recent versions of Python 3, it supports more features more robustly. The multiprocessing library is designed when CPU-intensive jobs need to happen in parallel and multiple cores are available (given that a four core Raspberry Pi can currently be purchased for $35, there are usually multiple cores available). Multiprocessing is not useful when the processes spend a majority of their time waiting on I/O (for example, network, disk, database, or keyboard), but they are the way to go for parallel computation.

The multiprocessing module spins up new operating system processes to do the work. On Windows machines, this is a relatively expensive operation; on Linux, processes are implemented in the kernel the same way threads are, so the overhead is limited to the cost of running separate Python interpreters in each process.

Let's try to parallelize a compute-heavy operation using similar constructs to those provided by the `threading` API:

```python
from multiprocessing import Process, cpu_count
import time
import os


class MuchCPU(Process):
    def run(self):
        print(os.getpid())
        for i in range(200000000):
            pass


if __name__ == '__main__':
    procs =  [MuchCPU() for f in range(cpu_count())]
    t = time.time()
    for p in procs:
        p.start()
    for p in procs:
        p.join()
    print('work took {} seconds'.format(time.time() - t))
```

This example just ties up the CPU for 200 million iterations. You may not consider this to be useful work, but it's a cold day and I appreciate the heat my laptop generates under such load.

The API should be familiar; we implement a subclass of `Process` (instead of `Thread`) and implement a `run` method. This method prints out the process ID (a unique number the operating system assigns to each process on the machine) before doing some intense (if misguided) work.

Pay special attention to the `if __name__ == '__main__':` guard around the module level code that prevents it to run if the module is being imported, rather than run as a program. This is good practice in general, but when using multiprocessing on some operating systems, it is essential. Behind the scenes, multiprocessing may have to import the module inside the new process in order to execute the `run()` method. If we allowed the entire module to execute at that point, it would start creating new processes recursively until the operating system ran out of resources.

We construct one process for each processor core on our machine, then start and join each of those processes. On my 2014 era quad-core laptop, the output looks like this:

6987

6988

```
6989
```

```
6990
```

```
work took 12.96659541130066 seconds
```

The first four lines are the process ID that was printed inside each `MuchCPU` instance. The last line shows that the 200 million iterations can run in about 13 seconds on my machine. During that 13 seconds, my process monitor indicated that all four of my cores were running at 100 percent.

If we subclass `threading.Thread` instead of `multiprocessing.Process` in `MuchCPU`, the output looks like this:

```
7235
```

```
7235
```

```
7235
```

```
7235
```

```
work took 28.577413082122803 seconds
```

This time, the four threads are running inside the same process and take close to three times as long to run. This is the cost of the global interpreter lock; in other languages or implementations of Python, the threaded version would run at least as fast as the multiprocessing version, We might expect it to be four times as long, but remember that many other programs are running on my laptop. In the multiprocessing version, these programs also need a share of the four CPUs. In the threading version, those programs can use the other three CPUs instead.

Multiprocessing pools

In general, there is no reason to have more processes than there are processors on the computer. There are a few reasons for this:

- Only `cpu_count()` processes can run simultaneously
- Each process consumes resources with a full copy of the Python interpreter
- Communication between processes is expensive
- Creating processes takes a nonzero amount of time

Given these constraints, it makes sense to create at most `cpu_count()` processes when the program starts and then have them execute tasks as needed. It is not difficult to implement a basic series of communicating processes that does this, but it can be tricky to debug, test, and get right. Of course, Python being Python, we don't have to do all this work because the Python developers have already done it for us in the form of multiprocessing pools.

The primary advantage of pools is that they abstract away the overhead of figuring out what code is executing in the main process and which code is running in the subprocess. As with the threading API that multiprocessing mimics, it can often be hard to remember who is executing what. The pool abstraction restricts the number of places that code in different processes interact with each other, making it much easier to keep track of.

- Pools also seamlessly hide the process of passing data between processes. Using a pool looks much like a function call; you pass data into a function, it is executed in another process or processes, and when the work is done, a value is returned. It is important to understand that under the hood, a lot of work is being done to support this: objects in one process are being pickled and passed into a pipe.

- Another process retrieves data from the pipe and unpickles it. Work is done in the subprocess and a result is produced. The result is pickled and passed into a pipe. Eventually, the original process unpickles it and returns it.

All this pickling and passing data into pipes takes time and memory. Therefore, it is ideal to keep the amount and size of data passed into and returned from the pool to a minimum, and it is only advantageous to use the pool if a lot of processing has to be done on the data in question.

Armed with this knowledge, the code to make all this machinery work is surprisingly simple. Let's look at the problem of calculating all the prime factors of a list of random numbers. This is a common and expensive part of a variety of cryptography algorithms (not to mention attacks on those algorithms!). It requires years of processing power to crack the extremely large numbers used to secure your bank accounts. The following implementation, while readable, is not at all efficient, but that's ok because we want to see it using lots of CPU time:

```
import random
from multiprocessing.pool import Pool

def prime_factor(value):
    factors = []
    for divisor in range(2, value-1):
        quotient, remainder = divmod(value, divisor)
        if not remainder:
            factors.extend(prime_factor(divisor))
            factors.extend(prime_factor(quotient))
            break
```

```
        else:
            factors = [value]
        return factors


    if __name__ == '__main__':
        pool = Pool()

        to_factor = [
            random.randint(100000, 50000000) for i in range(20)
        ]
        results = pool.map(prime_factor, to_factor)
        for value, factors in zip(to_factor, results):
            print("The factors of {} are {}".format(value, factors))
```

Let's focus on the parallel processing aspects as the brute force recursive algorithm for calculating factors is pretty clear. We first construct a multiprocessing pool instance. By default, this pool creates a separate process for each of the CPU cores in the machine it is running on.

The `map` method accepts a function and an iterable. The pool pickles each of the values in the iterable and passes it into an available process, which executes the function on it. When that process is finished doing it's work, it pickles the resulting list of factors and passes it back to the pool. Once all the pools are finished processing work (which could take some time), the results list is passed back to the original process, which has been waiting patiently for all this work to complete.

It is often more useful to use the similar `map_async` method, which returns immediately even though the processes are still working. In that case, the results variable would not be a list of values, but a promise to return a list of values later by calling `results.get()`. This promise object also has methods like `ready()`, and `wait()`, which allow us to check whether all the results are in yet.

Alternatively, if we don't know all the values we want to get results for in advance, we can use the `apply_async` method to queue up a single job. If the pool has a process that isn't already working, it will start immediately; otherwise, it will hold onto the task until there is a free process available.

Pools can also be `closed`, which refuses to take any further tasks, but processes everything currently in the queue, or `terminated`, which goes one step further and refuses to start any jobs still on the queue, although any jobs currently running are still permitted to complete.

Queues

If we need more control over communication between processes, we can use a `Queue`. `Queue` data structures are useful for sending messages from one process into one or more other processes. Any picklable object can be sent into a `Queue`, but remember that pickling can be a costly operation, so keep such objects small. To illustrate queues, let's build a little search engine for text content that stores all relevant entries in memory.

This is not the most sensible way to build a text-based search engine, but I have used this pattern to query numerical data that needed to use CPU-intensive processes to construct a chart that was then rendered to the user.

This particular search engine scans all files in the current directory in parallel. A process is constructed for each core on the CPU. Each of these is instructed to load some of the files into memory. Let's look at the function that does the loading and searching:

```
def search(paths, query_q, results_q):
    lines = []
    for path in paths:
        lines.extend(l.strip() for l in path.open())

    query = query_q.get()
    while query:
        results_q.put([l for l in lines if query in l])
        query = query_q.get()
```

Remember, this function is run in a different process (in fact, it is run in `cpucount()` different processes) from the main thread. It is passes a list of `path.path` objects and two `multiprocessing.Queue` objects; one for incoming queries and one to send outgoing results. These queues have a similar interface to the `Queue` class we discussed in *Chapter 6, Python Data Structures*. However, they are doing extra work to pickle the data in the queue and pass it into the subprocess over a pipe. These two queues are set up in the main process and passed through the pipes into the search function inside the child processes.

The search code is pretty dumb, both in terms of efficiency and of capabilities; it loops over every line stored in memory and puts the matching ones in a list. The list is placed on a queue and passed back to the main process.

Let's look at the main process, which sets up these queues:

```
if __name__ == '__main__':
    from multiprocessing import Process, Queue, cpu_count
    from path import path
    cpus = cpu_count()
```

```
pathnames = [f for f in path('.').listdir() if f.isfile()]
paths = [pathnames[i::cpus] for i in range(cpus)]
query_queues = [Queue() for p in range(cpus)]
results_queue = Queue()

search_procs = [
    Process(target=search, args=(p, q, results_queue))
    for p, q in zip(paths, query_queues)
]
for proc in search_procs: proc.start()
```

For easier description, let's assume `cpu_count` is four. Notice how the import statements are placed inside the `if` guard? This is a small optimization that prevents them from being imported in each subprocess (where they aren't needed) on certain operating systems. We list all the paths in the current directory and then split the list into four approximately equal parts. We also construct a list of four `Queue` objects to send data into each subprocess. Finally, we construct a `single` results queue; this is passed into all four of the subprocesses. Each of them can put data into the queue and it will be aggregated in the main process.

Now let's look at the code that makes a search actually happen:

```
for q in query_queues:
    q.put("def")
    q.put(None)   # Signal process termination
for i in range(cpus):
    for match in results_queue.get():
        print(match)
for proc in search_procs: proc.join()
```

This code performs a single search for `"def"` (because it's a common phrase in a directory full of Python files!). In a more production ready system, we would probably hook a socket up to this search code. In that case, we'd have to change the inter-process protocol so that the message coming back on the return queue contained enough information to identify which of many queries the results were attached to.

This use of queues is actually a local version of what could become a distributed system. Imagine if the searches were being sent out to multiple computers and then recombined. We won't discuss it here, but the multiprocessing module includes a manager class that can take a lot of the boilerplate out of the preceding code. There is even a version of the `multiprocessing.Manager` that can manage subprocesses on remote systems to construct a rudimentary distributed application. Check the Python multiprocessing documentation if you are interested in pursuing this further.

The problems with multiprocessing

As threads do, multiprocessing also has problems, some of which we have already discussed. There is no best way to do concurrency; this is especially true in Python. We always need to examine the parallel problem to figure out which of the many available solutions is the best one for that problem. Sometimes, there is no best solution.

In the case of multiprocessing, the primary drawback is that sharing data between processes is very costly. As we have discussed, all communication between processes, whether by queues, pipes, or a more implicit mechanism requires pickling the objects. Excessive pickling quickly dominates processing time. Multiprocessing works best when relatively small objects are passed between processes and a tremendous amount of work needs to be done on each one. On the other hand, if no communication between processes is required, there may not be any point in using the module at all; we can spin up four separate Python processes and use them independently.

The other major problem with multiprocessing is that, like threads, it can be hard to tell which process a variable or method is being accessed in. In multiprocessing, if you access a variable from another process it will usually overwrite the variable in the currently running process while the other process keeps the old value. This is really confusing to maintain, so don't do it.

Futures

Let's start looking at a more asynchronous way of doing concurrency. Futures wrap either multiprocessing or threading depending on what kind of concurrency we need (tending towards I/O versus tending towards CPU). They don't completely solve the problem of accidentally altering shared state, but they allow us to structure our code such that it is easier to track down when we do so. Futures provide distinct boundaries between the different threads or processes. Similar to the multiprocessing pool, they are useful for "call and answer" type interactions in which processing can happen in another thread and then at some point in the future (they are aptly named, after all), you can ask it for the result. It's really just a wrapper around multiprocessing pools and thread pools, but it provides a cleaner API and encourages nicer code.

A future is an object that basically wraps a function call. That function call is run in the background in a thread or process. The future object has methods to check if the future has completed and to get the results after it has completed.

Let's do another file search example. In the last section, we implemented a version of the `unix grep` command. This time, let's do a simple version of the `find` command. The example will search the entire filesystem for paths that contain a given string of characters:

```python
from concurrent.futures import ThreadPoolExecutor
from pathlib import Path
from os.path import sep as pathsep
from collections import deque

def find_files(path, query_string):
    subdirs = []
    for p in path.iterdir():
        full_path = str(p.absolute())
        if p.is_dir() and not p.is_symlink():
            subdirs.append(p)
        if query_string in full_path:
                print(full_path)

    return subdirs

query = '.py'
futures = deque()
basedir = Path(pathsep).absolute()

with ThreadPoolExecutor(max_workers=10) as executor:
    futures.append(
        executor.submit(find_files, basedir, query))
    while futures:
        future = futures.popleft()
        if future.exception():
            continue
        elif future.done():
            subdirs = future.result()
            for subdir in subdirs:
                futures.append(executor.submit(
                    find_files, subdir, query))
        else:
            futures.append(future)
```

This code consists of a function named `find_files` that is run in a separate thread (or process, if we used `ProcessPoolExecutor`). There isn't anything particularly special about this function, but note how it does not access any global variables. All interaction with the external environment is passed into the function or returned from it. This is not a technical requirement, but it is the best way to keep your brain inside your skull when programming with futures.

> Accessing outside variables without proper synchronization results in something called a **race** condition. For example, imagine two concurrent writes trying to increment an integer counter. They start at the same time and both read the value as 5. Then they both increment the value and write back the result as 6. But if two processes are trying to increment a variable, the expected result would be that it gets incremented by two, so the result should be 7. Modern wisdom is that the easiest way to avoid doing this is to keep as much state as possible private and share them through known-safe constructs, such as queues.

We set up a couple variables before we get started; we'll be searching for all files that contain the characters `'.py'` for this example. We have a queue of futures that we'll discuss shortly. The `basedir` variable points to the root of the filesystem; `'/'` on Unix machines and probably `C:\` on Windows.

First, let's have a short course on search theory. This algorithm implements breadth first search in parallel. Rather than recursively searching every directory using a depth first search, it adds all the subdirectories in the current folder to the queue, then all the subdirectories of each of those folders and so on.

The meat of the program is known as an event loop. We can construct a `ThreadPoolExecutor` as a context manager so that it is automatically cleaned up and its threads closed when it is done. It requires a `max_workers` argument to indicate the number of threads running at a time; if more than this many jobs are submitted, it queues up the rest until a worker thread becomes available. When using `ProcessPoolExecutor`, this is normally constrained to the number of CPUs on the machine, but with threads, it can be much higher, depending how many are waiting on I/O at a time. Each thread takes up a certain amount of memory, so it shouldn't be too high; it doesn't take all that many threads before the speed of the disk, rather than number of parallel requests, is the bottleneck.

Once the executor has been constructed, we submit a job to it using the root directory. The `submit()` method immediately returns a `Future` object, which promises to give us a result eventually. The future is placed on the queue. The loop then repeatedly removes the first future from the queue and inspects it. If it is still running, it gets added back to the end of the queue. Otherwise, we check if the function raised an exception with a call to `future.exception()`. If it did, we just ignore it (it's usually a permission error, although a real app would need to be more careful about what the exception was). If we didn't check this exception here, it would be raised when we called `result()` and could be handled through the normal `try...except` mechanism.

Assuming no exception occurred, we can call `result()` to get the return value of the function call. Since the function returns a list of subdirectories that are not symbolic links (my lazy way of preventing an infinite loop), `result()` returns the same thing. These new subdirectories are submitted to the executor and the resulting futures are tossed onto the queue to have their contents searched in a later iteration.

So that's all that is required to develop a future-based I/O-bound application. Under the hood, it's using the same thread or process APIs we've already discussed, but it provides a more understandable interface and makes it easier to see the boundaries between concurrently running functions (just don't try to access global variables from inside the future!).

AsyncIO

AsyncIO is the current state of the art in Python concurrent programming. It combines the concept of futures and an event loop with the coroutines we discussed in *Chapter 9, The Iterator Pattern*. The result is about as elegant and easy to understand as it is possible to get when writing concurrent code, though that isn't saying a lot!

AsyncIO can be used for a few different concurrent tasks, but it was specifically designed for network I/O. Most networking applications, especially on the server side, spend a lot of time waiting for data to come in from the network. This can be solved by handling each client in a separate thread, but threads use up memory and other resources. AsyncIO uses coroutines instead of threads.

The library also provides its own event loop, obviating the need for the several lines long while loop in the previous example. However, event loops come with a cost. When we run code in an async task on the event loop, that code must return immediately, blocking neither on I/O nor on long-running calculations. This is a minor thing when writing our own code, but it means that any standard library or third-party functions that block on I/O have to have non-blocking versions created.

AsyncIO solves this by creating a set of coroutines that use the `yield from` syntax to return control to the event loop immediately. The event loop takes care of checking whether the blocking call has completed and performing any subsequent tasks, just like we did manually in the previous section.

AsyncIO in action

A canonical example of a blocking function is the `time.sleep` call. Let's use the asynchronous version of this call to illustrate the basics of an AsyncIO event loop:

```python
import asyncio
import random


@asyncio.coroutine
def random_sleep(counter):
    delay = random.random() * 5
    print("{} sleeps for {:.2f} seconds".format(counter, delay))
    yield from asyncio.sleep(delay)
    print("{} awakens".format(counter))


@asyncio.coroutine
def five_sleepers():
    print("Creating five tasks")
    tasks = [
        asyncio.async(random_sleep(i)) for i in range(5)]
    print("Sleeping after starting five tasks")
    yield from asyncio.sleep(2)
    print("Waking and waiting for five tasks")
    yield from asyncio.wait(tasks)


asyncio.get_event_loop().run_until_complete(five_sleepers())
print("Done five tasks")
```

This is a fairly basic example, but it covers several features of AsyncIO programming. It is easiest to understand in the order that it executes, which is more or less bottom to top.

The second last line gets the event loop and instructs it to run a future until it is finished. The future in question is named `five_sleepers`. Once that future has done its work, the loop will exit and our code will terminate. As asynchronous programmers, we don't need to know too much about what happens inside that `run_until_complete` call, but be aware that a lot is going on. It's a souped up coroutine version of the futures loop we wrote in the previous chapter that knows how to deal with iteration, exceptions, function returns, parallel calls, and more.

Now look a little more closely at that `five_sleepers` future. Ignore the decorator for a few paragraphs; we'll get back to it. The coroutine first constructs five instances of the `random_sleep` future. The resulting futures are wrapped in an `asyncio.async` task, which adds them to the loop's task queue so they can execute concurrently when control is returned to the event loop.

That control is returned whenever we call `yield from`. In this case, we call `yield from asyncio.sleep` to pause execution of this coroutine for two seconds. During this break, the event loop executes the tasks that it has queued up; namely the five `random_sleep` futures. These coroutines each print a starting message, then send control back to the event loop for a specific amount of time. If any of the sleep calls inside `random_sleep` are shorter than two seconds, the event loop passes control back into the relevant future, which prints its awakening message before returning. When the sleep call inside `five_sleepers` wakes up, it executes up to the next yield from call, which waits for the remaining `random_sleep` tasks to complete. When all the sleep calls have finished executing, the `random_sleep` tasks return, which removes them from the event queue. Once all five of those are completed, the `asyncio.wait` call and then the `five_sleepers` method also return. Finally, since the event queue is now empty, the `run_until_complete` call is able to terminate and the program ends.

The `asyncio.coroutine` decorator mostly just documents that this coroutine is meant to be used as a future in an event loop. In this case, the program would run just fine without the decorator. However, the `asyncio.coroutine` decorator can also be used to wrap a normal function (one that doesn't yield) so that it can be treated as a future. In this case, the entire function executes before returning control to the event loop; the decorator just forces the function to fulfill the coroutine API so the event loop knows how to handle it.

Reading an AsyncIO future

An AsyncIO coroutine executes each line in order until it encounters a `yield from` statement, at which point it returns control to the event loop. The event loop then executes any other tasks that are ready to run, including the one that the original coroutine was waiting on. Whenever that child task completes, the event loop sends the result back into the coroutine so that it can pick up executing until it encounters another `yield from` statement or returns.

This allows us to write code that executes synchronously until we explicitly need to wait for something. This removes the nondeterministic behavior of threads, so we don't need to worry nearly so much about shared state.

It's still a good idea to avoid accessing shared state from inside a coroutine. It makes your code much easier to reason about. More importantly, even though an ideal world might have all asynchronous execution happen inside coroutines, the reality is that some futures are executed behind the scenes inside threads or processes. Stick to a "share nothing" philosophy to avoid a ton of difficult bugs.

In addition, AsyncIO allows us to collect logical sections of code together inside a single coroutine, even if we are waiting for other work elsewhere. As a specific instance, even though the `yield from asyncio.sleep` call in the `random_sleep` coroutine is allowing a ton of stuff to happen inside the event loop, the coroutine itself looks like it's doing everything in order. This ability to read related pieces of asynchronous code without worrying about the machinery that waits for tasks to complete is the primary benefit of the AsyncIO module.

AsyncIO for networking

AsyncIO was specifically designed for use with network sockets, so let's implement a DNS server. More accurately, let's implement one extremely basic feature of a DNS server.

The domain name system's basic purpose is to translate domain names, such as www.amazon.com into IP addresses such as 72.21.206.6. It has to be able to perform many types of queries and know how to contact other DNS servers if it doesn't have the answer required. We won't be implementing any of this, but the following example is able to respond directly to a standard DNS query to look up IPs for my three most recent employers:

```python
import asyncio
from contextlib import suppress

ip_map = {
    b'facebook.com.': '173.252.120.6',
    b'yougov.com.': '213.52.133.246',
    b'wipo.int.': '193.5.93.80'
}

def lookup_dns(data):
    domain = b''
    pointer, part_length = 13, data[12]
    while part_length:
```

```
            domain += data[pointer:pointer+part_length] + b'.'
            pointer += part_length + 1
            part_length = data[pointer - 1]

    ip = ip_map.get(domain, '127.0.0.1')

    return domain, ip

def create_response(data, ip):
    ba = bytearray
    packet = ba(data[:2]) + ba([129, 128]) + data[4:6] * 2
    packet += ba(4) + data[12:]
    packet += ba([192, 12, 0, 1, 0, 1, 0, 0, 0, 60, 0, 4])
    for x in ip.split('.'): packet.append(int(x))
    return packet

class DNSProtocol(asyncio.DatagramProtocol):
    def connection_made(self, transport):
        self.transport = transport

    def datagram_received(self, data, addr):
        print("Received request from {}".format(addr[0]))
        domain, ip = lookup_dns(data)
        print("Sending IP {} for {} to {}".format(
            domain.decode(), ip, addr[0]))
        self.transport.sendto(
            create_response(data, ip), addr)

loop = asyncio.get_event_loop()
transport, protocol = loop.run_until_complete(
    loop.create_datagram_endpoint(
        DNSProtocol, local_addr=('127.0.0.1', 4343)))
print("DNS Server running")

with suppress(KeyboardInterrupt):
    loop.run_forever()
transport.close()
loop.close()
```

This example sets up a dictionary that dumbly maps a few domains to IPv4 addresses. It is followed by two functions that extract information from a binary DNS query packet and construct the response. We won't be discussing these; if you want to know more about DNS read RFC ("request for comment", the format for defining most Internet protocols) 1034 and 1035.

You can test this service by running the following command in another terminal:

```
nslookup -port=4343 facebook.com localhost
```

Let's get on with the entrée. AsyncIO networking revolves around the intimately linked concepts of transports and protocols. A protocol is a class that has specific methods that are called when relevant events happen. Since DNS runs on top of **UDP (User Datagram Protocol)**; we build our protocol class as a subclass of `DatagramProtocol`. This class has a variety of events that it can respond to; we are specifically interested in the initial connection occurring (solely so we can store the transport for future use) and the `datagram_received` event. For DNS, each received datagram must be parsed and responded to, at which point the interaction is over.

So, when a datagram is received, we process the packet, look up the IP, and construct a response using the functions we aren't talking about (they're black sheep in the family). Then we instruct the underlying transport to send the resulting packet back to the requesting client using its `sendto` method.

The transport essentially represents a communication stream. In this case, it abstracts away all the fuss of sending and receiving data on a UDP socket on an event loop. There are similar transports for interacting with TCP sockets and subprocesses, for example.

The UDP transport is constructed by calling the loop's `create_datagram_endpoint` coroutine. This constructs the appropriate UDP socket and starts listening on it. We pass it the address that the socket needs to listen on, and importantly, the protocol class we created so that the transport knows what to call when it receives data.

Since the process of initializing a socket takes a non-trivial amount of time and would block the event loop, the `create_datagram_endpoint` function is a coroutine. In our example, we don't really need to do anything while we wait for this initialization, so we wrap the call in `loop.run_until_complete`. The event loop takes care of managing the future, and when it's complete, it returns a tuple of two values: the newly initialized transport and the protocol object that was constructed from the class we passed in.

Behind the scenes, the transport has set up a task on the event loop that is listening for incoming UDP connections. All we have to do, then, is start the event loop running with the call to `loop.run_forever()` so that task can process these packets. When the packets arrive, they are processed on the protocol and everything just works.

The only other major thing to pay attention to is that transports (and, indeed, event loops) are supposed to be closed when we are finished with them. In this case, the code runs just fine without the two calls to `close()`, but if we were constructing transports on the fly (or just doing proper error handling!), we'd need to be quite a bit more conscious of it.

You may have been dismayed to see how much boilerplate is required in setting up a protocol class and underlying transport. AsyncIO provides an abstraction on top of these two key concepts called streams. We'll see an example of streams in the TCP server in the next example.

Using executors to wrap blocking code

AsyncIO provides its own version of the futures library to allow us to run code in a separate thread or process when there isn't an appropriate non-blocking call to be made. This essentially allows us to combine threads and processes with the asynchronous model. One of the more useful applications of this feature is to get the best of both worlds when an application has bursts of I/O-bound and CPU-bound activity. The I/O-bound portions can happen in the event-loop while the CPU-intensive work can be spun off to a different process. To illustrate this, let's implement "sorting as a service" using AsyncIO:

```python
import asyncio
import json
from concurrent.futures import ProcessPoolExecutor

def sort_in_process(data):
    nums = json.loads(data.decode())
    curr = 1
    while curr < len(nums):
        if nums[curr] >= nums[curr-1]:
            curr += 1
        else:
            nums[curr], nums[curr-1] = \
                nums[curr-1], nums[curr]
            if curr > 1:
```

```
                curr -= 1

        return json.dumps(nums).encode()

    @asyncio.coroutine
    def sort_request(reader, writer):
        print("Received connection")
        length = yield from reader.read(8)
        data = yield from reader.readexactly(
            int.from_bytes(length, 'big'))
        result = yield from asyncio.get_event_loop().run_in_executor(
            None, sort_in_process, data)
        print("Sorted list")
        writer.write(result)
        writer.close()
        print("Connection closed")

    loop = asyncio.get_event_loop()
    loop.set_default_executor(ProcessPoolExecutor())
    server = loop.run_until_complete(
        asyncio.start_server(sort_request, '127.0.0.1', 2015))
    print("Sort Service running")

    loop.run_forever()
    server.close()
    loop.run_until_complete(server.wait_closed())
    loop.close()
```

This is an example of good code implementing some really stupid ideas. The whole idea of sort as a service is pretty ridiculous. Using our own sorting algorithm instead of calling Python's `sorted` is even worse. The algorithm we used is called gnome sort, or in some cases, "stupid sort". It is a slow sort algorithm implemented in pure Python. We defined our own protocol instead of using one of the many perfectly suitable application protocols that exist in the wild. Even the idea of using multiprocessing for parallelism might be suspect here; we still end up passing all the data into and out of the subprocesses. Sometimes, it's important to take a step back from the program you are writing and ask yourself if you are trying to meet the right goals.

But let's look at some of the smart features of this design. First, we are passing bytes into and out of the subprocess. This is a lot smarter than decoding the JSON in the main process. It means the (relatively expensive) decoding can happen on a different CPU. Also, pickled JSON strings are generally smaller than pickled lists, so less data is passing between processes.

Second, the two methods are very linear; it looks like code is being executed one line after another. Of course, in AsyncIO, this is an illusion, but we don't have to worry about shared memory or concurrency primitives.

Streams

The previous example should look familiar by now as it has a similar boilerplate to other AsyncIO programs. However, there are a few differences. You'll notice we called `start_server` instead of `create_server`. This method hooks into AsyncIO's streams instead of using the underlying transport/protocol code. Instead of passing in a protocol class, we can pass in a normal coroutine, which receives reader and writer parameters. These both represent streams of bytes that can be read from and written like files or sockets. Second, because this is a TCP server instead of UDP, there is some socket cleanup required when the program finishes. This cleanup is a blocking call, so we have to run the `wait_closed` coroutine on the event loop.

Streams are fairly simple to understand. Reading is a potentially blocking call so we have to call it with `yield from`. Writing doesn't block; it just puts the data on a queue, which AsyncIO sends out in the background.

Our code inside the `sort_request` method makes two read requests. First, it reads 8 bytes from the wire and converts them to an integer using big endian notation. This integer represents the number of bytes of data the client intends to send. So in the next call, to `readexactly`, it reads that many bytes. The difference between `read` and `readexactly` is that the former will read up to the requested number of bytes, while the latter will buffer reads until it receives all of them, or until the connection closes.

Executors

Now let's look at the executor code. We import the exact same `ProcessPoolExecutor` that we used in the previous section. Notice that we don't need a special AsyncIO version of it. The event loop has a handy `run_in_executor` coroutine that we can use to run futures on. By default, the loop runs code in `ThreadPoolExecutor`, but we can pass in a different executor if we wish. Or, as we did in this example, we can set a different default when we set up the event loop by calling `loop.set_default_executor()`.

As you probably recall from the previous section, there is not a lot of boilerplate for using futures with an executor. However, when we use them with AsyncIO, there is none at all! The coroutine automatically wraps the function call in a future and submits it to the executor. Our code blocks until the future completes, while the event loop continues processing other connections, tasks, or futures. When the future is done, the coroutine wakes up and continues on to write the data back to the client.

You may be wondering if, instead of running multiple processes inside an event loop, it might be better to run multiple event loops in different processes. The answer is: "maybe". However, depending on the exact problem space, we are probably better off running independent copies of a program with a single event loop than to try to coordinate everything with a master multiprocessing process.

We've hit most of the high points of AsyncIO in this section, and the chapter has covered many other concurrency primitives. Concurrency is a hard problem to solve, and no one solution fits all use cases. The most important part of designing a concurrent system is deciding which of the available tools is the correct one to use for the problem. We have seen advantages and disadvantages of several concurrent systems, and now have some insights into which are the better choices for different types of requirements.

Case study

To wrap up this chapter, and the book, let's build a basic image compression tool. It will take black and white images (with 1 bit per pixel, either on or off) and attempt to compress it using a very basic form of compression known as run-length encoding. You may find black and white images a bit far-fetched. If so, you haven't enjoyed enough hours at http://xkcd.com!

I've included some sample black and white BMP images (which are easy to read data into and leave a lot of opportunity to improve on file size) with the example code for this chapter.

We'll be compressing the images using a simple technique called run-length encoding. This technique basically takes a sequence of bits and replaces any strings of repeated bits with the number of bits that are repeated. For example, the string 000011000 might be replaced with 04 12 03 to indicate that 4 zeros are followed by 2 ones and then 3 more zeroes. To make things a little more interesting, we will break each row into 127 bit chunks.

I didn't pick 127 bits arbitrarily. 127 different values can be encoded into 7 bits, which means that if a row contains all ones or all zeros, we can store it in a single byte; the first bit indicating whether it is a row of 0s or a row of 1s, and the remaining 7 bits indicating how many of that bit exists.

Breaking up the image into blocks has another advantage; we can process individual blocks in parallel without them depending on each other. However, there's a major disadvantage as well; if a run has just a few ones or zeros in it, then it will take up more space in the compressed file. When we break up long runs into blocks, we may end up creating more of these small runs and bloat the size of the file.

When dealing with files, we have to think about the exact layout of the bytes in the compressed file. Our file will store two byte little-endian integers at the beginning of the file representing the width and height of the completed file. Then it will write bytes representing the 127 bit chunks of each row.

Now before we start designing a concurrent system to build such compressed images, we should ask a fundamental question: Is this application I/O-bound or CPU-bound?

My answer, honestly, is "I don't know". I'm not sure whether the app will spend more time loading data from disk and writing it back or doing the compression in memory. I suspect that it is a CPU bound app in principle, but once we start passing image strings into subprocesses, we may lose any benefit of parallelism. The optimal solution to this problem is probably to write a C or Cython extension, but let's see how far we can get in pure Python.

We'll build this application using bottom-up design. That way we'll have some building blocks that we can combine into different concurrency patterns to see how they compare. Let's start with the code that compresses a 127-bit chunk using run-length encoding:

```
from bitarray import bitarray
def compress_chunk(chunk):
    compressed = bytearray()
    count = 1
    last = chunk[0]
    for bit in chunk[1:]:
        if bit != last:
            compressed.append(count | (128 * last))
            count = 0
            last = bit
        count += 1
    compressed.append(count | (128 * last))
    return compressed
```

This code uses the `bitarray` class for manipulating individual zeros and ones. It is distributed as a third-party module, which you can install with the command `pip install bitarray`. The chunk that is passed into `compress_chunks` is an instance of this class (although the example would work just as well with a list of Booleans). The primary benefit of the bitarray in this case is that when pickling them between processes, they take up an 8th of the space of a list of Booleans or a bytestring of 1s and 0s. Therefore, they pickle faster. They are also a bit (pun intended) easier to work with than doing a ton of bitwise operations.

The method compresses the data using run-length encoding and returns a bytearray containing the packed data. Where a bitarray is like a list of ones and zeros, a bytearray is like a list of byte objects (each byte, of course, containing 8 ones or zeros).

The algorithm that performs the compression is pretty simple (although I'd like to point out that it took me two days to implement and debug it. Simple to understand does not necessarily imply easy to write!). It first sets the `last` variable to the type of bit in the current run (either `True` or `False`). It then loops over the bits, counting each one, until it finds one that is different. When it does, it constructs a new byte by making the leftmost bit of the byte (the 128 position) either a zero or a one, depending on what the `last` variable contained. Then it resets the counter and repeats the operation. Once the loop is done, it creates one last byte for the last run, and returns the result.

While we're creating building blocks, let's make a function that compresses a row of image data:

```
def compress_row(row):
    compressed = bytearray()
    chunks = split_bits(row, 127)
    for chunk in chunks:
        compressed.extend(compress_chunk(chunk))
    return compressed
```

This function accepts a bitarray named row. It splits it into chunks that are each 127 bits wide using a function that we'll define very shortly. Then it compresses each of those chunks using the previously defined `compress_chunk`, concatenating the results into a `bytearray`, which it returns.

We define `split_bits` as a simple generator:

```
def split_bits(bits, width):
    for i in range(0, len(bits), width):
        yield bits[i:i+width]
```

Now, since we aren't certain yet whether this will run more effectively in threads or processes, let's wrap these functions in a method that runs everything in a provided executor:

```
def compress_in_executor(executor, bits, width):
    row_compressors = []
    for row in split_bits(bits, width):
        compressor = executor.submit(compress_row, row)
```

```
        row_compressors.append(compressor)

    compressed = bytearray()
    for compressor in row_compressors:
        compressed.extend(compressor.result())
    return compressed
```

This example barely needs explaining; it splits the incoming bits into rows based on the width of the image using the same `split_bits` function we have already defined (hooray for bottom-up design!).

Note that this code will compress any sequence of bits, although it would bloat, rather than compress binary data that has frequent changes in bit values. Black and white images are definitely good candidates for the compression algorithm in question. Let's now create a function that loads an image file using the third-party pillow module, converts it to bits, and compresses it. We can easily switch between executors using the venerable comment statement:

```
from PIL import Image
def compress_image(in_filename, out_filename, executor=None):
    executor = executor if executor else ProcessPoolExecutor()
    with Image.open(in_filename) as image:
        bits = bitarray(image.convert('1').getdata())
        width, height = image.size

    compressed = compress_in_executor(executor, bits, width)

    with open(out_filename, 'wb') as file:
        file.write(width.to_bytes(2, 'little'))
        file.write(height.to_bytes(2, 'little'))
        file.write(compressed)

def single_image_main():
    in_filename, out_filename = sys.argv[1:3]
    #executor = ThreadPoolExecutor(4)
    executor = ProcessPoolExecutor()
    compress_image(in_filename, out_filename, executor)
```

The `image.convert()` call changes the image to black and white (one bit) mode, while `getdata()` returns an iterator over those values. We pack the results into a bitarray so they transfer across the wire more quickly. When we output the compressed file, we first write the width and height of the image followed by the compressed data, which arrives as a bytearray, which can be written directly to the binary file.

Having written all this code, we are finally able to test whether thread pools or process pools give us better performance. I created a large (7200 x 5600 pixels) black and white image and ran it through both pools. The `ProcessPool` takes about 7.5 seconds to process the image on my system, while the `ThreadPool` consistently takes about 9. Thus, as we suspected, the cost of pickling bits and bytes back and forth between processes is eating almost all the efficiency gains from running on multiple processors (though looking at my CPU monitor, it does fully utilize all four cores on my machine).

So it looks like compressing a single image is most effectively done in a separate process, but only barely because we are passing so much data back and forth between the parent and subprocesses. Multiprocessing is more effective when the amount of data passed between processes is quite low.

So let's extend the app to compress all the bitmaps in a directory in parallel. The only thing we'll have to pass into the subprocesses are filenames, so we should get a speed gain compared to using threads. Also, to be kind of crazy, we'll use the existing code to compress individual images. This means we'll be running a `ProcessPoolExecutor` inside each subprocess to create even more subprocesses. I don't recommend doing this in real life!

```python
from pathlib import Path
def compress_dir(in_dir, out_dir):
    if not out_dir.exists():
        out_dir.mkdir()

    executor = ProcessPoolExecutor()
    for file in (
            f for f in in_dir.iterdir() if f.suffix == '.bmp'):
        out_file = (out_dir / file.name).with_suffix('.rle')
        executor.submit(
            compress_image, str(file), str(out_file))

def dir_images_main():
    in_dir, out_dir = (Path(p) for p in sys.argv[1:3])
    compress_dir(in_dir, out_dir)
```

This code uses the `compress_image` function we defined previously, but runs it in a separate process for each image. It doesn't pass an executor into the function, so `compress_image` creates a `ProcessPoolExecutor` once the new process has started running.

Now that we are running executors inside executors, there are four combinations of threads and process pools that we can be using to compress images. They each have quite different timing profiles:

	Process pool per image	Thread pool per image
Process pool per row	42 seconds	53 seconds
Thread pool per row	34 seconds	64 seconds

As we might expect, using threads for each image and again using threads for each row is the slowest, since the GIL prevents us from doing any work in parallel. Given that we were slightly faster when using separate processes for each row when we were using a single image, you may be surprised to see that it is faster to use a `ThreadPool` feature for rows if we are processing each image in a separate process. Take some time to understand why this might be.

My machine contains only four processor cores. Each row in each image is being processed in a separate pool, which means that all those rows are competing for processing power. When there is only one image, we get a (very modest) speedup by running each row in parallel. However, when we increase the number of images being processed at once, the cost of passing all that row data into and out of a subprocess is actively stealing processing time from each of the other images. So, if we can process each image on a separate processor, where the only thing that has to get pickled into the subprocess pipe is a couple filenames, we get a solid speedup.

Thus, we see that different workloads require different concurrency paradigms. Even if we are just using futures we have to make informed decisions about what kind of executor to use.

Also note that for typically-sized images, the program runs quickly enough that it really doesn't matter which concurrency structures we use. In fact, even if we didn't use any concurrency at all, we'd probably end up with about the same user experience.

This problem could also have been solved using the threading and/or multiprocessing modules directly, though there would have been quite a bit more boilerplate code to write. You may be wondering whether or not AsyncIO would be useful here. The answer is: "probably not". Most operating systems don't have a good way to do non-blocking reads from the filesystem, so the library ends up wrapping all the calls in futures anyway.

For completeness, here's the code that I used to decompress the RLE images to confirm that the algorithm was working correctly (indeed, it wasn't until I fixed bugs in both compression and decompression, and I'm still not sure if it is perfect. I should have used test-driven development!):

```python
from PIL import Image
import sys

def decompress(width, height, bytes):
    image = Image.new('1', (width, height))

    col = 0
    row = 0
    for byte in bytes:
        color = (byte & 128) >> 7
        count = byte & ~128
        for i in range(count):
            image.putpixel((row, col), color)
            row += 1
        if not row % width:
            col += 1
            row = 0
    return image


with open(sys.argv[1], 'rb') as file:
    width = int.from_bytes(file.read(2), 'little')
    height = int.from_bytes(file.read(2), 'little')

    image = decompress(width, height, file.read())
    image.save(sys.argv[2], 'bmp')
```

This code is fairly straightforward. Each run is encoded in a single byte. It uses some bitwise math to extract the color of the pixel and the length of the run. Then it sets each pixel from that run in the image, incrementing the row and column of the next pixel to check at appropriate intervals.

Exercises

We've covered several different concurrency paradigms in this chapter and still don't have a clear idea of when each one is useful. As we saw in the case study, it is often a good idea to prototype a few different strategies before committing to one.

Concurrency in Python 3 is a huge topic and an entire book of this size could not cover everything there is to know about it. As your first exercise, I encourage you to check out several third-party libraries that may provide additional context:

- execnet, a library that permits local and remote share-nothing concurrency
- Parallel python, an alternative interpreter that can execute threads in parallel
- Cython, a python-compatible language that compiles to C and has primitives to release the gil and take advantage of fully parallel multi-threading.
- PyPy-STM, an experimental implementation of software transactional memory on top of the ultra-fast PyPy implementation of the Python interpreter
- Gevent

If you have used threads in a recent application, take a look at the code and see if you can make it more readable and less bug-prone by using futures. Compare thread and multiprocessing futures to see if you can gain anything by using multiple CPUs.

Try implementing an AsyncIO service for some basic HTTP requests. You may need to look up the structure of an HTTP request on the web; they are fairly simple ASCII packets to decipher. If you can get it to the point that a web browser can render a simple GET request, you'll have a good understanding of AsyncIO network transports and protocols.

Make sure you understand the race conditions that happen in threads when you access shared data. Try to come up with a program that uses multiple threads to set shared values in such a way that the data deliberately becomes corrupt or invalid.

Remember the link collector we covered for the case study in *Chapter 6, Python Data Structures*? Can you make it run faster by making requests in parallel? Is it better to use raw threads, futures, or AsyncIO for this?

Try writing the run-length encoding example using threads or multiprocessing directly. Do you get any speed gains? Is the code easier or harder to reason about? Is there any way to speed up the decompression script by using concurrency or parallelism?

Summary

This chapter ends our exploration of object-oriented programming with a topic that isn't very object-oriented. Concurrency is a difficult problem and we've only scratched the surface. While the underlying OS abstractions of processes and threads do not provide an API that is remotely object-oriented, Python offers some really good object-oriented abstractions around them. The threading and multiprocessing packages both provide an object-oriented interface to the underlying mechanics. Futures are able to encapsulate a lot of the messy details into a single object. AsyncIO uses coroutine objects to make our code read as though it runs synchronously, while hiding ugly and complicated implementation details behind a very simple loop abstraction.

Thank you for reading *Python 3 Object-oriented Programming, Second Edition*. I hope you've enjoyed the ride and are eager to start implementing object-oriented software in all your future projects!

Index

A

absolute imports 40, 41
abstract base classes (ABCs)
  @classmethod 81, 82
  about 78
  creating 79-81
  using 78, 79
abstract factory pattern 346-350
abstraction
  about 10
  defining 16
  examples 10
abstract methods 16
access control 46, 47
adapter pattern
  about 331-334
  Adapter class 332
  Interface1 332
  Interface2 332
aggregation
  about 13
  comparing, with composition 13
assertion methods 362, 363
AsyncIO
  about 409, 410
  AsyncIO future, reading 411, 412
  executors 417, 418
  executors, using to wrap blocking
      code 415, 416
  for networking 412-415
  implementing 410, 411
  streams 417
attributes
  specifying 5

B

basic inheritance
  about 59-61
  built-ins, extending 62, 63
  overriding 63, 64
  super function 64, 65
behaviors
  about 1
  defining 7, 8
  specifying 5
bottom-up design 58
built-ins
  extending 177-182

C

CamelCase notation 28
case study, object-oriented design 18-25
character classes 247
class 3, 4
code coverage 382
code coverage test
  verifying 382-385
command pattern 341-346
composite pattern 351-355
composition 11-13
comprehensions
  dictionary comprehension 276
  generator expressions 277, 278
  list comprehensions 273-275
concurrency
  about 393
  case study 418-424
constructor 34
context manager 203-205

coroutines
  about 284-286
  closing 289, 290
  exception, raising 290
  log parsing 287-289
  relationship, with functions 290, 291
  relationship, with generators 290, 291
Counter object 166, 167
coverage.py 382

D

data
  about 1
  defining 6, 7
  objects, defining 6, 7
data notation 258
decorator pattern
  about 301, 302
  Core 302
  example 302-305
  Interface 302
  uses 301
  using, in Python 305-307
decorators 134, 135
design patterns
  about 269-301
  abstract factory pattern 346-350
  adapter pattern 331-334
  command pattern 341-346
  composite pattern 351-355
  decorator pattern 301, 302
  facade pattern 335-337
  flyweight pattern 337-341
  observer pattern 307
  singleton pattern 320
  state pattern 313
  strategy pattern 310
  template pattern 325
Dewey Decimal System (DDS) 18
dictionaries
  about 160-164
  Counter object 166, 167
  defaultdict, using 164-166
  use cases 164

dictionary comprehension 276
docstrings
  about 35
  using 36, 37
dot notation 29
duck typing 17

E

empty objects 155, 156
encapsulation 9
exceptions
  about 97
  case study 114-123
  custom exceptions, defining 109-114
  effects 101, 102
  handling 102-108
  hierarchy 108, 109
  raising 98-100
expensive objects
  imitating 378-382

F

facade pattern 335-337
FIFO (First In First Out) queues 183, 184
file I/O 201-203
flyweight pattern 337-341
funcargs 373
functions
  about 213-217
  callable objects 218, 219
  using, as attributes 217, 218
futures 406-409

G

generators
  about 279-281
  data, yielding from another iterable 281-284
global interpreter lock (GIL) 398

H

hashable 163

I

information hiding
about 9
defining 9, 10
inheritance
about 11-16
case study 82-93
instance diagram 13
interfaces 16
International Standard Book Number (ISBN) 18
iterator pattern
case study 291-298
iterators
about 270
iterator protocol 271-273

J

JavaScript Object Notation (JSON) 257

L

LIFO (Last In First Out) queues 185, 186
list comprehensions 273-275
lists
about 167-169
sorting 169-172

M

mailing list manager, case study
building 219-226
members 6
method overloading
about 205, 206
default arguments 206-208
unpacking arguments 212
variable argument lists 208-211
methods 7
module contents
organizing 43-45
modules
about 37
absolute imports 40, 41

example 38, 39
organizing 40
relative imports 41, 42
multiple inheritance
about 17, 18, 65
diamond problem 67-72
sets of arguments 72-74
multiprocessing
about 399-401
drawbacks 406
pools 402, 403
queues 404, 405
mutable byte strings 243, 244

O

object-oriented
defining 1-3
object-oriented programming
case study 145-153
examples 14
objects
about 125
comparing, with class 3
defining 3, 4
duplicate code, removing 140-142
existing code, reusing 142-145
identifying 126-129
managing 138-140
pickles, customizing 254-256
serializing 252-254
web objects, serializing 257-260
observer pattern
about 307
example 308-310

P

package 40
parameters 8
patterns matching, regular expression
about 245, 246
characters, escaping 247, 248
multiple characters, matching 248, 249
patterns, grouping 249, 250
selection of characters, matching 246, 247

PEP 3101
  URL 239
pick action 8
pitfalls, threads
  about 397
  global interpreter lock 398
  shared memory 397, 398
polymorphism 16, 75
priority queue 186, 187
properties
  about 6
  using 136-138
  using, for adding behavior to
      class data 129-132
property constructor 133
property function 132
public interface
  creating 9, 10
py.test
  about 368
  cleanup 370-373
  setup 370-373
  testing with 368-370
  tests, skipping with 377, 378
  variables, setting up 373-377
Python 35
Python built-in functions
  about 197
  enumerate function 200, 201
  len() function 198
  reversed() function 198, 199
Python classes
  arguments 31-33
  attributes, adding 29
  creating 27, 28
  implementing 30
  object, initializing 33-35
Python data structures
  built-ins, extending 177-181
  case study 188-194
  dictionaries 160-163
  empty objects 155, 156
  lists 167-169
  named tuples 159, 160
  queues 182, 183
  sets 173-177
  tuples 157, 158

Q

queues
  about 182, 183
  FIFO queues 183-185
  LIFO queues 185, 186
  priority queues 186, 187

R

regular expressions
  about 244, 245
  case study 260-265
  information, obtaining from 250, 251
  patterns, matching 245, 246
  repeated regular expressions,
      making efficient 252
relative imports 41, 42

S

self argument 30, 31
sequence diagram 22
sets 173-177
simple command-line notebook application
  building 49-57
singleton pattern
  about 320, 321
  implementing 321-324
slots 156
stacks 185
state pattern
  about 313, 314
  example 314-320
  state transition as coroutines 320
  versus, strategy pattern 320
strategy pattern
  about 310
  Abstraction interface 311
  example 311, 313
  User code 311
  using, in Python 313
string formatting
  about 232
  braces, escaping 233, 234
  container lookups 235, 236
  keyword arguments 234
  object lookups 236, 237

string manipulation 230-232
strings
  about 229-240
  bytes, converting to text 240, 241
  mutable byte strings 243, 244
  text, converting to bytes 241-243
SyntaxError 33

T

template pattern
  about 325
  example 325-328
test
  need for 357-359
test-driven development
  about 359, 360
  case study 385-391
third-party libraries 48, 49
threads
  about 394-397
  pitfalls 397
  thread overhead 399

top-down design 58
tuples
  about 157, 158
  named tuples 159, 160

U

UDP (User Datagram Protocol) 414
UML sequence diagram 21
Unified Modeling Language (UML)
  about 1-4
  example 4, 5
unit tests
  about 360-362
  assertion methods 362, 363
  boilerplate, reducing 364, 365
  broken tests, ignoring 366, 367
  organizing 365, 366
  running 365, 366

W

web objects
  serializing 257-260

Thank you for buying
Python 3 Object-oriented Programming
Second Edition

About Packt Publishing

Packt, pronounced 'packed', published its first book, *Mastering phpMyAdmin for Effective MySQL Management*, in April 2004, and subsequently continued to specialize in publishing highly focused books on specific technologies and solutions.

Our books and publications share the experiences of your fellow IT professionals in adapting and customizing today's systems, applications, and frameworks. Our solution-based books give you the knowledge and power to customize the software and technologies you're using to get the job done. Packt books are more specific and less general than the IT books you have seen in the past. Our unique business model allows us to bring you more focused information, giving you more of what you need to know, and less of what you don't.

Packt is a modern yet unique publishing company that focuses on producing quality, cutting-edge books for communities of developers, administrators, and newbies alike. For more information, please visit our website at www.packtpub.com.

About Packt Open Source

In 2010, Packt launched two new brands, Packt Open Source and Packt Enterprise, in order to continue its focus on specialization. This book is part of the Packt Open Source brand, home to books published on software built around open source licenses, and offering information to anybody from advanced developers to budding web designers. The Open Source brand also runs Packt's Open Source Royalty Scheme, by which Packt gives a royalty to each open source project about whose software a book is sold.

Writing for Packt

We welcome all inquiries from people who are interested in authoring. Book proposals should be sent to author@packtpub.com. If your book idea is still at an early stage and you would like to discuss it first before writing a formal book proposal, then please contact us; one of our commissioning editors will get in touch with you.

We're not just looking for published authors; if you have strong technical skills but no writing experience, our experienced editors can help you develop a writing career, or simply get some additional reward for your expertise.

Expert Python Programming

ISBN: 978-1-84719-494-7   Paperback: 372 pages

Best practices for designing, coding, and distributing your Python software

1. Learn Python development best practices from an expert, with detailed coverage of naming and coding conventions.

2. Apply object-oriented principles, design patterns, and advanced syntax tricks.

3. Manage your code with distributed version control.

Python Data Visualization Cookbook

ISBN: 978-1-78216-336-7   Paperback: 280 pages

Over 60 recipes that will enable you to learn how to create attractive visualizations using Python's most popular libraries

1. Learn how to set up an optimal Python environment for data visualization.

2. Understand the topics such as importing data for visualization and formatting data for visualization.

3. Understand the underlying data and how to use the right visualizations.

Please check **www.PacktPub.com** for information on our titles

wxPython 2.8 Application Development Cookbook

ISBN: 978-1-84951-178-0   Paperback: 308 pages

Quickly create robust, reliable, and reusable wxPython applications

1. Develop flexible applications in wxPython.

2. Create interface translatable applications that will run on Windows, Macintosh OSX, Linux, and other UNIX like environments.

3. Learn basic and advanced user interface controls.

Learning Object Oriented Programming

ISBN: 978-1-78528-963-7   Paperback: 280 pages

Explore and crack the OOP code in Python, JavaScript, and C#

1. Write reusable code that defines and makes objects interact with one another.

2. Discover the differences in inheritance and polymorphism in Python, JavaScript, and C#.

3. Capture objects from real-world elements and create object-oriented code that represents them.

Please check **www.PacktPub.com** for information on our titles

23536621R00254

Printed in Great Britain
by Amazon

Python 3 Object-oriented Programming

Second Edition

Unleash the power of Python 3 objects

Dusty Phillips

BIRMINGHAM - MUMBAI

Python 3 Object-oriented Programming
Second Edition

First published: July 2010

Second edition: August 2015

Production reference: 1130815

Published by Packt Publishing Ltd.
Livery Place
35 Livery Street
Birmingham B3 2PB, UK.

ISBN 978-1-78439-878-1

www.packtpub.com